To Srinatha and the Twelve Elders
Who are my Master Teachers

And to
JBF
My Beloved King
Great Soul
He

# CHAPTER OUTLINE

# Preface

Humankind has been on a quest to search for the answers to the origin and nature of self and material things since it was first possible to pose the questions. In the broadest sense of the word, one could call that religion—to know and experience Ultimate Reality. When viewed from that broad definition, one could say that every field of study has, essentially, derived from religion. Science splintered from religion as the former sought to answer questions about the origin of the world by attempting to understand the origin of all things through observing and studying the visible, material world. Religion, which accepted on faith the origin of the world as derivative of an invisible world, would be fiercely at odds with the scientific world. Even today, the schism is large, but the disagreement is not as acrimonious as in medieval times.

Since ancient times, when astronomy and astrology were closely linked to religion, various fields of study have developed and splintered off as a way to answer the ultimate questions of the origin of existence. Assuming that truth was to be found in separateness, these divisions have resulted in physics, physiology, anthropology, archeology, astronomy, medicine, psychology and a myriad of other so called "sciences." By the very fact that they sought to arrive at, and understand, "truth" by the physical world alone, this is what made them "scientific" for science really only recognizes and gives homage to "the seen." Religion, and to some extent philosophy, is unscientific in the sense that it seeks to understand truth through the "unseen." In their own way, all disciplines seek the ultimate and, if possible, absolute truth of all of existence.

This book explores answers primarily through the lens of psychology although substantial attention is given to philosophical concepts. Since Western psychology split from philosophy in the late 1800s, the former borrowed its ideas and concepts from the latter and, indeed, virtually the entire idiomatic repertoire of psychological terms can be directly traced to concepts in Western and Eastern philosophy. It is my contention that the severance between psychology and philosophy, while having provided some benefit, must be healed because no authentic, whole and cogent psychology is possible without a simultaneous understanding of philosophy. The exodus of psychology from the domain of philosophy has allowed for the application of healthcare interventions which have helped many people who struggle with mental health issues. However, there seems to be no substantive Western mental healthcare effort which teaches and advocates the empowerment of the individual in regaining and sustaining her/his own mental health. This is where philosophy, particularly Eastern philosophy, plays a major role as it speaks frankly of the Self and the Soul along with modalities which place the individual as the responsible party in her/his health and, thus, eliminates the perceived power differential that exists today in current Western medicine between medical professional and patient. So it is this author's hope that this book may provoke deeper thought and consideration toward reconciling psychology and philosophy and, ultimately, in finding answers to Truth.

The Buddhists speak of how there are many paths that lead to Truth or Nirvana. Thus, this book should be viewed as only one of many paths as a search for answers we all yearn to know. It only takes an open and willing mind. Moving away from reductionistic and deterministic theories which attempt to speak of truth as "either/or," I make a paradigmatic and paradoxical shift into the nether world of "both/and." In that sense, this book is attempting to say that only by synthesizing many disciplines can humankind arrive at higher levels of truth. Only by psychology, medicine, theology, physics, philosophy and other disciplines collaborating and working together will humankind find the lost holy grail. With no guarantees that each person will arrive at Truth or arrive at it in exactly the same manner or method, this book attempts to say, as did Schopenhauer and Hegel, that Truth is knowable, yet paradoxically unknowable, as Kant posited. Since there are two levels of "knowing", we can say this paradox with certainty.

Erudition, intellect, rational thinking, reason and logic are, at the relative level, sufficient and necessary to provide comprehensive exegeses for what is otherwise unknown. However, at higher levels of consciousness and at the Ultimate level of Reality, Aristotelian logic becomes inadequate and irrelevant, making it obsolete as a scientific methodology. This is the Eastern admonishment which has been voiced for thousands of years which states that intellect alone, i.e., Aristotelian logic, is insufficient in knowing Absolute Truth and Ultimate Reality. Intellect teaches that A=A and, thus, A can never equal not-A. At relative levels of reality, this is accurate, however, at Ultimate levels of Reality, A equals both A and not-A. Until every discipline within the "sciences" arrives at this understanding, no comprehensive "theory of everything" is possible. This will shake the very foundations of masculine analytical thought which dominates and controls the world, but it is an ancient truth which will continue to resurface until the "intellectuals" embrace humility as a friend and intuition as a lover.

It is not possible to intellectually comprehend or verbally articulate Highest Truth. We can only "know" it by intuition and illumination. Indeed, the magnificent *Tao Te Ching* teaches us that "the Highest Truth cannot be put into words, therefore, the wisest teacher has nothing to say." The world is chock full of intellectual fools, the educated homeless and brilliant academicians yet war, violence, greed, hatred, prejudice and disease are rising at fever pitch levels which threaten the progeny of the human race. What can we say? It should be stating the obvious to say that intellect alone will never be the balm to soothe our Souls. In the end, Truth can only be found by hearing the Divine Echo within. This is where the all-knowing, Silent, Shining, Illuminating, Enlightened Self forever is. You need only seek it and it will find you. The unfettered and devoted Will to know is all you need.

You are honored in this sacred journey towards Truth. For in so beginning the quest, you have begun the search of knowing your Great Soul.

Namaste', Peace and Goodwill

# Introduction

The Soul Consciousness model was developed as a means for mainstream psychology to begin to study wholeness of Being. The model is a beautiful complement to Assagioli's transpersonal model of the Higher Self, Jungian's analytical model of the Self, Maslow's model of hierarchical psychological needs and some aspects of Wilber's model of the AQAL framework. Not meant to render any psychological models obsolete, the Soul Consciousness model is intended to expand, broaden and deepen consciousness theory such that every theory has a certain space within a continuum. When viewed this way, no one theory is entirely accurate, rather it will portray only one piece of an ever larger puzzle. In this case, the piece is understood to be a place on the continuum of evolving human consciousness and, as such, certain models are understood to represent lower and, hence, more narrow levels of consciousness than others.

The Soul must be more readily understood as a construct by large groups of people including researchers, academicians, psychologists, theologians and lay people in order to begin a systematic study of its nature, function, process and resultant behavioral and psychological outcomes. In this sense, providing an understandable operational definition of the Soul which can be standardized across multiple disciplines is the natural starting point by which we can begin the next phase of the study of higher psychological functioning. Only in this sense, will we be "singing the same hymn." With this objective in mind, it is intended that the Soul Consciousness model be used as a jumping off mark and that others will take this model and, over the decades, move even further than this model to yet another higher level of psychological functioning. As such, it is important to understand that the Soul Consciousness is not the highest level of psychological well-being or Truth, rather it is higher than the ego level of consciousness, but still lower than the level whereby no other teaching or learning is necessary. From Wilber's perspective, one could say that the Soul consciousness is beyond the First Tier and constitutes the Second Tier with existential issues of Being. As such, it is critical to understand the Soul as it stands on the cusp of the next major transformation in human consciousness. Having said this, what is sorely needed at the turn of the 21st century is a unifying and standardized concept of the Soul and Soul Consciousness which is broadly and generally accepted within the field which will yield a new phase of inquiry and research beyond the ego. Also needed is a new vision of psychotherapeutic treatment modalities as those which are utilized today have failed to result in mass utilization by society and high agreement within the field itself as to what constitutes optimal and effective therapy. It is with this intention of expanding current models that the Soul Consciousness model was conceived.

Also of note as we move beyond the ego consciousness is the paradox of simplicity versus complexity. The ego revels in complexity because it is within complexity that the illusiveness of the ego can successfully hide. On the outside, the ego seems initially very complex, but in truth, the ego is really simple being that mind which is split, unfulfilled and un-whole. Fear is its core emotion and all other negative, destructive emotions derive from the fear of the ego. All statements of explanation which have been stated about the ego such as Freudian and neo-Freudian theory are complex elaborations of what, essentially, is a simple construct. You might say that these voluminous works about the ego are a layer on top of another layer on top of another layer in an attempt to explain that which—at higher levels of consciousness—is understood to be an illusion, a puff of wind. At the higher level of consciousness, the Soul level, paradoxical logic becomes the only means by which this level of consciousness can be understood rendering any explanations in Aristotelian logic incomplete. For instance, you can say that the Soul is either an abstract which appears to be constructed or you can say that the Soul is a construct which is abstract. To argue which is foreground and which is background is moot. Both are accurate. In the beginning understanding of the Soul, people will likely attempt to superimpose complex thought upon what is, essentially, a simple theory. That is what the ego does; it finds the complex while overlooking simplicity. As we have a larger understanding of the Soul, we begin to have a dim awareness that the Soul is both complex and simple, but its simplicity is what is intuitively comprehensible and essential in moving to an even higher level where paradox itself is obliterated. At the highest level of Soul Consciousness, it is understood that everybody is right, therefore, using either/or logic to argue over who is right and who is wrong becomes totally moot, a futile exercise leading nowhere since the Soul can only be understood in terms of both/and logic. At the highest Soul level, everyone more or less just simply abides and peacefully co-exists realizing that ideas, concepts, perceptions and senses are all transitory and that humanity creates whatever it wants to create only for evolution to simply continue eternally. And in that creating, we have total free will to create a belief system which imprisons us or which liberates us. At this level, the only response that can be said to someone is: *"Is that so?"* The only sure thing is the eternal Mind, the "Nameless," the "Nothingness" from which all "Is." Think of it as the space between the light waves and between all the atoms. What can you possibly say about that? Nothing. It's unutterable, unspeakable. At the ultimate level, nothing can be stated because a personal self and consciousness do not exist *per se*. Taoists refer to this as "the Nameless"; Buddhists refer to it as "Emptiness" and "Nothingness." But for now, let us return to, and concentrate on, the Soul.

Any theoretical model which fails to identify the Psyche and all its expressions thereof as energy is not fully and wholly identifying the Psyche in its Wholeness and in its Ultimate state of Being. As such, the field of psychology must begin to think of the Psyche and its expressions as energic expressions or in terms of energy. This energy is the élan vital of human existence and is more compatible with the energy systems of Traditional Chinese Medicine and Ayurvedic medicine which considers the mind and body as inseparable units within a whole system of energy.

Everything that exists is energy and everything that "is" manifests as a vibrational frequency whether audible or not. This includes *everything*— light, sound, color, thought, emotions, actions, air, water, fire, earth, minerals, metals, plants, trees, animals, cars, houses, clothing and—yes—human beings. *You are energy.* Your physical body is energy. John Diamond, in his book, *The Body Doesn't Lie*, says it simply: "...the body itself is a system of electromagnetic energy." Your organs, blood, water and cells in your body vibrate at a certain frequency. Your thoughts and emotions are energy and vibrate at a specific frequency although those frequencies vary from thought to thought and from emotion to emotion. The clothes you wear and the house you live in vibrate with energy. The paper you write on, the book you read, the couch you sit on all vibrate to a frequency. Your essence is the frequency of light and sound because light and sound are the two fundamental, *yet indivisible*, "substances" of the entire universe. There is nothing that exists which does not have light and sound as an essential component.

John Beaulieu, in his book *Music and Sound in the Healing Arts*, refers to sound as "Sacred Sound." He says that "instead of using the word 'energy' the ancients used the concept of Sacred Sound." This Sacred Sound may be called by different names, but its essential meaning has been identical across all indigenous and civilized cultures. Christians refer to this as "the Word of God" while other cultures refer to it as "Kung, cosmic tone, soundless sound, the key note, the cosmic sound, and OM." Beaulieu also tells us that Pythagoras "called the Sacred Sound of the universe 'music of the spheres.'" Beaulieu refers to the concept of fundamental sound in terms of music by saying:

> "It was Pythagoras' view that sound was the link between the gods and man. Discovering Sacred Sound within ourselves is the basis for mantric yoga, Pythagorean intervals, Western classical and modern music, the Indian ragas, Buddhist chanting, the sacred rhythms of African tribes, the trance dance music of Bali as well as many other systems of music and sound. Audible sound is the gateway to the Sacred Sound. It is composed of three characteristics: Wave, Pulse, and Form. These terms have their origin in musical vocabulary and have a new and expanded meaning in the context of life energy."

If we look at the electromagnetic spectrum, we see that the visible light section is a higher frequency than is the audible sound section. Invisible light operates at even a higher frequency than visible light. Since ancient days, humankind has, in some way or other, revered light. Everything that lives responds to light and, since visible light contains all the colors, you could further say that everything responds to color. Ancient civilizations knew this and the Egyptians actually had healing temples where people entered to be healed by color. Color is a recognized concept in both Ayurvedic medicine and Traditional Chinese Medicine because of its energy properties. Light and sound are indivisible and can be thought of as the temple of the Soul so they are holy. In later chapters, we will discuss light and sound energy more fully as they are the indivisible "substances" of the Soul, therefore, any treatise on the Soul is lacking without proper attention paid to its "subtle substance."

We now move ahead in our epic of the Soul so we may now understand it more clearly and more fully. In doing so, we may also begin to have a clearer picture of the writings of historical philosophers and theologians who have, for thousands of years, given us such beautiful and eloquent words when telling us about the grandeur of the Soul.

*We must be the change we wish to see in the world.*
—Mahatma Gandhi

# I. THE FOUR DISCIPLINES

## PSYCHOLOGY

Freud, referred by most as the grandfather of psychology, was the first psychologist to posit a coherent and structured theoretical model of the mind. He opined, for the first time, that the Psyche is energy and it is structured and further expounded his theory of the epidemiology and epistemology of psychopathology. Quite simply, Freud's focus was on illness, not health. Absent from Freud's work is an adequate definition of optimal mental health as he chose to concentrate on the darker side of the human condition. Many believe, although he is said to deny it, that Freud drew from the ideas of philosophers such as Nietzsche when forming his theoretical principles.

Psyche is a Greek word meaning "soul" or in Freud's German language, *seele*. In truth, it is conspicuously and ironically missing from Freud's theoretical model. Psychology, if properly identified, is the study of the Soul although no one, to date, has posited a complete theory of what the field is, in actuality, intended to study. Indeed, though raised Jewish, Freud was a proclaimed atheist and referred to himself as "a godless Jew." He believed that people who professed faith in an unseen world and "God" were, at best, neurotic and, at worst, exhibiting a pathological projection. He would call it delusional thinking or pathological grandiosity or, quite literally, a "universal obsessional neurosis" in *Civilization and Its Discontents*. In layman's terms, he thought you were neurotic or mentally ill depending upon the specific symptomatologies that manifested.

Philosophers, virtually all male in ancient days, spoke freely of the Soul and had no reticence in explaining its nature. Socrates, Plato, Plotinus and Proclus were just a few of the Greek philosophers who spoke of the Soul and extolled the wisdom of its care. In fact, when reading Plotinus' *Enneads*, one feels that he communed often with the Great Soul and was intimately familiar with its expressions.

All current mainstream psychological models which are taught in the educational system ignore and dismiss the soul and, instead, study the mind and behavior which is not the Soul. Today, the Soul has been relegated by the field of psychology to a nebulous, irrational, misty ghost which simply does not exist. It is as though psychologists are intimidated by it or are so insecure in their inability to define it and relate to it, that the choice has been to simply ignore it and keep it buried.

Virtually the entire fields of psychology and medical science refuse to accept or even consider the existence of the Soul. While there are a number of philosophers and theologians throughout history who believed in the Soul, the most substantial information which does exist is largely through the writings of Plato, Aristotle, Marsilio Ficino, neo-Platonists such as Plotinus and Proclus, some historical religious leaders such as St. Augustine and St. Thomas Aquinas, Jewish mystics who honor the Kabbalah and Christian mystics such as Jacob Boehme, St. John of the Cross and Julian of Norwich to name just a few.

One of the first prominent psychologists who dared to write about the numinous was Carl Jung who was, initially, a student of Freud's until he began having serious doubts about Freud's basic premise---that sexual and aggressive instincts are biological drives which serve as the fundamental driving forces for all human beings and, further, that humanity is doomed to this animalistic existence, having no capacity to develop a higher consciousness. Forming his own theoretical model of psychology, which incorporated the numinous as a higher consciousness and a vital part of a person's optimal mental health and well being, Jung, who had been Freud's appointed heir apparent to the psychoanalytic throne, broke away from the psychoanalytic group. Freud would shun Jung, never forgiving Jung for disputing psychoanalytic theory. Freud would also eschew all others who deflected from his enclave. Indeed, the story is well known of how Freud refused to acknowledge Karen Horney as a professional and as a psychoanalytic member after she posited her theoretical model which displaced the father as a primary figure in psychological development and instead placed the mother as an equal, if not primary, factor in healthy development. So great was Freud's rage and arrogance that psychoanalytic thinkers during this time blacked out Horney's name in every document where she had previously been acknowledged in this elite intellectual circle. Horney's ideas challenged Freudian thought and cast substantial doubt as to the validity of some of Freud's core premises. Freud's verbal denigration of both Adler and Adler's theory is also well known. The rejection of anyone who dared question the theoretical underpinnings of psychoanalytical theory perhaps gives the reader a glimpse of the inflexible thought, if not intellectual narcissism and arrogance, of Sigmund Freud.

Considered by some as "the doctor of the Soul," Jung also drew from the ideas of philosophers like Schopenhauer, Nietzsche and Kant, especially the latter. Jung was convinced that humankind had a higher, loftier potential beyond being a bundle of biological drives and instincts that compelled the species toward sex and aggression. His unstinted belief that humankind strives for psychological health was his guiding force throughout his entire life. *Individuation*, a term Jung coined, which referred to a person's subconscious drive toward psychological wholeness, is a legacy he left to the field of psychology. He largely cast aside his concern with the atheistic academic community in his last years and wrote substantially regarding the Self, the archetypal God-image, *imago dei*, and referred to all problems of psychology as, ultimately, a matter of spirituality. It is my belief that he was the primary medical doctor who made the greatest inroads in moving psychiatry toward a psychological theory of the Soul.

## PHYSICS

Einstein still enjoys the sacred reputation in many people's minds as the greatest physicist of all time. It is said that Einstein's interest in physics really began at age sixteen when he was looking at light as it reflected off the surface of a lake. He asked himself what it would be like to ride a beam of light. And the rest, as they say, is history! He spent the remainder of his life studying the universe in terms of its relation to light and the speed of light. He was most famous for discovering the three laws of thermodynamics and for discovering that light is, paradoxically, *both* particle and wave. Before Einstein came along, scientists were in conflict over whether to define light as a particle or a wave since both had been theorized. Einstein was the first to prove that light is both. His first law of thermodynamics had profound implications stating that energy can never be created or destroyed, rather it only changes forms from matter to non-matter. Although Einstein denied the existence of what he referred to as a "personal God" or an anthropomorphic God, his works often refer to the religious reverence and awe he had toward the mystery of creation and the undeniable order which manifests in myriads of ways throughout the cosmos. Born into a Jewish family, Einstein rejected religious orthodoxy, but was awed by the ineffable. He once said:

> "It was the experience of mystery—even if mixed with fear— that engendered religion. A knowledge of the existence of something we cannot penetrate, our perceptions of the profoundest reason and the most radiant beauty, which only in their most primitive forms are accessible to our minds: it is this knowledge and this emotion that constitute true religiosity. In this sense, and only this sense, I am a deeply religious man...I am satisfied with the mystery of life's eternity and with a knowledge, a sense, of the marvelous structure of existence—as well as the humble attempt to understand even a tiny portion of the Reason that manifests itself in nature."

Most of us have been taught Einstein's equation of $E=MC^2$, but probably many do not know his deference to Spirit. Referencing familiarity with the ancient philosophers, Einstein was quoted: "The ancients knew something which we seem to have forgotten. All means prove but blunt instruments, if they have not behind them a living spirit."

## PHILOSOPHY

Most people recognize Socrates as one of the greatest Western philosophers who ever lived. Socrates debated topics such as virtue and justice through the use of logical dialogue. Some are unaware that he was sentenced to death for "corrupting the youth" due to his "not believing in the national gods and of introducing strange divinities." Socrates' spiritual ideas of the Soul, the transmigration and eternality of the Soul and the importance of nurturing Soul must have been considered threatening in that day. He faced death valiantly and considered his physical death but a luxurious return of his Soul to peace and a better existence than the pain and suffering on Earth. Given the choice of remaining on the earth by renouncing his ideas or staying true to his Soul and dying, he chose to drink hemlock. So strong were his convictions that he refused to ask the jury that convicted him if, instead of death, he could be exiled. Plato's *Dialogues* state that the jury would assuredly have accepted this plea. In the last paragraph of Plato's *Apology*, Socrates says to the jury members who have convicted him to death:

"The hour of departure has arrived, and we
go our ways—I to die, and you to live. Which
is better is known to God and only to him."

Lao Tzu is a Chinese philosopher, sage and mystic who, like the Christ and the Buddha, is considered as having transcended the ego and achieved enlightenment prior to physical death. He is thought to be the author of the *Tao Te Ching*, a book of wisdom consisting of eighty-one brief chapters. We know little about him and stories of his life are inconsistent and shrouded in mystery. According to the historian Ssuma Chien (100 B.C.), Lao Tzu lived in northern China as an archivist some time in the 6th century B.C. although others place Lao Tzu as living in the 5th and 4th centuries B.C. Ssuma Chien writes of Lao Tzu meeting Confucius whom he chastised as being full of pride, but it is unknown whether the meeting actually took place. Legend has it that, at age 80, Lao Tzu was deeply saddened that humankind was unwilling to live the simple, unfettered life which he espoused and so he set out for the western border of China. Upon reaching the border, a guard asked him to record his philosophy of life for posterity and, after 5,250 words, the *Tao Te Ching* birthed its wisdom for posterity. *Tao* ("way") *Te* ("virtue) *Ching* ("classic") is considered the true beginning of Taoism, a philosophical system of paradoxical thought which espouses following the laws of nature, seeking simplicity, truth and goodness and honoring the intuitive capacities which guide one through transcendency to the Tao. The transcendent Tao is the origin and sustainer of all things, being behind and within and through all things. It is nameless, according to Lao Tzu, and cannot be spoken of because it is ineffable, invisible and inaudible. It is the uncreated Creator.

The *Tao Te Ching* is perhaps the world's most translated classic writing next to the Christian Bible and there are literally dozens of translations in various languages. In some versions the Soul is mentioned in relation to the Tao with the Soul being that which points toward the Tao and unites with the Tao.

## RELIGION

Jesus the Christ is known by millions as a divine prophet. Even some religions which fail to acknowledge him as the proclaimed "Son of God" believe he had a connection to a grand spiritual panorama. His message of goodwill and love is ubiquitous to every human regardless of religious affiliation. Some believe that, during his lifetime and for three centuries after his death, many of Jesus' teachings were suppressed, edited or deleted by the religious and political patriarchy because of the serious threat his message posed to the egregiously corrupt political, religious and business hierarchy which wielded power and maintained control over the masses. Jesus' overarching message was the declaration that God is Spirit, not a man of wrath seated on a throne in a distant spiritual landscape. Instead, God— Spirit of Pure Goodness—resides within every human being. Realizing that many had come to anthropomorphize God, Jesus attempted to tell humankind that God was not man, rather an eternal, omnipresent Spirit living within and around us all. Jesus attempted to tell others that the Soul is God incarnate, the spiritual *imago dei*; and, similar to Socrates' message preceding him, that all knowledge and truth can be understood in relation to comprehending the nature of the Soul. Christ is a symbol of the Universal Spirit from which all humankind is molded and there is no major religion which does not speak of this same loving, kind, compassionate and unifying Spirit.

Many believe Jesus was a member of the Essenes, a small esoteric Jewish sect living near the Dead Sea whose teachings we know through Pliny the Elder, Flavius Josephus and Philo of Alexandria. Some believe Jesus, Mary Magdelene and John the Baptist were Essenes and that Christianity was foreshadowed by this sect which began in the 2nd century B.C. The Essenes were a close Jewish community of both celibate men and of married couples who denounced the exclusivity and elitism of Jewish orthodoxy and the rigid, inflexible dogma, rites and rituals of the religion. Essenes were pacifists who ate no meat, lived in a communal setting, condemned slavery and helped the poor. They wore white clothing to represent purity and believed in the immortality of the Soul. Philo of Alexandria called them "athletes of virtue" because the Essenes were vehement in their abhorrence of deceit, greed and corruption. They were known for their belief in telling the truth and denouncing liars. Their life was simple and frugal. Cleanliness was very important as were solitude, privacy and meditation. It is said that they studied androgyny, believing men and women are equal. They fought valiantly against the dark ego consciousness of avarice, deceit, oppression, hate and imprudence. The Essenes believed that the Pharisees, Sadducees, Scribes and Priests misused their power and control over the masses. The Pharisees were a Jewish religious group who were vigorous in their adherence to scripture and who were extreme in their attempts of exclusivity to keep Gentiles out of Israel. The Scribes, also known as lawyers, were experts in biblical law and associated with the Pharisees. Insisting on strict adherence to Mosaic Law, the Sadducees were a wealthy, aristocratic Jewish religious group opposed to the Pharisees. The Sadducees were affiliated with Jewish Priests who were the keepers of the rituals of the Temples in Jerusalem. It appears that Jesus, a Jew himself, was not opposed to Judaism as a religion and the misinterpretation by both Jewish and non-Jewish people that he was opposed has, in my opinion, been a gross and egregious source of unnecessary hatred between Christians and Jews. History does not reflect any statement by Jesus where he advocated for the annihilation of Judaism or the Jewish people. It is true that he spoke out against corruption and misuse of patriarchal power of religious, business and political leaders in that day. Here again, his thrust was not against religion, business and politics *per se*, rather against the shadow masculine ego consciousness of hypocrisy, corruption and deceit by an egomaniacal patriarchy. Let us be very clear on Jesus' message because an important step toward healing one of the most catastrophic and tragic rifts in the history of humankind rests upon the elucidation of this point. Jesus was not anti-Semitic. He was anti-ego. He was a serious threat to the powerful patriarchy because he was exposing the shadow consciousness, the darkness of abusive patriarchy and the hypocrisy, deceit and corruption in religion, business and politics. The way to combat this threat was for patriarchy to make repeated attempts to spread false rumors and lies about Jesus being a madman and a troublemaker and to catch Jesus making defamatory, treasonous and heretical remarks and disobeying biblical law because this was the way corrupt patriarchy could quell the threat Jesus posed. The ego consciousness of abusive patriarchy which seeks exclusion, division and elitist control can exist in any religion, any business and any political affiliation and, indeed, still exists in many religions, corporations and both major political parties today. If he were alive today, Jesus would be exposing the hypocrisy, deceit and corruption of abusive patriarchy in Catholicism, Corporate America and politics. Jesus never said or implied "Kill Jews" or "Eradicate Judaism" and, indeed, his entire message was "love one another." In fact, his next-to-the-last message on the cross, when he had every reason to be full of hatred and to vilify patriarchy, was "Father, forgive them, for they know not what they do," which is an explicit loving God consciousness toward a people who, because of their ego consciousness, were ignorant of a godly consciousness, a consciousness of Goodwill toward the All, the Whole of humanity.

Jesus was a troublemaker because he exposed those in power and he was crucified because his message seriously threatened abusive patriarchy, the shadow masculine ego consciousness. He was opposed to religious dogma and doctrines which were carried to such an extreme that the entire essence of a God consciousness of love, kindness, compassion and goodwill to all was grossly and sadly overlooked and lost. The heart of God was lost in the obsessive, intellectual attempts to obey biblical "law." Lost in the dogma and ritual of religion, the powerful leaders had put a God consciousness of love toward *all* people as a lesser priority to obeying biblical law. Ironically, the so-called "leaders of God" had buried God in dogma. God is not found through mind alone, rather through a mind *and* heart of love. God does not exclude; people elect to exclude themselves and others from a God consciousness. God is infinite and limitless in love toward humanity, therefore, what about exclusivity is godly? In their aggressive attempts to exclude part of humanity from the spiritual wealth of a God consciousness which could no more be divided than a ray of sunshine, Jesus exposed that the religious leaders were more lost from God than the masses to whom they preached. Jesus felt the God consciousness had been sacrificed at the expense of adhering to rituals and dogma. The concept of exclusivity in which only a portion of humanity would be loved and "saved" by God saddened Jesus who came to teach that the God consciousness of love is open to anyone who will awaken regardless of whether you are rich or poor, young or old, sick or healthy, Jew or Gentile. If God's love is infinite, how could God limit love? Either God is imperfect, limited love or God is perfect, limitless love.

During Jesus' day, political factions and numerous religious sects existed. In fact, politics and religion had become an insidious method by which a powerful patriarchy contrived laws and rules which allowed for the continued control of the people. With his message of spiritual truth and equality, Jesus seriously threatened that power base which ultimately led to his physical death. Jesus grew up a Jew and, as he entered adulthood, he drew people of all faiths to him and he accepted them all, so I'm of the conviction that he was never opposed to Jews or the Jewish faith, rather he was challenging the exclusivity, elitism and extreme dogma of Jewish orthodoxy. Every religion places value on a sense of community and the Jewish faith and culture is one of the best examples of actualizing and maintaining that essential spiritual value despite unthinkable hardships. Through the most atrocious crime against humanity, a holocaust, the Jewish people have maintained their dignity and culture and have never allowed the flame of their religious heritage to extinguish. A basic tenet of the Jewish religion, similar to Buddhists, Advaitans and Taoists, is the rejection of the concept of an anthropomorphic God and of a physical place called Heaven and Hell. Instead, there is the belief that God is an infinite, omnipotent consciousness, an energy, an invisible, loving consciousness which, when manifested, results in a consciousness called Heaven and, when not manifested, results in a consciousness called Hell. Jesus never opposed these spiritual values within the Jewish religion and, indeed, his messages, parables and the way he lived his life point toward his intense belief in this God consciousness. The focus of his life can be summed up in the spiritual law he asked others to follow: "love one another." This was his appeal to all people to bestow compassion, kindness and goodness to all of God's children, both Jews *and* Gentiles.

Jesus came to simply embody the authentic God consciousness, "love one another," which is the core and essential tenet in every religion. No more and no less. This is what made him a "son of God" because projecting this God consciousness makes him and anyone a "child of God." A Messiah is a person, like Jesus or the Buddha, who has attained enlightenment and illumination and who allows themselves to be put in service to show humankind the path toward that consciousness. The *Bodhisattva* is a similar concept within Mahayana Buddhism and refers to someone who has attained illumination and elects to defer Nirvana and, instead, to help others reach illumination. A Messiah and a Bodhisattva have achieved divine illumination and elect to show others the path so they may become that God consciousness or Nirvana consciousness too. God is pure love and the consciousness of love is surely the offspring of pure love. Jesus' message seems clear: there is no intermediary between your Soul and God. No one particular person or sect of people is limited in their potential inheritance of the God consciousness of love and compassion, rather every person has the capacity to assume this way of divine Being. Being a consciousness of love, God can never exclude you. *Only you can exclude yourself* from this loving consciousness which accepts and loves the All. Only you can deny yourself this consciousness when your consciousness excludes love toward others. That is the ego which forever excludes and divides people. Similarly, no other human being can deny you the inevitable return to the consciousness of God unless you allow them. *God and the Kingdom of Heaven are within you, therefore, who else but you can find what already exists within yourself?*

The Buddha is actually a title, not a name, and literally means "the enlightened one" or "the awakened one." His birth name was Siddhartha Gautama and he was the son of King Suddhodana and Queen Mahamaya in the Himalayan ranges near Nepal. Born around 566 B.C., he would be raised by his mother's sister because his mother died seven days after his birth. Legend has it that Siddhartha ("he who has attained his goals") was born fully awake and speaking, telling his mother he was born to free humankind of pain and suffering. At his birth, an astrologer predicted to King Suddhodana that Siddhartha would achieve one of two goals: 1) become a great king or emperor, or 2) become a Buddha, an enlightened soul, and save humanity. The father asked the astrologer what it would take for his son to seek the religious life upon which the astrologer replied: "Four signs—a decrepit old man, a diseased man, a dead man and a monk." Upon hearing this, the father set out to ensure that his son would not follow the ascetic life and sheltered him from all unpleasant things such as poverty, disease and death by not allowing his son to venture outside the large palatial area. Siddhartha would remain inside the palace walls indulging in extreme wealth and comfort. At age sixteen, he married a beautiful princess and had a son. Finally, one day he demanded to see his people outside the palace walls, so it was arranged by his father that every effort would be made to shelter Siddhartha from seeing anything unpleasant. As fate would have it, however, Siddhartha did see an old man, a diseased man, a dead man and a monk which, as presaged, caused him to pause and reflect upon these strange occurrences to which he had never been exposed. At age twenty-nine, he abandoned his life of wealth to seek enlightenment. After being dissatisfied with several teachers, he then took up the life of a severe ascetic by abstaining almost entirely from eating. One day, he saw a group of girls singing about the strings of a sitar being too tight or too loose and that the optimal way to tune the strings was neither high nor low. This is said to have been the moment when he adopted the

Middle Path or Middle Way in which harmony is achieved by avoiding extremes. Sitting under a boddhi tree, he meditated from morning to sunset going into a deep meditation in which he was tempted several times. Finally, at the age of 35, he achieved *samadhi*, the state of superconsciousness where Absoluteness is experienced with all knowing and joy. Oneness is attained. The Buddha spent the remaining 45 years of his life disregarding the caste system teaching the Four Noble Truths and the Eightfold Path to poor and wealthy alike explaining that achieving enlightenment was open to anyone regardless of religion, social or economic status, race, gender or ethnicity. The Four Noble Truths taught that the root cause of all pain and suffering is attachment and the Eightfold Path are those virtues which lead one away from suffering and to the goal of Nirvana, true enlightenment, true freedom from suffering.

One could say "in the beginning," there was essentially only religion as a means to understand ourselves, the world around and above us and the origin of existence, both human and otherwise. From that, there was a massive "split" with the emergence of science from the "rib" of religion, so to speak. This has resulted in our current two perspectives: the religious masculine perspective of the world and the scientific masculine perspective of the world. No feminine concepts, philosophies, tenets, values, methodologies or ideologies were accepted because females were considered inferior, if not insignificant. *Thus, the entire world has predicated its philosophies, concepts, tenets, values, ideologies and methodologies on a masculine perspective.* One might say in laymen's terms that the world is sustained by masculine rules, masculine rulers and masculine ways of ensuring that masculine rules are maintained. This is a key idea to keep in mind as you read this book, as you begin to question the current human condition and as we, as a human species, search for ways to alleviate human suffering.

Since this major split from "one" field of study, so to speak, there has continued to be split after split as one field breaks away from another believing that, by doing so, they will arrive at "truth" for, in the greatest scheme of things, humankind has been eternally seeking truth through knowledge.

From religion, philosophy blossomed as it sought to find the Highest Wisdom through the study of the mind and knowledge by means of pondering the metaphysical world. Before Aristotle, the Greek philosophers assumed the existence of a spiritual world as an accepted truth. Aristotle came along and, while still assuming the existence of a spiritual realm, began the first known systematic study of natural phenomenon. Most give Aristotle credit for the natural sciences unfolding approximately one thousand years later.

Astrology had always studied the heavenly bodies in order to understand the spiritual realm and its connection to humankind. Ordained priests and men of piety during the fifteenth and sixteenth centuries would have multiple interests including theology, astrology, philosophy and mathematics which led to great discoveries and would be the foundation upon which seventeenth through nineteenth century thinkers developed their famous theories. Because astrologists began postulating theories which were incongruent with the Bible (resulting in astrologists being put to death by the "Infallible Church Fathers" of the Catholic Church), astrology split from religion and what manifested was the field of astronomy we know today.

The field of science broke from religion for the same reasons that astrology split from religion—the scientists would discover something which was incongruent with the Bible or the dogma and doctrine of the Catholic Church. This resulted in the male leaders of the Catholic Church ("male leaders of the Catholic Church" is actually redundant since the Catholic Church does not espouse female leadership in the Church or females becoming priests) getting together to denounce the threatening theory, declare the scientist a heretic and put the heretic to death (or threaten the heretic to be put to death as in the case of Galileo). Since those dark days, all kinds of scientific fields have manifested such as psychology, psychiatry, medical science, physiology, physics, anthropology, archaeology, etc.

Most psychological theories have been postulated by men during the roughly 120 years since its inception. Klein, Horney and Satir are the few notable female exceptions, but, by far, psychological theory has been postulated by males and, for the most part, it has been a male dominated field (both psychiatry and psychology) until the 1970s and 1980s. Thus, you could say that, by and large, it was males who promulgated psychological theories and these same males who, in turn, critiqued, judged, authenticated and validated all new psychological theories to be accepted by the field. Then in the 1970s and 1980s, increasing numbers of females entered the field as clinicians, practitioners and researchers. According to a February 2003 issue of *Monitor on Psychology*, a publication of The American Psychological Association, since 1975 there has been a 43% increase in enrollment in graduate psychology programs and 74% of today's graduate psychology students are females. In spite of these substantial percentages, males still assume the majority of leadership positions in psychology and psychiatry. Prior to the 1930s, most females and minorities were either denied entrance to doctoral programs in psychology or the few who were admitted to universities and obtained their doctorate in psychology were then typically denied employment in many areas of psychology. The very psychologists in the field which advocated for, and guided clients toward, a more mature psyche, seemed little more mature in consciousness than some of the clients whom these psychologists served. It was common for white male professors to verbalize the proverbial, "We don't accept Negroes into this department" or "The professor won't accept females into this laboratory" or "Why don't you go into a field of study more suited to people like you?" Those few white male psychologists who fought to embrace females and minorities were sure to face ostracism. At the turn of the century, psychology, a field of study which purports in its very mission of existence to relieve human suffering, was as culpable in creating mental and emotional suffering through discrimination and prejudice as was the clientele from which it was accepting payment for services rendered. Today with the majority of clinical, research and academic psychologists who hold leadership positions being non-minority males, more opportunities are needed for females and minorities to penetrate the Glass Ceiling.

Modern psychology "split" from philosophy around 125 years ago as it began to utilize empirical methods to study the mind. The field of Western psychology—dominated historically by men—has elected to study the mind with its capacity to acquire and retain knowledge. The assumption that rational knowledge, reason and logic is primary in alleviating human suffering is a masculine-biased world view. A thorough study of Eastern psychology and philosophy will reveal more balance between the masculine and the feminine principles as it pertains to consciousness and psychological well-being. The majority of Western male psychologists, particularly those within the psychoanalytic, cognitive and behavioral schools of thought, have ignored and dismissed most attempts to broaden the field of psychology with a more authentic perspective which honors and validates the feminine energies as being an equally essential aspect of psychological well-being. In the characteristic manner of the prejudicial, abusive patriarchy, we can hear the masculine ego consciousness saying "I am superior and you, the other, are inferior." It is embedded within the foundations and tenets of Comte's positivism and Locke's empiricism. Positivism is a doctrine that recognizes only natural phenomena or facts that are objectively observed while empiricism only considers physical matter as a basis for facts. If something cannot be seen with the eyes, it is not real or valid, therefore, it is not valuable to study. We also recall the psychological foundations of Freud's determinism, along with his narrow and obstinate focus on aggression and sex as being the core drives of human nature. Determinism refers to the belief that a person's past determines present and future behavior and there is little, if no, potential to rise above past learning and behavior. Skinner's and Watson's highly reductionistic theories are strict masculine perspectives which only accept observable behavior which is learned through either reward or punishment as worthy of study. Emotions such as love and compassion are denigrated.

The sixteenth through the early twentieth centuries produced a cadre of philosophers who vehemently opposed each other's philosophical underpinnings. For the most part, one group postulated an explanation of existence solely through physical matter whereas the other group held fast to many of the ancient Greek philosophers who wrote of the governance of a spiritual realm in explaining existence. It is the first group of men, however, who have garnered most of the scientific leadership positions to date and have, thus, dictated what theories and concepts have been included in textbooks for academia to teach and for society to read. This dominant leadership group dictates norms and the punitive measures for falling outside these norms, in addition to ensuring that theories and methodologies which fall outside the rubric of scientism are summarily devalued and dismissed. For centuries, the shadow ego consciousness of the omnipotent, narcissistic and abusive patriarchy has exclusively monopolized and manipulated the zeitgeist so as to ensure that scientific methodologies, topics of interest and the leadership would continue to uphold and serve the best interests of the existing patriarchy.

There must be a higher level of consciousness than our existing collective consciousness which seems to be leading the human species for a global tragedy if it does not mature beyond ego. It seems painfully obvious that humankind must evolve to the next level of consciousness in order to avoid death of the human species. In order to do this, the mature masculine and the mature feminine must *share power* equally, honorably and respectfully. No one energy is superior over the other and all attempts at superiority and domination must be transformed into an energy of shared power. This will require the majority of males who currently dominate the leadership positions in psychology (in academia, professional life and professional associations) to recognize that the field of psychology must be reevaluated and transformed to include the feminine principle of a psychologically more mature human consciousness. The current masculine prejudice that exists in the psychological concepts, philosophies, values, ideologies, and research methods need to come under widespread question so as to include feminine perspective, epistemology and phenomenology. There appears to be some movement in this direction as phenomenological research is now becoming more generally accepted in the field of psychology, although it is still considered by male leadership to be considerably inferior to the masculine-biased quantitative research.

This collaboration, empowerment and sharing of power in leadership roles is a crucial step in order to save the field of psychology from becoming irrelevant. Indeed, the world may not survive at the rate that masculine aggression, domination and oppression is warring amongst itself. Psychology must evolve just as the human consciousness evolves. By developing a balance of feminine and masculine perspectives in the field, psychology itself may finally mature. It will be through the study of *both* the heart and mind of the human Psyche or Soul that this may be accomplished. Feminine aspects of the Soul such as intuition, love, collaboration, empowerment and nurturance must become viably accepted and substantially explored areas of research. The scope of research tools and methodologies must consider phenomenological research to be of equal value as the traditional masculine research which is empirically observable and measurable. Research into ontological consciousness and its outcome on the human condition, as understood by ancient Greek philosophers and by Eastern philosophers, should be viewed as an imperative endeavor. What does the ontological experience of someone like the Dalai Lama or Mother Teresa tell us? What mental and emotional patterns and cycles can be observed? Did Mahatma Gandhi and Mother Teresa exhibit a consciousness that manifests higher and more enhanced levels of pleasure and psychological well-being both intrapsychically and interpersonally? What if this consciousness could be experienced by large communities of people? Would the human condition be enhanced? The ontological experience of a loving, compassionate person and a person of wisdom *must* be viewed by the entire psychological field as a rich potential for research into ways of observing optimal behavior; how that behavior translates into more fulfilling and meaningful ways for humankind to interact and relate; and ultimately informing humankind on what treatment modalities enhance the human condition.

It is the historical masculine competitiveness and aggression which is indicative of the ego consciousness as it reflects the immature shadow of patriarchal superiority and prejudice. It is this fear-based consciousness of "superior I against inferior Other" that is predominately reflective of the evolution of human consciousness up to this point, has resulted in personal conflict and world wars, has resulted in the culmination of so many divergent, opposing stances within and between fields of study and untold human suffering and social ills. While we cannot ignore or forget contributions from thousands of people, regardless of gender or race, within these fields of study for the substantial strides in ameliorating human pain and suffering, we are now at a critical point in the evolutionary consciousness of humankind. After walking through the portal of the 21st century, our dim awareness is developing into a greater awareness that *it is only in the collaboration and synthesis of various fields of study and their major theories that humankind can make the next substantial leap in its evolution of consciousness.*

*We are not human beings having a spiritual experience; we are spiritual beings having a human experience.*
—Wayne Dyer

# II. THEORETICAL ASSUMPTIONS

There are theoretical assumptions we have as we engage in the study of the "Psyche" which literally means *Soul*. First, as Plato and Plotinus wrote about, as theologians such as St. Augustine and St. Aquinas believed and as mystics such as St. John the Cross and Jacob Boehme articulated, we operate under the assumption that the Soul exists. Though we cannot see the Soul with our physical eyes, we base the existence of the Soul on Einstein's first law of thermodynamics. Soul is in essence energy, therefore, it can never be created nor destroyed. It has always existed and it will forever be. It is alpha and omega within Spirit. Spirit is supreme. Soul is governor.

Psychologists study only one energic aspect of the Soul while theologians emphasize another aspect. Philosophy examines a third aspect of the Soul and science is the discipline which examines the fourth energic expression of the Soul. This split makes it impossible to study the wholeness of the Soul. Now is the time to synthesize Psyche and Soul into one concept, broaden the field of study and research under psychology and bring the study of the Soul under the rubric of an authentic psychology—its true focus. Still, there needs to be a collaboration with other related disciplines. As the four disciplines of psychology, religion, philosophy and science combine their energies, humankind can uncover and rediscover its essence, the Soul.

Second, we operate presuming that some spiritual Reality exists as well. Insomuch as quantum physics has reached the point of study to determine there is nothing between the electrons, protons and neutrons and seems to be saying that a universal consciousness of will and intent appears to be the "creator" of manifest existence, we may presume some spiritual governor of the Universe. When Bohr discovered the realm of quantum physics and the world of subatomic particles, it created a conflict between his theories and Einstein's theories that, to this day, remains unreconciled. With Aristotelian logic, insofar as you could accept Einstein's theory, you could not logically accept Bohr's and vice versa. While both men arrived at theories which the scientific community at large accepted, their theories could not be reconciled—*not by Aristotelian logic*. You were forced to apply paradoxical or Heraclitean logic in order to marry these two seemingly opposing theories. In fact, physicists are still searching for the theory which allows them to marry both of these seemingly mutually exclusive theories into what may be the Theory of Everything, TOE. Stephen Hawking is perhaps the most well known living physicist who has this goal in mind although there certainly are many others.

Einstein and Bohr's experiments led them to two different definitions of reality. Einstein believed there was some inherent order and pattern to the Universe and that everything could be coherently defined when this unified theory of the universe was developed. The implications of Einstein's theories were that there is a reality which exists somehow separate and distinct from the observer that is responsible for the order and pattern in the universe. No matter whether the observer is observing, there is a reality that exists, only it is relative. Bohr's experiments with the subatomic world led him to what is known as the Copenhagen interpretation. In simple terms, this interpretation means that there is no meaning to the objective existence of a quantum particle (a particle of light), unless it is observed. In simple terms, if you don't observe it, it does not exist! In a nutshell, Bohr would say that reality is, in part, based upon the observer. The philosophical and practical implications of this research and its theoretical underpinnings are mind boggling to say the least. Einstein's famous quote as a response to Bohr's theory was "Does the Moon disappear once we stop looking at it?" Debates between these two great scientists ensued and, to this day, science has been unable to arrive at reconciliation between these two theoretical positions. It is likely that one day science will find the "hidden variable" which Einstein often referred to as he spoke of the missing link in Bohr's scientific model. Perhaps science will understand the enormous power and influence of collective Will and a collective consciousness of Goodwill and maybe the mystery of the "hidden variable" of which Einstein spoke will be solved.

Just as we cannot study air, rather we seek to understand it by means of its effects, we explore the realm of spiritual Reality. The Soul, being energy that is eternal, is a spiritual Reality behind and beyond, yet within, the world of matter.

Our focus in this book is primarily the study of the Soul, but it is hoped that, through this theoretical examination, an interdisciplinary vista will be opened so people of all disciplines may unite their Will toward a common purpose of Goodness. Finally, we may begin to understand the power of the collective Will.

*"We are not going to have a soulful spirituality until we begin to think in the ways of soul."*
—Thomas Moore

# III. THE TEMPLE OF THE SOUL

To say the phrase "eternal Soul" is redundant. It is like saying "the slow turtle," "the wet water" or "the spiritual Saint." Soul is invisible to the physical eye making it difficult to use language to describe it, but because we live in a world in such need of reconnecting to its essence, we must attempt to reintroduce ourselves to whom we are. It is our essence of Being.

Universal Soul is Alpha and Omega. It never began, nor will it ever end. Soul is energy. As Einstein said—everything is energy. He might have described the human body as complex energy fields. This energy system affects every cell of your physical body such that your brain and the rest of your body reinvents itself over and over again throughout millennia. The sum total of this energy is responsible for all that has ever existed and all that ever will exist throughout eternity. Energy cannot be created or destroyed. It spends many eternities reinventing itself.

There is your Soul and my Soul and your neighbor's Soul. And, yes, that guy who jumped in front of you at the convenience store last week has a Soul too. And so does the homeless person you pass every day on the way to work. As well as the corporate executive mentioned on the front page of the newspaper who was indicted for fraud. It seems improbable, but it's true.

Every human being has a Soul regardless of whether they pay attention to it or whether they choose to ignore it. But that energy is indubitably there.

The body is the temple, or the vessel, for the Soul. To be more exact, as Plato and Plotinus argue, the body is actually *within* the Soul. As such, the body exists because of the Soul and deserves respect to the extent that the body incarnates and reincarnates in order that the body may experience sense perceptions until the Soul may come to remember and re-reveal itSelf. Yes, there is an "s" on the end of incarnation. The vast majority of humankind is willing to believe that a spirit or Soul of some kind enters the physical body upon birth. Many of them are also willing to believe that this same spirit or Soul leaves the body upon physical death. However, many refuse to question their religious system and wonder whether this process can happen more than once! Why is that? Edwin Schrodinger, one of the greatest physicists of all time, once said that it is easier to split an atom than to change a belief. Why merely accept everything you are taught? History is replete with millions of so-called "experts" whose ideas, opinions and statements have either become obsolete or have proven to be inaccurate.

It seems to be logical that, if the Soul enters and leaves once, it should be able to do it twice, three times or hundreds of times. It is difficult to have the courage to challenge long held beliefs and the religious dogma and doctrines which have been taught. This is especially so when seemingly high authority figures ostracize someone for not adhering to traditional dogma or, even worse, condemn a person to eternal damnation. Just because Rabbi Goldstein says it's true, does it have to be true? And just because Preacher Smith said it is gospel, does that mean it must be merely because he said it? Every person has a different interpretation of what is true. Additionally, we have interpreters who have interpreted interpretations which results in further distortions. Also, words are just symbols so every person has a different meaning for the same word. Words are symbols of symbols which has the further potential to distort truth from one person to another. For example, the word "house" is a symbol of what you live in which is, still further, a symbol of what that structure *means to you*. Words are like airplanes—they take you to different places. It should be no small wonder that truths become watered down over centuries due to people's varying interpretations. Authority figures throughout time have made proclamations that have later proven to be false. We live in a world that is obsessed with accepting information that comes only from a "credible" source, somebody who has a doctorate, has taught workshops, has studied the subject matter for thirty years or has some substantial worldly title such as doctor, lawyer, Judge, CEO, Dean, President, Senator, King or Queen. Typically this refers to a person who is highly educated, exceedingly wealthy, has a substantial secular or religious position, or has an abundance of experience. Without a doubt, someone with abundant experience is a credible and potentially good source for their particular area of knowledge. But who can say whether this person has integrity and is stating the truth or whether they are biased and withhold important factual information or, worse, are merely using their position to intentionally deceive others for self-gain? So a person who is simply "housewife," "carpenter," "electrician," "secretary," "janitor," "unpublished author," "aide," "junior associate," "graduate student," "gardener" or "young" is suddenly and immediately deemed ignorant and having little of value to say. We have come to believe that truth lies somewhere either outside of us or is only found in people who have substantial money, power and position. As a society, we have convinced each other that these are the only people who are able to articulate and validate truth. We oft forget that there have been relatively unknown figures who have courageously and boldly dared to test long held beliefs and have discovered, often to their own peril, that generally accepted "truths" are false.

Hopefully, after reading this book, you will learn to question and challenge your beliefs and hold them up to the sacred test of the Soul. You are not even expected to believe everything in this book. Perhaps the most significant point this book attempts to make is the value of questioning old beliefs. Don't take everything you've been told as necessarily the gospel. See if it resonates within your Soul. For it is within the vast kingdom of your Great Soul where all the answers you will ever need await your re-discovery. If truth were anywhere else besides within each and every one of us, we would, indeed, all be lost forever. The Kingdom of heaven is within us all. You need only seek and ye shall find.

# IV. THE EVOLUTION OF CONSCIOUSNESS

There are certain assumptions that are made when studying consciousness and one of them, in my opinion, must be that consciousness evolves. In fact, the concept of development is so pervasive within the field of psychology with respect to isolated aspects of our personhood such as cognition, emotions and behaviors that it bewilders me to think that mainstream psychology is so reticent to embrace, openly acknowledge and begin a systematic study of such an obvious psychological concept as evolutionary consciousness. It is perhaps a testimony to the difficulty of thinking about thinking or looking outside of consciousness, *per se* (even though that is impossible). Or better yet, the enormous difficulty in seeing the forest for the trees or in knowing higher truths even though they are all around us. It reminds me of the Eastern story of two men talking. The student asks the teacher: "Who discovered water?" The teacher replies: "I don't know who discovered water, but it is certain that the fish did not!"

And so we begin with some fundamental assumptions within our model. They are: there is an eternal evolution of consciousness which moves from a focus on Spirit to a focus on matter and then from a focus on matter back to a focus on Spirit (this could be conceptualized as an eternal evolution from a consciousness of One to a split consciousness and finally back to a consciousness of One). The three stages of consciousness are Pure Knowing (Spirit or Divine Mind) which merges the Many into the One; Being (Soul) which is mediator between Spirit and ego; and Ego (split mind) which perceives only the Many without perceiving or knowing the One.

The Soul is the mediator between matter (dense Light) and Spirit (Pure Light or Pure Blissful Knowingness); the ego can only manifest in a world of physical matter because the ego has a split mind viewing all things as separate and different. The Soul incarnates and reincarnates into matter; this is the realm of Being which forever seeks to illuminate Spirit.

The sacred or Holy Trinity is the tri-fold eternal energy of: 1) Will, 2) Love/Wisdom and 3) Knowledge/Creativity or can be thought of as: the Omnipotent, Omniscient, Eternal Divine Mind or Divine Consciousness (the Divine **Container** which holds all things and of which nothing exists outside because it is infinite), Knowledge/Love/Creativity/Wisdom (the Divine **Contents** within the Divine Mind); and Divine Will (the Divine **Conduit** which activates the Divine Contents).

Upon the unfolding of Soul Consciousness, human consciousness initiates its first authentic connection with the Divine Mind consciousness. The world of spiritual Beings is called the angelic kingdom and imbue pure knowledge, creativity, love and wisdom; this is called Pure Knowing or the realm of Union with God. The spiritual world is lord and governor of all that exists ;in the spiritual world, the *container* is Divine Mind, the *contents* are Pure and Sovereign Goodness, Truth and Beauty and the *conduit* is Pure Will (Dionysius the Areopagite referred to these as operation, essence and power, respectively).

Light or Will is the conduit of the Divine Mind (*arche*), a consciousness with Will, Knowledge, Creativity, Love and Wisdom as arche. These are the many within the One. One refers to the eternal and unlimited Divine Mind within which all thoughts and love exist and which has no boundary

Below is a simplified chart of the evolution of consciousness within the five kingdoms. We commonly get trapped into thinking of evolution in terms of a process in time, although in Ultimate Reality, there is no such thing as time. Time is an illusion just as is space. All of Reality exists everywhere and always and it has never not been. Thus, the only "time" that exists, *per se*, is *now* which really renders the word "time" as moot. For that which always has been and always will be is also that which is Uncreated and has no End. Therefore, what need is there to speak of time? A better, albeit still verbally inadequate and partial, description is that Reality is one continual succession of "now" moments. Ken Wilber speaks of the evolution of consciousness as "actually of the Moment, not of the past."

**Attachment I**

| Type | Possesses | Lacks |
| --- | --- | --- |
| Mineral | Life | "I" consciousness<br>"Other" consciousness<br>"Soul/Group" consciousness<br>"spiritual" consciousness |
| Plant | Life<br>"Other" consciousness | "I" consciousness<br>"Soul/Group" consciousness<br>"Spirit" consciousness |
| Animal | Life<br>"I" consciousness<br>"Other" consciousness | "Spirit" consciousness |
| Human (lowest self)<br>Primitive man<br>Ego | Life<br>"I" consciousness<br>"Other" consciousness | "Soul/Group" consciousness<br>"Spirit" consciousness<br>Self-reflection |
| Human (middle self)<br>Ego | Life<br>"I" consciousness<br>Self-reflection<br>"Other" consciousness | "Soul/Group" consciousness<br>"Spirit" consciousness |
| Human (Higher Self)<br>Soul (Being) | Life<br>"I" consciousness<br>Self-reflection<br>"Other" consciousness<br>"Soul/Group" consciousness<br>"Spirit" consciousness<br>Looks only to Spirit; but reaches<br>Downward to pull others upward | Duality |
| Angelic<br>(lowest spirit self)<br>Spirit (Knowing) | Life<br>"I" consciousness<br>Self-reflection<br>"Other" consciousness<br>"Soul/Group" consciousness<br>"Spirit" consciousness | Physical body<br>Duality |
| Archangelic | "I" and "Other" merge<br>(middle spirit self)<br>Spirit (Knowing) | |
| Oneness<br>(pure Truth) | Absolute merge with the One | |

At this time, little is known about the angelic kingdom and we can only speculate about the consciousness which exists there. One can postulate that, just as with human consciousness there are increasingly higher levels of consciousness, there could be one or more levels of consciousness within the angelic kingdom. Certainly, Christian theology infers there is by the distinctions between angels, archangels, principalities, powers, virtues, dominions, thrones, cherubim and seraphim. As humankind advances in consciousness to higher levels, there will come a time when humankind will unequivocally know these higher realms of consciousness through communion with this energic realm. Ultimately, humans return to this nonphysical dimension.

Let's take a look at the step-by-step process of consciousness beginning with the mineral kingdom and advancing to the Spiritual kingdom. We will see that, just like a circle, the evolution of consciousness returns where it begins such that there is no such thing as a beginning or an end, rather there is only an eternal ebb and flow of consciousness. It is always moving between these stages: 1. being aware of the many within the One, 2. being aware of only the many and not the One, 3. being aware of the One and not the many and finally back to 4. being aware of the many within the One. We could say it this way: being aware of the individual within the Whole; then moving to being aware of the individual, but not the Whole; and then moving toward the Whole, but losing awareness of the individual; and finally moving back to being aware of the individual within the Whole. In philosophical terms, we can say this is moving from an awareness of the particulars within the Universals toward an awareness of only the particulars and not the Universals toward an awareness of only the Universals and not the particulars and finally back to an awareness of the particulars within the Universals.

First, there is essentially and ultimately only the spiritual world where all particulars are simultaneously and paradoxically within the Whole or the One. Think of it as millions of rays of individual lights within One overarching, indivisible Light. Or you may relate it to the infinite colors within the One ray of Light. This world transcends all lower levels and is ultimately that which always *is*. In truth, it has no opposite because it is a conscious state of complete Wholeness and what about Wholeness is split? Ultimately, it is neither good nor evil because that implies there is some opposite Reality, but because it is best to define it in more easily understandable terms, Vedantins will label this consciousness as "good." It is *saguna* Brahma and is, ultimately, indescribable and unutterable. Within this spiritual world, there is no fear because there is no pain or sorrow. What about spirit could know pain? Ken Wilber describes it in *The Spectrum of Consciousness* as:

"...what there is and all there is" or "that which is always already." He further states that "there is no possibility or even meaning in 'trying to find It' or in 'trying to reach It,' for that would imply a movement from a place where Mind is absent to a place where it is present—but there is no place where it is absent. Mind, being everywhere present, abides in no particular place where we can finally grab it."

As we take each of the mineral kingdoms and examine consciousness, perhaps we can have a keener understanding of the evolution of consciousness. Minerals are embedded within the earth and have no conscious awareness of self or other. They simply just are. Minerals do have a certain "life" because they have a certain kind of "growth" process. Minerals do not see self, nor do they have an awareness of other so they can be considered as being embedded within the consciousness of Oneness, not being aware of self, other, difference or separation. In this sense, they can be likened unto the spiritual realm, although minerals are not Spirit because of their inability to have consciousness *per se* or to create all things out of themselves.

We then move into the plant kingdom. Plants are the first example of "splitting" between an upper and a lower self. The primary awareness exists above the ground and is forever pushing upward toward the Sun, a centre. The plant on the outside seems to have no awareness of the "subconscious" part of itself which lies beneath the surface of awareness. At this stage, the plant also seems not to have a sense of self, rather really only strives toward the "Other" which is the centre or the Sun. They can be likened unto the spiritual realm in the sense that they harmonize peacefully and tranquilly with all things simply being as they are, however, they are not spirit because they cannot create all things out of themselves.

Now we move to the animal kingdom where animals definitely have a dim awareness of self which I prefer to call simply the "me" consciousness. This is to distinguish it from the higher "I" consciousness which comes after the ability to master the environment and only with the capability of reasoning and logic. Animals certainly do "think," although it is to be sure that animals do not cogitate about themselves, nor do they have an even higher capacity of thinking about thinking. There is no ordered, systematic contemplation with their only capacity to concentrate being strictly related to that which arises from the physiological senses. Even in this kingdom, we begin to see a lower and higher order with animals such as amoeba and the jellyfish on the lower range and canines and apes at the higher end. Acknowledging different levels within this kingdom and limitations between lower and higher orders of animals, all in all, this world is primarily a world dominated by the biological senses with their ability to see, hear, smell, feel and crudely communicate in their own "language" whether that is chirping, grunting, neighing, cawing or other means. The point is not to begin to pick out all the various particulars that make this kingdom different within itself, rather to form a picture of the overarching similarities in this kingdom which demarcate it from the lower plant kingdom and which will, in turn, demarcate it from the higher human kingdom. For the most part, the animal kingdom is ruled by the physiological senses; their thinking is crude and lacking in logic, reason and judgment; their crude, base emotions are "split" between love within family and biological satiation on the one hand and fierce negative emotions related to a non-mastery of their environment on the other hand. Last, we note that animals seem to have no awareness of a spiritual realm and believe the only "reality" that exists is the material world. At the highest levels, we can say there is a beginning of a crude ego in that the animal has some dim, vague awareness of a "me" distinct from "other" and that the animal is unable to reconcile anything in opposition. The animals are totally incapable of forming a concept of the Universals which would give them an idea of the similarities (not just the differences) which exist between each other and between "me" and "other." For example, the father cougar in a clan is incapable of cogitating to arrive at the concept that he—just like his opponent and adversary, the antelope—desires many of the same things such as to be safe, secure and hunger free. Without reasoning and logic, without an ability to form an awareness of the self and the common Universals which exist between animals within their own kingdom, the crude ego remains forever "split" perceiving a world of separation, difference and lack and, thus, forever locked in a world of mostly negative emotions. Again, like the two preceding kingdoms, there is no consciousness awareness of creating things out of itself.

By this time, we should begin to develop some awareness of some of the overlaps between the kingdoms and understand that the lower order is always missing something that the higher order possesses, but that the higher order possesses—at least initially—some remnant of what the lower order retains. As we begin looking at the human kingdom, try to stay focused on the overarching universal characteristics unique to the entire kingdom and avoid getting caught into the trap of tiny details and particulars.

The human kingdom, as we understand it today, began with the Cave Man or Primitive Man. Wilber would refer to this as the pre-egoic level of consciousness. Notice that we still refer to this "first" human with the male gender even though Cave Woman existed alongside Cave Man. In fact, one important point to note about the Primitive Human is the wide split between the function of the Cave Man versus the function and role of the Cave Woman. As we understand Cave Man, he was the "hunter" and conqueror who wandered outside the security of the cave for wood to build the fire, to scour the dangerous land for food and loin cloths and to protect the family from encroachment of dangerous animals. His critical role was to master the environment which included utilizing those things within the natural environment which would sustain and protect the family from all things within the environment which threatened the life of the family. The warrior consciousness was absolutely critical for survival. Without this warrior consciousness, humankind as a species would not have survived.

On the other hand, we understand the Cave Woman's role as the domestic creature tending to the children and to the hearth. In postulating the consciousness of the Primitive Human, it is likely that she and he were not vastly unlike the highest order of animals within the animal kingdom. We examine the likely mind of Primitive Human.

The first man and woman definitely had a keen sense of "other" and a dim sense of "me" since there was little mastery over the environment at this time and the elements and the animal kingdom were strong, fierce opponents with which to deal. We assume there was a sense of "me" or lower ego, although it had not evolved to a distinct, competent, fully individual sense of "I" or "self" or higher ego yet. One may think of it as "me" fighting to gain a superior position from "Other", but not reaching a more mature "I" conscious state yet. Only until "me" gains a mental state of superiority over, or equality with, "Other" can the human fully develop an individual "self" or ego. We consider the mental-ego a halfway mark on the path to transcendence. So in the beginning, Primitive Human still maintained, as did the middle and higher animals, a sense of "me" in opposition to "Other." The tension of the opposites is high.

As for "thinking," a Primitive Human would begin to develop a sense of reason, rationalization, logic and judgment. In simple terms, the intellect would begin to form, blossom and crystallize. At the lower human conscious level, there is still the primary concern of survival and mastering the environment or as much of it as can be mastered. As the ego begins to develop more fully with its ability to study the particulars of life and all the myriads of ways in which it must maintain survival, it is still largely ruled by physiological sensations such as the desire to satiate hunger and thirst, sexual vigor and the mental and biological need for a minimal level of safety and security. Over time, humankind also begins developing the need for affiliation as it begins conquering more of its physical environment. Referring to the "beginning of the middle egoic" level of consciousness, Wilber points to fifth century B.C. Greece. With this developing mind when more physical safety and security from the harsh elements have been mastered, the consciousness of humankind would soon begin to contemplate higher things such as mental and emotional security and affiliation. Along with that, maintaining order would become important, therefore, justice would become a key consideration and how to create justice within an otherwise chaotic environment. Humankind's innate need to move toward homeostasis would allow for the development of basic laws which, in turn, would necessitate the need for rulers and governors to oversee these laws. This means that groups form and, quite naturally, groups which oftentimes opposed one another due to perceived inequalities. Maybe one group perceived the other group had more loin cloths or more stockpiles of food. Jealousy, envy, greed would lead to crime and war. The crude ego sees the world as "split," perceiving a world of separation, difference and lack, therefore, it fights for superiority. Because men were physically more powerful, they became the protectors of the remainder of the family and the harbingers of wealth and power. This physical superiority translated into a belief in the overall male superiority over females as males assumed roles which required logic, reason and judgment in maintaining peace and order within their own group and in securing safety from being harmed by an outside group, the "Other." These mastery roles left little room for kindness and compassion between groups of people since it was a world of eat or be eaten and serious laborious and dangerous competition to maintain the basic sustenance to live. The formation of a stronger ego was predicated on its ability to defend against the "Other" and to protect and bolster "self." It seems logical that the life of the male leader must have been deemed quite valuable since it was, in fact, his responsibility to ensure the safety and security of the entire family or clan.

Language developed as a means to more efficiently and effectively communicate ideas which, in turn, would allow for self-expression, establishing bartering rules and rules of conduct, protection of self or group and as a means of artistic expression. Fear must have been the ruling emotion in the ego because of the serious risk for mortal peril. The ego primarily views the world through a lens of "self" versus "Other" with little or no conscious awareness of the Universal similarities which exist between self and Other, therefore, there would be substantial tension between self and Other. In addition, it would be an issue of survival for the differences between the male and female roles to be clearly demarcated and upheld.

No one holds the final truth on how Primitive Human perceived the spiritual realm and how and when that consciousness developed. It is known, however, that there was a belief in some power or energy or Being (or Beings) which was (were) sovereign or divine, not human. Even though many different cultures developed over the centuries, we do know that by the time the Egyptian civilization formed, the belief in many gods was common and pervasive. One can say with relative assurance that this belief in the spiritual realm has existed in the human kingdom as far back as humankind existed and that even today a substantial number of humans maintain even though in varying degrees and concepts.

No one knows for sure who introduced the two primary concepts of "God" and how they were introduced to humanity, but these two predominant concepts are 1) God is anthropomorphic, a man who is Creator and rules over us, and 2) God is not a person, rather an energy, force or universal intelligence and this force lies within and around us all. The first concept is endemic within many Christians and Muslims while the second concept is inherent, for the most part, within Eastern philosophies such as Buddhism and Taoism. Unlike Western society, Eastern thought considers philosophy, religion, psychology and ethics to be inseparably bound so to speak of one discipline is to automatically infer each of the others. Buddhists do not believe in an anthropomorphic "God", rather they believe in Nirvana, a state of blissful consciousness. It is the Christian equivalent of God or Heaven. The first concept of God, more or less, places humankind at the whim of a governor, denies the role of personal responsibility in self-tragedy and allows for authorities within organizations such as churches and synagogues to maintain dominance over people through the utilization and enforcement of dogma and doctrines. Indeed, in some Western religions, there is a tacit understanding that the only way one can "reach God" is through the mediator of priest or pastor. Within this belief system, either God is responsible for both good and bad things or God is responsible for good and another entity, usually Lucifer, is responsible for tragedies.

The second concept of God being a universal energy or intelligence places humankind as a pivotal and dominant, although not entirely omnipotent, player in its own destiny; emphasizes humankind's free will to choose goodness or reject goodness; emphasizes the self-empowering role that humanity plays in creating a world of goodness or a world lacking goodness; and highlights the co-creative role that humankind plays in creating reality. There is no other person who can mediate between God and the individual because God is not a person, rather is the energy of Divine Goodness to imbue and carry within one's self. In a nutshell, humankind is primarily responsible for good or evil depending upon whether the free will of humankind elects goodness or rejects goodness. The importance of this higher mental aspect of the human kingdom over the animal kingdom is that, for the first time, consciousness is able to contemplate itself in addition to the powerful role it plays in creation and in the development of "reality."

In looking at the progression of the evolution of humankind, we can see that humanity became "civilized," that is, humankind created laws and attempted to live by them so that order could be maintained. As humankind began reaching for higher levels of mental states such as self-respect and self-esteem, so did the ego begin its ascent into a dim recognition and realization of the Universals which permeate all of humanity. One may say that, alongside satisfying the lower biological needs such as hunger and thirst, humankind also began to lift its awareness or broaden its awareness to the fact that there are common similarities amongst different groups. Understanding that some humans have more highly evolved consciousness levels than others, we can say that humankind, unlike the animal kingdom, has the capability to cooperate, collaborate and cogitate within larger and larger groups of people and to work toward common goals which are beneficial to both the individual and the group. As the ego consciousness evolves to higher levels, the wide "split" which is inherent within its awareness begins to diminish. In other words, as the ego begins to see more commonalities between self and Other, rather than concentrating and focusing on differences, the "split" diminishes. The "split" forms because the ego cannot reconcile, respect and equally value the opposites and, instead, elects to focus on difference, separation and lack at the relative level of existence. No awareness of the Whole exists.

At the Soul consciousness level, the "split" becomes more narrow as the mind begins to concentrate and focus its energies toward commonalities,

Universals and all that unites. What unites groups of people, as opposed to what divides people, is the primary mode of thinking. This is the merging of thought and feeling, female and male, minorities and non-minorities, rich and poor, old and young into a common bond of what makes these opposites similar. What can we say that minorities and non-minorities have in common? We can say they both wish for love, peace and harmony. What might we find in common between the young and the old? We can say they both wish for well being, happiness and comfort. These are spiritual Universals common to all human beings. As the Soul unfolds and views the world in terms of spiritual Universals and stops focusing on the particulars and the minutia which separates and divides, then humanity can finally begin its upward ascent back to the world of Spirit. And toward that end, greater levels of peace and harmony are inevitable outcomes.

*It is perfectly certain that the Soul is immortal and imperishable, and our Souls will actually exist in another world.*
—Plato

# V. THE SOUL AND SOUL CONSCIOUSNESS

The Soul is the ubiquitous, eternal, energic expression of the Divine *Nous* which incarnates and reincarnates into a physical body to express itself in and through matter. The fully embodied Soul eternally uses the Will to seek:

to know Truth ("I" as Self)—a primary *masculine* energy: **knowledge**

to create Beauty ("It" as Object)---a secondary *masculine* energy: **creativity**

to love Goodness ("We" as a Dyad)---a primary *feminine* energy: **love**

to be Wise about the Will ("All" or One)---a secondary *feminine* energy: **wisdom**

The Soul is your essence of Being. It is subtle light energy which is eternal and never dissipates upon physical death. Every human being *uses* knowledge, creativity, love and wisdom in order to *seek* knowledge, creativity, love and wisdom at the Soul level and it matters not whether you are female or male. Both genders have the equal *potential* and equal *capacity* to achieve these. Neither gender has sole, exclusive rights to expressing them. It is because we have split these energies and placed unequal value upon them between the genders that is the cause of rampant human pain and suffering. These energies can no more be separated than the color blue could be separated from the entire color spectrum. These energic expressions of the Soul are the ubiquitous energies inherent within all humanity, therefore, to divide them and separate them is ultimately impossible although humankind, particularly abusive patriarchy, has been attempting it for millennia. This division has resulted in untold human malaise.

The expression, function, structure, dynamic, purpose and goal of the Soul are identical. That is to say that the function of the Soul is no different than the Soul's purpose. And the Soul's expression is identical to the goal of the Soul. When you speak of one aspect of the Soul, you are simultaneously referring to every other aspect of the Soul. This is the merging of the Soul's Being of subject and object and means, or of thinking, feeling and willing, written about for thousands of years in philosophy.

When the Soul has not awakened yet, (another way of saying the individual does not yet know its true essence), the Soul has yet to discover what it is seeking. The simple, basic function is:

**1. TO KNOW** **(KNOWLEDGE)**
**2. TO CREATE** **(CREATIVITY)**
**3. TO LOVE** **(LOVE)**
**4. TO BE WISE** **(WISDOM)**

When the Soul is no longer split into the illusory ego and when the Soul is awakened, mature and fully embodied, it activates its Will to go a step further in order to:

know Truth ("I" as Self)—a primary *masculine* energy: **knowledge**
create Beauty ("It" as Object)—a secondary *masculine* energy: **creativity**
love Goodness ("We" as a Dyad)—a primary *feminine* energy: **love**
be Wise about the Will ("All" as a Whole)—a secondary *feminine* energy: **wisdom**

The fully embodied Soul uses Goodwill toward itSelf and other or, to borrow from a theological idea, the Soul always uses Goodwill toward the All. It seeks it and only knows itSelf through this primary goal and action. Love, at its most elemental definition, is simple, pure Goodwill toward Self and Other. Said another way, love is using the Will to obtain Goodness for Self and Other. The Will is the energic expression which precedes and merges with action. You cannot act without the Will. When we use the Will to achieve self-centered goals which deny others Goodness, we are using the will of the ego. An example is the seemingly rampant deceit and corruption at the top levels of Corporate America where CEOs use their power in order to benefit themselves, first and foremost, and they relinquish primary concern and care for employees and/or investors. When we use the Will to achieve Goodness for the All, we are using Divine Will. An example of this would be people such as Jesus the Christ, the Dalai Lama, Mahatma Ghandhi, Mother Teresa and Martin Luther King who used their own lives, at risk for immense peril, to better the lives of others. There are different kinds of human love such as platonic love, familial love and erotic love, but the most essential kind of love is simply Goodwill. Using our time and energy toward saving animals from abuse or toward saving our ecology are examples of simple, essential love or Goodwill. Goodwill is the *sin qua non* expression of a fully embodied Soul, therefore, the Soul cannot be fully expressed without love.

To use the word "structure" is somewhat misleading because the word implies that the Soul has boundaries. In reality, the Soul does not have boundaries. Structure is used as an attempt to help us better understand the concept of the Soul, but it should not be considered as a physical form with spatial boundaries and limitations. For what about energy could ever be limited? This is a good time to reemphasize how words are symbols of symbols and to remember how words can cause people to arrive at different ideas and interpretations which, in turn, create misunderstandings and conflicts. If we recall the instance of many rays coming from one light, we can perhaps eliminate much misunderstanding when a reference is made to the "structure" of the Soul.

Psyche or Soul has four *equal* functions or parts: to know, to create, to love and to be wise. Thus, knowledge, creativity, love and wisdom are the four (4) primary energic expressions of the fully expressed Soul. Plotinus, the greatest neo-Platonic philosopher, writes in the *Enneads* of the Soul having several parts in a hierarchical fashion. Plotinus' irrational Soul may be considered our modern version of the ego which is split between the lower and higher selves. Plotinus' rational Soul is the Higher Self which points toward, circles around and always moves toward Reality or the One because knowledge, creativity, love and wisdom are ever in its meditational focus. These four energies are unfettered and unblocked when the Soul manifests. These energies flow naturally and harmonically just as the melodic beauty of symphonies do. Things such as stress, poor diet, abuse, emotional neglect, pollution, deception, anxiety, depression, cruelty, unkindness, hate, anger, jealousy, envy, guilt, shame and a myriad of other factors inhibit and block the free-flowing, natural and harmonic expression of these energies. The more environmental insults the individual experiences, the more substantial is the blockage of the Soul's expressions. Children who are subjected repeatedly to sexual, physical and emotional abuse or neglect, poor nutrition, drugs and these types of severe psychological and physiological insults, the greater Soul poverty they will experience which, in turn, will almost always result in severe psychological problems.

One should understand knowledge, creativity, love and wisdom as four functions which are *equally valued* by the Soul and which are all naturally and fully expressed when the Soul is operative. The first two functions of the Soul are *masculine energies: to know and to create.* These energies are understood to be active, mobile and changing. This energy pushes outward and seeks individuality; it is in this sense that the masculine energy must compete in order to fulfill its principal function. The second two functions of the Soul are *feminine energies: to love and to be wise.* Since antiquity these attributes have been defined as feminine. These feminine energies are understood to be passive, immobile and unchanging. This energy pulls things inward into itself, always seeking to unite; it is in this sense that the feminine energy is collaborative and unifying. Both masculine and feminine energies are eternally co-existing within Reality in a perfect tension of the opposites. Neither energy ever began, nor will it ever cease. Plotinus writes of his belief that the Soul is paradoxically both in motion and at rest.

This is analogous to the concept of "complementarity" when writing of the dual and paradoxical nature of particles and waves in quantum physics. The Soul has the eternal paradoxical co-existency of motion and rest inherent within itSelf which is also simultaneously the essence of all that "Is."

Upon understanding the Psyche—which is forever whole---we see that the field of psychology, dominated by male leaders, has never studied the whole Soul, rather has only studied the masculine part of the Soul. Historically, the field of psychology has only studied the mind which is the masculine part of the Psyche, therefore, the field has failed to embrace and study the feminine energies of the Psyche which are love and wisdom.

When the Soul is expressing fully and naturally, all four of these energic expressions manifest within an individual. They are unfettered, thus, the person can express them freely. Societal norms, while some being necessary for a minimal level of social and moral order and decorum, are also the cause of much inhibition of the Soul. Some social norms are essential for a sustained civilization, however, others foster and support gender biases, discrimination, prejudice, abuse, oppression, suppression, arrogance, insecurity and greed. For example, males have, for thousands of years, fostered the concept that women are inferior to men. I hypothesized earlier how and why this belief likely developed during the time of Primitive Man and Woman. This belief is a "societal norm" that continues although it began to face serious erosion with the Women's Movement in the 1950s and 1960s. Societal norms are so embedded in the consciousness of society that going against societal norms, in many instances, results in devaluing, ostracism, ridicule, estrangement and outright rejection. We continue to face social norms of "women and minorities are inferior to white males" in American society and throughout much of the world. Little of the Great Soul has unfolded in the world.

What does the Soul seek to know? What does it seek to create? What does it seek to love? And what does it seek to be wise about? The fully embodied Soul forever seeks to know Truth. Not simply worldly truth, but Spiritual Truth. Knowledge is Truth in the spiritual realm. There is no distinction between the two. The perfectly embodied Soul eternally seeks to create Beauty. Not only worldly beauty, but Spiritual Beauty. There is no difference between creativity and Beauty in the spiritual realm. Forever and ever, the Great Soul loves Goodness or, as Plato and Plotinus referred to it, "the Good." Love can simply be defined as the Will toward Goodness for Self *and* other, or Goodwill toward the All. All other definitions are superfluous to this simple, core definition. This is the perfect state in the spiritual realm. And, without end, the Soul seeks the wisdom of the Divine Will because it knows that, only through wisdom, can it know Peace. Wisdom in the spiritual realm is aligning with the Divine Will, the perfect obeyance of all spiritual laws which manifests perfect Peace. This is the realm where having and being are consciously joined. What one *has* is what one "*is.*" This is the Soul and it forever seeks to remember and know itSelf. This is Perfect Goodness and the Will of the Soul is Perfect Goodness in the Spiritual Realm. Plotinus speaks of the three divine principles as God, *Nous* and the World Soul. God is "the Good" or that which is transcendent, ineffable, immaterial, eternal, unchanging and unmovable. Plotinus says that "the Good" is the king in the spiritual realm. Aristotle refers to the Absolute Good as the "Unmoved Mover." The Soul moves toward "the Good". According to Plotinus and Plato, there is a rational Soul and an irrational Soul. Aristotle would say there is a higher self and a lower self. In the myth in *Phaedrus*, Plato describes the Soul as a chariot of reason which is drawn by two horses, one which is obedient and powerful in its ascent, the other which is disobedient as it pursues its sensual desires. The rational Soul of Plotinus is always looking toward "the Good" and moving around it, seeking it. In addition, the Soul is incorruptible, therefore it cannot know or be evil. Thus, the Soul Consciousness model also sees the Soul as incorruptible, but instead of being split into a rational and irrational Soul, the rational Soul of Plotinus could be considered the Soul of the Soul Consciousness model whereas the irrational Soul of Plotinus could be considered the ego or ego consciousness which is, to be sure, a "split" mind. Aristotle's lower self could be considered the ego as well. The Soul which falls in love with its own images, i.e, physical things, becomes an ego. It is in that sense, that the ego is a "lower" energy because only the Soul with its authentic powers of knowledge, creativity, love and wisdom and then even higher divine principles of Spirit---Truth, Beauty and Goodness—have real and eternal power. All physical things are but symbols, images and presentations of a spiritual fruit. Plotinus refers to physical things as "shadows" because they are imperfect representations or emanations from "the Good." It is not the physical thing we seek, rather it is forever and ever the spiritual fruit which we seek. We delude ourselves into thinking that the physical object is what we want, but the truth is that we only seek the spiritual fruit within or behind the physical object. One day, science will acknowledge and humbly bow to the ineffable awesomeness of that which "*Is,*" the realm of the Spirit, the Uncreated Creator, the Divine Mind/Heart, the Infinite Boundless, the Invisible Oneness, Omniscient and Omnipresent Divineness that simply "*Is.*" This "Is-ness" can never be quantified or measured because it is infinite and boundless being everywhere at once.

Outlined below are the functions and gender of the perfectly balanced Soul:

| Expression | Function | Gender | Archetypal Role |
|---|---|---|---|
| To Know | Empower | Masculine | Teacher |
| To Create | Generate | Masculine | Carpenter |
| To Love | Share | Feminine | Lover |
| To be Wise | Integrate | Feminine | Counselor |

In order to express soulfully, the Soul must be balanced which means it functions as an *androgynous energy*. The Soul is the mind and the heart of what constitute, when combined, the collective androgynous consciousness of psychological health and wholeness. Even the medical community has developed an interest in the relationship between the mind and the heart which is given attention in the March and April, 2003 issues of *The Harvard Mental Health Letter* as it discusses research which suggests a link between heart disease and depression.

Androgyny is an ancient concept. Jung indirectly referred to it when he spoke of "the reconciliation of the opposites" and Eastern philosophy refers to it when they speak of the androgyny of Brahman and the Atman. The Soul is always guided by the Will toward Goodness. This is authentic Goodwill. Goodwill *always* moves toward the good of Self *and* the whole, therefore, the nature of the Soul is to include, embrace and unify while, paradoxically and simultaneously, also maintaining individuality. It is a kind of "both/and" experience which is why the Soul can only be understood through paradoxical logic. This is the antithesis of modern society where the ego self seeks only for itself at the exclusion of others which is an "either/or", Aristotelian logic. No balance of Goodwill is sought between Self *and* other. This imbalance is the cause of virtually all societal ills.

When the Soul is expressing itSelf naturally and fully, one can say that the individual is balanced **intra**psychically and **inter**psychically. *Intra*psychically refers to that which is within a person, so it refers to a person who is balanced between the four (4) primary energic expressions, knowledge, creativity, love and wisdom. They imbue these energies from within and project them equally and consistently outward and into the world. When a person is functioning at a high level *inter*psychically, this means the individual recognizes, respects and honors the interrelatedness of all that exists in life from the kingdom of nature to the animal kingdom to the human kingdom and up through the spiritual realm. One could say that the individual responds with goodwill to other people, but also honors and respects the interrelatedness that exists between the mineral, plant, animal, human and spiritual kingdoms. To affect one affects the others.

Here is perhaps a good time to introduce the difference between Goodness and the lack of Goodness. Goodness is the inherent ownership and essence of all positive energies of emotions and thoughts. Where Goodness is absent, there is a presence of all negative energies—emotions such as fear, anger, greed, envy, jealousy, guilt, shame and sadness. Goodness is an energy which arises out of itSelf, through itSelf, by itSelf and within itSelf. It does this because it is Whole. While the ego is furthest from spiritual Truth, Beauty and Goodness, the Soul always moves toward Goodness and, when it sees the Good, is stirred within itSelf. Truth, Beauty and Goodness always stir the Great Soul and brings its remembrance back unto itSelf. Plotinus speaks of the Soul as turning back towards itself. One can relate this to Eliot Deutsch's description of "*saguna* Brahman", in his book, *Advaita Vedanta: A Philosophical Reconstruction,* stating this is "*saguna* Brahman—Brahman with qualities....it is that about which something can be said. And it is also a kind of spiritual experience....state of being wherein all distinctions between subject and object are harmonized...a duality in unity is present here, and consequently, the power of love....*saguna* Brahman is a state of vital loving awareness."

The Soul is the Higher Self and is the closest energic link to the highest spiritual realm of *nirguna* Brahman which is Ultimate Reality. In Reality, *nirguna* Brahman is beyond both good and evil because it is the realm of complete, unlimited and infinite Wholeness. Because of humankind's limited consciousness, Advaitans refer to Brahman as good. For purposes of creating some minimal level of reconnection with the Ultimate Realm, my book will speak of Goodness as the realm of the spiritual world and to which the Soul always aspires. Once the Soul reaches the Ultimate Absolute Reality, the Soul becomes this Reality such that there is no longer a Soul Consciousness which moves toward something, rather it has reached its perfect state of Highest Self, Pure Knowing and Absolute "Is"ness. For purposes of the next practical step in what Wilber refers to as the "Great Chain of Being", however, we understand the Soul Consciousness as awaiting its reawakening so that it can, ultimately, move toward this re-manifestation and re-unfoldment of Highest Being and Pure Knowing. Like the ego, the Soul transcends although the Soul, unlike the ego, is not split. The Soul transcends and becomes *nirguna* Brahman which is Highest Self, the Ultimate and Absolute about which nothing can be said. It is, as Lao Tzu says, that which is unutterable because it transcends thinking.

Along this course of thinking, we say the Soul always and forever points to the spiritual realm of Reality and Goodness. Goodness is both cause and effect. Said yet another way, Goodness never began and will never end because it arises out of itSelf and turns back into itSelf or seeks itSelf in another. In Timothy Freke's book, Lao Tzu's *Tao Te Ching*, he refers to Tao by saying "emerging from the Source—returning to the Source. This is the way of

Nature." Stated another way, he says:

**TAO MOVES IN CIRCLES ALWAYS FLOWING BACK TO TAO**

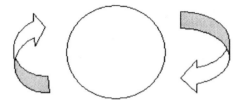

The Yang of the masculine energy moves away from Tao; the Yin of the feminine moves toward the Tao. This movement is eternal. Both are cause and effect of Tao. Love is both cause and effect. Truth is both cause and effect. Wisdom is both cause and effect. Love arises out of itSelf. All forms of Goodness lead to each other. Said another way, when you are experiencing love, you are simultaneously experiencing truth, knowledge, peace, joy, etc. These are the Many within the One that is referred to in ancient Greek philosophy. You cannot divide and separate any of these from one another. That which creates itSelf out of itSelf is eternal. Goodness never began and will never end because it simply extends itSelf forever. It is that which *"Is."*

Negative emotions such as fear, anger, hate, greed, envy, jealousy, shame, guilt and sadness do not come from themselves. It takes a physical world in order for these emotions to manifest. In fact, they can *only* manifest in a physical world. If you close your eyes and imagine you are a Spiritual Being with no physical body, then how could you possibly experience pain and suffering? Pain and suffering only exist from the existence you have while you incarnate in a physical body, experiencing the five senses. If you are pure spirit, pure light, then when would you ever feel pain? What would ever be lacking that would cause you suffering?

Negative emotions cannot create, cannot arise out of themselves and cannot unify. Negative emotions cannot create, rather they only destroy. Anger cannot arise out of itself; it must arise from being in a physical world and having a physical body which feels pain. As the ego looks around, it falsely perceives difference, separation and lack because it only believes in the reality of what it can see. Truly, it does appear that everything around us is different and separate, but everything around us is really only a dream that is here today, gone tomorrow. Physical things do not last; they constantly change. Spirit never changes. Your Soul, your spiritual Being, continues forever. That energy which creates out of itSelf is beginningless, real and eternal, therefore, Goodness is eternal and negative emotions are not. Goodness is that from which you came, therefore, you were born from a conscious state of spiritual Goodness.

If ill will is the guiding force, the ego is operative and the Soul is not expressing itSelf. With the ego in control, the Soul can be considered to be hiding in the background while the ego is in control in the foreground. Below is a table which portrays how the ego splits as it concentrates on the physical world of separation and division. This is the ego, a split or dual mind:

**Attachment III**

| Expression | Function | Gender | Archetypal Role |
|---|---|---|---|
| To Know | Empower | Masculine | Teacher |
| *To Deceive* | *Control* | *Masculine* | *Dictator* |
| To Create | Generate | Masculine | Carpenter |
| *To Destroy* | *Condemn* | *Masculine* | *Warrior* |
| To Love | Share | Feminine | Lover |
| *To Hate* | *Consume* | *Feminine* | *Villain* |
| To be Wise | Integrate | Feminine | Counselor |
| *To be Foolish* | *Ignore* | *Feminine* | *Fool* |

When the ego is operative, deception, destruction, hatred, punishment, oppression, suppression and foolishness is always an outcome to some varying degree or another. The punitive milieu in corporations is an example of the ego in control. The deception behind marital infidelity is of the ego. Sibling rivalry is ego. All kinds of abuses such as child, spousal, animal and ecological abuse are manifestations of the ego. All gender, racial, ethnic, religious, social and economic prejudices are warehouses of the ego consciousness which fears lack, cannot comprehend the interrelatedness of all that exists and believes in superiority and inferiority.

When the Soul is balanced and expressing itSelf harmoniously, this is authentic power. Authentic power manifests when there is a unification of purpose toward Goodwill, therefore, the Soul moves toward giving. When the ego is expressing itself, this is inauthentic, illusory or worldly power. Worldly power of the ego is built upon the false belief that the individual alone can have power; therefore, the ego only moves to take and hoard. The field of psychology has so strongly emphasized the strength and value of the ego that it is difficult to begin to unweave this long held conviction. Virtually the entire world power systems have bought into the concept of the value and supremacy of the ego. Spiritual bankruptcy has been its legacy.

In spiritual language, the Soul refers to the One that is contained within the many which ultimately makes up the One of the Universe or what is sometimes referred to as God, Brahman, the Universal Soul, Nirvana or Eternal Being. This Universal Soul or Being or God is the power or energy created by the unification of all Souls. This is authentic power. It always has been and always will be creating and recreating. There has never *not* been spirit or Soul.

Your Soul and your neighbor's Soul do not have rigid, solid boundaries like the edge of a chair or the rim of a drinking glass. Your Soul should be thought of as a mass of energy or light. Indeed, the "substance" of your Soul is light. Perhaps the best way of saying it is to say you are one ray of light and your neighbor is another ray of light and every person is a ray of light, but together you make up the Sun! Your Soul is intertwined with your neighbor's Soul, yet you still maintain your own unique identity. You cannot separate one ray of light from another, but we know that there are millions of rays of light.

When you combine my Soul and your Soul and all the other Souls on the planet, we have the Universal Soul or Over Soul. Yet there are many Souls that exist in the Spiritual world who have not incarnated in this world, so we must count those Great Souls as well. Think of all those Souls combined as One mass of energy. Your thoughts, actions and behaviors have an effect on all the other Souls. Their thoughts, actions and behaviors are all linked to your Soul. Just as you throw a pebble into a pond and there are ripples which manifest, so do your thoughts and actions have a ripple effect on the natural environment and other humans. Humans continue to use toxins that are destroying the ozone layer and are creating serious ecological disturbances which will, in time, create a critically dangerous environment for humanity.

Humans have created their own demise. What we give out always comes back to us. The responsibility for the environment lies with humanity so we can blame no one other than ourselves. We can create a healthy environment by respecting and honoring it, or we can create an unhealthy environment by dishonoring our planet. Corporations and their blind allegiance to greed have contributed substantially to our ecological demise. But corporations are nourished by the money that people give them when the corporate products and services are purchased; therefore, all of humanity has to share responsibility in this. Just like the ripple effect of toxins and waste, you cannot separate your Soul from influencing another Soul and, ultimately, from influencing the One Soul mass of energy—the Universal Soul.

Historically, many philosophers such as Heraclitus, Pythagoras, Socrates, Plato, Aristotle and Plotinus have written about the Soul. Theologians like St. Augustine and St. Thomas Aquinas have written about the Soul. Some ancient philosophers said that the Soul is in your heart. Others have believed that the mind is where your Soul exists. Both are partially correct. The Soul expresses itself primarily *within* and *through* two major bodily organs--your heart and your mind. But the Soul is *not* your *physical* heart and mind. The bodily organs are forms, representations or symbols of the Soul's masculine and feminine expressions. The organs are vessels or containers and, as such, should be honored and respected, but they are not the essence of the Soul. The functions of the Soul are expressed on a physical level through your bodily organs. All that exists within the spiritual world manifests itself, in some way, on a physical level. All positive thoughts and emotions reside within the spiritual realm, but in the physical world of matter, *both* positive and negative thoughts and emotions manifest. This is the birth of duality. Because the physical world of matter causes a kind of splitting in your mind, all negative emotions develop from this splitting. More about this will be discussed later.

Metaphorically speaking, there is a "structure" to the Psyche or Soul. Medical science and psychology have come to identify the Psyche as synonymous with the mind which is only one structural component of the Soul; however, Psyche refers to the entire structure of the Soul. The mind with its world of knowledge, thought and cognitive analysis is, to be sure, a component of Psyche or Soul. However, another *equally valuable* component of Psyche is the heart which expresses love and wisdom. Freud was a brilliant intellectual with what appears to be little understanding of universal love, compassion and kindness. He specifically wrote of the need for the "primacy of intellect" and told a personal friend that he had never felt, nor understood, the "oceanic feeling" which connects humanity in a universal spiritual feeling of oneness. In *Civilization and Its Discontents*, Freud conveyed his lifelong belief in the devaluation of the sacred feminine by saying:

> "...a universal love of mankind and the world represents the highest standard which man can reach....I should like to bring forward my two main objections to this view. A love that does not discriminate seems to me to forfeit a part of its own value, by doing an injustice to its object; and secondly, not all men are worthy of love...if this grandiose commandment had run 'Love thy neighbor as thy neighbor loves thee,' I should not take exception to it."

Neither did Skinner or Ellis (the founders of behavioral and cognitive psychological models) understand universal love. Like Freud, they were both adamant atheists and their psychological models and their writings are testimonies to their belief in the supremacy of intellect, logic and reason. This is why psychoanalytic, cognitive and behavioral theories and therapies will never serve as guideposts for humankind to move to the next level of Soul Consciousness since all three models were explicitly devaluing the feminine principle of life. In my opinion, we owe Freud a large debt for leaving posterity a brilliant exegesis of the split ego consciousness, but it is the dark half of humankind and his model, along with the cognitive and behavioral models, will never take psychology to psychological wholeness and fullness of Being, to the Soul. As Maslow stated, "Freud has given us the unhealthy half of psychology, now we must find the other healthy half."

The world's obsession with intellect as a god, particularly Aristotelian logic, must end and, instead, a broader, more embracing psychological wholeness must be incorporated in our world. Aristotelian logic is a masculine cognitive style because it divides; Heraclitean logic is a feminine cognitive style because it unifies. The world is literally failing to move to a higher level of consciousness and to experience greater levels of psychological peace because of our masculine leadership which is biased toward, and obsessed with, masculine ways of thinking. The world is stagnating because of the flooding of the masculine energy of the Psyche, or Soul, and the paucity of the feminine energy of the Psyche. Yes, intellect and Aristotelian logic are essential in understanding things at the relative, mundane level of existence and in surviving as a human being (you either stay awake while driving a car or you fall asleep, you either eat and survive or you starve and die), however, at the ultimate levels of Reality, only Heraclitean logic can provide a basis for understanding. The Soul Consciousness cannot be grasped or obtained through intellectual prowess alone. Consequently, intellectual geniuses may never attain this higher level of consciousness if they are unable to integrate the sacred and intuitive feminine. Without question, intellect is necessary and important. Nothing can be known or built without it. But without its feminine partners, love and wisdom, intellect is a clanging symbol. As Einstein once said: "We should take care not to make the intellect our god; it has, of course, powerful muscles, but no personality." We need only look around us at the abundance of intellect at the helm of corporations, political systems, educational systems and all fields of study to realize that intellect alone still has not solved the world's problems of unrest, chaos, violence, hate, intolerance, discrimination, greed and oppression. It is in that sense that humankind must awaken to the absolute necessity of transforming the inaccurate and limiting paradigm that "intellect is supreme" into a more accurate, inclusive paradigm that "intellect and love are *equally important* in the salvation of the world." This is the *Bodhiccita* or "Intelligent Heart" of the Bodhisattva of which the Mahayana Buddhists write. It is the Binah (feminine) and Chokmah (masculine) which results in the Kether (the One that is All and the One that is in All) of the Kabbalah of Jewish mysticism. Both of these ancient concepts are pointing to essentially the same transcendent, androgynous consciousness. They are simply two paths to the same destination. Only until the equality of the masculine and feminine is embraced by the leaders in politics, economics, education, religious institutions, science and all other aspects of life will this world ever finally make a solid gain toward peace. Much of the responsibility as to whether humankind remains in chaos or moves toward peace lies with the current leaders of the world who are presently virtually all male. If this mental shift in value does not occur within the next few decades, the masses of humanity will revolt because greed, war, intolerance, oppression, prejudice, hate and violence is escalating to unbearable levels and the growing distance between the "haves" and the "have-nots" is becoming increasingly intolerable to the mass consciousness. This growing disequilibrium must return to a state of psychological homeostasis.

To love and to be wise, energic expressions of the heart, are *not* subordinate to intellect and creativity, the energic expressions of the mind, although the ego consciousness of the world would attempt to have you believe they are unequal in value. In fact, knowledge and creativity without love and wisdom will always result in abusive power. This abuse of power by our current patriarchal society is due to an immature masculine ego which seeks to dominate and control society. This abusive, arrogant patriarchy was rampant throughout ancient times and, without doubt, currently exists in our political and business communities and even within many religions. The control, power, domination, greed and deceit in these systems are inherent in any abusive power structure and are the demise of all historical civilizations.

Earlier it was mentioned that masculine energy is active while feminine energy is passive. It would be a misunderstanding to consider active energy "good" and passive energy "bad." That is an erroneous judgment from a lack of understanding these two terms. Active could best be considered as that which activates whereas passive can best be understood as that which rests. The energies of knowledge and creativity cause changes in other things, other particulars. Knowledge and creativity focus on parts. This is the moving nature of the Soul consciousness. The energies of love and wisdom bring about rest and this is the restful nature of the Soul. These energies manifest a consciousness of Universal commonalities and bring the Whole to a state of rest. Love and Wisdom focus on the Whole. Activity and rest are *equally* important. This is the cyclical nature of the Soul consciousness.

Active and passive energies are not to be confused with being exclusively linked to the *physical body* of a man and a woman, respectively. That is yet another false belief. It *can* be that way, but it *need not be*. Humankind has the power to make up a set of rules by which to live. We can establish rules which limit or which create unlimited potential. That is the power of the Mind!

Because of the divisiveness that exists between masculinity and femininity, we associate men with being aggressive and women as being passive. Due to the social construct which men have promulgated, our world largely believes that men must be masculine and women must be feminine although this has begun to slowly change over the past two decades in some countries. Still, some people denigrate women who exhibit so-called "masculine attributes." Society has taught us that it is okay if men are aggressive, but women do not have permission. Who are the people behind the word "society"?

To be sure, in the business world, women in upper management face so much discrimination that they feel, in order to garner top positions, they must emulate men by being aggressive, demanding and controlling. Since many men believe that women do not have sufficient "masculine cognitive ability" nor do they have the aggressive, competitive masculine nature, some women change entirely and mirror the aggressive, arrogant patriarchy which controls the upper echelon of most corporations and political and economic organizations. The problem is when women mirror the behaviors and actions of men in order to be accepted and rise to top positions in business, men articulate the excuse that women are not supposed to act like men! In essence, women can't win because no matter what they do, men create an excuse to exclude women from the upper echelon. Below is a sequential, step-by-step illustration of the "no win" abusive psychological pattern in which women are placed as it pertains to reaching the highest positions within business, finance, politics, education, etc.:

*Male consciousness*: maintain power and superiority; discriminate against females because females are not competent to hold top positions

*Female consciousness*: angry and emotional because of being devalued and discriminated against

*Male consciousness*: females are too emotional

*Female consciousness*: become aggressive in an attempt to gain respect and share power

*Male consciousness*: females are not supposed to be highly aggressive

*Female consciousness*: females become emotional

*Male consciousness*: females are either too emotional or too aggressive

*Female consciousness*: it is a no-win situation

The ego consciousness limits because it wishes to separate and divide; the Soul consciousness expands because it seeks the Wholeness of the Good. The belief that only men can exhibit masculine energies and only women can exhibit feminine energies is limiting so it is an outcome of the ego consciousness. The belief that either a man or a woman can exhibit both is *de*-limiting so it is an inclusive belief from the Soul consciousness. A male can possess feminine energies while a female can possess masculine energies. As an ideal, it is referred to as *androgyny* when both energies manifest within a person. This does not mean that the physical body changes! It simply means that *both energies* are being manifested within one person. It makes the person a fuller, more expressive human because it is the consciousness of the Great Soul. To be sure, when a human being is expressing both masculine and feminine energies and willing toward Goodness, the Great Soul is manifesting in all its glory and grandeur.

There is nothing sacrosanct about feminine and masculine energies being limited to their respective gender, although it is true that, from a historical perspective, men have typically possessed active energies while females have traditionally possessed passive energies. History is riddled with examples of men being chastised for exhibiting feminine energies and women being ostracized for exhibiting masculine energies. It need not be that way, but the dominant patriarchal society held onto the primitive code of separating masculine and feminine energies and roles. For many centuries, male leadership has instituted mild to severe forms of punishment for those who violated these social norms. These rule makers were the authority figures in the world systems of society, education, business, finance, religion, science, etc. As we read further, we will, hopefully, begin to see that this has to do with the limiting beliefs that spring from the fear ridden ego. As part of evolution, humankind has the power to change that dynamic. Our beliefs are our only limitation.

We can observe history and see the reflection of masculine energies and the ego consciousness as the dominant consciousness since the beginning of time as we know it. It is this intrapsychic imbalance of the masculine and feminine energies, the permeation of the ego consciousness and humankind's failure to awaken to the interrelatedness of every existing thing that is responsible for wars, violence, chaos and destruction on this planet. As the dominant masculine energies and ego consciousness permeate and project out to the world, the evolution of humankind has now become stagnant. Men have evolved as the aggressive, controlling, active gender and have limited themselves by the denial of openly projecting the equally important feminine energies of love, kindness and compassion. This lack of love and kindness limits men and all others because an effect within one gender will always result in an effect on the other gender. This is an inviolable spiritual law of cause and effect. As a result, the masculine aggressiveness, competitiveness and hoarding mentality has transferred from the wilderness to Wall Street, business leadership, corporate boardrooms and political platforms. One could say that the masculine concept of "kill or be killed" which was essential for survival against animals in the wilderness lives on today in modern day businesses, corporations and politics. This masculine obsession for control and power has outlived its necessity, yet it remains in our society like an anachronistic nightmare where all of humanity is suffering from the hell it continues to produce for "the All". This masculine psychological pattern of cold and indifferent omnipotence, control and power has historically dominated what we know as the "thinking" professions such as medicine, science, math, law and business. Males continue to hold onto the positions in the highest echelon and, upon separation or retirement, legacy those upper positions to other males. Even in those professions where there are a substantial number of females such as in education and psychology, males are awarded positions at the helm. It is still virtually impossible for a female to garner a CEO or President title unless she is a sole proprietor. The human race has allowed this to unfold as we shape and reshape ourselves and, ultimately, our destiny.

Fortunately, the numbers are growing of what Jungian psychologists refer to as the "mature masculine." We understand the "mature masculine" to be a mirror image of the "mature feminine" because they both embody *equally* the feminine and the masculine energies of knowledge, creativity, love and wisdom. These energies are not "split" off. In this sense, mature masculinity and mature femininity become opposite sides of the same coin and, indeed, transform into androgyny. Today, we have relatively few "mature masculine" and "mature feminine," but since the "immature masculine" occupies leadership positions in all world systems, it is males who are primarily responsible for taking the lead in a transformative consciousness. If this effort is not undertaken by males and shared by females, a critical mass of adult females who have gained economic independence will overtake the project as a whole and, more or less, create the transformation by the power of their vote in democratic countries. One of the two strategies must occur because a wholesale transformation of leadership in every world system is required in order to move humankind to the next level of consciousness. We do have a few of the "mature masculine" occupying some substantial and visible positions, but notice I used the word "few." These are men who use their power to embrace, include and assist women, minorities and homosexuals into equal status and power in the world. Unfortunately, the "mature masculine" is a minority group and, thus, does not currently possess a critical mass of power which can induce change. But they are there. These men can be found in all segments of society and are awakening to the call of their Great Soul. They seek to use whatever power they have to empower, to honor and respect all of humanity, even sometimes at the expense of being ridiculed by other males. Some of these males were born in the 1950s and 1960s, however, many were born later. Those born in the 1980s have no experience of adult life as it existed prior to substantive anti-discrimination laws, such as the landmark Title VII Civil Rights Act of 1964, the Americans with Disabilities Act of 1990 and the Family Medical Leave Act of 1993. While many people still fail to see the inherent value in assisting people unlike themselves, these employment statutes have moved the consciousness of the human species to a higher level of awareness than existed prior to their passage. As more of the "immature masculine" age and leave their leadership positions, it is hoped that a burgeoning number of more psychologically mature males will use their soulful power to assist others and, in turn, teach their children the power of unification and collaboration.

Two great religious leaders who modeled Soulful expressions for humankind and attempted to integrate them into the human race were Jesus the Christ and the Buddha. Each man knew that the two least developed expressions of the Psyche or Soul within humankind were love and wisdom, so they incarnated in order to inform and teach the world that, not only masculine energies of knowledge and creativity are important, but also of equal importance are the two feminine functions of the Soul, love and wisdom. Both men were able to balance harmoniously these four functions by attending to, and nurturing, these attributes within themselves, so they were hearing the Divine Echo of the Soul. They were able to liberate Psyche or Soul and express the Soul's energies fully and naturally.

The ultimate, absolute and eternal yearning of the Great Soul is that it eternally wills itSelf toward itSelf. Another way to say this is the Soul seeks its essence, therefore, it seeks to know, create, love and be wise about itSelf which is the same thing as saying that the Soul seeks to know, create, love and be wise about Goodness. The Soul seeks to know Self and to imbue and express Self which is another way of saying that the Soul eternally seeks Goodness since Goodness is who you are. Humankind does not adore, worship and revere evil people like Hitler, Stalin, Jack the Ripper or Jeffrey Dahmer. Humankind has reverence for people who embody Goodness for the All. This has always been and always will be, no matter how chaotic the world becomes. Goodness is your essence and all you need do is rediscover this Truth and you have rediscovered your spiritual essence. Goodness is an expression of the virtues of truth, justice, honor, beauty, love, peace, joy, knowledge, creativity, wisdom. These are also referred to in the Christian religion as "fruits of the spirit" although all religions espouse them but perhaps refer to them with different language. When you speak of any of these virtues, you have spoken of the others. It is impossible to experience love without also experiencing joy. It is impossible to experience truth without also experiencing justice and honor. When you have experienced spiritual wisdom, then you have gained spiritual knowledge. Where there is peace, there is also love and joy. Beauty is always an expression of love, peace and joy. To create is to love; to love is to create. These are all inseparable and indivisible energies all from the same Universal Divine Source, the Oneness behind and around and within everything. Pure Goodness includes all virtues. Pure Goodness is the creator of all that exists and ever will exist. It is the Alpha and Omega and is eternally willing itSelf toward itSelf. All physical, mental and emotional human suffering ultimately results from a lack of Goodness flowing from the natural state of the Soul.

Most people in the world have not yet been given tacit permission by society to equally balance the four primary energic expressions of the Soul, therefore, most people are imbalanced and typically have a primary, secondary, tertiary and least developed function. Historically, males have been identified with having a primary and secondary function of knowing and creating as it pertains to the external world while females have been noted for a primary and secondary function of love and wisdom particularly as it pertains to the subjective or phenomenological world. This imbalance has resulted in disharmony in the physical world. Our next step as a species is to reevaluate and realign our Souls. As we reevaluate ourselves, we reawaken to our essence—our Great Soul—and begin reestablishing our identity as spiritual Beings who have elected to incarnate into a physical world in order to experience what it is like to know, to create, to love and to be wise in the temporal world. Ultimately, every physical thing that we can see with our eyes is but a symbol of a spiritual reality. As we begin to hear our internal Divine Echo and identify, once again, with our spiritual essence, we can work toward balancing our functions so as to bring about harmony within and outside ourselves. When we are listening more often to the internal Divine Echo as opposed to the chatter of the physical world, we will begin the process of honoring and respecting the Soul. As we begin developing an internal locus of control as opposed to an external locus of control, we become less dependent upon other people to make us feel valuable. Being Soulful, we feel our value from within and allow that light to shine outward. As we think and feel, so we are.

*The ego is a monkey catapulting through the jungle. Totally fascinated by the realm of the senses, it swings from one desire to the next, one conflict to the next, one self-centered idea to the next. If you threaten it, it actually fears for its life.*
—Lao Tzu

# VI. THE EGO AND EGO CONSCIOUSNESS

Ego can only manifest in a physical world because ego is a split or dual mind having no awareness of Ultimate or Absolute Wholeness. The dual mind believes in separation and difference, therefore, its power base is sustained by the belief in the superiority and inferiority of things in relation to each other. Having no consciousness of the Whole, the ego cannot cognitively or intuitively process all things (the Many) in relation to the Whole or to Ultimate Reality. You might say that the ego initially manifests and survives *because of* its narcissistic exodus and exclusion from the pre-incarnated, primal, interconnected Whole; its undeviated conviction in the supremacy of separation and division; and its urgent striving for independent control and power over Other. In this sense, we define "Other" as the natural, social and cultural environment, material objects and people.

The ego's entire existence is aimed at self preservation at the expense of Other. The ego will, therefore, sacrifice other people, the natural environment or objects which threaten its consciousness of supremacy. Seeing a visible world of more and less, all of its covert emotional defenses arrive primarily from the core emotion of fear, thus, its focus is to take and hoard so it may control and overpower. Its energic movement is to take, hoard, overpower, suppress, oppress, devalue, condemn, dismiss, divide, separate and exclude. This creates a dual world of superiority and inferiority because the ego is blind to the spiritual Wholeness and Oneness of the All of existence. The ego functions are in opposition to the functions of the Soul because the Soul always naturally expresses and Wills itSelf toward Goodness for Self *and* others, or the All. Its focus is to love. Its energic movement is to maintain a sense of autonomous sanctity while paradoxically sharing, giving, relating, communicating, creating, embracing, empowering, nurturing and uniting. The Soul does this because it knows that both Other and Self ultimately derive from the same universal consciousness source or, in Jungian terms, from the same collective consciousness. The world of Soul is acquiescent toward differences between objects in the material world, however, it possesses Ultimate Wisdom and always moves itSelf in response to this Ultimate Wisdom in knowing the Ultimate equality of all things *in relation to* the Whole. In this sense, "Ultimate" and "Absolute" are simply two words which are synonymous with "the All" or "the Whole" and will be used as descriptors of a whole, full and healthy consciousness.

The ego is the ruling state of mind on the planet Earth at this time. As has been stated before, it is the cause of all chaos. The next step in the evolution of the human species is to discover how to express the energy of the balanced, whole Soul. This will ultimately lead to harmony and peace for humankind and was, as said before, the ultimate message of Jesus the Christ, the Buddha and Mahatma Gandhi. Jesus the Christ and the Buddha were able to overcome the illusions of ego and carry a well balanced expression of Soul. The answer to world peace lies in our ability to disengage our values, priorities and obsessions with material accumulations, reconnect with our spiritual essence and then *reinterpret and revalue* material possessions as a means whereby we share in our abundance, help others and use the material gain to share our spiritual essence. When this occurs, Group consciousness will be the norm. Group consciousness is another term for Soul consciousness and simply means that humankind shifts from a I-It mindset to a "We" mindset. In order to make that shift in consciousness, humankind has to release the fear and prejudice that dominates in business, education, religion, politics, academia and society. Realizing that every action has an equal result, we must begin helping each other reach their potential. That is the Soul consciousness.

Presented again is the expression of ego, a split or dual mind. A dual mind is unawake to the knowledge of the relation of all things to the Whole, since the ego only perceives a world of physical matter. Thus, the ego is unconscious to wholeness since all objects in the world are its focus and are seen as either superior or inferior in relation to each other. The physical world is viewed as supreme with no conscious awakening of the spiritual aspect, or essence within, all that exists. In fact, the ego is slumbering; it is unconscious to the supremacy of the expressions of the Soul and, instead, is solely conscious of the physical and material world. It places highest value upon the objective world. One could say the ego is attached and devoted to objects as a means to maintain control and power. As we return to the prior chapter to examine the table which outlines the ego, the split mind, we see that the first line in each dyad indicates the Soul and its expressions and functions and the second line in each dyad represents what occurs when the Soul is ignored and dismissed, that is, when the ego is in control. Psychologists may refer to the "shadow" side as the immature dynamic within the ego. Noting the masculine 'shadow' energies, we can see that abusive patriarchy is that ego energy which deceives, controls, destroys and condemns. Perhaps the most infamous historical individual which imbued and projected this consciousness was Hitler who loved himself and hated his rivals. In a similar fashion, we can see that the feminine "shadow" energies of the immature feminine manifest in the archetypal evil queen in Snow White and the evil matriarch like the stepmother in Cinderella, both of whom hated themselves and were jealous of their female rival. All "shadow" energies are understood to develop from a belief in superiority and inferiority.

Let us clarify the warrior energy as a masculine concept since antiquity. In transcendent states of consciousness, there is no warrior energy in the sense that war means to separate, divide, conquer and oppress. Higher states of consciousness could be referred to as pure creativity, pure awareness, pure *transformational* energy. The word "war" literally means to be engaged in conflict or struggle, therefore, it is understood that at the egoic level, there certainly is a consciousness of conflict and struggle between inferiority and superiority and between all opposites. This psychological struggle and conflict does not exist at the higher Soul conscious level because the keen, silent, noetic awareness of Oneness exists, therefore, the concepts of war and warrior are masculine ego concepts promulgated by the immature masculine. The mature feminine and mature masculine understands that warrior energy is replaced with *transformation*, pure creativity, transmutation, and awareness which, inherently, absolves conflict through creativity. *Transforming the new from the old* is an entirely different conscious experience from the lower psychological egoic consciousness which is in conflict with itself and others and strives to *destroy with no consciousness of Goodness of the All*. Transformation through Soul energy is so scarce because of the few historical leaders who imbued this Soul consciousness and who, to this day, are unfamiliar with the power of transformation. We can best see the peaceful, transformational power of Soulfulness in the works of prominent figures such as the Buddha, Jesus the Christ, Mahatma Gandhi, Mother Teresa, the Dalai Lama, Martin Luther King, Sri Ramana Maharshi and Sri H.W.L. Poonja. Transformation does not destroy out of conflict. Transformation is a process of exhibiting Goodwill so as to dissolve conflict and transmute chaos in order for the creative energies of Goodness to spread. Destruction and deception at the egoic level is so pervasive on this planet in the male leaders of politics, business, and religion that it takes little reminding of the historical examples of corrupt politicians, avaricious corporate executives and hypocritical, condemning religious leaders to surface this painful truth. The masculine warrior, destroyer energy so dominates the pages of history and world leadership today, that one is left wondering how the warring ego consciousness has not already caused the extinction of the human race.

The genesis of the devaluation and suppression of the sacred feminine by the immature masculine can be surmised as having occurred as early as primitive man. Theologically and psychologically, we could say it began with "the Fall" of Adam and Eve from a higher state of consciousness which was in union with the Good, the All or the Whole. Seeing emotions as dangerous, lethal, and irrational, the immature masculine seeks to ignore, dismiss, oppress, sublimate and, in some cases, destroy the feminine energies of emotion. In Erich Fromm's book, *Sigmund Freud's Mission*, Fromm refers to Freud's "lack of emotional warmth, closeness, love" as resulting partially from Freud's reliance on reason. In tandem with enlightenment philosophy, Fromm further expounds on Freud's belief that:

> "...reason was confined to thought. Feelings and emotions were *per se* irrational, and hence inferior to *thought*. The enlightenment philosophers in general shared this contempt for feeling and affect. Thought was for them the only vehicle of progress and reason to be found only in thought. They did not see...that affects, like thought, can be both rational and irrational

and that the full development of man requires the rational evolution of *both* thought and affect. They did not see that, if man's thinking is split from his feeling, both his thinking *and* his feeling become distorted, and that the picture of man based on the assumption of this split is distorted."

This split to which Fromm refers is caused by the immature masculine ego consciousness which uses its power to declare the inferiority of the feminine. To feminists, it is a psychological insult that Freudian theory of sexual development is still taught in academia because of Freud's blatant patriarchal, sexist beliefs which are replete in his writings. His psychological model is so heavily biased toward masculine supremacy that there seems little doubt why classical psychoanalytical therapy is virtually nonexistent today. The model was promulgated by a man who, admittedly an intellectual genius whose legacy of the unconscious is unquestioned, reads as a Narcissist with a sense of omnipotence, control and power that is characteristic of the immature masculine ego.

The immature masculine ego operates in this split consciousness of superiority/inferiority as it seeks to be special, different and separate. This ego consciousness is at the helm of virtually every world system and is ultimately responsible for the bulk of our social ills. Until the immature masculine is transformed into the mature masculine and this mature consciousness manifests in leadership positions around the world, peace and harmony remain an illusive ideal. Unless the mature masculine and the mature feminine energies *value each other equally* and become a patently obvious consciousness, humankind will continue to experience war, conflict and chaos. Truly, as Wilber states, "the dragon we now must fight is simply the egoic structure itself." He further optimistically predicts in *Up From Eden* that the feminine energy is the potential future "hero" that may help rescue consciousness from the patriarchal masculine ego:

"The new Hero will be centauric (which means mind and body united and not dissociated), whole-bodied, mentally androgynous, psychic, intuitive *and* rational, male *and* female—and the lead in this new development most easily can come *from* the female, since our society is *already* masculine-adapted."


David Elkins is a writer, poet and psychologist who is past President of the Humanistic Psychology Division of the American Psychological

Association. As a past minister, he has written a book, *Beyond Religion*, where he speaks of the need for patriarchy to embrace the Soul:

> "When we repress the feminine—whether in ourselves, in our religion, or in our society—we do damage to the soul......A patriarchal society will never give women, feminine values, or the soul an equal place at the table, and with good reason. The feminine principle is dangerous to patriarchal systems, for feminine values subvert masculine assumptions, and the soul has more power than patriarchy ever dreamed. If soulfulness ever infiltrated our institutions of power, it could destroy them and leave them in rubble. But on those ruins the soul would build a more balanced and humane world."

It is this androgynous consciousness of Being which will lead the upcoming advancement from an ego level to the Soul Consciousness level, the next practical step in evolutionary consciousness. Again, I turn to Wilber to emphasize the need for the masculine and the feminine to look upon each other in awe and reverence as these two sacred halves marry to form a Beloved Oneness, a consciousness of mutual respect, a consciousness of wholeness. Wilber states in *Up from Eden*:

> "Until males stop killing themselves (and others) in order to be strong and silent; until females stop encouraging just this behavior as evidence of a "true man"; until chauvinists settle their accounts with their own masculinity and stop defensively exploiting their sisters; until angry feminists stop, on the one hand, reactivating chthonic "female only" matriarchal obsessions and, on the other, trying to co-op patriarchal obnoxiousness; until feminist intellectuals stop asking what it means to be truly female and start asking instead what it means to be neither male nor female but whole and human—then the patriarchy, the mental-ego, which has served its necessary, useful, but intermediate function, and which, for that, we have much to be thankful, will nevertheless soon prove, quite literally, to be the death of us all."

Actually, the ego is immature because it is disconnected from spiritual truth and Goodness toward *both* Self *and* others. Another way to say this is, at the deepest level, the ego is disconnected from its Higher Self. The optimal goal is not to have a stronger ego, rather the goal should be to transmute the ego and to reconnect with the Soul. Sustaining a healthy and strong ego will not result in optimal mental health for humankind. A healthy and strong ego is merely adjusting a mind to believe that falsehoods and untruths in the world of matter constitute the real world. By doing so, it is analogous to the Munsters convincing Marilyn that she is odd and abnormal. The abnormal Munsters believed they were "normal" whereas poor Marilyn—the only "normal" one in the group—erroneously carried around the false belief that she was abnormal! This comedy was able to capture the poignant point that, just because everybody says it's true, doesn't make it so!

Ego is an illusion created when the mind attempts to convince itself that only what you see is real and everything that is unseen is not real. This is the exact opposite to the truth of the Soul or Spirit. *Ultimate Reality is all that is unseen*. It is the world of the self-expressions of knowledge, creativity, love and wisdom, of blissful consciousness. For all eternity the Soul seeks to know, create, love and be wise. Its Will never ceases its movement toward this purpose. All matter changes and reaches an end and, after all, isn't that an illusion?

The ego is the author of all negative emotions. When you are experiencing negative emotions, your Soul is in the background, hidden and seemingly lost. Actually, your Soul can never truly be lost, rather your ego can only delude yourself into thinking the Soul is lost. A "lost Soul" is an oxymoron. "Lost" simply refers to a veil over the truth. It refers to a state of slumbering, a state of being un-awake. Psychologically, it refers to the unconsciousness of Ultimate Reality. The dominance and rule of the ego is a state of mind that is unconscious and unaware, therefore, you could say it is in a state of normative delusional trauma which simply means that society has erroneously taught that the ego is a "normal" consciousness for humankind, especially world leadership. The ego believes the illusory objective world is supreme and denies the reality and eternality of the spiritual realm. The ego rules by deception and can delude you into thinking that the Soul is lost, but the Soul is merely in the background, waiting quietly until you remember it, call upon it and express its energies. To "save a Soul" simply means to reawaken itSelf to its wholeness and Goodness and to restore its full, balanced energic expressions.

The ego, which attaches itself to the objective world, will defend itself out of fear. Fear appears to be the opposite of love, but in truth, only love exists because only love is eternal. Fear is an illusion of the temporal world. Fear produces other negative emotions such as anger, sadness, guilt, shame, envy and greed. When the mind splits, it is the choice of the world of ego (the physical world) over the real world of Soul (the spiritual unseen world).

The only Ultimate Reality is the spiritual world of virtues: love, peace, joy, truth, wisdom, knowledge, creativity, beauty, Goodness, justice and honor. These expressions of Soul have always been, are now and will always be.

Soul does not recognize time and space since Soul occupies the spirit world, the world of the unseen. Only in a world of matter—with beginnings and endings, separations and differences—can the mind split and ego rule.

All poor mental and physical health derives from the function of the ego whose preservation depends entirely upon feeding itself to the exclusion of others. It must exclude others because the ego believes in separation, difference and lack, thus, the ego thinks it must hoard in order to have. A world of matter generates this type of attachment. Ego violates spiritual laws consistently because if it were to obey spiritual laws, ego would cease to exist.

The ego believes that object and subject are separate and different and that one or the other is either more or less. Instead of understanding that all things are a beautiful piece of a Whole landscape of existence, the ego perceives all things only in relation to each other. This leads to a Master/Slave or superiority/inferiority consciousness. That, in turn, causes an individual consciousness and a collective conscious of conflict and chaos which is our current state of world affairs. This leads to the false concept of lack and scarcity. It is certainly easy to be deceived into believing that what you see with your physical eyes is separate and different, but, in truth, everything you see is, in essence, molecules of energy. The Soul knows that object is an extension of subject and nothing exists separate from, or outside of, the Divine Universal Soul. The Divine Soul is the culmination, or aggregate, of all spiritual energy. It is infinite, ubiquitous and eternal. Ego falsely believes in limitation. To the ego, the object is separate and different from subject since ego believes only the objective world is real. This is the belief of Western medicine and mainstream Western psychology. All projections manifest from this false belief.

Ego is made of both masculine and feminine "shadow" attributes of the Soul. These shadow expressions cannot exist unless fear exists. In a world of matter, we look around us and we perceive separation and difference, being unable to perceive the unseen interrelatedness of existence, the All. This illusion of disconnection to which the ego attaches itself is its survival mechanism. As we see separation, we fear that which is disconnected from us and particularly that which is unknown. As we perceive difference, we fear that which is unlike and dissimilar. Ego lies to us by convincing us that the world we see with our eyes is ultimate reality. Ultimate Reality is eternal and immutable, therefore, matter cannot be ultimately real. All material things change and end.

Let us move now to some examples of the ego believing in superiority and inferiority. Throughout history, different races of people have looked at each other and perceived difference. We recall how the Native Americans were slaughtered and the African Americans were sold as slaves. Many wealthy people perceive poor people as different from them, thus, creating an arrogant superiority which is condescending to those without wealth. We recall numerous examples throughout history of despots and dictators cloaked in royalty who greedily burdened the common people with excessive taxes so as to sustain the royal lifestyle. It is common for those holding executive positions in corporations to perceive employees in lower level positions as inferior. One need only work in the business world to note the arrogance, sense of entitlement and self-interest that exists in the top echelon of most businesses. Many well educated people view uneducated people in a demeaning fashion. The doctrinaire and elitist attitude in many educational institutions oftentimes sadly smothers the budding genius who develops a new thought or theory. Einstein commented in his 1946 memoir:

> "It's a true miracle that modern education hasn't yet completely smothered the curiosity necessary for scientific study. For without the required encouragement, and especially freedom, this fragile plant will wither. It is a grave mistake to believe that the pleasures of observation and inquiry can be induced by constraint and a sense of duty."

Medicine, and virtually every other branch of science, is dominated by the masculine energies and the ego consciousness. Men continue to foster the perception that cognition is the most important asset our species possesses. Science, dominated by males, has always searched for the origin of all things through the objective world. We call this "scientism" which refers to the belief that only the objective world which can be empirically tested and measured is of ultimate and authentic value. When a society constructs a value system or belief system, psychologists refer to this as *social constructivism*. Another word for this is "paradigm." In simple terms, it means that a group of people (usually the dominant group) construct an idea or a concept of how the world should perceive and value something. Then the idea or concept is disseminated by the dominant group until it is embedded in the collective consciousness and it is woven into the entire fabric of the social and cultural belief system. The subordinate party must accept and participate in the socially accepted norms. If the subordinate party attempts to reject the paradigm or the accepted norms which the dominant party created, the subordinate usually suffers some punishment, such as social or religious ostracism, exile or neglect, financial deficits or bankruptcy, even physical, mental or emotional abuse. Up until the 19th century, death was also a means used by the dominant party to ensure obedience by the subordinate party to the accepted "norms." It is usually extremely difficult to change a social construct and, while there are some examples of safe and calm transformations in consciousness, history provides us with a tragic littering of people who have attempted to change a belief system and suffered severe consequences up to, and including, death. We will proceed with a few examples.

For centuries, science and religion taught that the Earth was the center of the world until Copernicus published his work, *The Revolutions*, in 1540 stating his heliocentric, or sun-centered, theory of the universe. Out of vanity, fear and theological dogma, churchmen of that day would not accept that God had placed humankind anywhere other than the center of the universe. To those churchmen, Copernicus' view was sacrilegious because the accepted social construct (which was predicated on "infallible" religious dogma) was that the Earth was the center of the solar system. Even so called "religious authority" can manifest the ego consciousness. No person, even someone who is considered by worldly standards to be an authority figure, is immune from an ego consciousness.

Giordano Bruno was an ordained priest and a writer in the fields of theology, astronomy and philosophy in the late sixteenth century. Even though he was a deeply religious man, Bruno's studies led him to develop theories which convinced him that the Bible should not be followed for its astronomical teachings, but only for its moral teachings. He was openly critical of Aristotle's physics and, still worse, he rejected the Protestant principle of salvation by faith alone. The Roman Inquisition was intolerant to such heretical concepts and found Bruno's beliefs a violation against the Church and God, so Bruno was arrested in 1593 and put on trial which lasted seven years. After all that time, he was given a choice to retract his theories or be put to death by the Church. He refused to recant his theories and at the age of 52, he was convicted of heresy, bound to a stake and burned alive. Certainly those in power were not an example of the Soul consciousness expressing itSelf! He is remembered as a martyr for self-expression and freedom of thought.

Another example of a famous person who attempted to challenge a social construct was Galileo, who is considered today as the founder of the Scientific

Revolution. But in his day, he was derided as a religious heretic. Galileo's studies of the planets convinced him that he had proof of Copernicus' heliocentric theory. He published his results and was praised by many fellow philosophers and astronomers, however, was denounced by the church representatives because he supported Bruno's assertion that the Bible should not be used as a source for astronomical teachings, rather only used for moral teachings. Galileo's most important arguments were against the literal interpretations of the Bible. This was such a personal affront to the core premise of the infallibility of the Church Fathers and their sole authority for biblical interpretation that he incurred suspicion of heresy. Galileo innocently thought that if only some Jesuit priests could look through his telescope, they would see the proof of his discoveries for themselves. All but one priest refused the offer and when he saw what Galileo told him he would see, he was still adamant in his refusal to accept it. Instead, this priest gave an intellectual rationalization that it was the telescope that had altered reality! Sometimes we are so blinded by our beliefs that we cannot see truth even though we are looking straight at it! Galileo was arrested and brought to trial in 1632 by the Holy Office in Rome for defending the Copernican system. Operating from the ego consciousness of fear and vanity, the church did not allow him to be represented by an attorney and would not allow Galileo to see the evidence against him or to hear the charges brought against him. Giving Galileo the same choice as was given Bruno, the church told Galileo that he must publicly retract his theories or die. Galileo chose life and never taught Copernican theory again. It would not be until 1757—exactly 115 years after Galileo's death—that the church removed Galileo's works from its list of banned publications. Finally, in 1992, 359 years after Galileo was forced to renounce his theories, the Pope formally acknowledged the church's error to the Pontifical Academy of Sciences.

Joan of Arc was born a peasant in France and, at the age of 13 in the year 1425, she began seeing visions and hearing the celestial voices of St. Michael, St. Catherine of Alexandria and St. Margaret. This was during the Hundred Years War, when the English were laying claims to the throne of France and just before the English were about to capture Orleans. These voices began appealing to her to save Charles VII, the future King of France. In June 1428, she appeared before Baudricourt, a soldier who commanded for Charles VII, but was treated with rudeness and disrespect and ultimately dismissed. In January 1429, she appealed to Baudricourt again. She announced a great defeat at the Battle of the Herrings, just outside of Orleans. Finally, on March

6, 1429, Joan was allowed to appear before Charles VII. She did so in her usual male attire. Due to vanity, jealousy and envy, a strong party at the court, including La Tremoille, the royal favorite, denounced her as a crazy person. When Joan was able to provide Charles with a secret sign, he began to believe her. Although Joan never disclosed this sign, many now believe that the "secret of the king" was a doubt that Charles was from a legitimate birth.

Joan was sent to be examined by numerous committees of Catholic bishops and medical doctors. The theologians, while not attesting to the reality of her claims, could not find anything heretical in her mission. She was allowed to prepare for the military campaign against the English. Even though the king offered her a sword, Joan's voices indicated an ancient sword behind the alter at the chapel of Saint Catherine-de-Fierbols should be used. Indeed, it was discovered that the sword was buried there! More interesting than this, a letter from a sire was mailed to France prior to the Battle at Orleans which stated that Joan predicted she would save Orleans, be wounded during the battle although not die, and that Charles would be crowned that summer. As was predicted, Joan did take Orleans and was wounded in the breast by an arrow.

In another battle in 1430, Joan was taken prisoner by an English sympathizer and sold to the English. Charles VII and his advisers were unsympathetic to her plight and failed to ask for an exchange of prisoners although it seems likely they could have. A corrupt and ambitious bishop, Pierre Cauchon, invoked his authority to place her on trial for heresy. Once again, she appeared before Catholic theologians and medical doctors without being allowed an advocate. Even though it was illegal to imprison her in a secular prison because of being tried by an ecclesiastical court, Joan was imprisoned in the Castle of Rouen which was guarded by male soldiers. Initially Joan was in chains by the neck, hands and feet. She was refused spiritual privileges such as attendance at Mass due to her charge of heresy and her insistence upon wearing male attire. She complained bitterly and asked to be removed to the church prison where she would have had female attendants, but was refused.

She withstood several weeks of serious inquiry much of which was purposely and callously administered in attempts to confuse her and invalidate her visions. Knowing that Joan was unable to read and write, the churchmen and doctors used this to their advantage. At one point, she prophesized that in seven years the English would forfeit a larger prize than Orleans. Indeed, six years and eight months later, Henry VI lost Paris. Ultimately, the judges declared her visions to be "false and diabolical" and unless she retracted them, she would be burned at the stake. Private admonitions were made for Joan to retract her visions, but she held fast even after physical torture. When she was taken to the cemetery to be burned, she was finally worn down and signed a document. Many agree that what the church official told her was in the document was likely not what the document said. Being illiterate, Joan would have been unable to read the document and would be forced to rely upon whatever the church official told her it stated. Five witnesses at the trial including the official who read the document aloud, declare that the document was only a few lines, however, the official document which is held by the church is so long that it would take half an hour to read. It is almost certain that she had been deceived by male church officials. She believed she signed a document which stated that she retracted her visions only if it were God's will. As a result, she was not burned, but taken back to prison.

Catholic Bishop Pierre Cauchon and the English were not satisfied. Some historians allege that Cauchon set a trap for Joan by conniving with the jailers. Joan's women's garments were taken from her by the jailers, so she only had male attire to wear out of the prison. Since she had been condemned for two reasons—heresy and wearing male attire—if she wore male attire, she would be burned at the stake. This is exactly what happened. Just before she was burned at the stake, she embraced her crucifix, lifted it to the heavens and continuously cried out the name of Jesus. According to a recorder at the trial, "until the last, she declared that her voices came from God and had not deceived her." Twenty-five years after her death, her case was retried and she was pronounced innocent. It would take 489 years after her unjust death for the Catholic church to admit the unjustness. In 1920, Joan of Arc was canonized by Pope Benedict XV.

These are not only examples of the masculine ego consciousness, but are tragic stories exemplifying long-held beliefs and the extent to which the ego will go in order to defend a threat against its dominant position of power and control. The social construct which states that intellect, reasoning and logic are more important than love, kindness and compassion was created by a patriarchal ego consciousness. The social construct that concludes there is no spiritual world was also promulgated mostly by men who reflect the ego consciousness. These social constructs have existed since ancient times and, to this day, are fostered by virtually all masculine dominated world systems.

Another example of a social construct is the belief that women and minorities are subordinate and inferior to white males. Largely females and minorities have been overpowered, dismissed, abused and otherwise relegated to an inferior rank in the eyes of the non-minority patriarchy which is in power. Great strides were made in the 20th century, but there is still a greater potential for males, females and minorities to reach. Abuse is sometimes misunderstood to be overt abuse such as physical, verbal or sexual abuse which results in serious physical, mental and emotional harm. However, when people are dismissed, ignored and silently considered inferior, this is an arrogant, covert and insidious form of abuse. The same outcome of mental harm can result. The means are different, but the goal is still abuse. When slaves were physically beaten, this is a form of overt abuse whereas when females and minorities are silently dismissed, ignored and relegated to lower positions in the business world, this is covert abuse. Both kinds of abuse are outcomes of a pervasive ego consciousness which operates out of fear. Abuse is antithetical to the loving expression of the Soul which always seeks Goodwill to Self *and* others, so we can say apodictically that Soul does not collectively express itSelf in the corporate and political environments due to rampant avarice.

Females and minorities have responded to the arrogant domination of an abusive patriarchy by developing a natural compensatory defense system within the human body which responds emotionally. Those men who willfully and arrogantly assume positions of control and power over females and minorities with no intention to share power believe that only men and non-minorities are best qualified to be in the highest echelon within the political, financial, business, medical, scientific, legal, educational and religious structures. While gains have been made over the past thirty years as federal and state statutes serve as moral watchdogs and as some men are developing a more inclusive consciousness, the superior mindset of an arrogant patriarchy continues to exclude females and minorities from ranks of power and, hence, from sharing world wealth. Some common excuses are that "females don't think like men" and "minorities don't have the education." These subtle attitudes and prejudices are merely covert discriminatory practices which the ego utilizes as a means for continued self-aggrandizement and self-preservation and as a defense against loss of omnipotence.

Yet another social construct is the belief that homosexual individuals are morally deviant or perverted. This belief is held by both men and women and by some people of all races, colors and national origins. Fortunately, the vast numbers within the field of psychology have ceased to diagnose homosexuality as a pathology that needs to be cured. The only "cure" that needs to occur is within those people who invoke and defend a position of hatred, intolerance and violence. People who cleave to a fear and hatred against homosexual people must awaken to a fundamental and immutable fact: homosexuality is *not* a choice. People don't wake up one day and capriciously elect to like another person of the same gender. Same gender attraction cannot be turned on like a water faucet. In addition, being gay is not a moral disease of the spirit so the world must cease its moral indictment against the gay community. This ego consciousness of hatred, divisiveness and violence must be transformed into a loving, compassionate expression of the Soul. Jesus the Christ, the Buddha and Mother Teresa would never have sanctioned the hate and violence that has been generated by people who believe that homosexuals are deviants and need to be spiritually cleansed. These three wise Souls would simply accept out of compassion. That is the Soul consciousness.

The belief that there is no reality beyond the world of physical matter is still another example of a social construct. Even though surveys consistently report that two-thirds or more of Americans believe in a reality beyond that which is seen by the physical eye, it is largely ignored and dismissed as rubbish by the mostly male scientific, psychological and educational leaders. Of particular note is that this social construct has been created mostly by males personifying the ego consciousness. As long as masculine social constructs continue to be largely accepted, it guarantees males the prominent places and highest positions in the world economy. It allows for the continued masculine dominance of world wealth and power. These social constructs create the sufficient psychological milieu for the immature masculine ego to maintain unquestioned authority and to continue to play a dual role of gatekeeper and member of its own private club. The hierarchy of males in top positions is guaranteed as long as we limit our thinking. We limit our thinking by limiting our beliefs in our potential and in failing to awaken to the momentum of power inherent in a collective consciousness seeking transformation.

Patriarchy has sought, and continues to seek and maintain, control over worldly wealth and assets; to maintain control over religious dogma, doctrine and tenets; to garner prestige and power in developing the medical and scientific concepts which are taught within the educational system; and to dominate the political structures which, in turn, have control over the business and economic systems which control the worldly wealth. It is the fox watching the henhouse. Abusive patriarchy is pathological because it is the pathology of the entitled, omnipotent ego. It is narcissistic and does not seek to share control and power, rather seeks to hoard it as an autocratic monopoly.

Men created the myth that women are inferior to men so they could obtain and maintain world wealth through their position of dominance. White men created the myth that they are superior to people of color for the same reason. Superiority and exclusivity also exists within many religions. In Jungian psychology, these males are referred to as the "immature masculine" because they operate from the world of ego, not the world of the Soul. Indeed, the immature masculine projects its superiority across religious sects as is sometimes seen between the male leaders in the Catholic, Protestant, Jewish, Hindu and Muslim religious groups. The ego dismisses, excludes, separates and hoards. It does not believe in equality and will not make attempts to unify the whole. The Soul embraces, includes and unites because it knows that God consciousness, that is, a consciousness of the Whole, and Ultimate Reality are unseen and equal within every human being.

Worldly wealth, ethnicity, intelligence and education seem to be the primary determinants of a person's value and worth in the world as seen through the eyes of patriarchy. To the extent that an entitled patriarchy has created this myth, continues to uphold this value system and to the extent that everyone continues to allow this belief system to permeate our collective consciousness, the human race will continue to fetter the Great Soul. By doing so, we are stifling our psychological maturity and a future of abundance. For it is only in caring for our Souls, that we will ever be in harmony with ourselves and with each other. As the number of minorities and females escalate in the business, political and educational systems, all of these world systems based upon an exclusive patriarchy will come into question and be challenged and their very survival will be in serious jeopardy. Unless humankind focuses on the fullness of the Soul, recognizing the equality of all four functions and embracing them equally by bringing those psychic functions into balance, the human race will be in disharmony and will not survive. A house divided cannot stand.

So far, we have only discussed men who carry the ego consciousness. While it is far more detrimental to the world because men currently occupy most positions of power, it should be understood that females, minorities and homosexuals can, and do, operate from the ego consciousness as well. No one is immune from the temptations of the ego. It is the inner world which determines whether the ego or the Soul will express. Since males hold the keys to the largest world's treasure chests and wield control over the most substantial world's bank accounts, they are simply held most accountable for the human condition of the world. He who holds the top position also pays the price of being most accountable.

Females have been known for their nurturing instincts, but they also have a history of intense hatred, rivalry, envy and jealousy which is pure ego. By being fearful and seeing others as threats, females can behave in outrageous ways. The Queen in Snow White and the Seven Dwarfs portrays the archetype of the jealous, vindictive woman who is full of hatred for any other female more beautiful than she. Her hatred knows no bounds and the Queen is willing to go to all lengths to eliminate her threat, including killing Snow White.

It is not uncommon for females to feel insecure and inferior about their bodies and their intellect in a world that nourishes that insecurity. The immature masculine ego and the media (which is dominated by the immature masculine ego) create powerful arguments for pulchritude which continues to feed the fearful ego consciousness in women by reinforcing a social construct that the primary goal for women is to achieve physical beauty. This negates the masculine potentials for women to develop their intellect and creativity in building world. As women regain their core, healthy sense of "I" and find those ways which nourish their Great Souls, more women will achieve healthy balances and, in turn, reach out and collaborate so as to reach an equal status with men. By far, the greatest movement forward for females will be made by increasing education level, forming communities whereby their numbers are collectively seen and heard, and by using the power of the political vote. Females should consider strategizing by forming an alliance with each other and an even larger community with minorities and the gay community. The power of the collective mass consciousness cannot be underestimated. Indeed, statistics state that, by the year 2050, Caucasians will be a minority while people of color will become the majority. I am convinced that it is a larger collaboration between females, minorities and the gay community that will produce the greatest results and achieve the greatest good for the whole.

Minorities who have suffered centuries of serious overt and covert abuse also sometimes turn to the ego consciousness as a way of assuaging the pain felt by physical, verbal and emotional abuse. Sometimes turning this anger and resentment toward their own community, they can damage their own race when their actions and behaviors are an unconsciousness and unresolved feeling of inferiority fostered for centuries by non-minorities. Martin Luther King, Jr. was perhaps the greatest example of an African American leader who attempted, through peaceful means, to bring the heinous criminal and civil actions against the African Americans to the forefront. Mahatma Gandhi, being thrown off the train because of the color of his skin, also used peaceful means in order to expose the insidious racial prejudice in South Africa. Both King and Gandhi typified the manifestation of the peaceful Soul consciousness by refusing to use violence against those perpetrators who had used violence against them and their people. As larger numbers of minorities form a loving, united, peaceful community amongst themselves, they can peacefully seek to unite with females and the gay community in an effort to use the power of political vote to transform social constructs and, eventually, transform the world.

In the spirit world where Soul resides, the value system is based upon equality of spiritual growth and potential. Every Soul recognizes the capacity and potential of the Soul as equal with all Souls. Fame, fortune, job title, college degrees, worldly assets, age, race and ethnicity do not determine whether a person is aligned with their Soul. The world is full of highly educated, intellectual and wealthy people who are spiritually bankrupt. Believing that only they are in a position to convey knowledge and wisdom, they fail to realize a great Spiritual Truth taught by a simple Buddhist: every person is *both* teacher and student. There are no exceptions.

When you are jealous of your neighbor because they are wealthier, taller, more beautiful, smarter or more educated, you are basing your value system upon the value system of the ego because the ego, in order to survive, must hold onto fear. And ego fears because it only recognizes and values separation and difference. When you read a newspaper article about the indictment of a corporate executive who has pocketed millions by committing fraud, that person has neglected their Soul and bought into the value system of the ego. The ego would have you believe that more is better and to get is to receive. Nothing is further from the truth. You can only have by giving. Fear of lack and fear of scarcity feeds the greedy ego into wanting more and more. Soul knows that lack, separation and difference are only illusions and everything we need is within us, all around us and derived from the spiritual realm. It is only a matter of sharing and giving.

*The ego identifies itself with the body, and so loses sight of the Self, and the result of this inadvertence is dark ignorance and the misery of the present life.*
—Sri Ramana Maharshi

*The Self looks like the world. But this is just an illusion. The Self is everywhere. One. Still. Free. Perfect.*
—Ashtavakra Gita

*The Self is only Being, not being this or that. It is simple Being.*
—Sri Ramana Maharshi

# VII. THE FULL SELF AND THE EMPTY EGO

The Soul Consciousness theoretical model assumes, as does Jungian and transpersonal theory, that the ego is split from the Higher Self, so there is an illusion of more than one self. Ultimately, there is only One Self as taught in most Eastern philosophies. The Soul Consciousness model assumes, at the relative level of existence, there are three selves: the ego, the Soul (Higher Self) and Spirit (Highest Self). At the Ultimate level of Reality there is only One Self forever Whole, Full and in need of nothing. You may also refer to this as the Buddhists sometimes do when they speak of "Beyond Self". Highest Self, Beyond Self, Pure Knowing, Pure Consciousness, *nirguna* Brahman,

God, the Ineffable One, Pure Being, Absolute Truth, Ultimate Reality, Nirvana or Heaven is only assumed and known in a higher state of consciousness. In Truth, there really is only the Highest Self and the ego is an illusory consciousness not based in Ultimate Reality because the ego is a dream which dissipates upon awakening from the slumber of ignorance.

The ego is dependent upon Highest Self, but the Highest Self is not dependent upon ego. Ego is split thinking or dualistic thinking which makes the ego, in a sense, unreal. A better way of saying it would be "unwhole" or "not ultimately real." Think of it as a false consciousness because it predicates its thinking on false beliefs. Ego is that mind which tries to convince itself that what is not real is real and what is real is not real. In other words, it attempts to define itself in terms of the world of matter. I offer the analogy of a person who is looking through a pair of sunglasses that taints everything with a yellow hue. Yes, the person does see yellow. It is "there," but it is not ultimately real. When the yellow lens are taken off, the person can see the "true" surroundings. In this sense, I refer to the ego consciousness because it refers to a certain "way" in which the viewer "sees" the world. An even better analogy would be to think of a time when a certain experience changed your "outlook" on how you "saw" things. For instance, if you've ever experienced the death of a friend or the feeling of being in love, your concept of that experience is different prior to the actual experience. Your view changes because you have had a deeply felt experience which caused you to "see" those events in a deeper, richer and more meaningfully felt way. Prior to the experiences, you "saw" the world in a different way and after the experiences, it likely changed forever how you "saw" things. As always must be, words are really inadequate to describe what Wilber calls "Absolute Subjectivity" or "Level of Mind," but we must use them as a launching point to the silent place of Pure Being. Yet, there is really nowhere to go because Pure Being is here within you, therefore, there is no path to tread, no place to go. With intelligent humor in *The Spectrum of Consciousness,* Wilber states "there is no path to HERE, there is no path to NOW."

For purposes of simplicity and purposes of introducing the Soul Consciousness model, I will begin by saying that there is both the ego and the Higher Self. I will use the descriptor "Full" when referring to the Higher Self which exhibits the Soul Consciousness, but there are only minor differences between my concept of the Full Self and Jungian and transpersonal theories of the Self and Higher Self, respectively. Additionally, the Soul within this model is closely parallel to Plato's rational soul and Plotinus' concept of

Soul and Being. My concept of the Higher Self also closely follows the Advaitan concept of *saguna* Brahman. We may disagree over particulars, but at the Universal level of understanding, I believe, they are all virtually identical. We have to understand exactly what is the *substance* of the Full Self which makes it Full and what is lacking in the ego which makes it empty. This will be discussed shortly. We understand that it is this inability of the ego to become subsumed by the Full and Higher Self that is the cause of most mental and physical disease and illness, all chaos, war, violence, conflict, hate, anger, greed, jealousy, shame and guilt. Until this reconnection with the Soul occurs on a mass conscious scale, the planet will continue to move toward destruction attributed to the empty ego.

The ego forms when the self incarnates into a physical form and the memory of the Higher Self is lost. The ego cannot exist in the spiritual realm because there can be no possibility of a shadow in the spiritual realm. Shadow requires a physical object and the ego constantly seeks something "other" in order to fill itself. This "other" is always sought in the physical world because the ego, the subject, is always searching for an "other" separate object in an attempt to avoid feeling empty. One could say that it is unaware and unconscious of what it is seeking. Rollo May, in his book, *Man's Search for Himself,* refers to the "hollow people" because they are "empty" and lack the "courage to be." He refers to the lack of courage as automaton conformity which can be thought of as a process of comparing one's self to "other" instead of moving toward one's own inner Higher Self. One may think of this as the ego consciousness since the ego has separated from the Full Self, the Higher Self, the Divine Self which imbues the Soul Consciousness. Maslow would refer to the person who imbues the Full Self as a self-actualizing transcender because the individual transcends the ego. Some religions refer to the separation from the Higher Self or Full Self as "the Fall" or the separation of human from God. The ego is a state of separation from knowing its divine essence, from the subjective, ontological, phenomenological state of consciousness which imbues Highest Goodness. The fundamental drive in every human being is to reconnect with the spiritual realm of Pure Knowing, Pure Essence, Highest Self, Pure Light, Pure Love— this is Pure Being. This is the spiritual realm beyond the physical realm. The highest level of Being as an incarnated physical body is not understood to be the highest level of Being in the spiritual realm. There is a hierarchy of Being within the non-physical, spiritual realm just as there is a hierarchy of Being within the physical realm.

In a physical incarnation, the ego dissolves when it is subsumed by the Higher Self or Full Self which becomes fully conscious of itSelf, i.e., its Will toward Goodness for Self and others and the harmonious balance of the feminine and the masculine. This is when the Full Self knows its spiritual or divine essence, not just its human existence. Jung referred to God incarnating in man so that God can bring back a consciousness of Self, however, I prefer to think of it as God *re-discovering* and *returning back to* the original state or the primal state of pure knowing of Highest Self or Beyond Self. It is this cyclical process of full consciousness, followed by a split between consciousness and unconsciousness, and finally a return once again to the primal state of full consciousness which occurs throughout eternity. There is an eternity of eternities, therefore, there are an infinite number of eternal cycles. This eternal cycle is understood to be *both* a cyclical process, as the ancient Greek philosophers believed, and a dynamic process as Jung believed.

Kierkegaard refers to the three stages of human life as the aesthetic, ethical and religious. In the aesthetic stage, the individual is moved by the five senses and their resultant impulses and emotions. At the ethical stage, the individual assumes a moral position and is guided by a moral ethos. At the highest level, the individual is understood to have transcended the ego and reached the religious stage, the individual makes a commitment through the will and reconnects and actualizes the God Self, Higher Self, Pure Being, *saguna* Brahman. To Kierkegaard, the *quality* of existence is different at the egoic level (aesthetic and ethical) than it is from the quality of existence at the religious stage of consciousness. One might say that, according to Kierkegaard, at the aesthetic and ethical levels (egoic level), a person simply exists. There is little or no conscious awareness of a True Self, a Divine Self, a Whole Self. However, when the person, through faith, moves into a conscious awareness of the Higher Self, the individual moves out of the ego consciousness into the realm of Being, of Absolute and Knowable Truth at the religious stage. Transcendent values are imbued. These are the spiritual fruits of love, kindness, compassion, joy, creativity, wisdom, peace, truth, etc. This is the Will toward Goodness. "Religious" is best understood by Kierkegaard to be "God is *subject*," meaning the ontological, subjective experience of Godness as opposed to God as object or other or some physical entity outside of self. Hegel's concept of the evolving consciousness is more of a thinking model, where the individual advances through a thinking process and finally reaches "Absolute Truth" which appears to be a paradoxical combination of Absolute Being and Not-Being.

When the Full Self imbues knowledge, creativity, love and wisdom, one will reconcile the opposites and assume an androgynous consciousness and then there is a consciousness of Goodness for both Self and others which is reconciled. When the feminine and the masculine are *equally imbued and valued,* the Higher Self manifests the reconciliation of the feminine and masculine, the heart and the mind energies, the Holy Spirit incarnate. The Higher Self becomes itSelf upon the recognition that it is the subjective androgynous Godness, the embodiment of the Divine, the imbuing Being of Goodness, *saguna* Brahman. The ancient Greek philosophers such as Plato, Plotinus and Proclus referred to this simply as "Being". To return to this state of Being is the underlying fundamental drive in every human being. We are guaranteed to return to it because it is the primal state, *arche*, original essence that always has been and always will Be. This is a conscious state of Reality to be experienced and not a physical entity. Nietzsche describes it in his book, *The Gay Science*, when he states: "What does your conscious say?—*You shall become who you are*." The clear inference is that you will *return to* your essence. All attempts to give anthropomorphic qualities to this state of consciousness are an earnest, but feeble attempt to comprehend that which is invisible, eternal and life giving—the élan vital. All that exists in the physical world is but an illusion, an appearance, and a dream, what the Advaitans refer to as *maya.* Yes, you visually see the physical world, but you can never experience anything physical. *You can only experience the joy, love, peace, beauty which physical things give you*. This is all there is!

Having forgotten Goodness (which is our essence), we place highest value on the symbols and icons, the physical manifestations. Myths of ancient times were a way to remind humankind of the spiritual fruits, the Godness, inherent within the material world. Godness, or spiritual Goodness, is forever and ever. The Higher Self is eternal because it is the Self of supreme Goodness which *is* Godness. The Higher Self subsumes the ego which is forever split. The ego is split because it has not found its true Self and believes that what is missing is somewhere other than within. The ego has not rediscovered, owned and imbued its essence, its supreme Goodness, its divinity, its Godness where all spiritual fruits are both cause and effect and where the awareness of Beyond Self is total. The ego has an intellectual and emotional investment in physical matter instead of spiritual essence, therefore, it cannot "see" its Being or Higher Self. When you are in a state of seeking "other" in order to find yourself because you are unfulfilled, then you are not-Being, not-Self, ego, empty because you are not identified with your true and authentic nature which is the fullness of Being or the fullness of Goodness for Self and others. The false perception that you are missing something and that you need something "other" to make you whole is the cause of much disorder and illness. You *are* whole because your essence is the fullness of Goodness.

The ego can also be understood as the self with a small "s," the false self, non-Being, being with a small "b," the not-self, the empty self. At this level of consciousness, ego exists because it is not conscious of the Higher Self which projects the Soul Consciousness. In this sense, it is understood that the ego does not know itSelf! It is split from itSelf. May states in *The Discovery of Being* that "the real and fundamental trouble with the doctrine of the ego is that it represents, par excellence, the subject-object dichotomy in modern thought." There is an existence where body, cognition and emotions rule the self, but there is no spiritual awareness of the whole, of divinity, no awareness of the numinous, hence the Soul has not unfolded or manifested. This is a lack of fullness because the self is split off from its wholeness. The Will has not been activated toward Goodness. This disconnection creates illness, war, conflict, chaos, violence, hatred and prejudice.

The ego is never satisfied because you can never be wholly satisfied without love, Goodness, without knowing your essence. In that sense, the ego is forever empty. Material things can *never* fill; they can only delude you into thinking that you are filled by the pursuit and possession of them. Only spiritual fruits can create fullness of Being. *Only Goodness can fill and only Goodness can manifest a consciousness of abundance overflowing.* Goodness is a qualitative consciousness and can be experienced. Physical things cannot be experienced and this is why the bodily senses are not direct routes to Ultimate Reality. The bodily senses deceive you into thinking that you can obtain, experience and possess material things. You can never BE anything material. You can only BE the love, peace and joy which any material thing gives you. This is all there is and this is inseparable and immutable. You can only BE that Mind that contains all that is, ever has been and ever will be. This is the Oneness of the Divine Mind, the Godness behind and within and through and between and under and above. It is the indivisible "Is"ness that the person who has attained *saguna* Brahman consciousness will know and "see". It is in this way that Ultimate Truth is discovered because Ultimate Truth and Reality can only be experienced as a subjective Being. Only spiritual fruits can re-awaken you to your essence, therefore, spiritual fruits are not some pie-in-the-sky, unattainable, religious concepts. When authentically imbued and projected, they manifest as psychological health and well-being.

When they are withdrawn, withheld, oppressed or denied, psychological health and well-being decreases. There is a relationship between spiritual fruits and physical health and well-being. Finally, Western medical science is paying serious attention to the relationship between negative stress and psychological and physical health and the research indicates there is a strong correlation.

The Self seeks itSelf eternally because the Goodness of the Self *is* the Self and this is all that exists forever and ever. It is the highest reality spoken about in Eastern philosophies and in neo-Platonic theology. In the *Enneads*, Plotinus speaks of "the real drive of desire of our soul is towards that which is better than itself. When that is present within it, it is fulfilled and at rest, and this is the way of living it really wills." The Soul or Full Self seeks all that is "the Good" in a Platonic sense. Beauty, Truth, Love, Peace, Knowledge, Creativity all exist and the physical world is but a symbol of all these archetypes. Edward Edinger states, in *The New God-Image: A Study of Jung's Key Letters Concerning the Evolution of the Western God-Image,* "the very process of talking about archetypal contents constellates them, and suddenly they are in our midst." Edinger further elaborates on the Soul by stating "there is nothing else to be experienced except the psyche." The psyche or Soul holds within it and imbues the archetypes. Physical things are symbols, *not* realities. Your physical home is not an archetype. Your physical home is a *symbol* of an archetype. When you verbalize the word "home," it is a symbol of a symbol of an archetype. What your home symbolizes for you on a spiritual level, i.e., beauty, peace, certainty, safety, comfort, love, are the eternal Forms to put it in Platonic terms. They are archetypes to put it in Jungian terms. They are "things-in-themselves" to put it in Kantian terms. These Forms, archetypes and "things-in-themselves" are the highest reality because they exist forever and ever and never change. As pointed out by Plato, they are the Universals, not the particulars. Universals are what every human being can relate to because every person has different particulars in their lives which lead them to all these same Universals. Humankind is so bogged down in verbal controversy because everybody is polemically arguing, bantering, bickering about the ten thousand particulars instead of concentrating on all the simple Universals which unify humankind. Instead of two people bickering about whether da Vinci or Michelangelo created the most beautiful work, we should be uniting with each other in the ontological experience of the Universal: Beauty. What difference does it make whether da Vinci or Michelangelo has the most beautiful work? Symbols are perceived differently. Only the Universal ontological experience of Beauty is unchanging and uniting. Rejoice that you *experience beauty* by viewing da Vinci and your friend *experiences beauty* by viewing Michelangelo! Instead of arguing about whether Jews, Christians, Buddhists, Muslims or Hindus "have it right", we should be uniting with each other in the ontological experience of the Universal which they all teach: Love. Then and only then will any religion have it right and truly be True! We must honor religious liberty since all religions point essentially to the same loving consciousness. This is what it means to be divine. Benjamin Franklin had it right when he said that "to pour forth benefits for the common good is divine." Yes! This is what it means to be divine. What value can any religion provide humankind if its outcome does not lead to simple love, compassion and acceptance toward each other? Dogma and doctrine are simply symbols of the ultimate reality of Love, therefore, dogma and doctrine are two different paths to the same reality. Isn't it Love, not dogma, that should be our guiding outcome? Who gives a whit what the doctrine, method, path or process is as long as the outcome and the result is Love of Self *and* other, love of the Whole? Instead of bickering about whether writing, painting, sculpting, or building homes is true creativity, why not revere them all as practices which derive from the same sacred source of creativity? What difference does it make whether science, philosophy, psychology or religion is the most important area of study? They all seek, directly or indirectly, to answer the same question in a million different ways and in a dozen different languages, *What is the origin of things?* Each discipline seeks the same Universals, but argue over the thousand different paths to the same Universals which are within us and staring us in the face every day we live. All we need to do is awaken and BE. The polemic arguments between and within the disciplines are silly and needless in the grand scheme of life. Is it so incredibly difficult simply just to *Be* Goodness? If this is all there is, does it not sound silly that we will have spent millions of years arguing over the differences between dozens of religions and philosophies and ten thousand paths if each and every one of them lead to the exact same place—Higher Self of Goodness toward Self and others? It seems that humankind is so entrenched in finding truth in the most complex and difficult manners and methods when the truth of simply Being Goodness lies *within us* every second of every moment of our lives. That Goodness is not only within Jesus or the Buddha or Lao Tzu. *It is within you. The Kingdom is within.* All we need to do is awaken to that Beingness. Your Great Soul—not your priest, preacher or rabbi—is the mediator between you and Highest Self, *nirguna* Brahman, God, the Ineffable One, Heaven, Nirvana, Pure Being. And there is nothing and no one in this

Universe to keep you from finding this highest consciousness *except yourself and your beliefs*.

If we concentrate on Being Goodness, who cares which one of the ten thousands different paths each of us take to Be that Goodness? If our belief systems divide us and keep us from a simple ontological experience of Goodness, the Full Self, then there needs to be a wholesale re-evaluation of our long-held belief systems. It seems that it is the dogma, doctrine and tenets of belief systems that lead us astray, cause animosity and divide us more than unite us. These are the result of the ego consciousness. What conclusions can we draw from *any belief system including a religious belief system if the result is prejudice, separation, oppression, control, hate, violence, war, death and destruction*?

Beauty never changes. Only *symbols* of beauty can change. Creativity never changes. Only *symbols* of creation change. Truth never changes. Only *symbols* of truth change. Love never changes. Only *symbols* of love change. These spiritual fruits never change because they all unite. These *com*-pel, not *re*-pel. Forever and ever all spiritual fruits compel the Self to unite. The archetypes never change. They never began and will never end. When you hug your child and feel love, when you look at nature and feel its beauty, when you meditate and feel peaceful, these are moments in time when you are experiencing a highest reality because you are experiencing the fullness of an archetype, the "thing-in-itself." This is all that human beings ultimately seek—to experience and know Self, the Full Self, the "Fullness of Being" as the Advaitans refer to it. This is not only a philosophy, but it is most assuredly a psychology, a real and imbued higher consciousness if you can awaken to its truth. If you perceive Eastern philosophy as split from psychology, then neither have been fully comprehended and, more importantly, a higher consciousness than the ego has not unfolded. There is a real and higher consciousness than the ego and, until you actually have a spiritual awakening and self-actualize it, you will falsely perceive Eastern psychology as a philosophy unrelated to psychology instead of knowing it to be a new and higher level of psychological consciousness, an expanded awareness and a more integrated, healthy and whole way of perceiving the world which mollifies negative emotions. Advaitans refer to a higher way of "seeing" or knowing as Brahman or Reality and speak of the hierarchy of knowledge. Hierarchy could best be understood as an ever more increasingly expanded level of consciousness, awareness, insight or realization. In Eliot Deutsch's book, *Advaita Vedanta*, he states that "the final goal of knowledge, namely, spiritual intuitive insight, once attained, relegates all other forms and types of knowledge to a lower knowledge—lower at least because none of them is capable of bringing one to a realization of Reality." Deutsch continues by saying that:

> "Brahman is that which when known, all else is known. But this does not mean that a knowledge of Brahman carries along with it a knowledge of particulars, of individual objects and their relations in past, present, or future, time, for Brahman is incommensurable with the empirical world: the empirical world of multiplicity, according to the Advaitan, disappears from consciousness upon the attainment of the 'oneness' that is Brahman. *Para vidya*, the higher knowledge of Brahman, is thus not some form of supernatural, magical knowledge about Nature......The 'all else' that is known when Brahman is known, then, must necessarily mean 'all else of value.' In other words, when Brahman is realized, *nothing else needs to be known*. When the self has found itself at-one with Reality, there is nothing of real value that remains to be known."

It is that which knows itSelf as the "I am that I am" within. Let's see if I can give an example of the difference between the two *ways or types* of "knowing" referred to in Eastern philosophy. The two examples I will use are "knowing" that the cause of the First World War was the assassination of the Archduke Ferdinand of Spain and "knowing" the experience of loving your child, your spouse, your pet or your work. In the first instance, it can be said that you "know" intellectually that the assassination of Archduke Ferdinand initiated World War I. You do carry the "knowledge" of that inside you. In the second instance, however, you carry that love of your child or spouse at a far deeper level of Being, far deeper than a superficial intellectual level. In the first example, intellect grasps a part of relative reality. In the second example, when you "know" you love your child, it is grasped as a wholeness and fullness of knowing. There is a vast difference in the types and qualities of these epistemologies, the nature and way of "knowing." In the first way of knowing, you simply know on an intellectual level. This is the type of knowledge that is taught in all schools and universities today. You cannot Be that knowledge, feel it deep within you, imbue that knowledge within your Soul. It is superficial knowledge, worldly knowledge. You can only know it *intellectually*, not subjectively, ontologically or phenomenologically. This is why Eastern psychologies, philosophies and religions consider intuition to be a higher form of knowing than is intellect. Pure intellect can only understand parts, not wholes. Intellect requires analyzing which separates and divides, it requires Aristotelian logic, an either/or logic.

The second experience of loving your child or your spouse or of experiencing the creativity when you paint, draw, write or sculpt is a deeper kind of knowing, a deeper knowledge that you experience from within you. There is no school or university that currently exists which attempts to consciously teach students this way of "knowing" although Socrates, Plato, Lao Tzu, Buddha and Jesus the Christ likely taught their "students" and "disciples" this type of "knowing." You could say that you experience this "knowing" within your Soul. If someone asked you to define that experience, package it, sell it or reproduce it materially, you could not. You could only arrive at some *symbol* of that experience. You could not, however, convey your experience more than at an intellectual and superficial level or by some symbolic means such as drawing a picture to describe that love that you "know." No one can prove that love exists, yet we all know it does. How do we know it? We know it intuitively and we see it in the results that manifest when love is being felt and being projected. This intuitive "knowing" is called "noetic truth" and is a higher level of "knowing" than is intellectual truth.

Another example of the second type of "knowing" is when Carl Jung was interviewed in 1959 by the BBC and the interviewer asked Jung "Do you believe in God?" After a long pause, Jung answered thus: "Now? (Pause.) Difficult to answer. I know. I don't need to believe. I know." Believing is an intellectual and superficial way of knowing. Jung knew his Higher Self exists because he "knew" it deep within his Psyche, his Soul, which is an ontic reality for him.

It is impossible to subjectively be a diamond. It is impossible to subjectively be a yacht, a mansion, a flower, a tree, a car, a painting or any other material or physical thing. It is impossible to feel being $1,000,000. You can never feel the fullness of being a fur coat or a Rolex watch. The only experience you can ever experience is the fullness of the spiritual fruit *behind* that physical object. In other words, you can never experience a diamond, rather you can only ever experience the joy, beauty and love of owning or holding that diamond. The diamond is just a symbol. You can never experience being a luxury car, yacht or million dollar mansion. You can only Be and experience the spiritual essence—joy, beauty, love—behind that physical object. Would you reach for anything material knowing that it will cause you pain and suffering? NO! We delude ourselves into thinking that the things we reach for will bring us joy. In this sense, we have forgotten what it is we REALLY want. Taken one step further, we have forgotten WHO WE ARE. For you can never be anything material or physical. You are forever and ever spiritual essence. You have only forgotten this by valuing physical things. For what you concentrate on and what you focus on *will become reality for you*. But reality can never be the material and physical world because we can never BE matter. We can only BE essence and spirit. We certainly have free will to believe in our delusions and that is the power of the mind. And since the mind is very powerful indeed, we have grown to believe in the delusion that we value material things when the truth is that we only seek the joy, peace and love which is the essence of all things. In *The Discovery of Being*, May states that "this has much to do with the sense of isolation and loneliness which is endemic in the modern Western world; for the only experience we let ourselves believe in as real is that which is precisely not." We have deluded ourselves into thinking we want material things when in actuality it is only the spiritual essence *behind* the material thing that we want. And this is so forever and ever without end. For that which you cannot Be is not. You can never be an object; you can only be subject. Being is subjectivity. As Kierkegaard and Wilber point out, subjectivity can never be an object. Subjectivity can only be an experiencing subject. In Truth, *the only thing that exists is the spiritual realm of spiritual fruits because there is no way to ever experience Being anything in the material world.* You can only experience the effects of a material thing. You cannot subjectively experience the Hope diamond, rather you can only experience the joy and beauty which are effects of the diamond. You can never experience a chair or a table, rather you can only experience the safety, security, beauty and peace which a chair may bring you. You can never experience gold or silver, rather you can only experience the joy and beauty from these physical things. Negative emotions do not exist in Reality because they do not exist except on a physical plane. When you return to the spiritual realm of not having a physical body, you cannot experience negative emotions, therefore, negative emotions are transient and are not ultimately real. Only spiritual fruits are experienced forever and ever and ever. This is Brahman, this is Oneness and this is Reality. It is the illumined Divine One.

Plato and Aristotle disagreed as to whether the Form or archetype exists within the physical object or apart from the physical object. Plato argued that the Form exists apart from the physical object. Aristotle believed the two existed together. When viewed from the Soul consciousness model, archetypes are considered to exist everywhere since they are within the Divine Mind. These archetypes are the fabric of your Great Soul and are your essence. Nothing exists but your Higher Self and there is nothing else to experience but to rediscover your Psyche and know who you are in your spiritual essence. Scientism has attempted for centuries to lead you astray into the untruth of physical matter forming the basis of the only "reality". Science has deluded humankind into believing that if you cannot measure something and validate it against some physically known phenomenon, then it is not "scientific." And if it is not scientific, then it cannot be "real."

Be clear. Your Soul can never be measured by any current scientific measurement device and will never be validated by science as we know it today. Love cannot be measured by a scientific instrument. Love is an eternal reality and is the Authentic Power of the Higher Self. It transforms completely, wholly and eternally. Yet mainstream psychology and medicine ignore the subject for the most part and point their microscopes in all the places where the results of peace and harmony do not lie. Microscopes are pointed at physical materials which are but mere symbols and representations of Authentic Power—love, peace, joy, beauty, compassion, truth, justice, etc. How long will it take for science, which has been built upon the immature masculine ego, to make a quantum leap into the spiritual realm to search for answers? How long will the world allow the immature masculine ego to rule, dominate, control, oppress and divide the planet?

The immature masculine ego seeks to find answers everywhere but the one "place" that the answers lie. Every spiritual fruit lies within the Psyche and the Psyche projects spiritual fruits into the physically manifested world. Spiritual fruits of love, kindness, compassion, truth, beauty, honor, creativity, wisdom, etc. are the creators of all that is, ever has been and ever will be. There is no diamond, fur coat, yacht or mansion that has ever been created by itself. Only creativity, knowledge, love and wisdom can manifest physical matter. These are the eternal, energic forces of the Godness within your Great Soul. This is the eternal consciousness of the Great Divine One and it is that which simply "*is.*" It never began. Some Eastern philosophies refer to this as the "beginninglessness." Where humanity has gone awry is the obsession after the thing (the "other") and not the "thing-in-itself." When you go after the car, house, diamonds, furs, money and forget the spiritual essence, you have forgotten Ultimate Reality and you are seeking something that is not ultimately real. Seeking illusions will never give you completeness or fullness. This is why psychiatrists and psychologists have successful millionaires as clients arriving at their doorstep saying "I have achieved the pinnacle of worldly success, *but something is still missing, doctor.*" The ego seeks material things thinking that obtaining "things" is going to bring fulfillment. The Full Self seeks spiritual essence which is another way to say that the Full Self seeks itSelf which is yet another way to say that the Full Self eternally seeks to return to its original, primal conscious state of Being Goodness. Taoism speaks of the great eternal law: all things return to their original state or form. To return to the original state or form, however, is somewhat misleading because, in truth, Goodness never began. It simply always has been. It simply "*is.*" This is what I believe Socrates was referring to when he said "to know the Good is to do the Good." In reality, this is all there is. There is nothing else other than this. The physical world is but an experience of not being Full Self, not remembering your origin. The material world is a tool to rediscover the Full Self of Goodness. And the Full Self of Goodness is all there is. It is forever.

There are two paradoxes of the "knowing Self." On one hand, the Self is known ontologically, experientially within the deepest fibers of one's Being, through one's Soul. You will know Self as the Whole. In this sense, every human being will one day come to "know Self". On the other hand, in a paradoxical way, no one will ever "know" Self. What is meant by this is we can never answer the following questions through our intellect: Why does the Self exist? How does the Self exist? The Self simply "*is.*" It always has been and always will be. We cannot know why or how the Self exists through intellect because intellect operates through Aristotelian logic and the Self cannot be "known" except through Heraclitean logic. To ask why or how the expressions of the Divine *Nous* exist is to ask why mystery exists. They just do. We just know that it "*is.*" That is the ineffable mystery of Universal Divinity that pure intellect cannot answer.

The Full Self is always referred to with a capital "S" and can be referred to as *saguna* Brahman, the True or Authentic Self, Being, Soul or Higher Self. In Advaitic psychology, there are actually two Higher Selves—*saguna* Brahman and *nirguna* Brahman. *Saguna* Brahman arises when there is a harmony between the conflict of the opposites. Its result is a consciousness of loving awareness. *Nirguna* Brahman, considered highest reality or highest consciousness, arises when all opposites and distinctions are obliterated and its result is a mental spirituality or a state of pure loving knowledge. It might be said that the Christ, the Buddha and Lao Tzu attained *saguna* Brahman consciousness. It appears that these Great Souls knew no distinctions between opposites and were fully, calmly and serenely aware, and accepting of, a reality of paradoxical harmony.

Jung believed that there were two selves, but he believed that Divinity also had two sides: the *Summum Bonum* (supreme goodness) and the shadow. He referred to these as God with Christ on the right hand side and Satan on the left hand side. Believing that the fullness of the Self (*the imago dei*) empties into the ego, Jung postulated that the ego becomes divine and the Self becomes humanized. In my theoretical model of the Soul, I postulate that the Higher Self can never deplete itSelf of any Goodness, therefore, it can never be anything except full and abundant. The ego can never be divine because the ego is a conscious state which is split. Once it unifies, reconciles the opposites and imbues the Fullness of Goodness, the ego dissolves and becomes something greater, therefore, the ego can never be divine. Only the Full Self imbues divinity because the Full Self has come into the conscious awareness that it is the Godness, the *imago dei*. Emptiness is an illusion that the ego would have you believe, but fullness and abundance are your inheritance and these are the only Truths because they are the only Ultimate Reality. You can deceive yourself and place value in the material world and ignore the spiritual world, but you cannot serve both worlds. One must be supreme. If you place your value in the material world, the ego will reign and your consciousness, being powerful, will create a split world and not perceive the Whole. All negative emotions manifest when you place your value in the material world. Because your mind is a powerful thing, you have the ability to choose which world you will serve: the empty world of the ego or the Full world of Spirit. In truth, you can only deceive yourself into thinking that you are empty since you have free will. The Full Self eternally has knowledge, creativity, love and wisdom and eternally wills this for itSelf and others. These are lord and creator of all. Only consciousness creates. This consciousness of knowing, creating, loving and being wise and the will toward this conscious energy never had a beginning, nor will it ever end. Only you, as a human being in a physical world, can deceive yourself otherwise.

The Full Self or Brahman is whole and unified; it is not split. The Full Self desires only Goodness for Self and others. It only sees Goodness; it only *is* Goodness. The ego, on the other hand, vacillates constantly. The ego is understood as being jealous since the ego always believes that the "other" has something which the ego wants because the ego is never satisfied. That which is incomplete, lacking and empty surely will not be satisfied. And since only Goodness can bring fullness of Being, then the ego can never be full. The ego will, indeed, dissolve if the Full Self subsumes the ego. This process is what Jungian analysts refer to as the "ego-Self axis."

You have two ways of viewing the empty ego and the Full Self and the path between the two. One might say there is only a thin veil, so to speak, between the two since the removal of ignorance is an eye blink away. One might also say there is a continuum between empty and full, therefore, the consciousness of humanity can be understood as moving always toward fullness, toward abundance or toward the Full Self or Soul consciousness. Ancient philosophy and some modern theoretical psychological models refer to this process as "becoming" in order to stress the evolutionary process of the stages of self. Parmenides and Plato believed in the primacy of Being and they considered Becoming and change as illusions. Empedocles believed that Becoming and Being co-existed and, in fact, aided one another. Hegel believed that not-Being is ultimately subsumed into Absolute Being. Depending upon which view you take, they all can be considered accurate because both the Many and the One exist, but are forever a Whole. In the Highest Reality, the process operates much like the birth and death of all physical things. Once a human being is conceived in the womb, it begins to grow. Yet, simultaneously and paradoxically, it is moving toward its death. Yet, simultaneously and paradoxically, as it moves toward its death, it is moving toward life. Highest Reality is the congruence of all paradox and this is why the wisest on earth know that, ultimately, only the language of the Silence of the Soul knows truth since to speak one thing is to negate its opposite. Absolute Reality is both knowable, as Hegel and Schopenhauer believed, and yet paradoxically, it is unknowable, as Kant believed. In a Hegelian and Advaitic sense, you will "know" Highest Truth or Reality in the sense that you will become it and imbue it ontologically and phenomenologically. However, in a Kantian sense, it is "unknowable" because you can never measure, validate through "scientific" means, define, write down, verbally and wholly intellectually describe or contain Highest Reality.

The Soul Consciousness model is a model of psychological health and well being. It considers the Full Self as imbuing the Soul Consciousness of Goodness and considers the ego as empty (or not full), manifesting defense mechanisms and projecting all pathology. All other psychological models which de-emphasize or deny spirituality as a critical component of psychological health and well being are considered, paradoxically, both accurate and inaccurate. They are accurate in the sense that the ego is the first step among several steps toward psychological health and well-being.

The ego can only perceive a world through intellect and Aristotelian logic and no one who ever limits their cognition through these lens will ever know higher transcendent states of consciousness. It is in this sense that the ego has false beliefs and all psychological models which emphasize the ego consciousness as the apogee of psychological health are simply inaccurate. They are inaccurate in the larger scheme because the ego consciousness is always subsumed by the Higher Self which knows the ultimate Truth of spirituality; it knows the Many within the Whole. Thus, these prior models are incomplete and inaccurate from the standpoint that they are only reflective of one section of the spectrum of human consciousness—the ego consciousness. The ego consciousness is a critical and necessary part of the evolutionary chain of consciousness and a person must move through that part of the continuum prior to reaching the Full Self or Soul Consciousness although there are no set rules as to how long a person moves through the development. Some factors which determine the process of developing an integrated ego and the ego consciousness are family and social environment, culture, cognitive and emotional development, the desire and will to seek a fuller sense of self and prior physical incarnations. Prior incarnations have provided the self with a range of experiences which are embedded within the unconscious. As we will see later in the book, Jungian and transpersonal psychological models arrive at a broader picture of the evolution of human consciousness because they do recognize the Full Self or Higher Self, thus are considered more complete and more authentic psychological models. Some Eastern psychologies, particularly Advaita Vedanta with the concepts of *saguna* and *nirguna* Brahman and Buddhist psychology with the concept of Nirvana, also refer to a higher evolved state of infinite bliss.

The Full Self knows itSelf as subject and does not reach for and yearn for "other" to make itSelf whole. It is whole in and of itSelf because it is Full. It is Full because it has found the truth of its essence which are the expressions of knowledge, creativity, love and wisdom and the Will toward Goodness. It consistently projects this Goodness from within to the outside world. If we all were to imbue this, project this and respect all people of different races, gender, ages, religions, socioeconomic status as beautiful expressions of the Whole, our world would be a world of peace. The spiritual fruits of Goodness are the only energies which can give the Self its Fullness. This is referred to by theologians as "abundance," but you may also say it is the same as psychological abundance or well-being.

There can be no collective Goodness until all selves are experiencing their Full Self. It is also understood that the greater number of selves who have arrived at the evolutionary stage of the Full Self, the greater that each Self will experience its own Fullness, its own psychological and ontological state of abundance. This is the goal of the Higher Self—to return to this conscious state of Being.

The evolution from the ego consciousness to the Soul consciousness of the Full Self is not a fantasy. It is a fact. It *will* manifest. It will occur because it is an inevitable spiritual law that the Full Self will return to knowing itSelf in all its fullness and goodness because that is what the Full Self is! This Full Self is lord and governor over the ego because unity always triumphs over division. The Psyche or Soul has an inherent disposition to return to unity. One could say that it is an inherent structural component of the Soul to seek unification. Human consciousness seeks to find a unifying thread, if you will, behind all that exists. Individuality within unification was the state in the Spiritual realm and it is the state to which all Selves must return.

The ego has an inherent disposition to compete, divide, conquer and control. As we have stated earlier, the ego consciousness must develop and integrate prior to the Full Self manifesting. The ego must have arrived at its own recognition prior to becoming a Full Self. The ego must form prior to the formation (or return) of the Full Self. Such is the eternal evolution of human consciousness: first moving from the spiritual realm, then incarnating into matter, then back into the spiritual realm. Forever and ever, this is the cycle of the nature of consciousness.

When you incarnated into the physical world, you wanted to experience the physical world with all its multiplicity, diversity, difference and separation. There is a price to pay for this: you lose your essence as you become hypnotized by the allure of world glamour. You have free will to choose what you wish to worship and what you wish to value, therefore, there is no one to stop you from falling in love, so to speak, with material things. It is this love affair with material things to the exclusion of all things spiritual that is the manifestation of the ego and the root cause of all human suffering since the beginning of time as we know it. Once under the hypnotic sway of loving material things, the remembrance of your authentic essence--spiritual Goodness—has been lost. Salvation refers to the remembrance of your spiritual essence as your primary Being and the successful evolution back to your Full Self which is your reconnection with the Divine.

Let me repeat this because it is worth saying over and over: This is not a fantasy realm of consciousness. The Full Self is your essence and the Soul carries the memory of your Full Self. If you were not a Full Self in your essence and if you did not have a Soul, we would all indeed be lost forever and would never be able to find our way back to the pure knowledge of Goodness. The Soul is the recollection of the divine Goodness of who we are in the spiritual realm where no physical matter encompasses our Soul, therefore, no negative emotions can exist. This is the ontology of the Full Self or the ontology of Goodness. Plato and the neo-Platonists referred to this as Being which is a kind of merging or unifying of consciousness. One may view Aristotle's philosophy of Potential and Actual as the ego and the Self. The modern existentialist philosophers and psychologists spoke of Being. St. Augustine drew heavily on the Platonic philosophy of Being. For thousands of years, philosophers and theologians have been writing about and expounding on the Soul; they are all saying the same thing over and over, just saying it perhaps in different ways. Speaking as Pythagoras, there is nothing really new in the strictest sense of the term; just the same eternal cycle being repeated with varying expressions. If you turn away from the "busy-ness" of the material world, you will discover this in the world of nature which is all about cycles.

Goodness is the Godhead and the mysterious, living force by which all comes into existence. It is the essence of the Higher Self which imbues Soul consciousness. Plato spoke of the reality of Goodness or the reality of the Idea of Goodness. Plato spoke of Goodness *as* Being and the highest reality.

The Higher Self knows spiritual laws, obeys them and projects spiritual fruits of Goodness because the Higher Self knows that everything is related, interdependent and full in its spiritual essence. Only the spiritual realm can give a sense of fullness. The remnant from the ego that carries over into the Higher Self is that part of the ego that discovered the "I am" within, the Godness within, the Divineness within. The ego evolves to one day know that it is a separate, viable entity of consciousness just as you were a separate, viable conscious entity when you were in the Spiritual realm with no physical body, only consciousness. The ego, therefore, comes into an awareness of itself as distinct from "other." The Higher Self maintains this "I am" awareness, yet moves beyond it to remember that every Higher Self is interdependent upon each other in the spiritual realm. The Higher Self subsumes the ego and transforms the ego into something greater and larger in awareness. When the Higher Self begins to have a dim awareness of its fullness, its Goodness, its authentic power through spiritual fruits, it begins to know this Goodness is the author of everything. Goodness is truth.

Goodness is beauty. Goodness, truth and beauty are all one and the same thing. All spiritual fruits are One and indivisible. That which is Good is certainly true. That which is Good is most assuredly beautiful. It is what several of the pre-Socratic philosophers referred to when they spoke of "the many within the One."

The Full Self yearns, and is responsible, for creating, knowing, loving and being wise. It seeks to return to its essence. To return to a spiritual essence is to know that essence. The Full Self can never be truly lost from any human being. You can only deceive yourself into thinking the Full Self is lost. The ego, at its lower levels, will try everything to deceive you into thinking that fullness is a fantasy and that to experience divinity as a human being is impossible. The ego must do this because the ego will not exist if you transform yourself. The ego is the consciousness of despair, cynicism, criticism, ridicule, devaluation and hopelessness, so it will always tempt you into believing that Fullness is a fantasy. That way, the ego lives and Goodness does not manifest on our planet as a pervasive consciousness!

The ego seeks to distribute, divide, separate and to discover the particulars that exist in a world of matter. The ego seeks the minute, the tiny. The Soul seeks the Universals, as the ancient philosophers used to speak about. The Universals are love, wisdom, knowledge, truth, creativity and beauty. If humankind is projecting these qualities, poverty, discrimination, oppression, hate, greed, envy and wars would not exist. Capitalism, as we know it today, would have to transform into a more socialistic economic system since capitalism, in and of itself, is a political ideology which worships wealth for the individual, therefore, capitalism as we know it today is a bastion of mass ego consciousness.

Capitalism is built upon two primary ideologies: 1) material wealth is supreme, and 2) competition is the means by which material wealth must be gained. In a world ruled by the ego, greed is, vicariously, the means by which competition is fostered. Further, capitalism in America has evolved into a system whereby patriarchy controls all wealth, thereby disallowing the feminine from entering the upper echelon of the economic system. The greed which fuels capitalism is the same fuel for the ego, thus, capitalism separates, divides, conquers and controls. Capitalism (as we know it today) will be transformed when humankind evolves to the next higher level of consciousness. Democracy, as originally conceived by the forefathers in America as a political system "of the people, by the people and for the people," is a pristine system which has been bastardized, defamed and distorted by the immature masculine which controls it. As long as the mature feminine and mature masculine are unreconciled, the system will be corrupt and will not achieve its true goal. The education system must also integrate into its leadership positions the feminine energy. Education today has become mostly institutions of data dumping where masses amount of information is reciprocally exchanged from teacher to student and back to teacher. No schools exist like Plato's Academy and Aristotle's Lyceum, where there was a balance between ensuring students garner worldly knowledge, but also ensuring the student learns the nature of Soulfulness. Since the mind and intellect are worshiped on this planet and the feminine aspect is ignored and dismissed by the immature masculine, the Soul is left out of the world's education system. The "god" of education is intellect so the heart is ignored during all stages of educational pursuits. We teach knowledge and how to create worldly things, but there is no interest among the male leadership in education to teach the value of love and spiritual wisdom. Since the immature masculine perceives love and kindness as weaknesses and perceives only intellect, logic and reasoning as strengths, we have a psychologically incomplete and unhealthy world. We keep churning out incomplete humans as we push them through all our systems. The male leadership on this planet has given us much; it has also failed in this simple obligation. And yet these same male leaders wonder why there is world conflict.

The field of psychology has seen dozens of complex theories and models in attempts to find an answer to the pathology which consumes humankind and the psychological ill health of the world. Most of these theories are little understood by the lay person, hence, little, if any, of the theory and its application can be grasped by large numbers of people. Perhaps only Carl Rogers in his person-centered theory has developed a simple psychology and ontology which can be grasped by large numbers of people and which offer hope for a world starved for the feminine. His emphasis on empathy and unconditional positive regard toward the client are almost uncannily similar to the principles of love and compassion which Jesus and the Buddha taught. We feel the noetic truth of these energies within our deepest Being. It is common sense that the Truth must be simple since complexity seems only to divide and confuse. Seeking Goodness seems to be the one simple Universal Truth. We ask ourselves simple questions: Is oppression good? Is discrimination good? Is greed good? Is hate good? Is war good? How can anything be Good if the outcome reflects a society filled with hate, anger, crime and violence toward others? If it is true that the "kingdom of heaven is within" and that what is outside is always a reflection of what is inside ourselves, then truly our inward state of consciousness is hellish indeed. Again, it seems obvious that it is the duty and mission of the field of psychology to do everything it can in its power to work toward the goal of guiding humanity toward the Full Self which imbues the Soul Consciousness. The field of psychology must do the following to avoid irrelevance, to finally assume a respected and viable role in the eyes of the social world. The field will become irrelevant as a field of study unless:

1) professionals within the field (academic, clinical and research professionals) balance equally the feminine and the masculine, the *anima* and the *animus*, such that females have parity with male leaders,

2) the field recognizes that the ego is *not* the optimal state of psychological well being, rather it is a crucial developmental step toward the Full Self,

3) the field develops a cohesive, spiritual concept of Highest reality, away from a material, mechanistic model of human functioning,

4) the spiritual realm of spiritual fruits of love, kindness, compassion, truth, beauty, creativity, etc. are the overarching universal *psychological causes and results and behavioral outcomes* that psychology seeks as it develops a theoretical model of health and well-being and as it applies research methodologies,

5) research methodologies must include qualitative studies such that parity exists between the "within" and the "without";

6) the field accepts a comprehensive theoretical model which is exegetical of the evolution of human consciousness,

7) psychology begins a re-integration with his sister, philosophy, in its pursuit of wisdom of the Psyche, the Higher Self, and begins building an authentic bridge between psychology, philosophy and spirituality,

8) the field of psychology develops an ethos to include a larger, broader and much more significant world perspective in advocating for all viable states of consciousness which foster social change toward Goodness for Self and others, hence, for society as a whole,

9) psychology heals the split between Eastern and Western psychologies and philosophies and seeks to collaborate toward a unified theory of consciousness,

10) educational curriculums integrate Jungian and transpersonal theoretical models into their psychology programs, along with fundamental concepts of Eastern psychologies, epistemologies, methodologies and various psychotherapeutic techniques such as meditation, hypnotherapy,

chromatherapy, sound therapy, music therapy and aromatherapy,

11) psychologists write in simple language for large audiences of lay people to understand,

12) the American Psychological Association reinvents itself and moves toward these twelve (12) objectives.

To accept the simplicity of the Full Self, the Good Self, is to move away from the complexity of the ego. Psychology has studied the cause and effects of the *lack* of Goodness *ad nauseum*. Yet we are still seeing droves of the mentally ill check into the Psychiatric Unit of hospitals to be put on anti-psychotics and masses of the "normal neurotics" spending billions of dollars every year on anti-depressants and anxiolytics. We know that fear, anger, hate, anxiety, sadness, guilt, shame have a positive relationship with mental illnesses and disorders. As one increases, so does the other. Is this so surprising? Do we need one more research study validating this simple, common sensical truth? *Mainstream psychology ignores and dismisses a study of the common traits, characteristics and lifestyles of people like the Dalai Lama, Mother Teresa, Jesus the Christ, Lao Tzu and the Buddha who happen to be honored, adored and revered by millions of people on the entire planet.* Instead, mainstream psychology studies the ego for 125 years. When will the pendulum swing toward the study of Goodness in order to make the study of the Psyche an authentic psychology? What will it take?

Complex psychological theory after complex theory has been proposed, developed, studied, written about, debated, critiqued and researched. Until psychology begins to write simple theories so that large numbers of lay people can understand them and until a large-scale, systematic and collaborative study of Goodness and its relationship to psychological health and well-being is begun, the field will be taken over by other practitioners and will become irrelevant by the 22nd century. What ultimate good is any theory if the masses of people cannot comprehend it? The immature ego is responsible for a social construct which says that only something written in language barely discernable to more than a few elite people within that field of study is worthy to be honored and revered. Otherwise, if the theory is simplistic, it must be invalid and irrelevant. And so we continue to give validation to a few who control through elitism. We have so many complex theories which are written in verbiage that is verbose, dense and barely comprehensible to mainstream society. Is it any wonder that the public fails to grasp the value, worth and validity of the field of psychology?

The Soul is mostly simple, the simple way of Being which gives the Soul its greatest allure. The theory is simple as well. Humankind must return to the simple. Humans have become so obsessed and consumed with complexity that it is virtually impossible to present simplistic concepts today because it threatens the ego consciousness, particularly the dominant ego masculine consciousness. Virginia Satir was a prominent female social worker amongst mostly male psychiatrists in the 1950s. She is among the founders of the family therapy movement and identified her therapeutic approach as the Human Validation Process Model. Satir believed that all humans strive toward growth and development and possess all the resources necessary to fulfill their potential. She related to clients in a warm, nurturing way believing in the inherent goodness of people and in the healing power of love. She firmly believed that practicing this "love" with her clients was a necessary condition for actualizing a client's capabilities and, indeed, was the ingredient which best facilitated change. Looking for the healthy within clients even when they were exhibiting unhealthy symptomatology, she believed that every person has this inherent capacity to grow under the right circumstances. She believed that the spiritual level, or the Soul or life force, was a fundamental level of functioning within all human beings, yet her ideas were devalued and considered simplistic and "polly-annish" by her mostly male critics whose theories were far more dense and complex than hers.

People yearn for that which is simple. The Soul yearns for simple because the Soul *is* simple. Goodness is simple. Simple truths are Universal and eternal. Every person has a Soul which yearns for these simplicities of life. When psychology arrives at a unified theory of human consciousness which presents a range from non-spiritual to spiritual consciousness, presents it to the world in simple concepts and arrives at effective, natural and simple therapies, then perhaps the world will value psychology.

Each of the aforementioned twelve objectives are critical for the field of psychology if it wishes to be in existence as a viable field in 100 years and if it wishes to garner the broad-scale social, economic and political support which the field has pursued since its divorce from its sister, philosophy, roughly 125 years ago. Psychology must be recognized as *an art, a science, a philosophy, an ethos and a spirituality.* The field must recognize itself as encompassing all of these under the rubric of health and well-being. All its tenets and methodologies of research must come under scrutiny and be revisioned in order to keep up with the evolutionary change in the consciousness of humankind. The past 125 years of psychology have been dominated mostly by a masculine cognitive style, a masculine perspective of the world, a masculine method of studying human behavior, a masculine approach of establishing rules, a masculine way of research methodologies, a masculine style of relating, a masculine view of developing theories, a masculine vision of developing constructs and a masculine manner of criticism. *It is time to integrate feminine with masculine, a reconciliation of the opposites so we may stop analyzing ourselves to death and, instead, we may begin to unify amongst ourselves.*

If the field is unable to achieve these objectives and unify under the rubric of these common goals, the ego consciousness will continue to lead mainstream psychology and the field, therefore, risks obsolescence. Much like the concept of entropy in physics, the closed-minded thinking of the current mainstream psychological associations and organizations will create an implosion. The ego is closed-minded because only spiritual fruits bring authentic freedom. The ego, particularly, the immature masculine ego, is responsible for virtually all of the following: world and civil wars, serial killings, genocide of groups of people, murders of individuals, pedophilia, rapes and robbery. Certainly, the immature feminine ego has participated in white collar crimes, but the bulk is understood to be committed by males, particularly at the corporate executive level. The immature masculine has been in power and control of this planet since time began and is responsible for the murder of over 6,000,000 Jews in the holocaust, the decimation of the Native American race and culture in the United States, the oppression and murder of African American slaves and African American people for over a century, the murder and torture of innocent Buddhist monks and nuns, the heinous slaughter of Muslim women and their unborn children and the arrogant abuse, devaluation and egregious discrimination of females for over 4,000 years. How long can we continue to tolerate this outrageous leadership? How much longer can the world experience the deleterious effects of the immature ego masculine? For over a thousand years, the immature ego masculine in the male leadership in the Catholic Church was responsible for the murder and torture of people because they dared to have a different belief system than set down by Catholic dogma and doctrine. More recently brought to light are those Catholic priests responsible for the sexual exploitation of countless of numbers of young boys and yet the Catholic Church at the highest levels appears reluctant to assume candid ownership and noble accountability for this unholy travesty. The immature ego masculine is responsible for hundreds of years of arrogant, narcissistic corporate greed resulting today in thousands of innocent people losing their life's savings, yet it continually

114

appears that the immature masculine within the legal and politic systems oftentimes fail to avidly pursue justice. Many times these powerful males are connected through personal alliances or business deals which makes it almost virtually impossible for indictments to result and for any truth or justice to be seen. The business and political world today seems to have culminated into one mass of interconnected personal and business male relationships which are held together through self-gain, self-aggrandizement and the tacit agreement that all the wolves in the pack will ensure that the unsuspecting public and investment community will only see the fabric of the sheep's cloth. The immature ego masculine is responsible for the wholesale dismissal and patriarchal abuse of females as the latter have been historically discriminated against and denied opportunities to pursue social, economic, financial, business and political goals. The immature ego masculine is responsible for the brutal oppression of millions of African Americans and the heinous lynchings and murders of thousands of them throughout history. The immature masculine ego in psychology has given us a conceptual edifice by which the field has begun its ascent from the narrow "I" or ego toward a higher transcendent consciousness, but the field has failed in its responsibility for recognizing and honoring the Whole Psyche, the Soul. Hence, mainstream psychology has failed to study what it is intended to study. You could say that the psyche of dominant, mainstream psychology (psychoanalyatic, cognitive and behavioral theories) is the immature and unwhole psyche because the field has not only failed to acknowledge and honor the sacred feminine, it has even denounced love as a primal part of wholeness and fullness of Being. This is why psychoanalytic, cognitive and behavioral theories and therapies, while essential and valuable for understanding part of the Soul, are partial, at best, but will never provide a guiding ethos for self-transcendence and for optimal mental health.

When the Soul Consciousness manifests, the ego consciousness is afraid of it or attacks it. The world is so full of ego consciousness that when a person imbues Goodness, the ego looks upon it as suspicious. All negative emotions are defense mechanisms used by the ego to substantiate itself. Greed, jealousy, envy, shame, guilt, anger and fear cannot exist unless the ego perceives lack, separation or division. All defense mechanisms derive from fear and the ego's ultimate fear is that it will cease to exist. The empty ego lives the life of hell because it creates a world of fear, anger, greed, jealousy, envy, shame, guilt which leads to all war, conflict and chaos. Where else could hell be if not the hellish, painful, sorrowful life we humans have created for ourselves?

The ego is destructive. The Soul is constructive. The ego destroys. The Soul transforms and creates. War is the state of mind in which the ego operates. To be in conflict is to be at war. War is a state of division and separation. In Webster's dictionary, it states that war is a "struggle or competition of opposing forces" and to "be in active or vigorous conflict." Only the energy of creativity and transformation exists at the higher level of psychological functioning of the Full Self. When two men are on the battlefield shooting at one another that is a state of psychological warfare because the ego is fearful. The ego is operating because it cannot perceive any Whole, rather it only perceives difference and separation. When you are working to manifest your dreams from an abstract idea into physical form such as when you are working to build your own business, you are exhibiting the divine creative energy, not the warrior energy. Only the immature ego masculine attempts to teach the world that the warrior instinct is within the essence of human beings because the ego is a warring consciousness. That which is split can only be at war. That which is whole experiences balance and harmony. Your essence is not war; your essence is peace and the resolution and harmony of all things.

Every person on this planet can and will reach the Soul consciousness state that Jesus, the Buddha and Lao Tzu attained. It is not a matter of whether it will happen, rather it is only a matter of *when*. You have free will so you can take the next 17,000,000,000,000 years to reach that state if you want because you have total free will to return to your essence. This is the inevitable, eternal evolution of consciousness. You are destined to return to your Full Self and there is no force on this earth or beyond which will forever prevent that from occurring. Fullness is not a fantasy. This is your destiny because this is your eternal essence. Love yourself no more or no less than your neighbor. Both of you are equal in your potential to return to your Full Self.

The Psyche, in its fullness, forever seeks itSelf, therefore, it forever seeks to know Self. This is the state of Being and Fullness when the Self projects itSelf which is to say when the Self projects its Goodness, its essence, its spiritual inheritance. The ego is unaware that all desire to have physical things is a metaphor for, and symbolic of, the Soul seeking to remember and rediscover itSelf.

Everything that exists follows a stream, a cycle, and goes through stages. You may think of cycles as evolutionary and at the highest universal level, the same cycles occur throughout eternity. The flow or evolution of the self and the Self, the not-Being and the Being, the self and the Soul, the self and the Higher Self follows an eternal cycle. This eternal cycle moves from unification to separation back to unification. This is the eternal evolution of consciousness and unconsciousness.

Let's take a look at a chart below to give a better visual to this process.

**Attachment IV**

THREE STAGES OF THE EGO

FIRST
Dominant: biological/sexual
Recessive: social influences

Primitive
Largest split between I and Thou
No awareness of "I am"
Environment is the stimulating and overwhelming Master

Goal:   Master the physical environment
Psychoanalytic model

SECOND
Dominant: social influences and
　　　　Biological/sexual
Recessive: psychological awareness,
　　　　the "I am" (moderate awareness)

$6^{th}$ Century B.C. through $17^{th}$ cent.
Schism still exists between I and Thou
Growing mastery of "I" over the environment
Social environment largely molds the "I"
$17^{th}$ century is seen as when a mass of people reached this stage

Goal: Master social environment
Neo-Freudian, Adlerian, cognitive/behavioral, Family systems models

THIRD
Dominant: psychological awareness of

　　　"I"; intellect (logic and reason) are
　　　supreme
Recessive: social and biological/sexual
　　　Influences

$17^{th}$ century until present
Highest awareness of "I" versus Thou
"I" is seen as supreme, but I and Thou are still viewed as separate
There is only a dim awareness of the interdependence and interrelatedness of all of life

Goal: Know the egoic self
Humanistic/Existential, Gestalt Models

THREE STAGES OF THE FULL SELF

FIRST

| Dominant: psychological awareness of "I"; Intuition (knowledge through the Unconscious)<br>Recessive: psychological awareness of "I"; Intellect (knowledge through logic/reason) | The "I" constructs society, not visa versa<br>Biological/sexual drives become background; Soul is emerging<br>Dim awareness of self-governance<br>Dim awareness of "I" related to "Other" (the group or Soul consciousness) |

Goal: Master over the egoic self; healing of the split

SECOND

| Dominant: Reconciling of opposites, Particularly feminine/masculine<br>Recessive: splitting of consciousness | Intuition and intellect are given equal status and usage<br>Mastery of "I" over social and biological<br>Minimal influence of biological/sexual |
| Goal: Unification of consciousness and Unconsciousness; transformation Of Self through collective Self-Governance | Mass group of people reaching Soul consciousness; individuation Substantial decrease in disease and illness |

THIRD

| Dominant: Androgyny; integration of Anima and animus within the Individual Higher Self within the Collective whole; all of life is viewed As an interdependent, interrelated Whole of many individuated Higher Selves | Collective individuation, self-actualization; Full Self of Goodness Soul/Self is divine and human Grandeur of the Soul manifests "Glory" of the God-image manifests Consciousness of Christ, Buddha, the Group manifests on a global Scale<br>Virtually no disease or illness exists |

Goal: Re-integration with spiritual realm

As we look at this model, we hypothesize that 97-99% of the current world population functions at the egoic levels of consciousness. Most world leaders of politics, business and education function at this level. Approximately ¼ of 1% of the current world population functions at the lowest level of the Soul consciousness. If any leaders in politics, business and education exist at this level, they are virtually unnoticeable by society. It is likely that there are less than a few hundred people on the entire planet who are functioning at the mid-level of the Soul consciousness and these are most probably Eastern yogis or gurus living in ashrams or monasteries or Buddhist monks who meditate consistently and do not intermix with society to any significant degree.

We understand evolution as more of a fluid, dynamic process than a simple "Step 1," then "Step 2," then "Step 3," yet the evolution of consciousness is understood to be cyclical as believed by the ancient Greek philosophers. At the lowest level of ego functioning, there is little or no movement forward. This is the lowest level of human conscious experience. Once the next level of consciousness is reached, the person can slip back and forth between Stage 1 and Stage 2 until a sort of equilibrium is reached that calms at the next highest stage. The person will stay at the next level for a period of time, then begin to be compelled to move forward as the energy frequency rises. Once again, the rocking back and forth begins so that now we experience movement back and forth between Stages 2 and 3. Finally, there is another calm experienced. You may think of this rocking back and forth as analogous to leaning a glass of water to the side. At first, the water is calm. Once you move the glass, the water starts rocking back and forth until finally it rests again when it reaches equilibrium. Each person has free will and each person incarnates into this world at varying levels of spiritual advancement, therefore, some people stay in a stage longer than others. The law of equilibrium applies to this movement back and forth and as the energy pull of the next higher stage becomes a greater force than the lower stage energy pull, the next higher energy pull will eventually cause the person to move completely out of the lower stage and eventually completely into the next higher stage. The rocking back and forth stages can also be seen throughout the human development stage models of theorists such as Piaget and Erikson. For example, age two carries a rocking back and forth as does puberty, middle age and the elder years. A person does not simply move one day from one stage into the next higher, rather there is a kind of rocking back and forth until the next energy cycle has a greater frequency than the lower one. At each stage, the fundamental paradoxical dilemma is always the desire for dependence, yet the desire for independence. It is the desire of the self to be a whole Self, yet to retain connectedness with a larger unified collective Self. The unified collective Self is a composite of many whole Selves, so true independence is gained, but paradoxically it is only gained upon the recognition of independence within a dependent whole. No one person can ever rule the world although it seems that countless males keep trying to do just that. That is a myth which has caused the death and suffering of millions of people on this planet for thousands of years and, if left unchecked, will be the death of us all. Each person finally attains a point in consciousness where they are self-governed, but always within a larger context of other Selves. At the highest evolutionary step of Soul consciousness, each Full Self cooperates, co-creates and peacefully coexists with other Full Selves. It can be no other way. This is the reality in the spiritual realm. It is the perfect diversity within absolute Unity.

At each successively higher evolutionary point, the Self becomes fuller and is expanding in awareness and knowingness. The fuller the Self becomes, the more it looks upward to the next higher stage. It is perhaps best to say that "higher" really means "more inclusive." It is not intended to mirror the superiority of the ego. More inclusive translates into acceptance and fullness. Paradoxically, at higher, more inclusive levels of consciousness, there is a growing Will to assist those at lower, less inclusive levels of functioning in order to return the collective consciousness of Absolute Goodness. In that sense, the Full Self works in service to the Higher Collective Soul to bring humankind to fullness. This can only be achieved through sharing and community. There is no other way.

Many writers have referred to the "dark night of the Soul." This is considered a pivotal point and usually occurs at the point of highest ego functioning when the ego has caused much suffering due to its conscious outlook of the world. The Soul is considered buried or has a sort of veil over it whenever the ego is functioning, but there always comes a time in a person's life (either in this incarnation or a future incarnation) when the person must face the Soul and its memory of the Higher Self.

The Soul pushes to express itSelf in all its Fullness. The ego suppresses the Soul. There exists a mass of people on the planet today whose Soul is pushing to express itSelf as a critical mass is reaching the highest levels of ego consciousness. The extraordinarily visible levels of greed and abuse which lead to conflict and war are causing greater numbers of people to awaken to the need for another way for humans to relate to each other. This is truly a turning point in the evolution of humankind.

Let's go back to the stages of the evolutionary model. The first and second stages of egoic level fit within Freud's psychological model of the ego in service of the Id. Freud did not believe in a Higher Self and believed that the ego was in total service of the Id, that part of the self which was always driven by biological drives and always said "I desire". At this level, in line with the Freudian model, sex, war and aggression are instinctual so Freudian's theory is accurate at the lower levels of consciousness. Freud believed these energies were forever instinctual within the human being. The Soul consciousness model refutes this and believes that sex, war and aggression are predominate throughout the ego consciousness, however, as the ego evolves, these instincts become less prominent.

As the second level of the ego consciousness proceeds, the environment is largely conquered and the social and familial influences begin to have profound effects on the self. The self is struggling to find itself and to recapture its fullness, however, the ego is unaware of this at this stage. The ego is shaped and influenced by outside and external factors and functions through an external locus of control. There is a slight diminishing of the biological/sexual factors as the social and familial influencers become dominant.

At the third stage of the ego consciousness, there is a dim, but growing awareness of the self. The ego begins to have an awareness of "I am" and the power that the "I" has over its environment. Intellect is prominent in the struggle for the "I" to reconnect to its essence and all intellectual inquiry based on this method of knowing is considered valid. The intellect is split off from intuition, the anima and animus are split off from one another and the "I" and "Thou," subject and object, remain split from each other.

In other words, at all these levels, the ego is empty although it does not even have a conscious awareness of its emptiness or of what it is seeking. It is seeking something that it is not because the ego always perceives a world of lack as it seeks all answers outside of itself. The ego is the subject and it is constantly seeking the objects of its desire in order to make it feel full. It is seeking fullness because it is seeking a remembrance of its essence although this seeking is totally unconscious at these stages.

The ego projects fear into the world and perceives a false reality; all negative emotions manifest from this conscious state of emptiness and lack. The ego is afraid of finding the Soul, the Higher Self, the essence of Being because the ego will be dissolved and transformed if the Higher Self, the Full Self, is rediscovered. You might say that the ego is lost, does not know what it is searching for and has no awareness of its spiritual essence. In this lost state, the ego has a veil over it because it is really only a breath away from knowing its Full Self. Only the Soul can bring to memory the essence of the Full Self. Ego can do nothing on its own because it is the consciousness of emptiness and not-Being. It is empty because it cannot stop seeking something other or something else. Believing that the other always has something that it lacks, the ego defends against lack. Through greed, the ego attempts to become full although it does not have a conscious awareness that physical matter will never give it psychological fullness. Upon obtaining something other, the ego either feels guilty or shameful that it has more or the ego feels sad or angry because it is still does not have enough. The Other is always perceived as having more or less through the eyes of the ego. Power is seen as unequal energy with self or other, but is always based on something material. The ego is always angered, threatened and intimidated by the Other because the Other is always seen as having more or less. Unaware that the ego creates its own false reality of scarcity and lack by not sharing, the ego blames the Other for its problems and denigrates any optimism or hope for a better world.

The Higher Self, Full Self, Being Self or Soul consciousness are all one and the same. It is the essential awareness of the "I am" in relation to all other Selves. Everything is related within the spiritual realm. All individuals are understood to, one day, return to the Higher Self so that superiority and inferiority are only in relation to being asleep (the ego) and being awake (the Highest Self) with the full understanding that everyone will awaken to the Highest Truth of who they are. No one is excluded except by their own ignorance and free will. Only on the physical plane can things appear to be in a fixed superior or inferior state and this is a dream world that is here today and gone tomorrow.

The Full Self recalls the spiritual awareness of Self as Goodness and knows that there is no higher state of consciousness than Highest Goodness for Self and others. "Others" includes people, animals and nature since nature provides humankind with its sustenance. The Full Self knows Reality as the Source of Authentic Power and that it is this Source that forever flows and never decreases. Only the ego can delude a self into thinking that power lies in matter as opposed to Soul and Spirit. The Full Self knows authentic unlimited power, hence, does not perceive a world of lack, scarcity, separation or difference. All things are interrelated, interdependent and precious as part of the grand cycle of consciousness.

The Full Self is the Grand Self or the Grand "I am" and is understood to be a whole within a larger interconnected whole of Highest Goodness. If you have reached the Full Self consciousness and your neighbor has reached it as well, you have whole Goodness, your neighbor has whole Goodness, but there is also a whole Goodness greater than the two of you. Projecting into the world its fullness, wholeness and goodness, the Full Self seeks to see itSelf in other Full Selves.

The Full Self knows itSelf fully because it knows its Goodness. This is its Source and its power and from whence all things come. It only wills to awaken others to a Full Self because Goodness forever seeks itSelf. The Full Self, the Good Self, eternally seeks to return to itSelf, its essence which is the Being of Goodness. This is understood as an ontological state of Highest Goodness where nothing of real value is lacking. Whatever is full of Goodness lacks nothing!

Psychologically mature Kings and Queens manifest all over the earth when humankind returns to a conscious state of the Full Self, the Good Self. The Full Self only Wills toward Goodness for All. Truly this is the hallmark of any beloved Queen or King. Dictatorships or monarchies which only seek to fill their own coffers with material wealth and seek power and control in order to rule the masses with arrogant oppression are not manifesting the Full Self. Religions without this Goodness are not operating from the Divine, Full Self. Religion has unfortunately become little more than segregated masses of people with ego consciousnesses seeking to laud its superiority over other religions as a means to be superior in the eyes of that religion's so-called "loving God." Jesus' message was simple when he said "The Kingdom of heaven is within" and "Love your neighbor as yourself." You may interpret this as "Peace comes from the Full Self of Goodness" and "Love Highest Goodness for All." This is why Socrates said "the unexamined life is not worth living" and "Know ThySelf." The lost consciousness of Goodness for the All will be the extinction of the human species. The regaining of the Full Self, the Higher Self, the Self of Goodness is our hope of reconciliation with our deepest essence—our divine Self.

*The Kingdom of Heaven is within.*
—Jesus the Christ

# VIII. THE PSYCHE OR SOUL OF JESUS THE CHRIST

Perhaps no other historical figure, mythological or real, has been written about, spoken of, debated over and questioned more than Jesus the Christ. Many of his spoken words and loving spiritual intentions have been lost to humankind as religious, political and business leaders of Jesus' day were threatened by his simple, yet profound teachings. He attempted to reach humankind through parables which have been taken literally, misunderstood, lost or distorted. In fact, many believe that much of Jesus' message was insidiously and intentionally hidden from humankind by the powerful and wealthy patriarchy of the Catholic Church (the "Infallible Church Fathers" as they called themselves) whose patriarchal supremacy would crumble if the authentic messages were read and if humankind were to finally learn that the Bible which exists today is full of patriarchal bias, distortions and half truths. It is an unquestionable fact that the Church patriarchy did select which writings would comprise the final version of what we now refer to as the Christian Bible. Many other books and writings which articulate Jesus' words, it is believed, have purposefully been left out by the "Infallible Church Fathers" of the Catholic Church.

It is my unstinted conviction that many of Jesus' teachings have been misinterpreted and overlooked by millions of people who are both Christians and non-Christians. Esotericists believe that Jesus' messages had symbolic meanings which are far deeper than the literal interpretations which many find. As best as I can ascertain, it seems Jesus attempted to convey seven simple and fundamental messages to humankind, although the masses were not psychologically ready to hear and understand the message. They are:

1) God is not a man; God is a consciousness of love: this is why Christ said "I and my Father are One."

2) Since God is not a man and, instead God is a consciousness, God does not have a "chosen people," rather it is better said that only *those people who choose God* are special.

3) the Christ consciousness is the consciousness whose thoughts, feelings and actions are in alignment with "Love your neighbor as yourself" which is the God consciousness.

4) Jesus the Christ was a living embodiment of the Beingness of God consciousness.

5) Religious dogma and doctrines are meaningless if a person fails to imbue Christ consciousness.

6) In order to know God consciousness, it is unnecessary for a rabbi or priest to serve as mediator between yourself and God since "the kingdom of heaven is within."

7) And every human can attain God consciousness and may do so without a mediator such as a rabbi or priest.

By the powerful elite editing and deleting much of Christ's message, the masses would continue to be dependent upon the patriarchy which dominated the religious, economic and political systems, a controlling wealthy patriarchy which abused its power for continual self gain and would go to any lengths to ensure its sovereign position. Based on Jesus' intentions, were he alive today, he would be speaking out against the hypocrisy of the Catholic Church and the fundamentalists of the Islamic faith because neither of these religions embody the authentic, loving, accepting Nature of the Soul which yearns for the Good of the All. Instead, the Catholic Church has failed to take appropriate action against child molesting priests, continues to adopt the belief that females are unequal to males, and continues to relegate homosexuality as a moral deviance. Likewise, the fundamentalist Muslims continue to wage "holy wars" in the name of a Loving God and they continue to think of women as little more than housekeepers and child bearers. If Jesus were witness to our existing planetary consciousness and the resulting divisiveness, he would be grieved, as he was in his own day, to see the inhumanity against humanity which is so antipodal to a God Consciousness of love and compassion toward the All.

Jesus seemed to be calling attention to the incongruency between the punitive nature of not adhering to extremely strict doctrines and dogma versus the basic, simple tenets of a God consciousness which only seeks to love everyone. Jesus' message threatened the overemphasis on strict, unloving and contradictory man-made rituals and dogma which exclude part of humanity from God's kingdom and which keep the common person bound to a false perception that doctrines are more important than love, kindness and compassion to *all of humanity*. Based upon the story of Jesus, Jesus would have opposed *any* dogma or doctrines which caused a person to lose their heart by getting bogged down in the details and minutia of law. The Law is not the goal. Love is the goal. The Law is *the guidepost along the path*; Love toward All, a God consciousness, is *the destination*. If Christ were alive today, his message from the heart of compassion would be opposed to any concept, rule, law or admonition that was diametrically opposed to the act of imbuing a God consciousness of *equal* love toward your self and your neighbors. He seemed to be saying an almost painfully obvious admonition: "BE my consciousness" which was another way of saying to imbibe and reflect to others a consciousness of love, compassion, humility and kindness. If every person on the planet were to simply BE the Christ consciousness, wouldn't we all be in an optimally mentally healthy state? I'm of an equally potent conviction that Christ never wanted or intended all these splits between religions because division, separation, exclusion and disunity were antithetical to his entire thesis of love within the God/Christ consciousness.

An example of a strict religious doctrine during Christ's lifetime was that it was forbidden to do work on the Sabbath. Rescuing a dying cow from a ditch was considered work so the poor cow just had to die if it happened to be dying on a Sunday. If the cow happened to still be alive on Monday, the person could rescue it. Today, that kind of absurd rule is considered patently ridiculous by most people, yet 2,000 years ago people were in spiritual peril and were subject to admonishments from the male religious leaders if they did not obey. Jesus' simple message implied that these kinds of dogma and doctrine were not God's commandments, rather were man-made rules and, thus, they were antithetical to a message from a God of Pure Love. Much of the sanctity of simple, divine Goodness was lost as the religious, political and business leaders became intoxicated with the worldly power they held over the masses which is an inebriation that continues today after 10 millennia. Jesus preached his simple message of equality and love and told people that they can have this Christ consciousness too. As he embraced openly all levels of the socioeconomic strata, the masses of common people responded with a fervor which drew Jesus to a position of prominence that threatened to topple the religious, political and economic systems dominated exclusively by a greedy, ruthless and deceitful patriarchy.

Outlined below are the four functions or expressions of Psyche or Soul, their gender energies and their related archetypes as exemplified by Jesus the Christ:

**Attachment V**

| Expression | Gender | Archetype |
|---|---|---|
| To Know | Masculine | Teacher |
| To Create | Masculine | Carpenter |
| To Love | Feminine | Lover |
| To be Wise | Feminine | Counselor |

Jung wrote in *Aion: The Phenomenology of the Self* of Jesus the Christ as the archetype of the Higher Self, the *imago dei*, and when Jesus is understood from a psychological perspective, we can examine his mind set and his resultant behaviors as the perfect embodiment of the Soul Consciousness. Below is a chart of the authentic Nature of the Soul and how Jesus the Christ and his message can better be understood when considered through a psychological lens:

**Attachment VI**

| Expression | Function | Gender | Christ Archetype |
|---|---|---|---|
| To Know | Empower (Self) | Masculine | **Teacher** |
| To Create | Generate (Other) | Masculine | **Carpenter** |
| To Love | Share (We) | Feminine | **Lover** |
| To be Wise | Integrate (All) | Feminine | **Counselor** |

Perhaps we see why Jesus the Christ was revered as divine royalty because he was able to utilize and integrate all of these masculine and feminine expressions and the full expressions toward the Good for the All, hence, the phrase, "love your neighbor as yourself." When understood psychologically, humankind will never know psychological health and authentic well-being until the Good of the Whole of humanity and the ecological system is finally unilaterally agreed to be the goal of all of humankind. Until that time, rampant mental illness and psychological stress will be in existence and a collective healthy Psyche will forever remain out of reach.

Because the Soul seeks balance and harmony, Jesus' message has resonated within the Souls of millions of people because his message was simple: Be Love toward yourself *and* others. Do not love others more than yourself; neither love yourself more than others. Be Love toward yourself *and* others. Be at One with this. This is your essence because it is your divineness and your core Being, *no matter what religious affiliation.* It is that which makes you Whole and is your Divine Nature.

Soul consciousness, with its Full Self, is a higher, healthier level of psychological functioning because it overrides the split consciousness of the ego and knows itSelf as both object *and* subject combined into one unified subject—the Full Self. When Jesus the Christ stated "I and my Father are One", he had integrated the Godness within and was projecting this inner consciousness toward the outside world. This is what made him an authentic "King" because he infused the quaternity of femininity (love and wisdom) and masculinity (knowledge and creativity) and exuded this energy toward Self and others. Utilizing the Divine Will, energies were channeled toward Highest Good for the All. The Christ animated the love and wisdom of the feminine in *equal unison* with the knowledge and creativity of the masculine and used these energies toward Highest Good for the Whole. This is what made him Wonderful, a Prince of Peace, Counselor, a Mighty King. Everyone was viewed as having equal capacity to evolve to a higher level of consciousness by transcending the ego.

Queenship and Kingship can be considered as the reconciliation of the opposites or the perfect embodiment of the Soul Consciousness. Queen and King energies are two sides of the same coin. They carry the balance between knowledge, creativity, love and wisdom and use the Divine Will to manifest Goodness not only to Self, but also to others. This can be referred to as the benevolent King and Queen because self-interest is not valued more highly than the interest of others. There was nothing "split" within the Christ. He was nonviolent, totally accepting and simply loving of Goodness for the All. This was why the Christ incarnated so he could reflect this divine consciousness to the world and be an example of that bright light which lights up the world in shining Goodness. This is the light which draws people to itSelf because it is the Light of the Full, Whole Soul. This is the *Bodhiccita* or "Intelligent Heart" of the Bodhisattva of which the Mahayana Buddhists write. It is the Binah (feminine) and Chokmah (masculine) which results in the Kether (the One that is All and the One that is in All) of the Kabbalah of Jewish mysticism. The "Intelligent Heart" of Mahayana Buddhism, the Binah and Chokmah resulting in the Kether of the Kabbalah, Brahman of Advaita Vedanta, Jesus the Christ, the Buddha, and Lao Tzu all point to essentially the same transcendent, androgynous consciousness of the Soul. They are simply different paths leading to the same destination: a royal, divine consciousness of Goodness for the All. Which path we choose matters not; that the whole of humanity get there is of utmost importance. It is our salvation, our inheritance of psychological abundance and wellness and it literally determines whether we live in heaven or hell on earth.

You have queenship and kingship within your essence because Goodness of Being is *truly* queenly and kingly. This is another way of saying that a state of Being which imbues Goodness toward Self *and* others are truly a self-governing, benevolent queen and king where right order exists. Both Queen and King energies (mature feminine and mature masculine) occupy *equal* status on the throne. Jesus' divine nature caused him to treat every person with dignity and to relate to all human beings as having the *same and equal potential for Goodness*. Every person, although different and separate at the relative level, is considered as an equally important part of the Whole of Humanity. In the physical world, we relate things *to each other*; in the spiritual world, everything is an equally beautiful part *of the Whole of Humankind*. These are two entirely different ways of perceiving and, as a result, produce an entirely different consciousness. Perceiving everything in relation to each other, we have conflict and chaos; perceiving everything as a beautiful part of a harmonious Whole creates tolerance, acceptance and peace. The spiritual world of Goodness was primary for Jesus; the physical world was secondary to this royal conscious state.

Essentially, all religions, regardless of the doctrines, dogma or tenets within that religion, teach the simple message of love. This is why large amounts of people gravitate toward some type of religion or philosophy which has at its root this fundamental direction: to love. It is largely due to the man-made religious doctrines, dogma and tenets, however, that causes people to lose interest in religion. That teaching which causes a person to lose a connection to Goodness is not, by nature, a spiritual Truth. For instance, killing another person in the name of some deity or religion does not imbue Goodness no matter what deity is used as an excuse. Thus, "holy wars" is mutually exclusive. It is an oxymoron. We do not need to search in any book to know intuitively that war is unholy because war is conflict and division which is not a conscious state of unification and love. Any religion which teaches that God destroys is not teaching the truth of the Soul since it is impossible for Soul to destroy. Only a split mind--the ego--deceived by an illusory world of matter can destroy. Soul is incapable of violating its own spiritual essence which is to love and create.

It should be noted while Jesus the Christ is considered in the West to be the only person who embodied the Soul Consciousness, the Eastern cultures recognize the Buddha and Lao Tzu as imbuing this same consciousness. These historical figures were interested in Being Goodness, not in arguing semantics or in getting into arguments about whether a religious doctrine or tenet was right or wrong such as whether or not you were supposed to wash your hands or rescue a sick animal on the Sabbath. An individual expressing the Soul consciousness finds it largely unimportant whether you are Christian, Jewish, Buddhist, Taoist, Hindu or Muslim. Rather, the importance is whether you are imbuing Goodness toward Self *and* others. After all, the Soul is ubiquitous and may or may not identify itSelf with any religion. People who elect not to identify solely and exclusively with one religion may recognize there are many paths to living a spiritual life, thus, the Soul may or may not affiliate with the Christian, Jewish, Hindu or Islamic religion or any other religion. Soul is simply spiritual and Spiritual "Being" simply means expressing and sharing knowledge, creativity, love and wisdom within yourself and sharing that with "Other"; seeing humankind and all of existence as interrelated, thus, using the Will toward Goodness. The Soul resonates not toward religion *per se*, rather it resonates toward love---a community of love and loving-kindness. The community of people who embrace and welcome one another in the common spirit of love, compassion and kindness are unified.

All religions have spiritual people in them, however, not all spiritual people are religious. We seem to have reached a point in our evolution where we are now defining religion and spirituality as two different concepts, although no one seems to be able to provide an operational definition of both which large numbers of lay people, academicians, psychologists, researchers and theologians accept. The inability to arrive at a consensus creates a problem for research purposes since operational definitions are a core feature of research. Paul Tillich, in *My Search for Absolutes*, prefers to define religion as a state of "being grasped by an ultimate concern." If research into religion, religiosity and spirituality as it pertains to psychological ill health or well-being is to become common and less controversial, a generally accepted definition of "religion," "religious," "spirituality," "Soul" and "numinous" must be derived. These are my definitions of these words. "Soul" I have already defined earlier in the book. "Religion" can be defined as a set of rules, tenets, dogma, doctrines and conditions which provide a cognitive schema whereby an individual has *the potential* to embody Soulfulness and perceive, experience and express the numinous. "Religious" or "religiosity" can be defined as a strict cognitive and behavioral adherence to a religion which seeks, but does not result in, an authentic, actualized, ontological, phenomenological merging with the numinous and, therefore, does not manifest in a consciousness of acceptance, compassion and goodwill for all existence. "Spiritual" can be defined as the authentic, ontological, phenomenological merging of cognition, affect and will whereby the individual actualizes Soulfulness, is subsumed by the numinous and whose consciousness results in an overall joyful loving awareness and a general acceptance, compassion and goodwill for all existence. "Numinous" can be defined as Ultimate, Absolute Wholeness and Reality, also as God, Tao, Brahman, Nirvana, Kether, Allah, the All, the Good, the One, That from Which the All is derived. As we note, "religion" is objective whereas "religious" and "spirituality" are subjective experiences. Additionally, of importance is that a person who is religious is primarily characterized by religion, the external object, whereas a person who is spiritual has an authentic inner experience which results in acceptance, compassion and goodwill toward all existence, not just select portions of existence such as someone who is in the same religion, a person of the same color, nationality, education level or socioeconomic status. Religion is an external tool, so to speak, to arrive at its ultimate goal, inner spirituality. Throughout history, we have seen millions of "religious" people, but few "spiritual" people.

All religions have people who are operating within the ego consciousness of exclusion, specialness, separation, superiority and inferiority. This is why it is accurate to say that all people who are religious are not spiritual since we have millions of "religious" people who delude themselves into thinking that only their religion includes "the chosen" and, thus, these so-called "religious" people have a consciousness which fails in its goal of universal love because it excludes and divides rather than unifying humanity. It is in this sense that many religions fail in their intentions and their overarching goal of universal compassion and goodwill. Indeed, if religions are unable to overcome this ego consciousness of exclusivity, they will reach the end of their usefulness and, in the future, will be transformed or entirely replaced by a unifying consciousness of spiritual communities.

The Soul or Psyche does not identify with a single religion to the exclusion of others because exclusion and division is not a manifestation of the Soul or Christ or God Consciousness. The Soul seeks to unite; the ego seeks to disunite. Exclusion, and that which seeks to exclude, can only be from the ego. The Soul can only forever and ever yearn for, and resonate toward, its purpose: to know, to create, to love and to be wise. To the extent that any religion has a doctrine or tenet which opposes these expressions or functions or opposes Goodness for the All, then that religion is not in alignment with spiritual truth or the true nature of the Soul. Let me give you some examples.

In a society dominated by masculine energies, we have come to define loving-kindness as a weakness whereas we consider aggressiveness and competition as strengths. This is not in alignment with the true nature of the Soul. Love is strong because it is inclusive; aggressiveness and competition are weak because they are exclusive. As a human race, we must unlearn these masculine distortions and myths which have permeated our world since time immortal or we will not survive and it is certain we will not achieve optimal psychological well being. Until we learn to respond to each other, on a large scale, with loving-kindness and compassion, our natures will be little better than that of the animal kingdom. We must begin to embrace each other for their spiritual gifts and help one another grow in spiritual harmony. This is the Soul's call if we are to be a flourishing species.

What is divinity? What is the sacred? How do we define these terms which are so commonly used? It is that which is expressed through the Soul. It is the sum total of the fruits of the spirit. It is Goodness. It is the immeasurable, unlimited and eternal energy of Goodness for the All. This is the energy that is authentic power. The ineffable mystery of the Soul is that we can never see it, touch it or hear it. We can never pin it down to a certain spot or scientifically measure it. We cannot create it or destroy it because it has always been and always will be. But we can *experience* it and *know* it.

And when we experience it, we know, deep within our Souls, that we have experienced the Goodness of the sacred and the divine fruits which only Soul and spirit can know.

Jesus was incarnated so as to assume the role of the well-balanced Soul and demonstrate its reality to the world. These energies were balanced within himself so we call that being balanced *intra*psychically. He also obeyed all spiritual laws, so he was balanced *inter*psychically with the world around him and with spiritual Beings—angels, archangels, cherubim and seraphim— who assist humankind many times unbeknownst to us. This meant he was able to understand and honor the interrelatedness of all that exists in the world from the nature kingdom to the animal kingdom to the human kingdom and up through the spiritual kingdom. He honored and cherished all of existence and considered it good, thereby projecting outwardly his inward belief in Goodness. By expressing these spiritual fruits of Goodness—love, joy, peace, kindness, compassion, patience, truth, justice, honor, knowledge and wisdom—Jesus drew thousands to him. Who is not drawn to the person who is imbuing total love and acceptance? Only the ego consciousness could reject this.

The devotion of the Soul is to extend Goodness toward self and others. Jesus exhibited what has come to be known by some as the Christ consciousness or the Group consciousness. This consciousness is what made him the archetypal benevolent, humble King and why he was revered. When the Soul is expressing fully and naturally, a human can be thought of as a benevolent, humble king or queen!

Below is the Holy Trinity which Jesus the Christ manifested psychologically:

**Attachment VII**

**The Good**

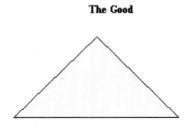

**Love/Wisdom**                    **Knowledge/Creativity**

This consciousness was the "image of God," *imago dei*, incarnate. Divine Goodness is Love and Goodness for Self *and* others: *Goodness for the whole*. With Jesus, divinity and humanity greeted each other. This is what is meant when we say that Jesus was both divine and human and his entire message was intended to inform us that we, too, can rise to this level of conscious Being. Providing humankind with the blueprint of the human that is in harmony with the Soul and the spiritual realm, Jesus' legacy of Goodness demonstrated to the world the archetypal embodiment of knowledge, creativity, love and wisdom and the Divine Will toward Goodness. Jesus was living proof that humanity can reflect the Soul consciousness from the Godness within and still be human. The outcome would be right human relations (literally, "righteousness") and, ultimately, peace. The Buddha reflected this consciousness, too, as he taught the Middle Path which is the essential path that does not excessively fall on either side of caring for Self or caring for Other, nor is it excessively masculine or excessively feminine. The consciousness they reflected is the hope, the salvation, of humanity and the psychological wholeness and fullness of Being.

Any person, regardless of their religious affiliation, can exhibit this consciousness in the world. There is no requirement to be affiliated with the Christian religion and any person who is Jewish, Hindu, Buddhist or any other religion can rise above the ego consciousness to the Soul consciousness. Indeed, it is this Soul or Group or Christ or Buddha consciousness which is the next step in the evolution of human consciousness. What we call it or designate it is of little concern; that we imbue it is of critical importance. Getting caught up in semantics and words will only cause us greater delay and more conflict. The evolution of humankind, nay, its survival, depends upon this unfolding consciousness.

Jesus' message of love excluded no one since exclusion is not of the Soul or Christ or Group consciousness. Living in a world of ego consciousness which seeks to separate, divide, exclude, control and oppress, Jesus instead exhibited the Soul consciousness and invited, welcomed and embraced every person regardless of gender, race, religion or social, economic or political status.

When men are able to balance their functions of thinking and creating with the more feminine expressions of love and wisdom, the Soul will be in harmony and it is this harmonic balance which makes women and men the queens and kings of Goodness. As women are accepted and embraced by a more mature male society, more women will balance their functions of loving and being wise with their more masculine expressions of thinking and creating. It is with the development of a more androgynous human race, one where all four expressions of the Soul are balanced and harmonious, that we can hope for the salvation of humankind and the amelioration of human suffering.

*By their own theories of human nature, psychologists have the power of elevating or degrading that same nature. Debasing assumptions debase human beings; generous assumptions exalt them.*
—Gordon Allport

*Human existence is not authentic unless it is lived in terms of self-transcendence.*
—Victor Frankl

*There is no science of the soul without a metaphysical basis to it and without spiritual remedies at its disposal.*
—Ken Wilber

# IX. THE VERTICAL AND HORIZONTAL AXIS OF THE SOUL

In Freud's later years, he was queried by a student about whether marital partners should be considered equal, to which Freud replied, *"that is a practical impossibility. There must be inequality and the superiority of man is the lesser of two evils."* In *Civilization and Its Discontents*, Freud speaks of how man has "become dependent in a most dangerous way on…his chosen love-object" or he restates, as his "sex object," the latter he specifically declares as "woman." Freud's arrogance also manifested in his flagrant disregard for spiritual matters and, indeed, in *The Future of an Illusion*, he is referred to in the Preface as a "convinced, consistent, aggressive atheist."

I am in agreement with feminists who argue that Freud, albeit an intellectual genius, promulgated a masculine biased theoretical framework within psychology from which, even today, the feminine continues to attempt to extricate herself. Jung, who would all his life challenge the Freudian concepts of sex and aggression as the major instincts and drives of humanity, wrote prolifically on the reconciliation of the opposites—the aspects of the hidden feminine underlying males and the hidden masculine underlying females, the *anima* and the *animus*. Today, Jungian analysts such as Robert Moore, author of *King, Warrior, Magician, Lover: Rediscovering the Archetypes of the Mature Masculine,* refer to the "mature masculine" and the "immature masculine," the latter which could be considered as parallel to the Freudian concept of the masculine ego consciousness. While agreeing with Moore's overarching concept of a quadrated psyche and of the King and Queen energies of the psyche, he has, in my opinion, neglected to interpret the warrior energy as an unhealthy and immature expression of the masculine ego. Moore has also omitted the mature teacher energy who teaches mature selfhood as the beginning step toward that which is beyond selfhood, beyond the "I," to the full maturation and wholeness of the fully embodied Soul. Additionally, Moore's theoretical model reflects King and Queen energies as equivalent to each of the other three expressions of lover, warrior and magician, so Moore's model does not articulate King energy as an apogean or pinnacle energy. In line with all revered religious and philosophical figures throughout history such as the Buddha, Jesus the Christ, Mahatma Gandhi, kingship is a cumulative, pinnacle energy. King and Queen energies are not a *part* of the Soul, rather are a *culmination of* the perfectly balanced *four* energic expressions of the quadrated Psyche or Soul. It is only the combination of the teacher who knows selfhood, the creator of building beauty through form in the world, the loving energy of beloved partnering and finally the ultimate maturation of wisdom and discernment of Beyond Self to the All which culminates into the beneficent, generative, loving, truly wise King and Queen. This is Jesus the Christ and the mature consciousness he carried within and projected outwardly and it is the crucial message which he came to share as being the authentic salvation of humankind. It is authentic because it is the whole, full, healthy, peaceful Soul or Psyche. There was nothing war-like about the Christ's Being or his message and in fact his entire ethos was one of love, so warrior energy is not a mature expression of the Soul. Instead of saying "spiritual warrior" which is still implying the lower ego consciousness, it is best to say "spiritually transformative." War never has been, nor never will be, mature although the immature masculine would attempt to convince us of it. Mahatma Gandhi, the Buddha and Mother Teresa were vehemently opposed to war and everything in their messages conveys that. Only the gentle, yet resolute energies of creative transformation are mature.

Before expounding on the feminine and masculine concepts, it is imperative to ask: "Where is the mental health field today?" Paul McHugh, M.D., Professor of Psychiatry at Johns Hopkins University School of Medicine, had this to say of the implicit near death of psychoanalysis in the November 2002 issue of the *Harvard Mental Health Letter*:

> Psychiatry is in crisis…surrounded by vigorous and growing fields of knowledge but does not know how to make use of them or contribute to them. **Now that psychoanalysis no longer provides an overall guide for reasoning about mental disorders,** psychiatry has been proceeding ad hoc.

Ken Wilber predicts the death of psychology when he stated in a Shambhala interview in 2000 which is posted on www.wilber.shambhala.com:

> '…the four forces of psychology are slowly dying…psychology as we have known it…has been dead for almost a decade…and will never again, in any of its four major forms, be a dominant influence in culture or academia…These four schools…are in ideological warfare…in a state of self-cannibalization…ignored by the larger world…a negative cultural pressure is moving them to extinction, so these major forces are one jot away from dinosaur status…Western history is going through a period of…rampant scientific materialism (the orange meme)…nothing but surfaces of the extreme postmodernists (the green meme)….this puts an intense selection pressure against any sort of psychology that emphasizes solely or mostly the interiors (psychoanalytic, humanistic/existential and transpersonal)…this is compounded by numerous social factors such as the medical/insurance and 'managed care' industry supporting only brief psychotherapy and pharmacological interventions…the only acceptable approaches to psychology are increasingly the Right-Hand approaches including behavioral modification, cognitive

*therapy...an increasing, almost epidemic, reliance on the use of medication....which focus almost exclusively on Right Hand interventions.....the only interior psychologies that will survive are those that adapt to an AQAL framework....which paints a much broader picture of consciousness and the Kosmos...from matter to body, to mind to spirit...such a psychology is not really a psychology as we have known it.'"*

Wilber states that within the next decade, seven to ten percent of humanity will move from what he refers to as the First Tier level of consciousness (Centauric Early vision logic) to the Second Tier (Centauric Middle and Late Vision logic) which will result in "a major, major cultural shift." This corresponds to Beck and Cowan's Spiral Dynamics as a movement from the Green/Relativistic meme (Wilber's top of the First Tier) to the Yellow/Integrative and Turquoise/Holistic memes, respectively. Additionally, this corresponds to Dr. Clare Graves' movement from the Materialistic and Personalistic Subsistent levels (Wilber's top of the First Tier) to the First Being and Second Being levels of consciousness which correspond to Wilber's Second Tier.

It is my hypothesis that the defining characteristic of those seven to ten percent of humanity is their ability to shift into an androgynous consciousness which I have articulated and defined as "Soul Consciousness." This is what Advaitans refer to as "fullness of Being," "joyous loving awareness," *saccindananda* or *saguna* Brahman and what Mahayana Buddhists refer to as the *Bodhiccita,* or "Intelligent Heart," of the Bodhisattva. Taoists would simply refer to it as the balance of the yin (feminine) and the yang (masculine) energies. The feminine and masculine energies are ubiquitous in the plant, animal and human kingdoms just as they are at the Ultimate level of Reality—the Spiritual level—which has been studied by physicists such as Einstein, Planck, Bohr, Heisenberg, Schrodinger and de Broglie when studying light phenomena, i.e., the particles and waves of light.

Humanistic-existentialists such as May, Maslow and Rogers would refer to Soul as "Being," as taken from ancient Greek philosophy and Eastern philosophy, while transpersonalists would refer to it as the "transcendence of the ego consciousness" which is also borrowed from Eastern philosophy. Since psychology split from philosophy roughly 125 years ago, it should come as no wonder that, once again, psychology comes full circle back to his sister, *sophia,* or *philo-sophia,* which derives from the Greek meaning, "the love of wisdom." Once again Pythagoras' famous statement rings true: nothing is really new or original in the strict sense of the term, rather only reinterpretations, reconceptions and new ways of expressing what always is and ever will be throughout the Eternal Now of which the Taoists speak.

If psychology does not lead, or take serious participation, in this major shift of human consciousness which Wilber predicts, I opine that the field of psychology, like psychoanalysis, will be largely irrelevant by the 22nd century (at least as we know it today). Hypnotherapy and Rogerian therapy will exist for severe disorders such as Dissociative Disorder and for trauma resulting from serious sexual, physical and emotional abuse. Cognitive Behavioral therapy will likely exist (at least for some time) for disorders of a neurological basis such as biological based depression and autism and mental retardation. Psychologists will continue to conduct psychometric testing. However, the remaining client population in need of some type of psychotherapeutic intervention will be taken over by practitioners who own clinics which promote natural, self-healing, thousand year old modalities such as meditation, music therapy, color or light therapy, Tai Chi, Qigong, Reiki, acupuncture, acupressure and other more holistic techniques. With no research to provide an informed estimate on how many clients do not have serious disorders, I will take an educated guess and say that anywhere between 40% and 60% of the current population receiving services from psychiatrists and psychologists could likely resolve their issues through self-healing, natural interventions such as proper diet, exercise, meditation, creative visualization, affirmations, music therapy, color therapy, etc. If this percentage is accurate, the provider of services for this particular client population will change from the psychiatrist or psychologist to a provider who offers natural, self-healing modalities. The degree to which the general population appears to be gravitating toward natural, self-healing modalities is surprising and startling and it is anticipated to burgeon. It is as though the collective conscious seems to be saying "Self heals Self" or "Seek thine own counsel from my Higher Self." Having said this, it is my contention that the next major epoch of psychology is an exegesis of the Soul and Soul Consciousness; its manifestations, nurturants and antithetics; and its next-level psychotherapeutic treatment modalities. The defining moment for psychology in the 21st century appears to be whether or not psychology is able to:

—accept that human consciousness evolves along a spectrum, move beyond the ego consciousness to embrace a larger span of humanity which honors spirituality as a core, essential and undeniable part of "psyche" or

Soul and psychological health and well-being;

—articulate and agree upon an operational definition of the Soul and Soul Consciousness;

—develop and execute self-in-relation-to-Higher Self treatment modalities;

—conduct and publish research regarding the efficacy of advanced treatment modalities; and

—garner a widespread acceptance and respect by lay people.

To the extent that psychology is able to achieve these objectives, psychology will remain a viable field and enterprise, although, as Wilber states, it will not be "a psychology as we have known it," rather it will have been transformed and will, *in itself,* have transcended. Simply put, unless psychologists themselves move beyond the ego consciousness toward a higher level of consciousness on Wilber's spectrum of consciousness, the field will fall behind the masses who will, indeed, be evolving along that spectrum of consciousness.

Soul seems to be a word that keeps manifesting in books being published and in commercials selling cars, clothing, shoes, toiletries, etc. One could say that Soul is an idea whose time as come. One way to understand this is to explain it as humankind's unconscious yearning to know and to love Soul. For thousands of years, mostly males have written extensively about the Soul from Plato to Plotinus and Porphyry to theologians such as St. Thomas Aquinas and St. Augustine to more modern philosophers such as Kierkegaard, Heidegger, Hegel to psychologists such as Jung, Fromm, Rank, Frankl, Hillman and Wilber. However, in spite of thousands of years of writing volumes on the Soul, no one has been able to articulate a concise, clear, operational definition of the Soul which is largely accepted by both lay people and by multiple disciplines. Heidegger stated that, if anyone ever did arrive at a definition of the Soul, it would be very general. It is with Heidegger's comment that this author largely agrees and it is with this agreement that the general definition of the Soul is now found. Perhaps, finally, humankind can bridge the gap between the physical world of ego and the spiritual world of the Great Soul. This theoretical model of the Soul and Soul Consciousness carries with it an implicit and explicit radical revisioning of psychology *as we have known it.* Furthermore, implications for social, economic, political, religious and scientific endeavors must be seen through an ever widened lens.

When defining Soul, we operate under two basic assumptions: 1) the

Soul exists, which is based upon Einstein's first law of thermodynamics (energy eternally changes from nonmatter to matter and back to nonmatter, and 2) the Soul transmigrates, which is implicitly understood as a Reality within most Eastern philosophies and within ancient Greek philosophy. And so we define Soul as the ubiquitous, eternal, energic expression of the Divine *Nous* which incarnates and reincarnates into a physical body to express itSelf in and through matter.

The Soul, as stated earlier, when fully expressed is androgynous and always uses the Will toward Goodness for *both Self and Other*, therefore, it is understood that Goodwill toward humankind is the *sin qua non* expression of the fully embodied, soulful human. You may say that the Soul is quadrated, however, not in the sense that Soul has physical boundaries since the Soul is invisible and indivisible energy. Einstein may have used the term "frozen light" from the perspective of his second law of thermodynamics. The Soul has two axes: a horizontal axis of masculine and feminine and a vertical axis of Self and Other. The fully embodied Soul or Higher Self may be pictured as a star as symbolized by the Judeo-Christian religions:

**Attachment VIII**

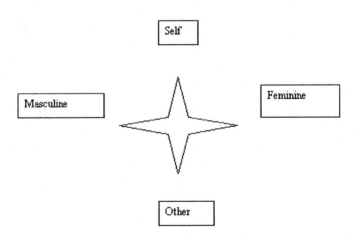

When the masculine and feminine energies integrate on the horizontal axis and when the Self/Other dichotomy is integrated on the vertical axis, the Soul has fully embodied into a Whole Soul or into a Full Being or what Advaitans refer to as *Saguna* Brahman where there is a consciousness of "joyous loving awareness." The Star of David is an esoteric symbol of sacred geometry which symbolizes the harmonious psychological union of these two axes.

Soul or Being is the level of consciousness which the Eastern philosophers, sages and mystics have referred to for thousands of years as the "enlightened". This is not the highest level of consciousness, but is the authentic level of Being written about by philosophers for millennia. At the highest level of consciousness, Self is understood to be not only enlightened, but also "illuminated" and there is no more need to learn anything else since *Ultimate* Truth and Knowledge have been achieved. Advaitans refer to this highest level of consciousness as *Nirguna* Brahman or non-duality where all distinctions are obliterated.

Since the four energic expressions of the fully embodied Soul are ubiquitous, it is understood that these energies can and do manifest, to some degree or other, within the entire human species regardless of how bifurcated they exist between genders within our current levels of mass human consciousness. In *The Enneads*, Plotinus stated that "all things have some share of Soul", therefore, even the mineral, plant and animal kingdoms have some essence of Soul as seen within the Soul Consciousness model.

As was stated in an earlier chapter, the Soul seeks to know, to create, to love and to be wise. The Soul seeks to know Truth (the "I" or Self), it seeks to create Beauty (the "It" or Other), it seeks to love Goodness (the "We" through which, Wilber states, the "I" can only be authentically understood), and it seeks to be Wise about the Will (the "All" or collective consciousness). When the Soul expresses these fully, it can be understood as a "whole psyche" or "full psyche" or "Full Being" to use an Advaitan concept. Epistemology implies ontology and ontology implies epistemology and this is why Socrates stated that "to know the Good is to do the Good." Plotinus also stated in *The Enneads* that the Soul "eternally circles around the Good or the One", so we say that the fully embodied Soul yearns for the Good or the One. Plotinus stated that "the Good is that on which everything depends and to which all beings aspire; they have it as their principle and need it." Understood this way, the Soul seeks itSelf and cannot exist separate from a consciousness of Goodwill. Indeed, it *is* a psychologically healthy consciousness of "Goodwill toward Self and All" or love of self *and* other to borrow from a theological perspective.

Knowledge and creativity are masculine energies whereas love and wisdom are feminine energies. To interpret these invisible energies as synonymous with the physical, biological genders of male and female is a gross error for, as the ancient Greek philosophers taught us, the world of particulars is a different and lower world of relativity from the Ultimate and Absolute level of Reality, the world of Universals where no difference or separation exists and only Oneness or only One consciousness exists. It seems that Einstein implicitly confirmed this when he gave us the theory of relativity and he told us that, at the speed of light, time does not exist. Biological gender falls within a physical world of separation and difference, therefore, it can only be understood to be a relative level of existence. Conversely, masculine and feminine *energies* are unseen, indivisible, immutable and eternal, therefore, we speak of them within the language of Absolute and Ultimate Reality as spoken so beautifully and eloquently within Eastern philosophies of Buddhism, Taoism and Advaita Vedanta. Westerners have come to understand them simply as the yin and the yang energies, but these are real energies studied in physics when studying light and also in the biological fields when studying cellular structure. At the most fundamental levels, we have what we may term as pure feminine and pure masculine energies which are paradoxically only understood to be two halves which comprise a beautiful, indivisible, harmonic whole. At the human level of existence, the ego consciousness has bifurcated these two energies (even though in Reality these can never be split), devalued the feminine as subordinate and distorted these two energies so that we no longer can comprehend the purity of the "mature" or "wholeness" of the harmonious balance of these two energies.

As June Singer states in *Androgyny: Toward a New Theory of Sexuality*, "the psychic qualities that we have come to conceive of as 'masculine' and 'feminine' are grounded in mythologems that follow patterns laid down by nature." From a Taoist perspective, the Soul could be understood to eternally move away from itSelf (Wilber's concept of the *evolution* of human consciousness) and returning back to itSelf (Wilber's concept of the *involution* of human consciousness). Said another way, this is the yang which moves outward and the yin which forever pulls inward. From a biological perspective, you could say that the outward expression of cellular growth is masculine whereas the integrative/holistic expression of the cell in maintaining its integral wholeness is the feminine expression. From a physicist's perspective, you could say that the masculine energy is that of the particles of light which are the individualistic, competitive tension from the zero point of the nucleus whereas the feminine energy is the wave of light which manifests as process and interrelatedness within the phenomena of light. These are eternal, ubiquitous and immutable energic expressions of all that exists within both the material and spiritual realms.

The process of the evolution from "I" to "It" to "We" to "All" is natural, *mature* human development because it is development away from the "I" toward the "All," beyond the narrow Self toward the full Soul. These developmental stages should be understood as moving in a paradoxical manner which means they move in a linear fashion, yet spirally and concentrically at the same time. In the first few months of birth, the infant perceives herself to be merged with the Other and little or no distinction can be discerned as she intuits the Primal Oneness, the "All," she had within the womb and prior to incarnation which has now, upon physical birth, been disturbed. This refers to Margaret Mahler's stage of "symbiosis" and Daniel Stern's stage of "the emergent self." Moving toward the toddler stage and early childhood, the cognitively and emotionally immature individual begins to develop some semblance of an independent "I" as seen during the "terrible two" stage. Vacillating between needing the primary caretaker and, paradoxically, vying for complete independence, the child begins to perceive an outer world of objects or of "It" and so a world of "I-It" is formed as much of the external world is objectified. The social norms of an ego-driven world which places much emphasis upon materialism further supports and upholds the "I-It" perception. This is the rudimentary beginnings of Buber's psychologically immature I-It relationship. In normal development, once the core "I" begins solidifying and forming, there can be a healthy development toward understanding an even more psychologically mature I-We relationship (the I-We relationship of Wilber or the I-Thou relationship of Buber). Some conscious awakening to this usually begins forming in adolescence and becomes increasingly fuller through the 20s and, in our current mass consciousness, is not commonly fully developed, if at all, before the 30s. It is important to note that this I-We consciousness is not fully developed on a large scale when considering the entire global consciousness, rather only pockets of this consciousness exist and, even then, is not fully mature. Finally, if the individual continues to develop along normal lines and there have been little or no environmental insults, traumas or negative cultural, religious and/ or ethnic beliefs promulgated by the community group consciousness (which does not exist on the planet today), she may move to the next level of the widest, expansive consciousness of the "All" which encompasses, yet transcends the individual "I." There can be no individual Self *alone* or as has been stated, "No man is an island." Each individual is a part of the "All" in optimal psychological states of mind which has been experienced by humans such as Jesus, the Buddha, Lao Tzu and more recent 20th century enlightened humans, Gandhi, Mother Teresa, Sri Ramana Maharshi and Sri H.W. L. Poonja. This psychological consciousness, once assumed, needs no empirically objective evidence, rather stands firm in her conviction of noetic truth that there can be no individual Self which is completely autonomous and superior, rather the Self—in and of its Ultimate Ontology—is a part of the "All," the Eternal Now, of existence which has been understood, embodied and written about for thousands of years by Eastern philosophers, ancient Greek philosophers and Christian and Jewish mystics.

**Attachment IX**

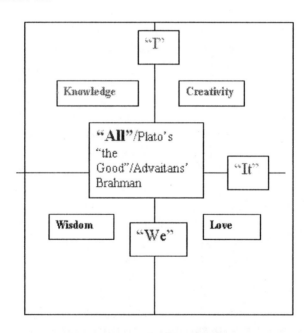

The Ground of Being (The Soul): The Development of the Soul/Psyche (from split ego to Whole Soul) toward the Highest Good (All or One or Brahman, the Ultimate Wholeness)

It should be emphasized that the Soul is depicted symbolically through sacred geometry and various other symbols throughout history since the Soul is not a person. The Soul is not anthropomorphic; it is an energic expression. Having said this, Brahman or God is neither a biological male nor a biological female, yet has inherent "pure" feminine and "pure" masculine expressions when understood morphologically and fundamentally.

It should become evident when viewing this model that, without *both* the masculine and the feminine energy, a psychological development toward Soul Consciousness, or wholeness and Fullness of Being, will not manifest. One could say that, as we examine the entire canvas of the collective consciousness of humankind, humanity, on a large scale, has today only reached childhood or, at best, adolescence with the male gender being primarily stalled within the narcissistic "I-It" trajectory and the female gender being primarily stalled within the "We-All" mode. Perhaps the most salient and important point to be made in the entire exegesis of the Soul Consciousness model is that *there is no evolutionary advancement of consciousness, and, thus, ultimate psychological maturation toward Soulfulness or Full Being or Higher Self, unless the feminine energies are introjected, imbued and openly projected by males and the collective consciousness of humanity.* Additionally, there is literally no Full Being or Soul Consciousness unless the female gender initially develops her essential, healthy, Core "I". However, until the omnipotent Narcissist matures psychologically creating a collective consciousness, a social and cultural consciousness, of the equality of the masculine and feminine energies, it is unknown whether the unworthy Borderline pathology can finally mature either. Time will reveal that. However, we can be safe in our prediction that the male will fail in psychological maturation toward wholeness and full maturation of Soul unless he is able to merge *both* masculine and feminine energies within himself. Further, since the male gender has assumed world leadership since time began, he is, quite logically, most culpable for pervasive psychological malaise. When viewed wholistically, should the masculine and the feminine merge their Soul expressions and should this occur on a global scale, it could be said that the psychological development of the collective consciousness would finally reach adulthood.

A key aspect of understanding the Soul is the conceptual understanding of Heraclitean logic and how it is the only logic that can be utilized when studying and comprehending the Soul. Within the Soul Consciousness model, the Soul can only be understood within Heraclitean logic, therefore,

Aristotelian logic no longer is applicable. Just as Einstein established the paradox that light is *both* wave and particle, so, too, the Soul can only be understood as a paradox. Below is an exegesis of masculine and feminine energies, both their mature and immature expressions:

Attachment X

| Masculine Energy (neutral) | Feminine Energy (neutral) |
| --- | --- |
| Active energy | Passive energy |
| Pushes outward (outer/exterior/objective) | Pulls inward (inner/interior/subjective) |
| Goal oriented (toward "It") | Process oriented (inner and intersubjective) |
| Individualistic, competitive energy ("I") | Collaborative, interpersonal ("We") |
| Seeks to be individual One against the Many (wants to be "I") | Seeks to be a Unified One amongst the Many (wants to be a collective "All") |
| Natural expressions are freedom and Autonomy ("I") | Natural expressions are intimacy and interdependency ("We") |

| Immature Masculine (Shadow) | Immature Feminine (Shadow) |
| --- | --- |
| Overly aggressive and pushy | Indecisive and needy |
| Goal oriented ("It") at the expense of the process (how) | Unable to establish or attain goals (no "It") |
| Individual, competitive ("I") which overpowers, ignores the Collective Whole ("All") | Excessive dependence on "Other" for focus and direction |
| Excessive focus on self and self interests | Lack of self-focus or self-interest (no "I") |
| Excessive focus on freedom and autonomy and away from intimacy | Excessive need for intimacy |
| Superior position of the "I" | Inferior position of no "I" and all "We" |
| Archetype: Narcissist/Hitler—control, power and perfection of the Superior "I" | Archetype: Borderline/Queen in Snow White—no core "I" or Self |

| The Delusion of the Immature Masculine | The Delusion of the Immature Feminine |
|---|---|
| Cognition: Thinks that by condemning, deceiving, devaluing and oppressing "Other", he can maintain superiority (his "I" is superior to "Other") | Cognition: Thinks that by consuming "Other" and concentrating on "We", she can love herself and find her core self (her "I" is inferior to "We") |
| Affect: Deifies self and devalues, condemns, deceives or destroys "Other" | Affect: Self-loathing and vacillates between deification and hate of "Other" |
| Behavior: Controls, devalues, deceives, condemns, oppresses "Other" to maintain superiority | Behavior: Ignores self because there is no core "I" so she consumes "Other" in an attempt to find her core "I" (as Wilber states, there can be no discovery of "We" unless there is a core "I") |
| Result: Excessive rational thinking (intellect and logic) and no authentic feeling (love and compassion) for "Other" | Results: Excessive irrational feelings (hates herself and is jealous of "Other") and no rational thinking (reason and logic) |
| Clinical Diagnosis: Narcissistic Personality Disorder | Clinical Diagnosis: Borderline Personality Disorder |
| Archetype: Hitler, the Dictator, intellectual who loves himself and has no feeling or compassion for "Other" | Archetype: Queen in Snow White, the Evil Queen who hates herself and is jealous of "Other" |

The immature masculine has been overtly denigrating the immature feminine for thousands of years, whereas the immature feminine has been silently and covertly demeaning the immature masculine for millennia. The immature masculine, being in the omnipotent role, has been afforded the opportunity to openly denigrate the feminine whereas the immature feminine, at risk for punishment or censure due to the power differential between her and the dominant group, has been forced to secretly voice her disgruntlements. Even her disgruntlements were used by abusive patriarchy as an excuse to accuse the feminine of irrational emotionalism. As understood from the Soul Consciousness model, it suddenly becomes understandable, if not plausible why each has belittled the other. As for the former, one may call it the masculine derision of the "irrational, hysterical, needy, neurotic woman" from a Freudian viewpoint and, quite suddenly, we see the genius of Freud for leaving posterity the psychological roadmap of the immature ego masculine and the immature egoless feminine. Unconsciously, it has been the immature masculine (abusive patriarchy) which has literally been the *cause of* the manifestation of the immature feminine and the immature masculine since the immature masculine has been primarily responsible for ensuring that little boys' process of psychological growth is stunted. By only allowing little boys to develop two primary energies of sex and aggression and by disallowing overt feelings such as love, kindness, shame, guilt, fear and sadness, the immature masculine has created, and continues to perpetuate, the varying degrees of narcissistic, arrogant and abusive patriarchy that has hauntingly characterized "real manhood" for centuries. Sadly, but mostly due to either ignorance or the fear of further abuse, oppression or disenfranchisement (or both), the immature feminine has, until the 20th century, by and large, assisted in the perpetuation of split consciousness which has had tragic global social, ethical, political, financial and psychological consequences.

We must all be informed as to how abusive patriarchy is primarily responsible for the psychological demise of both males and females. For as science teaches us, only by knowing the cause of problems are we able to arrive at effective resolutions. How does abusive patriarchy cause psychological demise? By teaching and perpetuating a myth of male dominance and superiority, that predominately Western myth that intellect, reason and logic are far superior to love, wisdom, intuition, collaboration and interrelatedness. By promulgating the myth that feminine energy is sinful, tempting and dangerous; by denying little boys the right and privilege to develop into whole human beings; and by denying males the fullness, wholeness and health of an integral consciousness which would encompass relating to, and connecting with, "Other" not as an "I-It" relationship, but as Buber would eloquently define the "I-Thou" relationship. In a 1995 journal article from *Psychoanalysis/Psychotherapy/Psychology of Men*, William Pollack, Assistant Clinical Professor in the Department of Psychiatry at Harvard Medical School and author of *Real Boys: Rescuing our Sons from the Myths of Boyhood*, provides a cogent explanation of what he terms "normative developmental trauma," the experience of males who live in a world where it is a socially accepted "norm" or expectation that "boys must dis-identify from their mothers in order to achieve adequate masculine engendered identity" and a healthy sense of self. Pollack gives a psychological description of the male who successfully dis-identifies from the feminine:

"In all likelihood, he would be obsessionally concerned about maintaining a rigidly independent self and have a matrix of intrapsychic defenses something like the following: unconscious anger or rage toward women, defensive condescension of anyone in a caretaking role, overvaluation of independence (defensive autonomy), devaluation of the need for connectedness or interdependence, stoic denial of sadness or pain with an inability to grieve loss or to mourn, a walling off of a vulnerable but hidden core self and the need to externalize inner conflict and take refuge in impulsive action in order to avoid anxiety. Interestingly enough, this is remarkably similar to the description of a prototypic 'narcissistic' character structure."

This pathology and unhealthy milieu has haunted humanity and resulted in millions of women who have been murdered, raped, physically, sexually and emotionally abused, neglected and, in general, dismissed, ignored and summarily devalued. This same narcissism has also been the primary cause of racial prejudice and discrimination. One is reminded of Martin Luther King's book, *Why We Can't Wait*, where he tells of how long the black race had waited for parity and, upon the lack of evidence of economic, legal, social and political parity being *given to them*, saw as the only solution to begin a revolution to *take it*. Is that not what happened with the Women's suffrage movement led by women such as Elizabeth Cady Stanton and Susan B. Anthony at the turn of the century? Until the latter part of the 19th century, abusive patriarchy and its endemic narcissism sat in silence, refused to honorably acknowledge fathership of the human tragedy it birthed thousands of years ago and quelled virtually all serious efforts at equality. In some ways, this is shocking, however, in other ways it is but symptomatic of the narcissistic character disorder. Any psychologist knows that the hallmark of a narcissist is the excessive need for control, power, omnipotence and perfection and, in fact, a sense of arrogant entitlement to this power differential over others. The narcissist can rarely admit imperfection within self since he is obsessed with appearing to be "in control," he demands that he retain ultimate power, and his ego usually is so pronounced that he has great difficulty conceding that he has erred. In fact, so great is the unhealthy need to be perceived as in control, powerful and perfect, that the narcissist has a common psychological defense pattern of shifting the blame for any imperfections onto another person. This is why in Corporate America and politics we have an endemic and pervasive pattern of those who actually make poor decisions or execute unsound business or political strategy assume little or no blame while some lower party in the chain of command serves as the scapegoat. It is the pathological defense that wife batterers use when they commonly say, "Well, she made me beat her." The wife batterer beats his wife and says, "But she made me beat her because she nags me," as though that faulty and arrogant logic somehow justifies assaulting and physically beating her. These are many times narcissists who like to believe themselves to be omnipotent and special when, in actuality, they are quite impotent and ineffectual. The senior executive of the multi-million dollar company who has been indicted on charges of fraud will state an equally narcissistic and flawed logic when he says: "But every other CEO buys $6,000 shower curtains," which is an implicit way of saying that white collar crime is justified as long as it is tacitly understood by senior corporate executives that at least 51% or more of these same senior executives are fleecing investors, employees and consumers out of millions of hard-earned dollars. This egregious, pathological consciousness can only come from a person who falls somewhere on the Narcissist continuum. The fact that only 1% of CEOs in America are females and that males still remain overwhelmingly in political leadership positions in spite of intelligent, highly educated and competent females points to this "Old Boy System" or what could be colloquially described as "The Narcissist Monopoly" or "The Narcissistic Monarchy."

The truly sad commentary is that Narcissists rarely change. It usually takes a monumental wake-up call, something many times no less than a financial bankruptcy, serious detriment to his business or personal reputation, substantial personal loss or a spiritual awakening, for this person's ego to deflate so he can finally look himself in the mirror and, instead of thinking he is infallible, at last perceive his own destructive, insidious pathology which has been all too patently obvious to everyone around him who has had to suffer (usually in silence) from the decisions he made from his pathological position of power. In fact, the very thing that needs changing the most in a Narcissist is the very thing that prevents the Narcissist from changing—his arrogant belief of masculine superiority within virtually every realm of human experience and functioning; the narcissist's insatiable demand for power and control; his intense belief in his own omnipotence and specialness; his perception of entitlement to maintain this unnegotiable, exclusive position in the world; the narcissist's overall denial of imperfection; the obsessive need for others to live by his made-up rules; and, last, his demand that only he can be the authenticator and judge of his own self-made rules. It is, indeed, a pathology of ego inflation, the Superior "I," the self-perception of specialness, exclusivity, omnipotence and entitlement which largely dominates politics, business, academia, religion, law, medicine and science. It is this very pathology which is going to be the death of us all if we allow it to continue to flourish in world leadership.

The wholesale lack of ownership and accountability of a narcissistic and abusive patriarchy and their unwillingness, as a collective group, to humbly and nobly share power should signal to the rest of the world that massive changes at the world leadership level is critical if the human species intends to survive. Since Narcissists firmly believe their sovereign reign must continue and that, indeed, the world is a far superior place because of their omnipotence, the moment is now for females, minorities and the gay community to unite, gather all its numbers and become vocal and active in world change. The time has never been better for females, minorities and the gay community to unify in purpose and use the power of their numbers to:

–boycott products from companies whose executives do not have legitimate mentoring programs which promote competent, educated females, minorities and homosexuals into senior executive corporate positions;

–boycott products from companies who have poor ecological sensitivity and who fail to implement ecological awareness into their corporate ethos;

–use the voting polls as a means to elect political candidates who are particularly sensitive to human rights issues.

By the very fact that only 1% of females are CEOs in America, no minorities are in CEO positions of any Fortune 100 companies in America, no females or minorities have ever been elected as Vice President or President in America, only one state in America recognizes gay marriages, these facts and these facts alone are screaming testimonies to the covert discrimination that is still pervasive throughout the political, business and judicial systems in America and should be constant motivators for females, minorities and the gay community that their collaboration and unification is critical if they are to gain authentic parity with non-minority males. Not unlike Martin Luther King's day, the subordinate groups are still forced to unify their numbers and use their collective power to peacefully take what is rightfully theirs as part of the human race. In spite of major federal legislation which has been passed to prevent discrimination, the fact is that rampant discrimination remains in politics, business, academia and law, particularly at executive levels. This patent observation that the dominant group is unwilling to relinquish their exclusive position, mentor the subordinate groups and share their power should become a marching call for every person who is in a subordinate group.

The feminine seems to be unable to win against a pervasive pathology in male world leadership which erroneously and tragically (to the peril of the opposite gender *and of its own gender*) believes it is healthy. Is it any wonder that females have become "hysterical, neurotic and emotional" as a result of thousands of years of the superiority of the oppressive, derisive and abusive immature patriarchy? Of thousands of years of being denied equal access to academic knowledge, higher education, economic, social and legal parity? It does not take an intellectual giant to deduce the emotional and mental consequences of this kind of treatment. Caucasian Americans can perhaps gain a clearer understanding of the African American silent "rage" which exists today and the turning of that rage on their own community.

Until the 20th century, it has been with the help of the immature feminine that the myth of masculine superiority continues. It should be conceded a fact that, during primitive times when physical superiority was, by nature, of critical and essential importance to the survival of the human species, the male had to take the lead and protect the female and the children. We acknowledge to mankind that were it not for his aggressive protector role, the human species would likely not have survived. We genuinely thank mankind for that dangerous and arduous responsibility. But today we have no major threats from beasts of prey. Although there are no large-scale threats against wild beasts in the wilderness, the myth of masculine superiority remains pervasive as we examine the immature masculine energy of narcissism thriving in corporate boardrooms, on Wall Street, in medicine and science, in families and even within certain fundamental religious groups. As stated earlier, even though anachronistic, most societies and cultures maintain this superior masculine construct. We also continue to see many Borderline females desperately searching for their Core "I" and it manifests in self-destructive behaviors such as cutting, head banging and eating disorders. With the masculine emphasis on morphic Beauty, as opposed to Spiritual Beauty, it should come as no surprise to see an ever growing number of females develop obsessions with body dysmorphia. Until the feminine discovers, honors and learns to love her Core "I," she will continue to move through the world via an external locus of control in order to find psychological peace. We could also say that, until the masculine discovers, honors and learns to love and value "Other" as equal to "I," the narcissistic immature masculine will continue to perpetuate mythic, distorted and unwhole psychological concepts of what it means to be a fully functioning, healthy human being and present it to society as "normal gender identity development." We are thankful that the past twenty years have seen some appreciable movement in the right direction and, hopefully, the feminine can resist the temptation toward revenge and, instead, assist mankind in assuming the equal rights to be a whole, full human being. Further, we hope that females can convince, allow and give explicit permission to mankind (and mankind can take that offering) to fully participate in the process of the development of little boys and little girls; both genders giving each other express permission to embody an androgynous consciousness which simply means giving each other express permission to reflect what every Soul naturally desires to express, knowledge, creativity, love and wisdom.

Until the Soul begins its ascent upward, humankind will only stay in the quagmire of psychological chaos which the ego perpetuates. Below is a drawing which represents Soul as the mediating principle between the lower ego consciousness and Brahman:

**Attachment XI**

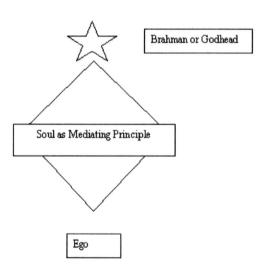

As understood from the theoretical model of the Soul, the fully embodied Soul is the human being capable of integrating and equally expressing two sides of *the same coin*: the mature feminine and mature masculine; the Self and Other. What appears above is the sacred geometrical figure of the triangle which eventually turns into a shining circle of Pure Light, the Pure Light of Goodness. Once the human is able to integrate both the feminine and the masculine (*intra*psychically), along with Self and Other (*inter*psychically), there can be no perceivable or discernable difference between them, rather they simply become One whole, balanced, harmonious consciousness. We may say this is the "I-Thou" relationship or perhaps the "I-I" or what Eastern philosophers refer to as the "eye seeing itSelf". When these two energies are split, however, the ego manifests into a split psyche which results in the Platonic and Hegelian concept of the Master/Slave dichotomy. There can be no narcissist consciousness (master) without a borderline consciousness (slave). Karl Marx borrowed heavily from Hegelian philosophy and based his social and economic theories upon the concept of the Master/Slave (dominant/subordinate) relationship which is why some African Americans like William Dubois gravitated toward Marxian theory. As long as the immature masculine ego perpetuates the myth of masculine superiority, males will rely on a mythic structure upon which the entire world must hang its belief system. This, in turn, continues to perpetuate the masculine superiority in virtually all world systems from financial, business, political, social, scientific and academic arenas where the masculine maintains complete power and control over all world resources. For the dominant group which has exclusive control over world resources is the group which maintains the position of Master over "Other." This Master/Slave relationship is built upon the hoard/greed mentality of the immature ego consciousness.

As I see it, the masculine energy was destined to be the leader in the process of the evolution (unfolding) of human consciousness with the outward, separating energies of knowledge and creativity. When seen this way, we say that we owe the creation of virtually all world systems to both the masculine *energy and the biological male,* since it is a fact that males vehemently, overtly and pervasively denied females academic knowledge and the ability to create (or participate in creating) systems until roughly the 20th century. It will probably be unknown how many females throughout history did attempt to make intelligent contributions, but since females were thwarted in intellectual efforts and most creative efforts in the social, business and political arenas, it is also unknown how many females' ideas were stolen by males who would take those ideas and turn them into reality.

As humankind continues to evolve and the Soul begins to manifest more, i.e., when more humans begin to exhibit androgynous consciousness, more females will become involved in the creative process of using knowledge and building form in the world. We have seen the beginning of this to an appreciable degree only in the twentieth century, although virtually all world wealth remains in the hands of males. Oprah Winfrey and Madonna seem to be two famous, wealthy females in their own right who do overtly use their wealth to enhance the equality of females and/or to promote the cause of other subordinate groups. To be sure, the world is in desperate need of more Oprah Winfreys as politicians, as CEOs in Corporate America, as heads of academic institutions and as executive administrators in healthcare. She seems to be a shining example of someone who expresses Soulfulness as she seeks to use her knowledge and creativity in order to love and be wise about the All of humanity. Her balance of masculine and feminine energies is a beacon for us all as she uses her personal wealth to unite humankind.

In the process of involution (enfolding) of human consciousness, where humanity transcends ego consciousness and moves closer to Soul and Spirit, it must be the feminine energies of love and wisdom (inward, collaborative, interpersonal energies) which must be allowed to take the lead. *Both feminine and masculine energies, however, must be expressed equally in the world and within genders.* Without this, humankind will remain at Wilber's First Tier level of consciousness and humankind will remain in a stalled revolution.

The ego consciousness could be understood as the split psyche or split Soul since *Psyche* literally means "Soul". *Psyche* in the 6th century meant "the study of the Soul," however, since the masculine dismissed, and pushed away from, philosophy in the 19th century in order to form a separate psychology, "psychology" has, in modern times, come to be defined as "the study of mind and behavior" which is, by and large, a masculine construct. By considering the founders of virtually all our theoretical models of psychology and also reviewing our modern definition of psychology, we realize that psychology is a masculine dominated field and it has failed to study what the very word "psychology" means. Modern psychology has only studied ¼ of the Psyche or Soul because it has dismissed the feminine part of Psyche and only studied the human mind. It does not even seriously study creativity, the other half of the masculine expression of the Soul. Mainstream psychology, begun and perpetuated by Wundt, Titchener, Freud, Watson, Skinner, Ellis and Beck, continues to emphasize intellect, logic, cognition and behavior and consistently ignores and dismisses ways that humankind expresses creativity, love and wisdom. Cognition and behavior without creativity, love and wisdom appear cold and inhuman. When we add creativity, love and wisdom to our personhood, we add the warmth of what it means to truly "Be," in other words, what it truly means to "Be" a whole human. In fact, the humanistic, existential and transpersonal theorists developed their ideas in contradistinction from the mechanistic or deterministic model of the human by these aforementioned theorists.

As seen from the Soul, we can picture how our four primary disciplines each symbolize or represent a portion of the Soul. Psychology has been inauthentic in its quest since it has only been studying ¼ of what the "Psyche" truly is. Modern psychologists have attempted to study the mind and behavior, the mechanical "I." If we review the definition of the Whole Soul, it becomes obvious that modern psychology is masculine biased in its study, its focus and its methodologies and the field largely denies feminine inter-subjectivity its rightful *equal* place of value. Instead, ultimate and supreme value is placed only on masculine, objective, empirical data, the "It" of the external world.

Physics, until Einstein came along, seems to have been largely bent on finding the "Creator" of the Universe as the "It" of the Universe. The burning question for physics was always to examine all of the "Its" in the physical subatomic world in order to finally arrive at the author of the manifest world. Denouncing all religious proclamations which stand on simple faith that there is an "I" who created the manifest world, the world of physics prior to Einstein was truly an "It" discipline. It presents as ironic that Einstein, an intellectual genius, has said "we should take care not to make the intellect our god; it has, of course, powerful muscles, but no personality" and "by painful experience, we have learned that rational thinking does not suffice to solve the problems of our social life."

The overarching quest of theology, no matter which religion was involved, has always been to motivate humankind to develop a divine love toward one another, between self and neighbor. This is the "We" of loving energy.While it has largely failed in its efforts to unify the world, religions reflect a long, solid and successful history of building community amongst members within its own segregated clique.

And philosophy, the "All" of existence which literally means "the study of wisdom," seems to be the one discipline which attempts to wrap its arms around the entire cosmological existence. As Alfred North Whitehead stated: "Philosophy asks the simple question, What is it *all* about?" Each discipline represents a different quadrant of the expressions of humankind, all being part of a composite whole.

**Attachment XII**

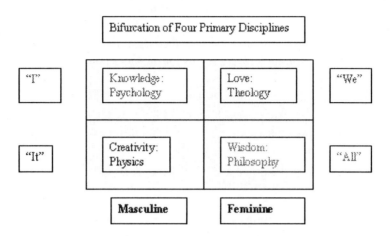

It was the unification of the feminine and the masculine, its resultant manifestation of Goodwill toward All and its equality (at the Ultimate level of Reality) of all humanity which resulted in the crucifixion of the Christ. This psychological mindset, if fully expressed on a large scale in the world and especially 2,000 years ago, would have culminated in the complete dismantling of the narcissistic masculine ego consciousness which can only continue to exist if there is an inferior counterpart to its existence which tolerates and accepts it as the dominating consciousness in world leadership. If this book seems overly harsh toward the immature masculine ego, here are some sobering 1995-2001 statistics from the FBI Uniform Crime Reporting Program and from the Bureau of Justice Statistics which is the statistical agency of the U.S. Department of Justice. All but the last statistic is representative of the U.S.:

–91% of murders are committed by males.
–77% of murder victims are males.
–33% of all female murder victims are murdered by a former spouse, spouse or boyfriend.
–In America, a woman is battered every 15 seconds.
–In America, a woman is raped every two minutes.
–97% of reported rapes are perpetrated by a man against a woman.
–64% of the women who are raped and physically assaulted are done so by a spouse, former spouse or boyfriend.

159

–Boys who witness their fathers' violence are ten times more likely to engage in spousal abuse in later adulthood than boys in non-violent homes.

–21% of women who are raped for the first time are below age 12 and 32% of women who are raped for the first time are between ages 12 and 17.

–Women are ten times more likely to be attacked by a spouse, former spouse, boyfriend, parent or child than are men.

–18% of women who were attacked by an intimate do not report to the police because of fear of reprisal.

–Globally, at least 33% of women and girls have been beaten or sexually abused in their lifetime.

This is a small sampling of statistics which speak loudly for the dire need for the feminine in the world to become recognizable, valued, honored and openly expressed in both women and men. An earnest plea is made to all parents to begin to teach and allow the free expression of *both feminine and masculine energies in both genders*. Responsibility lies with the father and mother to ensure their children, regardless of biological gender, are given express permission to develop both the masculine and feminine energies. Bifurcation of these energies within and between the genders must stop. Adult males in leadership are challenged to take responsibility and allow for the expression of both the mature masculine and mature feminine energies when conducting business, making political decisions and passing legislation. It is parenting and world leadership which has the most accountability and which holds the most promise for positive change in the world today. It barely needs pointing out that leadership is a pivotal change agent, positive or negative, because it is this group whose consciousness uses its influence, power and control in order to affect and manifest systemic change. For 10,000 years, the immature masculine has controlled world resources and has ensured, through every conceivable overt and covert cognitive, emotional and behavioral tactic, the use of financial, political, judicial and social power and even through unthinkably horrible acts such as physical abuse and rape, that the feminine would remain disempowered, disenfranchised and inferior to the masculine. This guaranteed that the feminine had no formal voice of influence or power in building or sustaining world systems. This is not to say that the immature feminine has not played a role as *contributor* to the social and psychological ills which permeate society. To be sure, she has been, and is, a tragic actor on the stage of life, albeit she has been cast, by the immature masculine, into an inferior acting role during every act of the human epic. The point is to say that the immature masculine has abused, oppressed, devalued, dismissed and ignored her to the extent that she has had little, or no, collective self-worth, thus, she has never collectively had the ego power, the strong sense of "I," which is a requisite if she is to ever assume a leadership role. The irony in the story of female subjugation is that she has never vied to be a Master, rather has always only fought for parity. That is her goal: shared power, not dominant power. For if she sought to be Master, the feminine would only turn into that which has subjugated her for thousands of years— the immature, arrogant ego masculine. This immature, arrogant masculine has relegated her to "Slave" until the 20th century and, even now, the Glass Ceiling continues to keep her in an inferior role in business, politics, academia, science and law. While this prevents her from being esteemed as a creator of world systems, neither can she be held as culpable party in the pervasive greed, deceit, corruption and crime which is, literally, destroying the same world systems that the masculine has built. Having said all this, it is an undeniable fact that patriarchy sits and reigns over every world system on this planet, hence, *primary responsibility lies with masculinity to change.* Anything other than this is the abstruse analogy of blaming slaves for being caught, oppressed, devalued, abused, beaten, raped, hanged and murdered. Such charge that the subordinate is to blame for her own oppression and discrimination and, likewise, is responsible for her own emancipation could only come from the voice of an arrogant, abusive Master. Only an ignorant or narcissistic mindset could opine such an illogical absurdity.

Domination, oppression and suppression, if unchecked and unresolved by the leader who is dominating, will always eventually lead to revolution initiated by the subordinate group. Unfortunately, what has happened is that the subordinate group, upon assuming the leadership role after the revolution, has become a mirror image of the despised leadership which led to the oppression and revolution. History has born out this simple truth repeatedly, yet humankind has been cognitively dull in its capacity to learn such a simple lesson. This is why the feminine does not wish to assume the Master role, rather seeks only shared power with the masculine. It is only in sharing power between the masculine and the feminine that humankind can be redeemed psychologically and spiritually. In fact, were the Christ Consciousness or Soul Consciousness to gain a mass following, it would wreak havoc on virtually every masculine-dominated world system. As noted in an earlier chapter,

Elkins in *Beyond Religion*, speaks of the social, political, economic and even religious structures as becoming "rubble" should Soul manifest on a widespread level of consciousness. This Soulfulness or fullness of Being would be the benevolent queen and king in the kingdom of humanity. Maslow, May, Frankl and Rogers understood Soul as presence of "Being" since it is only Being— with a divine and broadened presence and awareness embracing and accepting all of humanity—which is authentically Soulful as it yearns for The Good for the All. What more could Ultimate Truth and Beauty be than the Good for the All? Roberto Assagioli would call Soul the "Higher Self" and Carl Jung called Soul simply "the Self" spelled with a capital "S." Both theorists point to essentially synonymous concepts. To borrow a Wilberian phrase, we are all using different cameras with different lens, but we are all pointing toward the same thing.

The Advaitan concept of *Saguna* Brahman or "Fullness of Being" can be pictured as below:

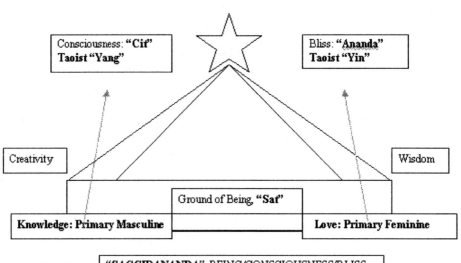

At the base of the sacred pyramid, we find the Ground of Being which is the Soul with its four energic expressions of knowledge, love, creativity and wisdom. At the Soul level, we have *Saguna* Brahman which is a state of consciousness where there is a loving, joyful awareness within. We may still have something to say at this level of consciousness, although it is to be sure it will be paradoxical. The energy of knowledge, when ascending, actually transforms into a purer form of energy which is the Pure energy of Consciousness, whereas the energy of love, when ascending, transforms into a purer energy, the Pure energy of Bliss. At this level, bliss and consciousness cannot be separated and there is a complete union with God or Brahman or Tao. This is the level of consciousness above the Soul Consciousness and could be referred to as *Nirguna* Brahman where all distinctions are obliterated. Everything is complete, One and Whole. No split consciousness exists. One may say that everything "Is" at this level and, therefore, the only response is silence in confronting this ineffable mystery, the Great Mystery of the All.

To return to the ego consciousness, we may use the table below to outline how the psyche has been split for millennia as we refer to the Platonic phrase of "Not-Being" or the Hegelian concept of the Master and Slave or psychologically speaking, the Narcissistic Master and the Borderline Slave:

**Attachment XIV**

| Expression | Function | Gender | Archetype |
|---|---|---|---|
| To Know | Empower (Self) | Masculine | Teacher |
| To Deceive (other) | Control (other) | Masculine | Dictator |
| To Create | Generate (Other) | Masculine | Carpenter |
| To Destroy (other) | Condemn (other) | Masculine | Warrior |
| To Love | Share (We) | Feminine | Love |
| To Hate (self) | Consume (other) | Feminine | Villain |
| To be Wise | Integrate (All) | Feminine | Counselor |
| To be Foolish (toward self) | Ignore (self) | Feminine | Fool |

The ego is empty because it is split from its Ultimate Essence, the spiritual, yet unseen, Realities of knowledge, creativity, love and wisdom which are shared equally by all and which move us in the direction of heartfelt community and, ultimately, if meditated upon, toward a whole consciousness—a consciousness of bliss. For only a consciousness of wholeness can ever experience psychological health. Instead, the ego focuses on the physical and material world which divides and separates humanity into an "either/or" mentality of superiority and inferiority. At the Soul level of Consciousness, all of humanity is seen as sharing in the Soul and as expressing Soul in the world in what the Buddhists refer to as the "ten thousand paths" which lead to Nirvana (or God) or what Plato and Plotinus would consider as the "emanations" from the Divine *Nous*. Plato's Allegory of the Cave is a beautiful pictorial representation of the Divine *Nous* all the way down to the ego consciousness which is forever in chains and forever experiencing pain and suffering due to its emphasis and focus on the material world, the world of duality. The ego is split and searches outside of itself for confirmation of its identity. Hence, the ego has an external locus of control and it can only recognize separation and division since the physical and material world do, indeed, appear to our senses as separate and different. Advaitans would refer to this ego consciousness as *apara vidya* or lower knowledge in the world of *maya* or "illusion" or "appearance" whereas they would speak of *para vidya* or higher knowledge (intuition or illumination or self-revelation) as Ultimate Reality of Brahman or God or Highest Self.

The Soul is not anthropomorphic, therefore, concepts such as race, color, ethnicity, culture, social status, economic status, job title, education level, religious affiliation and sexual preference are all understood by the Soul to be one of ten thousand expressions or emanations or projections of Brahman or the One. Thus, these concepts hold only relative importance or satisfaction since they manifest only at the relative (material) level of existence. In fact, things such as race, social status, education level or religious preference are only meaningful to the extent that they are understood as expressions of the One, the All. Different races should be perceived as different colors of the light spectrum, different social or educational levels should be considered as varying levels of the Whole, a religious preference could be considered as one path out of hundreds of paths which lead to the One, the All. If perceived in a superior/inferior way at the relative level of existence, it is the ego consciousness which is in control since the ego deifies the physical world, only perceives a physical world of separation and division, superiority and inferiority and cannot grasp the All, the One, the Whole, the Good. Perceiving the physical world as lord and governor will forever alienate humankind and, as stated earlier, distance the human species forever from psychological health and well-being. The Soul imbues a holistic, integrated consciousness because it perceives from an internal locus of control and understands, contemplates and places ultimate value only on that which is *ultimately* meaningful—the eternal, indivisible and immutable. The Soul recognizes the physical world as *maya*, transitory and ephemeral. While respecting the physical world and its necessity for living a human life, the Soul places only relative, not ultimate or absolute, value or meaning on it. All consequent actions and behaviors derived from the Soul Consciousness are in alignment with this Truth, therefore, peace and well-being are natural expressions from the fully embodied Soul. This is what it means to be divine, yet human. It is truly the grandeur of the Great Soul, not the grandiosity of the ego.

As stated previously, in order for humankind to shift the level of consciousness from a split psyche to a Full or Whole Soul (psyche), both the horizontal axis of the Soul (*intra*psychic: masculine and feminine opposites) and the vertical axis of the Soul (*inter*psychic: Self and Other) must be integrated. When this occurs, I'm in agreement with Wilber's prediction that there will be a major cultural shift. And that shift in human consciousness will be, in my opinion, the integrative, holistic expression of the Whole Soul or Full Being.

*It is also part of the cosmic law that what you say and do determines what happens in your life. The ordinary person thinks that this law is external to himself.... The superior person recognizes that he and the subtle law are one. Therefore he cultivates himself to accord with it.*
—Lao Tzu

*Mysteriously existing before Heaven and Earth. Silent and empty. An unchanging oneness. An everchanging presence. The Mother of All Life. It is impossible to really give it a name, but I call it 'Tao'. Without wishing to define it, it could be called 'The Whole.' The Whole moves as if in a circle: Turning away and returning to itself. Tao is the Whole.*
—Lao Tzu

# X. THE FOUR FUNDAMENTAL SPIRITUAL LAWS OF THE SOUL

There are scientific laws which have an equivalent or correlating law in the spirit world. Just as the scientific laws are inviolable and govern the material world, so are the spiritual laws inviolable in their governance of both spirit and matter. Walt Whitman, a poet who wrote prolifically on nature, said this:

"I hold it as a changeless law,
From which no soul can sway or swerve,
We have that in us which will draw,
Whate'er we need and most deserve."

The law of cause and effect: that which is a cause will always produce an effect. All other laws can be subsumed under this law. Eastern religions refer to this law as the law of karma. Many people say: "What you give out comes back to you." Some western religions say: "Whatsoever you sew, that shall you also reap." In the spiritual world, cause and effect are the same. Being and doing are one and the same. Love produces love. Joy produces joy. It is spontaneous. To say that the Soul *acts* with love and joy, is the same as to say it *is* love and joy. In the physical world, energies are slower and denser, frequencies are lower. In the physical world, the effect sometimes is seen far apart from the cause, however, the law will still govern and it is inviolable. If the effect is not experienced in one lifetime, the Soul must incarnate into another lifetime in order to complete that karmic debt. This is why the Soul seeks love, peace and joy since it seeks to reawaken to its essence. Jesus admonished us to love one another because he was keenly aware of this spiritual law of cause and effect. This law is directly related to the expression of love.

The law of vibration and attraction: all things gravitate toward, or vibrate around, a center. Its corresponding physical law is the law of gravity. Your Soul may be thought of as a Divine Center of energy although, in Reality, your Soul is everywhere. Empedocles said "the nature of God is like a circle whose center is everywhere and circumference is nowhere" referring to the brilliance of light which is the "body" of your Soul in the spiritual world. When you are in tune with your Divine Center, you are nurturing your Soul and your essence. Your Soul is always attracted toward itSelf which is ultimate Goodness. You are also diminishing the lower energies of negativity and increasing the higher energies of positivity.

The law of cycles: this refers to the cyclical process of energy. Some refer to the yin and yang of life. Its physical equivalent is the first law of thermodynamics that says energy cannot be created or destroyed, rather only changed from matter to nonmatter. In the scientific world, this refers to molecules and how molecules, which are unseen, make up the world we see. Molecules cannot be created nor can they be destroyed. The governing force of both the seen and unseen world is Tao, the Great Mystery, unseen to the physical eye. It is the real world of knowledge, creativity, love and wisdom and the Great Will which forever produces. From this, all matter is formed.

The law of abundance: The more you give, the more you have. This spiritual law has been turned on its head and transposed on a physical level and, instead, in the world of matter, we deceive ourselves by thinking that the more we take, the more we have. Soul knows that giving and having are the same since the Soul only recognizes abundance. If you want humility from others, give humility. If you want arrogance, give arrogance. If you want joy from others, give joy. If you want a miserable, sour attitude from others, give that to others and you will surely begin to receive it back. What you give always comes back to you even if it takes time. Only the ego, with its delusional belief in lack, scarcity, superiority and inferiority, difference and separation, can have a value system which believes in taking as a way of getting more.

*Tao gives life to all living things, and its Natural Goodness nourishes, tends, comforts, feeds, shelters and protects them.*
—Lao Tzu

*Nurture Natural Goodness within yourself, and you will feel its benefits. Make it part of the family, and it will grow from generation to generation. Make it the centre of your community and it will flourish. Make it the leader of your nation, and it will be abundant. Make it the whole of your world, and whichever way you turn, you will meet Natural Goodness.*
—Lao Tzu

# XI. THE SPIRITUAL VALUE SYSTEM OF THE SOUL

According to the dialogues of Plato, Socrates spoke often of virtues and called the Idea of Good "the highest truth of all" and "the guiding star of the Soul." And so the idea of the Will toward Goodness is actually an ancient, yet timeless concept. The value system of the Soul is a world of virtue where Goodness, not worldly power, reigns supreme.

Not every person who is well educated or wealthy is arrogant. Likewise, not every person who is arrogant is wealthy or well educated. There are masses of people from both genders, all ethnicities, educational levels, socioeconomic and political backgrounds and religious affiliations who feel superior or inferior to others. Superiority and inferiority derive from a basic belief that people are forever unequal and that only something worldly like money, assets, social or political position, job title, pulchritude or educational degrees can give you superiority over others. This inequality, in turn, is founded upon a worldly value system—a conviction which says that something contrived by man is the yardstick by which we must measure ourselves and others. For instance, many people predicate a hierarchical value system on physical attributes such as age, gender, beauty, height, weight, sexual orientation; worldly knowledge such as the amount of knowledge you have about medicine, law, science or business; education level in terms of whether you have a high school diploma, undergraduate degree or multiple graduate college degrees; worldly wealth such as income, financial investments and assets; social, professional or political status such as which social or professional organizations with which you have membership or the political connections you establish; and religious affiliation such as whether you are Protestant, Catholic, Jewish, Hindu or Islamic.

These are worldly—not spiritual—yardsticks by which to measure a person. Your Soul is a spiritual yardstick and cares not one whit about worldly yardsticks except to the extent they are used for Goodness for both yourself and others, for the All. The spiritual value system of the Soul is Goodness for All—love, peace, joy, loving-kindness, truth, honor, justice, beauty, knowledge, creativity, wisdom. The Soul is devoted to these spiritual fruits. The Soul—your Soul—does not give one iota about any of the worldly systems listed above if you are not in harmony with your Great Soul. Let's repeat that.

*Your Great Soul does not give one whit about whether you are old or young; woman or man; tall or short; heterosexual or homosexual; a doctor or car mechanic; have a high school diploma or have a doctorate; have billions or are on welfare; are Jewish, Hindu or Catholic; are Republican or Democrat; belong to the American Psychological Association or the local union organization; or whether your hobby is fishing or collecting paintings by Picasso and Van Gogh.*

Every one of these distinctions can manifest the ego consciousness; therefore, the Soul does not recognize them as having ultimate value, only relative value. When I speak of ultimate value, I mean the Whole, the All. When I speak of relative value, it refers to pieces of the Whole. Your Soul does *not* measure itself and its value on worldly things. Neither does your Soul pursue worldly things as an end unto themselves. Worldly things are merely expressions or emanations or projections from the Soul. To the Great

Soul, worldly things are only *means to spiritual ends*. So your Soul seeks worldly things as an *ultimate means to enhance spiritual well being*. Psychological well being is an outcome of spiritual well-being. If worldly things are pursued merely as a means to another worldly end, the Soul is not expressing itSelf and the ego is in control.

Your Soul and your neighbor's Soul and every other Soul on this planet is totally indifferent to these man made systemic affiliations except to the extent you are able to experience them and use these systems for the Good of your Soul *and* for others. Using them solely for your own benefit which devalues another person is not Soulful. Neither is giving away all your energy to others without reaping joyous benefits for yourself. Self-denigration and self-deprecation are not values of the Soul; neither are self-inflation and excessive self-involvement. A consistent pattern of giving your energy to others that continually results in depletion of your own energy and overall self-esteem is no more welcome to the Soul than is self-absorption and self-involvement to the extent that you expect the world to revolve around your needs, wishes and desires. I see the former admit themselves to the psychiatric unit where I work and the entire world has to endure the painful consequences of the latter as they currently hold leadership positions and govern the decisions which create our social, political, judicial and economic conditions. These are two extremes on the axis of Self/Other and only the Middle Path, as the Buddhists speak, is worth treading. In fact, only the Middle Path will give this world peace. Only to the extent that man made value systems contribute to the nurturance of your Soul and your neighbor's do they have any value whatsoever. *The value from these systems is not in the system, rather the value is derived from the Goodness which they engender*. Otherwise, their value is zero on the spiritual balance sheet of life. As Einstein once said, "try not to become a man of success, but a man of value." Millions and millions of people know this on a subconscious level, but do not know exactly from whence this spiritual knowledge comes. Perhaps the following examples will enlighten your path.

Have you ever come home at the end of a long, particularly stressful week at work, read your company proxy statement that stated your company is in a financial slump, laying people off and not meeting its targeted financial goals for two years in a row, however, the board of directors has voted themselves large bonuses totaling millions of dollars? Did you sit down in silence feeling an overwhelming sense of injustice and ask yourself: "Why do I keep doing this every day? What is all this for?"

When you read the newspaper about another corporate executive who has failed to be indicted for absconding with millions of dollars by committing fraud off the backs of millions of middle class employees and investors who have lost their life savings, do you read it and wonder: "Do the greedy and dishonest control the world? Has the incest between today's politicians and corporate executives become yesterday's version of the lack of division between church and state? Is there any justice anymore?"

Doesn't it seem that road rage is becoming commonplace? How many times are you simply minding your own business, driving along to your destination, when the car behind you jumps suddenly in front of you, cutting your car off and barely maintaining his road rage? Do you ever ask yourself: "Are we all going to end up in the psychiatric unit from anxiety and depression?"

Do you see the news events of terrorist attacks, with people killing and injuring each other, all in the name of a "loving" God? Or some serial killer who is randomly killing people for seemingly no reason at all? Do you wonder to yourself: "Are we all just going to kill each other?"

Unless you live in total isolation, you're likely to relate to these situations and experiences. If so, then your Soul is speaking to you. Your Great Soul is gently and quietly telling you that the world is in a state of disharmony. As we mentioned in the earlier chapter on Spiritual Laws which govern both the Spiritual world and the physical world, we, as humans, receive exactly what we have given; it just takes less time in some situations and more in others. There is nothing in the above situations that the Soul would sanction. Absolutely nothing. Your Soul can only value that which is Goodness because your Soul *is* Goodness. And anything which is antithetical to this essence— your essence—will not be condoned by the Soul. The Soul will *only* guide and direct you toward Highest Good for yourself and the whole of humanity.

Abraham Maslow and Victor Frankl began as humanistic-existentialist psychologists from a theoretical standpoint, however, in the last several years of their lives, they moved into the transpersonal theoretical camp of psychology as they both began to understand that the psychological salvation of the human race is predicated on the ability to transcend the ego. Frankl, already a medical doctor, spent three years in four different Nazi concentration camps during WWII where all family members were murdered except for his sister. His theory of logotherapy is based, in simplistic terms, on healing through finding meaning. Frankl believed that it is only through finding meaning and purpose in life that we are able to move toward authentic psychological health and well-being. He had to discard much of what he had learned in the field of psychology in order to arrive at logotherapy in the late 1920s since, at that time, the edict of Freudian psychoanalysis taught that spiritual beliefs and a belief in a spiritual after-life were signs of pathology or sickness in the individual. This is not dissimilar from today where medical science and mainstream psychology, with their primary emphasis on sickness, disease and prescription drugs, needs to be overhauled, transformed and a broader paradigm needs to take its place. Frankl had to reach inside his own Soul and rediscover truths that we all know intuitively in the depth of our Souls. As a result, he published his book, *The Doctor and the Soul,* after surviving one of the most hellish results of the immature ego masculine that one can experience. It is his Soul's testimony to the indefatigable Spirit that is within us all.

Maslow arrived at Theory Z near the end of his life. He had coined the phrase "self-actualization" to refer to the person who has an integrated ego, but Maslow began studying, with greater interest, what he referred to as "non-transcending self-actualizers" and "transcending self-actualizers." Even though he reported that even psychologically *un*healthy people can have "peak experiences," his focus became those people who are self-actualized and have transcendent experiences, i.e., the "self-actualizing transcenders". In his book, *The Farther Reaches of Human Nature,* Maslow outlines what he refers to as B-Values or "Being Values" which are the values of those people who are self-actualized transcenders. They are:

Truth
Goodness
Beauty
Wholeness
Dichotomy-transcendence
Aliveness
Uniqueness
Perfection
Necessity
Completion
Justice
Order
Simplicity
Richness
Effortlessness

Playfulness
Self-sufficiency

Maslow refers to those who prefer and carry these Being Values as "fully human people." One could say these are the values of the great and fully embodied Soul. Note that these are all positive and optimistic attributes. William James, in *The Varieties of Religious Experience*, has this to say of the positive mind:

> "'Pessimism leads to weakness, Optimism leads to power.' 'Thoughts are things,' as one of the most vigorous mind-cure writers prints...and if your thoughts are of health, youth, vigor, and success, before you know it these things will also be your outward portion. No one can fail the regenerative influence of optimistic thinking...Every man owns indefeasibly this inlet to the divine. Fear, on the contrary, and all the contracted and egoistic modes of thought, are inlets to destruction. Most mind-curers here bring in a doctrine that thoughts are 'forces,' and thoughts draw to themselves as allies all the thoughts of the same character that exist the world over. Thus one gets, by one's thinking, reinforcements from elsewhere for the realization of one's desires; and the great point in the conduct of life is to get the heavenly forces on one's side by opening one's own mind to their influx."

Maslow and James knew of the great power of thinking, the realm of spiritual values, because they knew these are the thoughts which create Goodness. Much like Jung when he stated that archetypes constellate when you begin talking about them, there is a power inherent in Goodness. Its force is real and gathers all like things unto itSelf. This is the realm of the Soul as it looks Spiritward. For Goodness is the value system of the Soul.

What do you value? Soul's essence is Spirit and subject to all Spiritual Laws. Soul may use some physical matter toward some Higher Good, but it is the Higher Good which is of highest value, not the physical matter. An example would be winning the lottery. If a person places value only on the physical possessions which are brought with the money and uses those possessions in order to establish superiority over others who possess less, then Soul is not expressing itSelf and, thus, the Soul is not nurtured. If a person pursues worldly knowledge only for the sake of establishing superiority over those who are less educated or as a way to attain worldly goods with no consideration of what nourishes the Soul, the Soul is not being honored and the person is not expressing energies from their Soul. If a person pursues fame merely to proclaim superiority over others or to garner worldly possessions, the Soul is not operating. Always remember that the Soul does not denigrate, demean and devalue others because the Soul always knows the real essence of a person is their spirituality, not their education or income level, political or social status, religious affiliation or any physical attribute. The Soul only ultimately values spirit, therefore, what about that which is unseen could ever be unequal?

You can ignore and deny your Soul exists, but your Soul merely exists in quiet, divine silence. You can never diminish your Great Soul. You can only *think you can*. Just like the corporate executives who delude themselves into thinking that they can get away with unlawful white collar activities. Having violated both worldly and spiritual laws, what they give out will have a ripple effect to the world around them and, sooner or later, to themselves. They are actually contributing to the eventual demise of the entire economic and ecological system whenever they use power to primarily bring them self-gain. In the case of corporations that dump toxic waste, these corporate executives are destroying, little by little, the very ecology which sustains them and their family. That is a law just like the law of gravity. It is inviolable. For every action, there is a consequence and this Spiritual Law is that by which your Soul is governed. Spirit *"is,"* *always has been* and *forever will be*. You have free will to believe whatever you wish, but in your free will of believing in whatever you want, you establish your value system. In turn, your value system determines whether you and others live in harmony or disharmony. Your mind is the most powerful energy that exists and your mind is part of your Great Soul, just as a ray of sunshine is a part of the Sun. Your mind creates every moment and there is never a moment when it does not create. With your free will, every second of your life you are given the freedom and the power to create harmony or disharmony by your beliefs.

The Soul has a spiritual value system, just as we humans have developed our own worldly value system. The spiritual value system of the Soul never changes, so it is certain. But the value system of the world does change, so it is a system of uncertainty. The value systems of the world have been created, primarily sustained by, maintained and dominated by a masculine cognitive style. Throughout history, men have placed value upon these man made systems and have continuously struggled, largely through dominance, strife and wars, to keep control of, and power over, their manufactured world systems. The most recognizable world systems created by men are the political, financial, business, educational, religious, medical, scientific, legal and marital systems. Without exception, each of these systems has been, and is, dominated by male leadership. We measure the success of these systems by the harmony that either exists or does not exist within their structure. If there is substantive harmony within a world structure, then it can be said that the Soul is being nurtured and cared for. If, however, there is abusive and controlling power, chaos and corruption, then it can be said that the Soul, and its value system, are being ignored. When we get to the chapter on the functions of the Soul, we will examine why there is so much disharmony in the world today.

Unlike the physical world where multitudes of different value systems exist, the spiritual realm of the Soul has one primary value system. The overarching value system of the Soul is contained within one word: Goodness. Goodness for the Soul is the value system by which it operates. Every subsystem in the spiritual realm is derived from this value system. The value system of the Soul is a mirror of the functions of the Soul. And the functions of the Soul are a mirror of the essence of the Soul. Slow down here and please don't get lost! Think of it this way:

Functions of the Soul = The value system of the Soul = The essence of Soul

They are all three one and the same! If you talk about Soul's functions, you are also talking about Soul's value system. And by doing this, you simultaneously are referring to Soul's essence. Each is inextricably intertwined.

*When the mind is examined, its activities cease automatically. Look for the source of mind. That source may be said to be God or Self or Consciousness.*
—Sri Ramana Maharshi

# XII. THE GOOD AND BAD

By now, it should begin to be apparent that the ego is "split" between thoughts, feelings and acts of goodness and thoughts, feelings and acts which deny pure goodness. The ego is split and cannot see, perceive, comprehend, appreciate or Be the Whole, the All, the Infinite One. When the ego is acting out of a state of superiority, it considers itself as more valuable and worthy than others and cannot perceive the wonderful and diverse rays of light emanating from the One Source, therefore, it considers only itself while denying, devaluing and dismissing others. The ego denigrates and eschews the rights of others so it, alone, the individual "I," can be supreme. This is what we refer to as selfish or self-absorbed or excessively self-involved. It is different from self-esteem which merely healthily looks upon itself as one, unique, but equal, ray within many rays of the One sun! The ego deceives itself into thinking the "I," the individual, can be alone and supreme without and above others. One may say that this is a state of ego believing that only itself deserves Goodness. Ego has no recognition, awareness or appreciation of the interrelatedness of everything on the entire planet, that every action creates an impact on others whether that is an animal or nature or another human being.

Fear of lack forces the ego to constantly hoard and compete for a position of superiority and for lone control and power. This ego consciousness refuses to allow others their own grandness for, in so doing, that would mean this ego would be forced to relinquish power and control and, instead, *share* power and control. In this exclusive state of mind, the ego is fed and kept alive by fear. Within the field of psychology, this is considered the apogee of the narcissist personality and statistically speaking, these personalities exist, by far, within the male population. Psychologists speak of these narcissistic personalities as pathologies or, said in another way, they are deviations from good mental health. When viewing most of the world leaders, we see narcissistic tendencies as these people compete and strive to be omnipotent, to have worldly power and use this power to maintain control over others. Collaboration, cooperation and sharing power is considered a threat to the survival of this ego inflation.

When the ego is acting out of a state of inferiority, it believes itself less worthy than others or unworthy altogether, therefore, it denies its worth and value, acts and submits to the rights and wishes of others and essentially sacrifices itself to others. We often refer to this as complete selflessness. One may say that this is a consciousness of low self-esteem whereby the self believes that only others are worthy of Goodness. Fear of believing in its own greatness and deserving of Goodness, this self gives itself away and allows others to have control and power over itself. In psychology, this is the hallmark of a borderline personality and, statistically speaking within the field of psychology, this tendency exists, by far, within the female population. This pathology is also considered a deviation from good mental health. You may think of narcissistic personality disorder on one end of the unhealthy continuum and borderline personality disorder on the opposite end of the continuum. Both are equally unhealthy and destructive with the focus of destructive behaviors for the narcissist being largely directed at others through narcissistic rage whereas the primary focus of destructive energy with borderlines is toward themselves as manifested in suicide attempts and cutting. As we consider the historical discrimination and wholesale degradation, abuse and dismissal of the female gender by the male gender, one may have a clearer picture of why females are typically borderlines and males are typically narcissists. Narcissists and borderlines are made, not born.

To explore this "split" thinking and its outcome on the human condition further, we can consider the duality of superiority and inferiority within the realm of race relations, religious differences, socioeconomic relations and also into the realm of sexual preferences. As has been stated before, it is this split thinking of "I versus other" with no conscious awareness of the universal principles which connect all of humanity that leads to all prejudice, discrimination, hate, violence, crime and war as those who seek to compete for power and control also seek to have dominion over the masses. The belief in the supremacy of the Aryan race has fostered centuries of hate and violence. The erroneous belief that only one religion contains all Truth has bred egregious tragedy in the form of hatred, wars and prejudice, all sadly under the distorted guise of an anthropomorphic God of "perfect love." We all seek love, but we fail to simply *Be* love. In our quest to find Truth, we fail to see that the path to Truth is to simply *Be* love. As one banner in my community reads, "There is no w*ay* to Peace; Peace *is* the way." Jesus the Christ attempted over and over to simply say "be love," but that message has been so diluted and the focus on his life has been so distorted, that humanity fails to realize that the answer to suffering lies within us all. It is the capacity to Be love that will save us. It is our vengeance of hate that will be our demise. One could say that we focus on the dogma and fail to understand the importance of the entire ecology of love. The ecological system of love is to simply *Be love*. For it is only in *Being* that we give and receive. To think of love and to feel love are part of *Being*. To *feel* love is one step away from reaching out to your neighbor and saying "let me help you." It is in the essence of *Being* that we find our next shift in human consciousness. This is the dawning of authentic and optimal psychological health.

Both the narcissistic and borderline ego states of mind of superiority and inferiority are unhealthy and may be considered the root "split" of the mind. They may also be thought of as the root "split" within the entire human race. Jesus the Christ had a simple message: "to love others as yourself." He did not say love yourself *more* or love yourself *less* than others. He said "love others *as* yourself." When we can begin to look upon others and concentrate on *Being love*, this will be a major shift toward collaboration and cooperation.

When couples can begin to look upon each other as equal partners who each bring unique gifts to the partnership and realize that it is only in helping the other person realize their potential that the partnership will grow and thrive, then marriages will last longer because we will enter into relationships at a higher maturational level. As long as one partner believes they are overall superior to the other, the marriage will not possess spiritual wealth and will, therefore, not experience an optimal state of happiness. Instead of each partner focusing on what the *other* partner lacks and deriding them for it, each partner must take responsibility for Self first. This responsibility means to look within and take responsibility for becoming a Full Self. This is what will bolster and strengthen the person and the partnership. Growth, not deficiency, becomes the focus of the dyad.

When various races begin focusing on what each race can do to help the other race instead of focusing on what the other race is lacking, then it is this very collaboration and cooperation that will enhance the mental and physical well being of each group. For it is only by helping other that self advances. When oppression and prejudice of another race is maintained, the dominating group will, sooner or later, either dissipate from hate or perish in war.

Humankind must relinquish its fear of lack and it must extinguish its subsequent virus of greed or the world will not survive. Those who are blessed with material wealth must seek ways to give back to those who are in need in order to create a balanced economic system. Unless this happens, the schism between the wealthy and the poor will only widen which will then ultimately result in the same revolt that has occurred time and time again when the few rich are obscenely more prosperous than the numerous poor. One need only look at the plethora of historical examples of revolutions to understand the necessity of sharing. We see these revolutions occur again and again yet we remain locked in the cycle of greed and oppression by the oppressors, then revolt by the suppressed and then the suppressed take power and become the oppressors.

You cannot expect to feed the Soul, a nonphysical energy, with matter. Thus, buying a fur coat, diamond ring, expensive automobile and palatial residence is not, and never will be, food for the Soul. It is *the value and meaning we place on* physical things and whether we obey spiritual laws in relation to material possessions that determine our Soulfulness. In other words, it is our *mind*, not the material thing which is either good or bad. For example, there is nothing inherently wrong with owning a diamond ring. After all, a diamond ring is only as good or as bad as we choose to define it. The diamond ring means nothing unless we put meaning behind it. The meaning of a diamond ring is potentially beauty and comfort. That is the meaning we have elected to give the possession. What our hearts possess defines who we are. Let's take a simple kitchen knife as another example. To those of us who use knives on a daily basis to cut our food, a knife is a wonderful, indispensable tool which conveys the meaning of convenience and utility. However, for the person who was stabbed by a criminal, a knife is surely to be perceived in an entirely different light. We choose every day what meaning we give things and we have the power every day to change that meaning. With our minds and hearts, we create meaning. And we create the world around us.

Many people have been erroneously taught that money is the root of all evil. While it certainly seems to attract quite a bit of criminal activity and negative emotions such as greed, envy and jealousy, money is neither inherently good nor evil. For a moment, imagine that the article for world bartering was salt, not money. Quickly, money becomes meaningless and all the value is placed on salt. Then, people with an abundance of salt would be envied. Those who did not have salt would be valued less than those who had much salt. It is all where our minds place value which determines whether we live in heaven or whether we create hell on earth. Abundance is an outcome of nurturing the Great Soul since Soul loves and honors the universal principles of all Souls. When we place our highest value on truth, love, joy, kindness, and fruits of the Spirit, and our secondary value on material things, we will manifest peace on the physical level. If, however, we place our highest value on material things to the exclusion of the fruits of the Spirit, we will continue to have violence and unrest as a human species. Money is not the root of all evil, rather it *is the value we place on money* and *how we elect to use it* that gives it power whether good or bad.

If money is used as a means by which a person is able to bring Goodness to herself and/or others, then there is care for her Soul and another's Soul. Money, in and of itself, the cold, hard form in your hands, is neither good nor bad. Its value, good or bad, is determined solely by the person in whose hands it lies and the use it is given. The person has the choice of using money for Goodness which means sharing, embracing and unifying. Or the person can choose to use money for ego so as to exclude, separate and hoard. Money is neither evil nor spiritual. People's minds and hearts are. A thousand dollar bill has no inherent qualities of Goodness or evil, but the person whose hand it is in will have the power to use that money for good or for evil. It is always the *way in which money is valued and how it is used* that establishes its Goodness or lack of Goodness. All power lies within you.

A person can have lots of money and use it for good or for evil purposes. Certainly, Americans have selected capitalism, an economic system which promotes inequality of wealth. However, even in communist countries, the system is intended to spread wealth, but the actual outcome remains much like capitalism where only a few possess wealth. To be sure, people in democracies which espouse capitalism have more opportunity than do those in communist countries. But systems are as good or as evil as the people who lead them. Surely this is an indication that it is not systems, rather it is ultimately people who are in them, which create social ills.

Another well known and important arena where money can be used for Good or evil is in the world of politics. The politician has two choices: to use that political position to further Highest Good of the whole or to use that position to primarily advance self-interests and only secondarily benefit others. A political position is neither good nor bad, *per se*. Rather, it is *the person* in the job that is either promoting Goodness or not. So it is a combination of the politician, his values and his priorities which establish whether the entire political system is good or bad.

Some people obtain more wealth than others; some by honest means, others by dishonest means. If money is obtained through spurious or nefarious means, that person has violated a spiritual law and she/he will either have to balance that spiritual debt or some reciprocal effect will result to themselves. If money is obtained by honest means such as through honest, hard work or through an inheritance, the person has a choice to use that money toward continued good purposes or to use it for evil purposes. Generally speaking, when wealth is obtained, the spiritual law of giving comes into play. In order to retain wealth, one must give something of that blessing back to those in need. It may be in the form of creating an organization which helps battered women, donating to a charity that helps orphaned or disabled children or volunteering at Habitat for Humanity. The person who has wealth must be guided by their Great Soul in terms of how and what proportion can be used to give back as a means of gratitude.

The Soul knows that as you help others, you will be helped. There are many kind, giving wealthy people who do help others, just as there are many unkind, selfish wealthy people who do not help others. It has been said that Rose Kennedy, the mother of John F. Kennedy, had a mantra. It goes something like this: "To those who are given much, much is expected." This reminds me of the spiritual law of giving and having. When we help others who are less fortunate than ourselves, no matter what our economic status may be, we are obeying a divine law. If, however, as a society, we refuse to assist those less fortunate even though we are capable of helping, we fall prey to violating divine laws by which the Soul is governed. The cumulative result over generations is what we see around us today which is a growing population of poor and homeless people and people who are led to a life of crime and violence. Also as a result is the abuse and neglect of the ecological environment which is now resulting in the global warming. If continued, this growth will lead to the destruction of the human species for, as was mentioned earlier, a house divided cannot stand.

It is only through giving up or transforming the ego and assuming the qualities of the Full Self that the human race will experience greater levels of peace on earth. This will require, first and foremost, substantial cooperation between both genders since the split between masculine and feminine is the most essential split in the Psyche or Soul today. Second, it will require people of all races, ethnicities, colors, ages, religions, political affiliations and socioeconomic levels to shift the consciousness to a level of activating the Will toward Goodness for the whole while still honoring and maintaining a sense of individuality. The litmus test is to determine if one's individual needs impede or infringe upon the well being of another.

Some simple, everyday examples of balancing individual needs with group needs are as follows. One example is the person who bangs a set of drums in his garage with the door wide open creating noise that can be heard several houses away. The person banging on the drums is infringing upon others' right to peace and quiet and is not operating from a sense of Goodwill toward others. He only cares about himself. If that same person played the drums in his house, then no one in the neighborhood can hear it, therefore, the person is not infringing upon his neighbor's peace and quiet, yet his needs are being met. Another example would be the African American who dresses in the cultural attire of native Africa. The litmus test is to ask who is being impeded in their right and in what way is this hampering neighbors or society? What is the African American actually doing that is detrimental to others? If the only response from others is that the native cultural dress does not conform to others likes, then one cannot say that the African American is impeding upon others' rights or that society is being hampered. The African American is simply using the attire as a means of individual self-expression which in no way harms others. Indeed, it would be those individuals who harass or ostracize the African American for dressing in native attire that would be those who are infringing upon the right of the African American. A last example would be a Buddhist who moves into a neighborhood of predominately Christian people. Do the thoughts or actions of the Buddhist impede upon the rights of the Christians or hamper or endanger the Christians? Not merely by the Buddhists' beliefs. The actions of the Buddhist are what determine the answer to the question. If the Buddhist has a way of Being which demonstrates kindness, compassion and tolerance, then what about the Buddhist should be criticized or judged harshly?

These are rather simple examples, but they open our eyes to what our focus usually is when we decide to impose harsh judgments on others and ostracize them for being different. The ego loves to focus on difference and what separates us instead of perceiving difference as a beautiful tapestry of One Whole Humanity. By doing so, the ego survives and is assured center stage. If, however, the human race begins to identify with each other based upon what unites us and makes us whole, in other words, universal principles, then the ego begins to transform into the Soul consciousness.

The ego (self) has both masculine and feminine energies just as the Soul (Higher Self) does, however, the ego seeks to separate and divide these energies between the genders. Remember, that the ego's entire existence is predicated on dividing, separating, splitting and disconnecting. Division is necessary in a physical world because there are single units and individuals at the relative level of existence, so it is important to point out that division must still exist to some degree. However, division has so dominated the human consciousness, with no regard or value for the Whole, that we must now embrace a broader perspective of the individual "many" within the interconnected Whole of humanity. Let us not lose sight that both the mature masculine and the mature feminine are ubiquitous and essential to our existence. The entire ethos of this book is not intended to advocate for a reversal of what currently exists, rather it is to expose the pernicious effects throughout history of the severe bias toward the masculine energy which has caused the sacred feminine to be in peril. This has been the root core cause of human suffering.

The ego is the voice in the crowd that says "It can't be done". The Soul is the voice in the crowd that says "Humankind can do anything it wants. Humankind has endless possibilities as long as we direct our Will toward Goodness." The ego knows that by saying "It cannot be done," that truly it will not be done. This maintains the split and the divisiveness and ensures the continued survival of the ego since the ego survives because of divisiveness. The ego said "We can never fly." The Soul said "Yes, we can." And so we now fly. The ego said "We can never land on the moon." The Soul said "Yes, we can go to the moon." And so we now have the experience of being on the moon. The ego says "Utopia will never exist." The Soul knows that only the ego prevents it.

How the masculine and feminine energies are directed and activated is one determining factor in what is manifested in the physical world. The masculine energies of knowledge and creativity are active and they seek movement. We speak of them as being in motion. Their primary focus is on the parts. While knowledge and creativity themselves are energies that do not change, the energies do *generate change* at the physical level. One could say that, in the spiritual realm, these energies are changeless, but on the physical level, these energies are responsible for change. In the spiritual realm, knowledge and creativity are known to be part of the Great Self, not separate from it. To *have* knowledge and creativity are to *be* knowledge and creativity. In the world of ego, the lower ego self forgets and separates from its authentic essence of Being, therefore, the ego begins to think of itself as being separate and distinct from knowledge and creativity. The ego begins to think of itself as merely a body composed of earthly matter. This is its primary identity and only secondarily does the ego think of itself as a knowing and creating Being. To the ego, matter and all things seen are lord and governor.

The feminine energies of love and wisdom are resting energies or what has been referred to as passive. Passive, however, is a word that has come to have a negative connotation as though it means lazy. Passive is not lazy in the spiritual realm rather it is a state of peaceful, blissful contemplation. Love and wisdom seek to be at rest and immobile. Their primary focus is to unite, bring together and make Whole. Like knowledge and creativity, both love and wisdom are immutable in and of themselves. All four energic expressions are what animate the physical body. Without these four energies, the body would not exist nor would any other thing visible to the eye. These four energies are lord and governor; matter is their subject.

The first challenge of humanity at this time is to comprehend that both males and females have these energies within their Soul. These are *energies*, not anatomical body parts, thus these energies permeate the entire human kingdom regardless of a person's gender, race, ethnicity, color, religion, socioeconomic status, etc. What has occurred in the evolution of the human species is that men, on the physical level, have dominated because of their sheer physical superiority and ability to protect those who are in weaker physical positions. This physical dominance has further translated into a myth of male superiority. Because of men's physical dominance, they evolved to be the primary gender which sought knowledge and sought to create outside the domestic sphere. These are both highly active roles in human society and literally involve creating and leading the human species toward external greatness. Females being physically weaker were forced to succumb to those roles which did not involve building and creating the society at large, namely, she was relegated to domesticated roles of homemaker, parent, wife or caretaker roles such as nurse or secretary. As a result of this energic manifestation, males developed a dominant tendency to know and to create while their recessive tendency has been love and wisdom within the interpersonal sphere. Seeking knowledge and displaying creativity have had throughout history an individualistic quality to them, so it is not surprising that the spirit of competitiveness arose on a physical level from these two energies. It is an expansive energy and one could say this is the spirit of the individual. To know and to create can also be thought of as goal energies while feminine energies are predominately process energies. It is masculine to focus primarily on goal, secondarily on process. It is feminine to focus predominately on process first, secondarily on the goal. This should not be misunderstood to mean that men do not consider process and females never consider goals. Rather, the subtle difference in the *focus of the energy* is what should be underscored. For example, in a group of men and women, men are far more likely to initially think in terms of goals and a vision to arrive at these goals and only secondarily as to how those goals will be achieved. Then it is common for males to compete for the leadership position. Females, on the other hand, have a stronger tendency toward collaborating with the team in order to determine what tools, resources, methodologies are necessary to achieve the goal. It is not that men are unconcerned with the process nor is it that females are indifferent to the vision. But the energy and focus tend to vary somewhat between females and males. Hopefully, by the end of this book, we will see how much choice we have in developing these energies between genders and what our next step in the evolutionary ladder will be.

Due to the evolutionary process, females' dominant energies have been to love and to be wise while their recessive energies have been to know and to create the world at large. It is important not to misinterpret this to mean that no females have ever had masculine energies to know and to create because we certainly can cite known examples such as Madame Curie, Amelia Earhardt, and Helen Keller. But in viewing things at the broadest level historically, we must concede that the bulk of those who have led the world in politics, business, science, education, religion and society have to date, unquestionably, been men. For purposes of looking at humankind at a macro level, it is critical that we initially take a landscape picture instead of getting lost in the microcosmic aspects of evolution. Females' dominant energies have always been to love and to be wise which manifests as a nurturing, collaborative, sharing and empowering role. One could say it is the spirit of inclusiveness or the inclination toward forming a group of shared power. What better example is the historical fact that women have literally sacrificed themselves (their sense of self, career, independence, financial freedom) in order to maintain harmony with the husband and to ensure the needs of the whole family are met?

While much of this book will reflect upon and discuss the proliferation and domination of the shadow, immature masculine energies and the simultaneous absence of both the mature masculine and mature feminine energies, it is important to first acknowledge the tremendous advances that humankind has experienced due to the manifestations of the masculine ego.

First, virtually every discovery on this planet has been made by man and essentially all major thought in every academic field has been advanced by men. It is certainly not my intention to ignore and dismiss females who have made contributions to the world because they do exist. Indeed, throughout this book it is my intention to cogently and passionately argue that it is because of the historical imbalance of the mature feminine and masculine energies within the individual and between the genders, humankind's unwillingness to recognize the inherent equal worth and value of each of these energies, and humanity's unwillingness to integrate both of these mature energies *within each gender,* that is, in large part, responsible for psychological imbalances. We begin to see that it is not a foreign entity, but ourselves and our belief systems, which are responsible for the suffering we endure. However, before we move forward, it is first important to recognize what the ego consciousness has given us to date.

The dominance of the masculine energies has given us the focus on the individual and the subsequent knowledge and creativity necessary to imbue this individualistic spirit into the Psyche. The sheer numbers alone are a testimony to the debt we owe to great men of history for their desire to know and to create a better world. Socrates, Plato, Aristotle, Pythagoras, Confucius, Lao Tzu, Jesus the Christ, Moses, St. Augustine, St. Thomas Aquinas, Siddhartha Gautama (the Buddha), Mohammed, Martin Luther King, W. M. Du Bois, Booker T. Washington, Galileo, Newton, Beethoven, Mozart, Tchaikovsky, da Vinci, Michelangelo, the Wright brothers, Ford, Edison, Einstein, Heisenberg, Bohr and Hawking are just a handful of thousands of famous men who have made our lives better for having made their discoveries or having posited their theories. We owe the bulk of the existence of cars, airplanes, architecture, governments, laws, music, sculpture, paintings, medical cures, electricity, telescopes, literature, math and personal computers to male leaders within their fields of expertise. Yes, there were women who contributed, but mostly men have dominated in discoveries and theory. There are also countless others whose identities we will likely never know simply because these people were ahead of their time and their ideas and discoveries fell upon the ears of the narrow-minded or the jealous. Minimally, we can say that these thousands of men have garnered knowledge in order to create something that is useful and valuable to the world. Through these discoveries, inventions and ideologies, humankind has advanced and evolved from a primitive, uncivilized and lawless condition to our current civilized and cultured state.

We can say that men have dominated in knowledge and creativity of world affairs. What we cannot definitively know is, had females been given equal respect and equal opportunity to pursue any field of endeavor as men have been given and this had been given since antiquity, how would the history of the world be written? What would women's contribution to discoveries and inventions be? To what extent would females have developed the intellectual curiosity, energy and aptitude to know, to create and to lead in building world? Would females and males working side by side in a collaborative milieu and equally sharing power have resulted in females assuming more masculine energies and males developing more feminine energies? If the psychological development of little boys had included integrating the feminine energies of love, kindness and compassion, would the world be different today? Would the *human condition* be different? If females and males had been sharing power for millennia, would humankind have waged fewer wars? Would Hitler have ever risen to power? Would the percentage of murders and rapes be as high? Would there be such pervasive corruption at executive levels in Corporate America? Would politics have become as corrupt as the general population believes it to be?

While it is pure speculation to assume how the past would be different, these are compelling questions. What we can definitively say today is that our current level of human functioning has not brought us a warless society, nor has it resulted in any decrease in social ills or any appreciable movement toward optimal mental and physical health. Why is this so? I believe it is largely due to the masculine shadow energies of deceit and destruction which have counteracted and overshadowed the mature masculine energies of gaining knowledge and utilizing creativity as the means to activate the societal Will toward Goodness. These same leaders dismiss and ignore the restorative and generative power of the mature feminine energies of love and spiritual wisdom; therefore, these energies do not surface to any substantial degree in global leadership. The societal Will toward Goodness of balancing the individual with the whole is lost and waiting to be uncovered and rediscovered. Females are placed in a subordinate role and are denied leadership positions so that the immature masculine ego can maintain power and control. Even within most religions, the male holds tightly the reins of power and control. History has shown that only when the subordinate groups gather to form a powerful mass does the dominant group take notice and even begin to consider adjusting rules, customs and overall culture. Usually the dominant group will attempt to appease the subordinate group in such a way that the latter are temporarily satisfied, yet they gain no equal status and, thus, no real power is relinquished by the dominant group. The outcome, no matter how much time goes by, is eventually: 1) revolt by the growing minority and forced acceptance by the majority or 2) acquiescence and willing acceptance by the dominant group because of a perceived inevitable threat to, or erosion of, their power.

Females are not the only example to highlight. Minorities, the gay community and disabled persons currently seek to obtain equal status and rights within the larger dominant groups. Both the immature masculine *and* feminine shadow energies are expressed as men *and* women focus on racial lines, sexual preferences and disability status. A far more personal and visceral hatred manifests in these instances as opposed to the largely cold, impersonal masculine shadow energies of corruption and deceit. Males have traditionally begun wars and competed for omnipotent control and power because of an impersonal narcissistic need to assume and maintain the superior position of power. It is not uncommon to bury greed for personal power and wealth underneath the excuse of some religious or economic justification, but the core truth is still there. By and large, masculine narcissism wishes to be perceived as the sole leader in power. To be sure, it was a time of biological preservation as primitive man faced the very real daily danger of being eaten by, or pummeled by, beasts of prey in the animal kingdom. During this period, aggression was an instinctual survival method and, without it, it is hardly arguable to say that the human species would not have survived to enjoy the relative state of "civilization" that we live in today. But those days of competing against a dangerous "other" ended, for the most part, centuries ago. Yet men still retain this aggressive nature. With rampant male violence and aggression in a so-called "civilized" society, what will it take for man to curb his desire to hoard wealth and kill people? In my estimation, the immature masculine has to be transformed; the masculine has to mature. Men must grow up and take responsibility. The human species depends upon it.

The masculine energy is predominantly individualistic and the immature masculine ego tends to be perceived as rational, cold and impersonal to others. It is cold and impersonal because the heart (love) is devalued and denigrated. Generally speaking, the feminine energy is about relationships and the shadow feminine energy of jealousy is a rather personal, passionate, irrational hatred.

Expressed simplistically, the immature masculine energy will overlook the group's needs, or destroy a group if it must do so, in order to be dominant and in control of others. The immature masculine ego perceives love as irrelevant to the goal of obtaining and maintaining supremacy. Indeed, the immature masculine consciousness is highly psychologically threatened by love since love, by its very nature, establishes a unifying, subjective equality between the subject and the other. This equality is, of course, antithetical to the entire ethos of the immature masculine ego which can only survive if it remains superior to other. Therefore, the immature masculine is indifferent to, if not threatened by, love and, indeed, would rather obtain power and control through fear since fear separates and divides, thereby ensuring the immature masculine energy remains omnipotent. The immature masculine ego is perceived as cold and impersonal because it has no heart since it is only through the denigration and devaluing of the heart (the feminine and love) that it can deceive the other into thinking that it is lord and governor. It does not easily and naturally seek love because love is a threat to the supremacy of the immature masculine ego. The immature masculine ego eschews and sacrifices love whenever it threatens its primary goal of supreme power and control. It can do this only through deceiving the world into thinking that intellectual knowledge is supreme whereas love, kindness and compassion (the sacred feminine) is unnecessary in world affairs.

Masculine energy is individualistic. Ensuring the he always has more knowledge than "other" and deluding himself into thinking that worldly knowledge is authentic power, the immature masculine ego hoards worldly knowledge so he can hoard resources and power and, in turn, he can be in control of what is created in the world. Power, control and omnipotence through hoarding knowledge and through creativity are his psychological sustenance; he cares not whether he is loved. He deludes himself, the individual, into believing he is a god and deifies himself through the denigration of one group and the control of another group. The group is never perceived as equal to himself, the individual. The group is only there to serve the needs of this narcissistic king. Lacking authentic love, he is callous and indifferent about being loved by "other" except to the extent that he receives adequate praise and mirroring so he can love his false superiority more. His so-called "love" of his partner is, in truth, a shallow means whereby he loves himself more and more in her nearness. It is shallow because he does not love, honor and respect the feminine, rather he only subconsciously uses her love so he can love himself more and more. His cold, impersonal power is used to maintain his sense of control, power and omnipotence, his inflated sense of superior "I" versus the inferior "other." His sense of self and personhood is sustained through abundant worldly knowledge and through the control and power of creating material wealth. Hitler exemplifies the archetype of this dark shadow energy although there is an abundance of male corporate executives, male politicians, male scientists, male medical doctors, male academicians and male judges with a similar narcissistic psychological construct. The consciousness of the immature masculine ego has ensured that love (the feminine energy) is exiled from business, science, Western medicine, academia and law because if love were to enter these arenas, the immature masculine ego would no longer be the omnipotent leader in the world.

It is this psychological construct which poses the most substantial threat to the human species and to the ecological equilibrium on the planet. If this rampant narcissism fails to mature into a fuller, androgynous consciousness, the human species is in jeopardy. The difference between males in leadership today and Hitler is that Hitler sought to destroy Soul *and* body; the males in leadership today, for the most part, don't physically kill people, but they are definitely destroying the potential for the unfoldment of Soul consciousness.

Jung, in *Aspects of the Feminine*, speaks of the feminine energy having a more personal flavor than the masculine energy. I am in agreement with this because, unlike the immature masculine, the immature feminine energy seeks love (which is highly personal), not power and control (which are highly impersonal). The immature feminine energy will typically focus on the "other" individual and seek to possess what the other has so she can finally be loved. This dark energy hates and envies the "other" individual who embodies love. This is what the immature feminine energy wants; she wants to be loved by "other." Sadly, the immature feminine energy falsely believes that she can be loved through hatred and jealousy. If the immature feminine energy can only possess what the "other" has, she can garner love of "other" and finally love herself. She deludes herself into thinking that, through the adoration of the "other," she can finally love herself. Love and adoration of "other," not control or power, is her psychological focus and sustenance. Thus, the love and adoration of other is psychologically vital for her discovery of her sense of self, her personhood. She equates personhood and sense of self with love from "other." The Queen in *Snow White*, the Wicked Stepmother in *Cinderella* and the Wicked Witch in *The Wizard of Oz* stand as psychological archetypes of this dark, shadow energy although there are many borderline females who match this archetype as well.

Again, it is crucial that these generalizations be understood as energies, not as biology. Men, who are flooded with feminine energy, can exhibit the dark, shadow feminine energy; women who are flooded with masculine consciousness can exhibit the dark, shadow masculine energy. The elucidation of the shadow feminine and masculine energies is intended as a guidepost to understanding the underpinnings of the bifurcated Psyche, along with how and where it has manifested as a consciousness in the collective consciousness of the world today. These are opposing, yet complementary, energies.

Hopefully, we arrive at a picture of two energies which have given us both the best and the worst that humankind has been—and is—today. We also come dangerously close to arriving at the conclusion that these oppositional energies have little chance for reconciliation. In fact, many people who have much to lose in terms of power, control and status and many people who simply are not informed have arrived at that conclusion. I am reminded of a local preacher who authored a book on solitude who stated at his book signing: "Men are men, women are women and human nature simply cannot change." With this type of mythical patriarchal belief system, the feminine and the masculine will, for sure, remain unreconciled. We can hold onto this type of archaic patriarchal myth and fail to move forward or humankind can change its belief system and change itself. This is the awesome power of Psyche.

Human nature *can* change and *has* changed. We change when our belief systems change and when we mature psychologically. Over the last two decades, great strides have been made as females have assumed more traditionally "masculine" roles in American society and in some parts of Europe. As males allow females more opportunities, more females enter the fields of law, math and science. These societies have also seen greater numbers of men become more comfortable integrating and reflecting "feminine" emotions of love, kindness and compassion. If we compare our society of today with society five hundred years ago, we open our eyes to the fact that human nature can and does change *when our belief system changes*. We are, ultimately, in charge of our own evolution as we create a belief system, incorporate it into our environment, respond to the environment and then further evolve our belief system. To a large degree, over time, we become what we wish to become. It is unknown at this time what role genetics would assume were collective humanity to achieve the next level of Soul consciousness where society exudes a Group consciousness and utilizes the Will toward Goodness for Self and others and the environment. Recognizing that every act and intention has a ripple effect even down to our very cells of our bodies, were humankind to begin to respect the role our bodies and our natural environment play in sustaining our health, one wonders what the mental and physical state of humanity would become.

Suffice it to say as we begin to use the unlimited powers of imagination to create a different world, we can see both the long-term and short-term Good which is created, yet we also recognize the short-term birth pains that many would experience. Were society to begin looking through the lens of the Soul, the individual-within-the-group becomes the mode of living. The lone voice of the ego is at peril. Those who operate largely through the limited ego consciousness would be threatened since their very power and control would be threatened. Men would no longer hold virtually every leadership position, rather females would share power with them. Men would no longer garner and possess all world wealth; females would share world wealth. Men would not hold 97% of leadership positions throughout the world; females would provide balance in these leadership positions. Women would no longer be primary caretakers of children; men would share equally in that critical role. Additionally, there would be a sharing of power between females and men, minorities and nonminorities, heterosexuals and homosexuals, disabled persons and nondisabled persons. The yardstick by which leadership positions were obtained and by which they would be sustained would be the ability of the individual to maintain individuality, yet motivate and activate group Will toward Goodness for the group and, ultimately, for the greater Good. The uniqueness of the individual ego must not be lost entirely, yet the power of the group consciousness must become the focus. And its devotion must become the Greater Good for the Whole.

The greatest responsibility and debt is carried by men who are in current leadership positions and in those men who aspire for those roles tomorrow. For as females, minorities, homosexuals and disabled persons begin to combine their mental focus, mount their mutual offenses, and collaborate toward a common goal of sharing power, it is inevitable that the face of the world will change and the consciousness of humankind will evolve. No greater time than now has existed for humankind to re-evaluate its prejudices, judgments and ideologies and to shift the narrow consciousness of the ego toward a broader, more inclusive and empowering view of the Soul.

Men who are our current leaders can make this shift in consciousness. Indeed, they must. The masculine ego shadow drive for dominance, power and control over others must be transformed. Leadership in the 21st century must include the feminine aspects of the Soul.

Every evolutionary step forward carries with it both the excitement of a higher level of existence and the simultaneous anxiety of how that step forward is implemented. It is inevitable that human evolution will proceed. It is only a matter of how long we prolong it and in what manner it proceeds. Either way—slow or fast, chaotic or smooth—we decide.

*There are those who imagine God to be like a man, composed of a body and soul and subject to passions; but it is clear...how far off men who believe this are from the true knowledge of God...For all men who have looked into the divine nature deny that God is corporeal. That He cannot be so they conclusively prove by showing that by "body" we understand a certain quantity possessing length, breadth and depth, limited by some fixed form; and that to attribute these to God, a being absolutely infinite, is the greatest absurdity.*
—Baruch Spinoza

*If you want to eliminate the suffering in the world, then eliminate all that is dark and negative in yourself. Truly, the greatest gift you have to give is that of your own self-transformation.*
—Lao Tzu

# XIII. THE SOUL AS SECOND PRINCIPLE

Spirit is the First Principle, Soul is the Second Principle and Matter is the Third Principle. Spirit is the Alpha and Omega, the *arche*. *Arche* means original principle, beginning or ruling element. Spirit is Pure Light and is experienced as the consciousness of Pure Knowing, Self-illumination, Self-revelation, *nirguna* Brahman, the Ineffable One, God, Highest Being, Nirvana or Heaven. At the lowest level of consciousness, matter involves a conscious splitting and separation of thinking, feeling and doing. It is at this level that Aristotelian logic, reason and intellect make sense of the world. At the next highest level of consciousness, the unfolding of the Soul consciousness is the merging of *thinking* and *feeling* and *doing* into *Being*. It is at this level that Hericlitian or paradoxical logic and intuition manifest as the ways of knowing while intellect alone is inadequate and insufficient to comprehend the nature and fullness of Being. Any psychological, philosophical, scientific or theological system of thought which attempts to define and comprehend Soul or Being or the Full Self with *pure reason or intellect alone* is a cognitive schema using Aristotelian logic which, as I have repeatedly stated, is a lower level of logic and, thus, is irrelevant in describing and comprehending higher levels of consciousness.

All "doing" at the Soul or Being level is essentially creating and loving or, said another way, is essentially creating through a loving consciousness. At this Soul Being level, all power manifests from the activation of the Will toward Goodness. At the highest level of consciousness, Spirit is the further merging of Being (Soul consciousness) and knowing into Pure Knowing.

For purposes of this book, we investigate and discover the Second Principle: the Great Soul. We must begin to develop an understanding and a deep knowing that the Soul is an experience, a subjective experience, not a body or a physical entity to be measured and quantified. God is Being, not "a" Being. Many people confuse the Soul with a physical body. This is called anthropomorphizing the Soul which means it is the tendency to think of something that is not a physical body and transfer and project anatomical and human characteristics onto it. Many people anthropomorphize God by thinking of God as a person with arms and legs and envisioning a man with a white beard. For centuries, this has been the archetypal image of God which people of many Western religions carry in their minds. God is Spirit, the Spirit of a consciousness of Love, therefore, Spirit does not have arms, legs and a beard, nor does Spirit have a skin color. The image of God would not be a physical person, rather it would be the invisible, loving consciousness of the All within the person. Spirit actually is a force, an energy, a Will of universal totality of creativity, knowledge, love and wisdom within and around everything that exists, but many people still project anthropomorphic characteristics upon an invisible élan vital which is responsible for everything.

The Soul, as Second Principle, should be thought of as a consciousness of "Being." The Soul is the eternal, ontological, divine energy which results from the Willful conscious merging of both thinking and feeling toward a spiritual Goodness. Remember that spiritual Goodness is spiritual fruits of love, creativity, kindness, joy, truth, wisdom, honor, etc. Jesus the Christ

196

understood clearly the ability to carry the Soul consciousness and was ultimately crucified for imbuing that consciousness. He was both God and man because he carried the spiritual fruits within him and he was a Being whose consciousness used his Will toward Goodness for All. Socrates understood the experience of Beingness and spoke of it frequently when he referred to the greater Good and humankind's capacity to focus on that. In fact, he essentially was sentenced to death for exemplifying it and for attempting to teach it to his students since the state of Soul consciousness carries with it overwhelming practical implications for dramatic overhauls and transformations in the world. For that, Socrates was forced to drink the hemlock. It would be left to Plato, Socrates' student, to serve as the genius who would conceptualize for the world the two human states of consciousness: the Beingness, or Being consciousness, of the Soul and the non-Beingness, or not-Being consciousness, of the ego. Plotinus, the father of Neo-platonic philosophy and a lover of Platonic philosophy, expounded greatly on the nature, function and dynamic of Being.

In the psychological world, ontology refers to a person whose awareness of self is beyond ego or beyond self in the sense that ego is no longer split between feminine/masculine and Self/Other. Being is a kind of merged affect/cognition/will. It is a sense of *Being* as opposed to simply *doing*. People merely going through the motions of religious rituals are simply doing and may not be feeling or thinking in a holy (whole-y) manner at all. This is why religious rituals, in and of themselves, mean little if not done with holy reverence for the All. You can perform religious rituals and be obsessed with performing these rituals every day of your life and yet be devoid of a consciousness of love toward the All. This persona's consciousness can be referred to as the pious indignation of a religious zealot. They do everything externally that is according to biblical "law", but they are spiritually bankrupt because they use their religion to divide and separate themselves from others. This is where religion is more important than God, a consciousness of love toward the All. Conversely, you can be filled with a consciousness of love for the All and never perform a single fundamental religious ritual in your life. This can be considered authentic spirituality.

If you feel joy while walking through a scenic part of nature, you are "Being" joyous. Your sense of Being is about joy, not about the separate aspects of actually walking, listening and perhaps talking with your friend. In this sense, the Soul is about *Being* which is a merging phenomenology of both thinking and feeling Goodness. Close your eyes and begin thinking about something that brings you great joy. It could be the rapture you feel listening to your favorite classical music; the peaceful serenity you imbue while walking through a pasture and smelling the fresh, clean scent of honeysuckle; gazing adoringly upon Botticelli's famous painting, the *Annunciacion;* or the ecstasy you feel while making love with your beloved. While you imagine these, it's important to close your eyes, since the Soul does not speak in the same language that the ego does, rather the Soul has a silent voice—the voice of symbols and the voice of Beingness. Once you close your eyes, begin to feel throughout your entire Being what that feels like to experience those inner thoughts and feelings. What happens is that your thoughts of Goodness and your feelings of Goodness merge together so that they are indistinguishable from one another. Stated more specifically and accurately and with more in-depth meditation, there is an awareness of the "place" or "state" *behind* and *beyond* thoughts and feelings which is a state of merged silent, infinite consciousness and bliss and these two cannot be separated ontologically. This state is a higher consciousness than intellect because at the intellectual level, the knower (subject) becomes split from the known (object) and means (will) such that knowledge, creativity, love and wisdom are "thought" rather than ontologically merged as in the state of Soul Consciousness. To carry and sustain this ontological state of consciousness is what it means to imbue the Soul consciousness. It is a true state of Being. These are the "true Beings" to which Plotinus referred because they are an actual content of subjective/objective experience where knower and known and means of knowing become one. In this state of true Being, neither thought (consciousness) nor feeling (bliss) are separate or distinct or unequal from an ontological perspective. A sense or perception of Oneness emerges. In fact, the tri-fold beingness, consciousness and blissfulness of this "state" is referred to by Advaitans as *saccidananda* and is the nature of *saguna* Brahman or the realm of Ultimate Reality with attributes. In meditative states, this is the consciousness that is sought. When you are conscious of that sense of "Being," that is the world of the Soul. You may feel it throughout your body like an adrenalin rush or you may experience it as outside of your body. Abraham Maslow referred to these Being states as "peak experiences" and I am confident he understood clearly why people who have had them seek that experience again and again. This is the state that all humankind seeks and, indeed, what yogis experience in intense meditative states. It is during sexual climax that a merged sense of Being is experienced. It is this Being experience that is the unconscious focus of using illegal drugs and of alcohol consumption. The Being experience is mimicked while experiencing the "high" of various illegal drugs such as cocaine, LSD and heroine and also when inebriated and intoxicated due to alcohol consumption. Those who use illegal drugs and abuse alcohol are unaware that their addiction is a kind of adrenalin rush to seek divine Being. Their unconscious goal is to have a merging experience with the Divine Soul. Uninformed as to what authentic Being is and how to manifest that Being consciousness in their lives through healthy, natural means, the ego turns to drugs and alcohol as a way to seek the merging experience. The tragic outcome is that millions of people have become addicted to an unnatural, temporary experience and, further, that millions of dollars on healthcare are spent combating these addictions. As a result, most nonusers feel unsympathetic toward people with drug and alcohol addictions and the harsh, critical judgments toward people with addictions does nothing but reinforce the addiction.

Let's go back to the world of ego. If you recall, it's the consciousness of separateness. It's the world of feeling, but not thinking *about* feeling. And it's the world of doing, but not giving great *thought* to doing. And, most of all, *it's not connecting thinking, feeling and doing into a cohesive Will toward Goodness which results in Being.* The ego just goes through the motions, so to speak. This means the Soul is in retreat. Concentrating your focus, attention and intention purely on the surface of physical things alone will prevent you from experiencing the "Beingness" of Soul consciousness. The retreat of the Soul also occurs when the negative emotions of the ego manifest such as when you are fearful, angry, jealous, envious, guilty, shameful, greedy or hateful. The Soul never leaves you, but you may think of it as receding behind the veil of the ego. Thus, the Soul is best thought of as *an experience of Being conscious Goodness* while the ego is understood as a being of *acting or doing in a state of unawareness.* The ego experiences the thinking and feeling processes as separate and distinct because that is what the ego does: it separates and divides. The primary emphasis with the Soul is always on Being; the primary emphasis for the ego is to just think *or* to just feel *or* to just do or act. The Soul is, for the most part, consciously choosing Goodness because it perceives the Whole, the All. Its consciousness is, therefore, expanded. By consciously choosing this path, it is in a state of Being. The ego, for the most part, moves through the world doing discrete and separate acts without connecting thoughts or feelings to them, nor does it ponder and contemplate thoughts or think about feelings. One could say the ego largely acts and does in an unconscious manner. By the very fact that the ego is "disconnected" from Soul, the ego also remains disconnected from the natural kingdom within which it moves. The ego does not consider the plant and animal kingdom as a conscious and integral part of the ongoing evolution of the human kingdom. The sacred interrelationship is unrecognized. Animals are killed for sport and plants are denied their intrinsic value as nutrient and medicinal. Overall today, humankind holds little honor and respect for these two kingdoms, therefore, portions of both, and ultimately all, become at risk for endangerment. Here again, the ego sees the world as split and dichotomous, thus, harmony remains a distant horizon.

The "splitness of the ego" either thinks or feels or does, but cannot integrate these into Being, and the "Being of the Soul." All humans perform these three functions. We all think. We all feel (to varying degrees). And we all certainly act or do. What is important to note is that, throughout history, many philosophers have bifurcated thinking and feeling and relegated feeling to an inferior position. Mainstream psychology (Freud's psychoanalytic, John Watson's and B.F. Skinner's behavioral psychology, and Albert Ellis' and Aaron Beck's cognitive psychology), which based its main concepts and ideas upon the mechanistic, materialistic, empirical and rational philosophies of Bacon, Hobbes, Locke and Hume, has also segregated and split these functions, relegating love to an inferior, irrelevant position. Hobbes is noted for his famous statement, *homo homini lupus est* which means "every man is a wolf to every other man" and is surprisingly similar to the ego consciousness.

With the ego, it is a state of consciousness in which you *un*consciously think and feel and act without really pondering, examining or evaluating what you are thinking, feeling or doing to any great degree. These mental and heart activities have largely been segregated. Men became leaders and, for the most part, viewed all the spectrum of feelings (negative and positive) as irrational and, thus, inferior. As the primary intellectuals, men viewed females as the primary containers of all feelings, both negative and positive, and this, along with the fact that most women are not as physically as strong as men, led to the belief that females are subordinate. Whenever females attempted to challenge this masculine view, it is no small wonder that these females were emotional about being considered inferior! Thus, even though it's logical that a person would become emotional about being considered inferior, men attacked the female emotionality that resulted from being thought of as inferior! This "no win" situation creates yet another level of emotional reaction and the female is left all but mute in her frustration with attempting to have a voice, be heard and be respected on equal par with men. These men certainly do not think about their thinking, think about their feelings or think about what they are doing. There is no contemplation or care about this kind of psychological construct. This book is to expose how the ego goes to great lengths of deception and destruction in order to separate thinking and feeling and to continually fortify the masculine myth that cognition is superior to affect. Certainly to create equal value for them both would place the ego at risk for transformation into the Soul consciousness of *Being*. This would be a form of meditative consciousness and could eventually lead to enlightenment. Indeed, His Holiness, the Dalai Lama, in *Awakening the Mind, Lightening the Heart: Core Teachings of Buddhism*, states that "we can achieve enlightenment only through the practice of meditation; without it there is no way we can transform our minds."

It should go without saying that most of us in the world operate at the egoic level. Most of us do not spend substantial amounts of our time giving serious contemplation and serious thought to thinking, feeling and doing and making attempts to merge these experiences into an ontological experience. We simply move through the world going through the motions of what the world expects us to do. Rollo May, in *Man's Search for Himself*, speaks of the masses of people as "the hollow people" and as operating in "automaton conformity." In a simpler phrase, most of us are on auto pilot following the dictates of what our jobs, our bosses, our schools, our laws, our spouses, our children, our parents dictate for us. We never really check in with our Souls to see if what we're doing is in alignment with our Higher Self. We wake up, go to work at a job that most of us feel dispassionate about, pick up our paychecks, buy groceries, pay the mortgage and car payment, send our kids off to school, socialize with our close set of friends and then go to sleep only to wake up and do it all over again the next week. We do not self-examine and "think about our thoughts," "think about our feelings" and "think about our actions." Rather, we simply think. We feel. We act. All performed in mostly a segregated fashion.

The man who beats his wife is not thinking about his thoughts, thinking about his feelings, thinking about his actions or thinking about his wife's either. He most assuredly is not activating his Will toward Goodness. This narcissistic ego-driven husband is only thinking about how frustrating his life is and externalizing the blame for his own sorrows onto his wife. He is unable to make the connection that he is projecting onto her his own feelings of inadequacy, frustration, anger and disappointment because he lacks the willingness to spend any time thinking about his thoughts, thinking about his feelings or thinking about his actions. He just moves through the world. Higher Good is lost to him and the only means in finding it entails the one thing he refuses to do—look within. Unwilling to self-examine and self-contemplate, he lives a miserable existence which entails making others' lives as miserable as his own.

The CEO of the large corporation who is charged with malfeasance and insider trading is not thinking about what he's thinking, thinking about what he's feeling or thinking about what he's doing and it is certain to say that he lacks the conscience to be concerned about his employees either except to the extent that high productivity is maintained so the company can make higher and higher profits so his compensation package will be richer. This man is just moving through the world in not a dissimilar manner from the previous wife beater. The higher Good is not to be found with him.

The corporate wife who is an ornament on the arm of a highly paid corporate executive goes through her days planning, organizing and implementing at her husband's directives without claiming any of her own inner passions, dreams and goals. Having given up her early dream of having a successful career, she buries these aspirations underneath a mountain of social dinners and country club meetings intended to woo clients to her husband's client roster. She does little thinking about her thoughts, thinking about her feelings or thinking about her actions. If she did, she would likely come dangerously close to reconsidering her choices. She is moving through the world by a false self with inauthentic intentions and an unrealized personal vision.

The Baptist preacher's wife who fearfully sides with her husband when they discover their daughter is a lesbian feels some maternal instinct that contradicts what the dogma and doctrine of the Bible teach. Feeling innately that "love one another" cannot be reconciled with rejecting her daughter who has decided to live an authentic life, the wife feels some incongruence within her. Despite this, she decides to ignore that dissonance and follow the Bible's teachings without stopping to question the fact that males were the sole authority in determining which books were included and which were excluded from the Bible we know today. As a result, both father and mother stand together and give the daughter an ultimatum: "Stop being gay or leave the household and live on your own." Pathetically and erroneously perceiving homosexuality as an intellectual choice, the parents make a decision which will forever cast a division between parent and child. The spiritual law of "love one another" must be cast aside in order to justify their rejection. This wife is electing not to sit down, think about her thinking, think about her feelings, think about her actions and determine where the deepest truth lies. She certainly is not giving great consideration to her daughter's truth and the possibility that the Bible may have some error in it. This wife pushes her maternal instincts aside and plays the preacher's wife. She is moving through the world and her Soul, which only seeks the joyful Goodness of All, remains behind the veil of the ego.

Now, let's consider again the geometrical shape of the Soul and review the triangular shape of thinking, feeling and doing. The interactions between these three facets of human life represent the *consciousness* of interacting between them. In other words, at the Soul consciousness level, the human begins:

thinking about thinking,

thinking about feeling and

thinking about acting/doing

Over time, these three are in sync with one another and, slowly, this process begins to alter how we think, what we feel and what we do because we realize something very basic, but very profound—we have power. In time, this brings with it an awareness of the power that we have in creating what we wish to create. In turn, this brings the awareness that humankind possesses great power *per se*. The only question is whether we activate this power toward Goodness or away from Goodness. Humankind has the choice to either use its great power for Goodness or away from Goodness. This means that we can activate our Will toward spiritual fruits of love, kindness, compassion, truth, honor, etc. or we can activate our Will toward ego thoughts that are led by fear such as anger, hate, envy, greed, shame, guilt and all negative emotions. Every day, *you have the choice as to what you think.* Every moment, *you choose how you wish to feel.* Each second, *you have the power to decide how you wish to act. What an awesome awareness!!! You have POWER TO SELF-GOVERN!!*

At a global level today, we mostly act based upon what society has come to deem as right or wrong, but we have the power of choice to choose to act with consciousness toward Goodness. Every moment of living, we choose either to move through the world "going through the motions" that someone else has taught us or to consciously begin a life of being attuned to our Soul. Our thoughts, feelings and actions determine whether we create heaven or hell on this planet. If we give love, we get love. If we give hate, we get hate. Wealthy, middle class and poor parents all share in the psychological and physical crime of neglecting and abusing children. There is no specific socioeconomic status for the father who never tells his son he loves him or the mother who delegates nurturing to the household nanny. Rich and poor parents alike spend an inordinate amount of time at work to the detriment of providing the needed love and nurturance to children. Is it any wonder that these children grow up full of anger, insecurity, greed, jealousy, shame, hatred, prejudice and intolerance? Many leaders in the business and political community fail to hear the divine echo of the Soul which seeks to find the good of the whole. If any political decision is a threat to their self-interests, the good of the Whole is neglected. It seems no one who is honest and considers what is best for the whole can get elected today and, even on the off chance they did, they couldn't survive in politics because politics has, by its very nature, become synonymous with greed and self-gain. This disastrous and gloomy depiction of politics is reflected in the all too common saying: "Which candidate is the lesser of two evils?" Big business and politics are in bed with each other and the males who dominate feed off each other's greed. The ego is rampant and pervasive in the world; both men and women and people of all colors carry some culpability to varying degrees. The good of the whole is left out in the cold. Quite literally, it is homeless. Is it any wonder this world is in the mess that it is in? Who has created this world we live in but ourselves? It is *WE WHO CREATE HEAVEN OR HELL ON EARTH.* We need not look above or below. All we need do is look within to find the source of what we see outside us.

The hope of rising above our current human condition is self-examination, self-reflection and activating the Will toward Goodness for the All. This is the Being consciousness of the Soul. Once the process of self-examination and self-reflection become more integrated into every day life, the Soul manifests more and more. When the Soul begins manifesting, the conscious awareness of the interdependence and interrelatedness of every thing that exists begins manifesting as well. This very act of the mind being self-reflective and, simultaneously, becoming connected with the lower kingdoms can be considered as moving to the next level of ***Being***. Once you make this mental shift from being led by your unconscious to leading your world consciously, then your world begins to shift. After you begin incorporating these self-examinations in your life and begin making choices toward Goodness, these become more and more embedded into your unconsciousness. Then your unconsciousness and your consciousness move toward a state of Soul consciousness. It becomes more and more of your conscious nature.

The Soul uses its energies of love and creativity in order to more fully experience Being and to more fully experience a relatedness and connectedness with itSelf and with the world around it. In its purest sense and when fully awakened, it only knows its individuality through its connection and unity to the larger whole. The ego uses its energies of fear in order to do and act and to have more of the physical world for itself. It is delusional because it believes that only through getting more and more can it have and only through establishing difference can it live, therefore, it only knows disconnection and division.

The Soul is the mediator between the "unseen order" (the spiritual Kingdom) where the Highest Self resides and the ego consciousness. Soul as mediating principle between the ego which seeks to separate and divide self from object, self from the whole, self from a spiritual real, self from plant/animal/spiritual kingdoms. Ego consciousness, in its arrogance of self, seeks to compete, dominate and conquer all kingdoms and completely denies the existence of a higher spiritual kingdom. The plant and animal kingdoms are only perceived as an inferior tool by which the ego masters its environment. There is no higher awareness of a connectivity which binds all kingdoms together, therefore, the ego disrespects and ravages these two kingdoms for primarily material benefit. The same psychological dynamic occurs within human relationships. The ego simply cannot see and know the ubiquitous connection between every thing that exists. The physical world is the only world that the ego consciousness recognizes; therefore, it is only natural that the ego would see a world of difference and separation. Material gain is the end and any means to securing that end for itself is considered and used. There is no obeying of spiritual laws.

The ego consciousness is less inclusive than the Soul consciousness. The ego always operates from fear. Out of fear, the ego exists, quite literally. The Soul knows the eternal laws that are inviolable; therefore, the Soul desires that which will bring harmony. Harmony can only be attained through obeying spiritual laws.

The ego consciousness is in conflict with the Soul Consciousness, but the Soul Consciousness is not in conflict with the ego consciousness. You ask how that can be. The Soul, metaphorically speaking, only looks upward toward the spiritual realm of love, joy, peace, truth, beauty, creativity, etc. Even when the Soul is observing a flower, it should be understood as "looking upward" since the Soul manifests and flourishes in a state of Beingness, a state of Being and merging with Good. Its Will always moves in the direction of Goodness, therefore, it is understood that the Soul moves in the direction of inclusiveness. Goodness is understood as love, joy, peace, compassion, honor, justice, etc. Again, this *is* the spiritual world. Many people have historically stated that the Soul moves downward. In a sense, one could say that is true, but only to the extent that it is temporarily connected with the physical body and the physical body is understood to be descended spirit in its lowest and densest form. Einstein's theories came closest to proving that matter is but another form of light. Light Being pure; matter being dense and impure light. The frequency of light is high; the frequency of matter is low. Both are energy, however.

The Soul's glance is forever constellated upward toward a "higher," broader, more inclusive level of consciousness. Plato and St. John of the Cross have spoken of the Soul as moving downward or descending. This has been referred to as the "dark night of the Soul." To use the word depth is often misunderstood to mean a darkness of the Soul, rather than a darkness *surrounding* the Soul. The darkness surrounding the Soul is the veil that the ego places over it. When the ego manifests, you may symbolically imagine a dark veil being placed over the Soul when the Soul is no longer in view and cannot be stirred and activated. The Soul itSelf, however, does not become dark. Only the ego can become dark and cover up, metaphorically speaking, the Soul. In that sense, one may arrive at an understanding of the Soul somehow descending or moving downward in its direction. Think of the Soul as an energy frequency. Remember, everything is energy. If your ego is manifesting, your energy frequency is low. If you begin using your Will toward purely selfish means, never take responsibility for your actions and never seek to help others, then your vibrational frequency will be low. Your body may be on the go all the time, but your frequency will be sluggish and low. This is the domain of the ego. As you use your Will toward Goodness for self and others, then your vibrational frequency increases. Oddly and paradoxically, when this happens, there is a tendency for you to physically begin to slow down the pace at which you lead your physical life. The Soul surfaces, is found and is stirred within this vibrational frequency range, so to speak. If this were not so, humankind would be lost forever and would never be able to reconnect with the spirit world for all of eternity since the Soul carries the memory of Spirit.

While the Soul is never truly lost and cannot be destroyed, it can retreat and it can be (and often is in today's world of massive material focus) "pushed" aside by the ego. All the while, the Soul remains there, silently and peacefully, only awaiting remembrance when the veil of ignorance or *avidya* is lifted.

The ego seeks to hold the mind chained toward the earthly realm of all things visible to the physical eye. The Soul seeks to merge with the unseen order where the Ideal forms of truth, beauty, love, creativity, peace, joy, honor reside. When speaking of "above" or "higher," we simply refer to richer spiritual content and a broader, more inclusive, wealthier level of awareness, consciousness and enlightenment. The world of Ideas is the invisible world within your mind and heart and, essentially, throughout the entire cosmos. This is the ontological world of Being that we mentioned earlier. For where could you possibly draw a line to say that "Being" starts here and ends there?

The "doing" experience of the ego is different from the ontological or "Being" experience of the Soul. The ego:

–recognizes, concentrates and fixes itself upon the material world
–uses the physical world as both means and end
–denies or ignores a spiritual realm
–denies or ignores a spiritual connection with the mineral, plant and animal kingdoms
–merges with only that which the ego perceives as physically similar with itself
–perceives superiority and inferiority based upon the physical appearance of existence
–disconnects from, dishonors or disrespects other humans unlike itself
–disobeys spiritual laws

This leads to psychological pathology and, hence, all negative emotions, violence, hate, crimes and wars. One could say that the ego is unable to resolve the conflict between the spiritual and physical worlds. Material possessions are perceived to have more power than the knowledge, creativity, love and wisdom which are the ultimate truths responsible for their manifestations. The ego, with its constant seeking to do and act, could be thought of as a false Soul, a pseudo-Soul. When the Soul consciousness begins to manifest, the ego begins to transform and disappear. At that point, you could say that the ego recedes and the Soul comes to the foreground. This has sometimes been referred to as the Soul Being "stirred." That simply means that the Soul is taking front stage while the ego is receding. It also refers to the higher vibrational frequency of the Soul.

Whether the ego or the Soul manifests is a question of free will for humankind. Constantly faced with the free will to choose between electing goodness or denying goodness, humankind faces the choice every day as to its evolutionary direction. In reality, humankind can only *ultimately* return to the spiritual world, but how long it takes and the amount of suffering along the way will determine *when*. We can continue to destroy the physical world over and over again through the lower evolutionary consciousness of the ego, but one day, perhaps millions of years from now, humankind ultimately evolves back to spirit. Once humankind finally learns the difficult lesson of disobeying spiritual laws and then moves to the next level of consciousness—the Soul Consciousness—we will look behind us and see how unwise we have acted toward ourselves and each other for aeons.

You get to choose every day whether you want the ego or the Soul to be in control. That's the gift of free will. Since humankind is the only species on this planet with the capacity to think about thinking, then only we—of all the kingdoms on earth—have free will. The animal kingdom certainly has a will, but it is a manifestation of physiological states and the bodily senses. Humankind has the choice to choose, in spite of what our bodily senses are telling us, which direction we wish to move in—goodness or not. This is because humanity has evolved to the point that we have reasoning capabilities. Another way to say that is we can think about thinking and think about actions and the consequences of our actions. Animals are not evolved enough to do this. Over centuries of choosing the ego consciousness to guide humankind and seeing the disastrous and unpleasant consequences of this choice, we are on the cusp of the next level of consciousness. Through repeated centuries of the outcome of an ego consciousness which breeds hate, violence, prejudice, crimes, war and overall destruction, humankind is finally beginning to feel the stirring of the Soul consciousness pushing its way up from the subconscious world into the conscious world. Remember that the Soul carries the memory of the Spirit world. This is what makes the Soul the mediator between the physical and spiritual worlds. If we did not have Souls, we could never begin to recall the spiritual world and begin our ascent upward to the next level of human consciousness. One could say rather simplistically that when enough people on the planet finally get tired enough of the hate, fear and violence that we have made for ourselves, that is when we begin to look inward to the Soul for its remembrance of a higher consciousness, then we can experience psychological health *en masse*. This takes, however, a critical mass of humankind to have this awareness and create this shift in consciousness. It is simply not enough for one, two or ten people out of billions of humans to have this awareness. In this way, it functions just like the energy that it is. You simply have to have a certain number of people manifesting the Soul Consciousness in order for it to have an effect upon the entire globe. This is what makes it so critical that as many people as possible develop an awareness and move toward the next higher level of consciousness. Remember, even Jesus the Christ and the Buddha couldn't change the world in a blink of an eye. They were the Wayshowers for the mass of humanity. It takes the collective consciousness of a critical mass of people. Examples of this critical mass are strewn throughout history. Finally, when enough people raised the awareness of racial and gender parity, the laws changed. Some nonminorities still discriminate against minorities, some men still discriminate against females and some heterosexuals still discriminate against homosexuals, but the energy is slowly, but surely shifting away from the negative energy of prejudice and discrimination. As more and more adults unlearn prejudice and as more children are taught the evils of prejudice, the greater numbers of those who are not prejudiced in these areas will outweigh the numbers of those who are. The outcome will be a broadened consciousness and, ultimately, greater levels of cooperation and peaceful co-existence on the planet. It is only by raising the level of consciousness which entails obeying spiritual laws that humankind will return to a harmonious existence. Any law, religion, biblical statement, philosophical belief, social opinion, political stance, educational premise or idea which states or implies that potential for Goodness for the All is inaccessible, this is an untruth. Spiritual fruits are not derived from, caused by, unique to, or in any way related to the color of a person's skin, the religion they practice, the birthplace of a person, their anatomical gender, their sexual orientation, the amount of worldly education attained, weight, height, shoe size, clothes style, automobile preference or home address. The Soul really knows none of these worldly things because it only knows and makes a connection with the spiritual world behind them. It was this unifying principle and reality which both Jesus the Christ and the Buddha came to know and which made them enlightened when put into daily practice. Humankind can attain this level of consciousness. We do it by connecting with the Great Soul.

*Silence is the perennial flow of Language.*
—Sri Ramana Maharshi

*In the attitude of silence, the soul finds the path in a clearer light, and what is elusive and deceptive resolves itself into crystal clearness. Our life is a long and arduous quest after Truth.*

—Mahatma Gandhi

# XIV. THE LANGUAGE OF THE SOUL: SILENT BEINGNESS

Quite simply, the language of the Soul is the same as that of the spiritual realm: the Voice of Silence. The language of the Soul is not vocalized words with nouns and predicates, verbs, adjectives and adverbs. In fact, the Soul does not speak in human words. It does not speak English, Italian, Spanish, German, Russian, Hebrew, Arabic, Dutch, Swedish or any other human verbal language. The Soul operates within the nether world of Silence, therefore, it communicates and comprehends through geometric, mythic and morphic symbols. Spiritual symbols are understood to be sacred forms and numbers; while the material world has secular symbols.

Form, in its simplest and most sacred shape, is a geometric shape so it could be a circle, square or triangle. In the material world, a form turns into a tree, a car, a table or chair. The entire physical world is but some rendition of a geometrical shape. You have already been introduced to the holy shape of the triangle since it represents the holy trinity. The four energic expressions of the Soul could be geometrically expressed as a perfect square. The circle is actually representative of the One behind the many that we see with our physical eyes. In fact, Empedocles stated that the nature of God is a circle whose center is everywhere and circumference is nowhere. In this sense, the circle is considered to be the highest expression of divinity, followed by the triangle which represents the holy trinity of will, mind and heart and the square which represents the four energic expressions of knowledge, creativity, love and wisdom all of which are activated by the Great Will toward Goodness. Sacred mathematicians and geometricians speak of the harmony and beauty of numbers and forms, regardless of whether they are consciously aware or not of the sacredness and divinity of what they study. This is why the ancient astronomers closely studied the heavenly bodies of sun, moon and stars. Locked within them are the spiritual cycles and patterns which run throughout all of existence. It was their quest to find the answers to the mysteries of creation by studying this vast panorama.

We all have the capacity to "hear" the language of the Soul whenever we dream for it is within the subconscious world that the Soul communicates to us and attempts to inform, guide and direct us. Sigmund Freud was perhaps the first well known psychologist to be recognized as focusing, and placing importance, on the subconscious realm. In actuality, mystics and sages had for centuries, but Freud has received the credit and recognition because of his systematic and serious study of it as a function of the Psyche. The field of psychology owes much to Freud and even though today much of his theoretical model has been discounted or invalidated and is losing its foothold as a viable theoretical model, his debt to humankind will most likely one day be his naming of the ego and its defense mechanisms, along with his focus on the unconscious and dreams. Freud's thought was limiting as he declared the subconscious as a vast land of sexual and aggressive wishes, hopes and fears. Some have come to refer to Freud's account of the subconscious as a sort of garbage can of unconsciousness. In simplistic terms, he believed the subconscious was a vast warehouse of the negative with repressed, suppressed and unfulfilled sexual and aggressive wishes. This was the world of negative psychic activity. In the typical Freudian fashion, he perceived this as set and determined by childhood problems and conflicts. This mindset is what labeled his theory as "deterministic" since he postulated that a person does not have a spiritual potential, cannot rise substantially above their current level of consciousness and is, largely, not going to move substantially beyond the existing level of pathology. One could say that Freud believed psychic "damage" was not "curable." If you had experienced a traumatic childhood of sexual, verbal and physical abuse, it was not likely that you would ever rise far above the pathologies which typically manifest because of experiencing that type of environment. For most in the psychological community today, Freud is considered a spiritually bankrupt intellectual who refused to acknowledge the psyche's innate potential to seek wholeness.

Carl Jung, Milton Erickson and Roberto Assagioli are three very prominent medical doctors and psychologists in modern times to posit the untapped positive potential of the subconscious and to place the subconscious at the core of their theoretical assumptions and therapeutic interventions. Far more optimistic than Freud, these three men saw the glass as half full when it came to humankind's potential. Humankind not only is capable of higher levels of consciousness, but they posited that humankind innately *seeks* these more self-actualizing levels of Being and relating. In other words, humankind seeks to restore wholeness of Being or Soulfulness. This, in turn, leads to greater psychological maturity and overall functioning. Jung said that all psychological problems are, ultimately, of a spiritual nature and origin. He believed in the power of the subconscious to heal itself and utilized therapeutic techniques such as guided imagery and dream interpretation in order for clients to access the subconscious realm. A prolific writer, a voracious reader and an extraordinary intellectual genius, Jung's theory of the Higher Self was heavily influenced by his belief in the restorative powers of the psyche.

Milton Erickson arrived later on the scene than did Jung, but was equally fascinated with the power of the subconscious. Erickson began utilizing hypnotherapy in his clinical practice and, as a result, became known as the founder of hypnotherapy. Erickson thought little of diagnostic labels and, in fact, preferred not to place labels on people, rather concentrated on helping a person find their own inner potential. He did so by means of hypnotherapy. Erickson believed that most of what we learn as humans is learned by our unconscious mind. He placed substantial importance on nonverbal communication, believing that our bodies always convey the truth which is in our subconscious.

Roberto Assagioli, considered the father of transpersonal psychology, developed a transpersonal theory of human development which stated that humankind subconsciously desires to move beyond the ego consciousness.

In fact, *trans* means "beyond," so transpersonal means to *move beyond the personal* or in more psychological terms, to *move beyond the ego*. Assagioli acknowledged all other psychological theories such as psychoanalytic, cognitive, behavioral and humanistic, but believed these theories were narrow and limiting as they were only pieces of the larger puzzle as it pertains to human consciousness, the human potential and psychological wholeness. One of the most important legacies of Assagioli is his theoretical development and study of the Will and the critical role it plays as humankind experiences pathology or as humanity moves to higher levels of psychological integration. Like Jung and Erickson, Assagioli focused largely upon therapeutic techniques which enhanced the unconscious as he, too, believed that this archetypal landscape was the key to reaching optimal mental health and well being.

As was stated earlier, the Soul does not know how to speak in words. It can only relate in terms of *Being*. Being is a state of connecting with the spiritual realm and incorporating spirit within. To the outside world of physical matter, this is the world of subjective reality. To the Soul and the spirit realm, this is understood to be the only True Reality because it is the world of diversity within Unity. Let's try an experiment and see if you can connect to this concept and actually have a "wow, I got that" moment. Close your eyes and imagine that you have no knowledge whatsoever of any words. This will require some effort, but you can do it. You will need to stay with that moment until you can begin to grasp what that must be like. As your eyes remain closed, imagine that you are standing in a vast, peaceful, serene meadow on a bright, sunny day in springtime. Several hundred yards away, you see a pond with no ripples, just quietly being peaceful with willow trees surrounding the banks. You are surrounded by acres and acres of green, lush trees, wonderfully bright, scented flowers and budding bushes. You see pink and coral azaleas, fuchsia rhododendrons, white gardenias, bright golden-yellow forsythia, deep purple irises, yellow sunflowers, orange day lilies, yellow daffodils and dozens of other favorite flowers surrounding you and enveloping you in their colors of beauty. The aromas of the flowers are wafting all around you so that you are also filled with fresh scents. You've had to read this, so now it's time to put the book down and start imagining this experience. Once you spend about two or three minutes standing in that reverie, then open your eyes and read the next paragraph.

It's time to remind you that you do not know any words. You have never learned a language, so you cannot speak nor can you even imagine in your mind any words to speak. You'll likely have to close your eyes once again and re-enter that sacred space of beauty, wonder and peace. If you try it again, perhaps you'll be more successful just standing in the beauty expressing no words. What you should be able to do, if done successfully, is to have a *Being* experience, not a solely *thinking* experience. If you're like most people, it truly is difficult to articulate to someone that *Being* experience of standing in and *Being* peaceful, calm and joyous. If you did not know any words, but you had to convey to your friend (who also does not know words) what your *Being* experience was, how would you do that? Remember, you and your friend don't know words, so you can't say words or write down words on a piece of paper.

If you're like most people, it's almost irresistible to tell your friend some word to convey your experience. I can imagine as you're sitting and reading this how tempted you must be to blurt out to your friend "I saw a meadow with bright, colorful flowers." It would be tempting to say that the flowers are "peaceful" and "beautiful" and "joyous." But words are either symbols or they are symbols of symbols. Anything material or physical is a symbol of a symbol and when you say those words, you are two levels away from a *Being* experience. For instance, the word "car" is a material thing. It is, therefore, a symbol of a symbol. The word "car" is a *symbol* of security, safety, comfort, joy, beauty, etc. These spiritual words of security, safety, comfort, joy and beauty are yet *symbols of a Being experience*. A *Being* experience is a direct knowing experience. A thinking experience, what we commonly call intellectualization, is not a *Being* experience. It is only a thinking experience of the ego that intellectually sees the object as separate and different from itself. The ego cannot *feel* the connection that is created when a Being experience occurs. Only the Great Soul can do this and this is why the Soul is considered the mediating and connecting principle to the spiritual realm.

When you speak of physical and material things in words, you are two levels away from a *Being* experience! When you use words to articulate a spiritual fruit, you are still one step away from a *Being* experience. To say the word "love" and to think about the word "love" are not a *Being* experience. It is a sterile, intellectual ego experience of *non*-Being to simply articulate the word "love." You are still one step away from the actualized *Being* experience. This is why all great sages and mystics have emphasized silence and meditation as a means to higher consciousness. In the world of psychology, Abraham Maslow coined the word self-actualization and Carl Jung coined the word individuation. In very simple terms, these are *Being* experiences, not solely thinking experiences.

So we're back to square one. You are still stuck on how to convey to your friend the Being experience of the meadow and the flowers and the peace and joy because to say that you were in a meadow with colorful flowers means you are two steps away from a Being experience. To go further and tell your friend that you had a peaceful and joyous experience means you are still one step away from a Being experience.

What the Great Soul would do in conveying that Being experience is it would simply *be* that experience to your friend. You ask how in the world can you do that. Let's think about this carefully. If you can't use verbal language, then you must utilize *non*verbal language. That means that you use your body to convey a message. Varying ways and mannerisms you might use to tell your friend would be smiling, dancing, lifting your arms to the heavens and smiling, skipping, frolicking or rolling in the meadow, standing on your head and smiling, turning cartwheels and smiling, closing your eyes and smiling. Ways of contact would be to hug your friend, pat their arm, give them a flower as you're smiling, put a flower under their nose and watch their reaction, gently rub the soft petal of a flower on their arm, hold their hand and walk through the meadow or lie down next to your friend and hold their hand. It is likely that your friend would have a Being experience. You will be connecting with each other and connecting with the spiritual, sacred realm where all spiritual fruits are experienced. Love, peace, joy, comfort, safety, beauty, truth and every spiritual fruit would be experienced in those moments.

You should begin to start forming an idea of what it means to have a Being experience. I suspect that Stevie Wonder has lots of Being experiences. The entire world for a person having a Being experience is a kind of merging of thinking and feeling processes into a symbiotic oneness with everything. You may test that for about five minutes. Close your eyes and don't speak and imagine being in that space as you are with someone you love or as you sit in nature. Aaahhhh! The sacred appreciation you would have as you move into a heightened state of consciousness and awareness realizing that everything you do is in reliance upon everything and every person around you. You would be forced to rely on your imagination and in your states of imaginative power, you would be merging both *thinking* of something with the immediacy of *feeling* that thought as well. If you were able to carry the Will toward Goodness and all its spiritual fruits, this would be the apogee of Beingness. It is simply being totally consciously aware of incorporating a spiritual fruit within your Soul. It is *Being* a spiritual fruit and being totally conscious of that *Beingness.*

It is also the Being experience of connecting with every thing around you and being consciously aware that separation and difference is really an illusion. Jesus the Christ, the Buddha, Lao Tzu and Ramana Maharshi were able to self-actualize and individuate and carry this higher Being experience and consciousness within them. They accessed the positive spiritual fruits, connected with others and the plant and animal kingdom and exemplified the Being consciousness or Soul consciousness of these spiritual fruits of love, kindness, compassion, creativity, generativity, wisdom, etc. Their Will toward Goodness was activated and, thus, they accessed the world of Truth, Beauty and Goodness where All is One. This can be thought of as a substantially more optimal level of human consciousness and of mental health and well being.

The Soul, as we know it today, operates and functions within the subconscious or unconscious world. Our next step is to bring the unconsciousness of the Soul to the consciousness level. As we operate at the egoic level, we remain largely detached from this subconscious world. When the Soul consciousness manifests in greater magnitude within our lives, our dream world will become less a wasteland of fearful dreams and more of a wealthy landscape of spiritual guidance and symbols by which we are informed and make choices. When we allow our Souls to guide our lives, our dreams will inform us of past lives and, thus, give us important clues as to the emotional and mental patterns we have in this incarnation. Our dreams will also provide us with symbols which we can read and interpret, then guide and direct us.

*If you look to others for fulfillment, you will never truly be fulfilled. If your happiness depends on money, you will never be happy with yourself.*
—Lao Tzu

*Those who try to control, who use force to protect their power, go against the direction of the Tao. They take from those who don't have enough and give to those who have far too much. The Master can keep giving because there is no end to her wealth. She acts without expectation, succeeds without taking credit, and doesn't think that she is better than anyone else.*
—Lao Tzu

# XV. THE SOUL: HAVING, BEING AND SHARING

In the physical and material world, when you have something material, it certainly does not mean that you become that thing. In other words, what you have is *not* what you are although the ego certainly attempts to convince you of this falsehood. If you hold a diamond in your hand, you are not a diamond. By hugging your fur coat or grasping a $100 bill in your hand, you do not suddenly become these things. If you hold a gun in your hand, you do not become a gun. In all instances, you are still a person with a Soul. To have and to be are two different things in the material world.

In the spiritual realm and in the domain of the Soul, *what you have is what you are.* If you hold a flower in your hand and you are full of joy and love, then you can say that you *are* joyous and loving. If you are sitting on a quiet beach and have a feeling of peace and joy come over you, then you can say that you *are* peaceful and joyous. When you experience a spiritual fruit, you ARE that spiritual fruit. *To have is to be in the spiritual realm. Having and Being are one and the same.* In the spiritual world:

**Attachment XV**

| WHAT YOU HAVE | = | WHO YOU ARE |
|---|---|---|
| HAVING | = | BEING |
| HAVING SPIRITUAL FRUITS | = | BEING A SPIRITUAL FRUIT |
| HAVING LOVE | = | BEING LOVE |
| HAVING JOY | = | BEING JOYOUS |
| HAVING PEACE | = | BEING PEACEFUL |
| HAVING TRUTH | = | BEING TRUTHFUL |
| HAVING HONOR | = | BEING HONORABLE |
| HAVING JUSTICE | = | BEING JUST |
| HAVING COMPASSION | = | BEING COMPASSIONATE |
| HAVING COURAGE | = | BEING COURAGEOUS |
| HAVING WISDOM | = | BEING WISE |
| HAVING CREATIVITY | = | BEING CREATIVE |
| HAVING KNOWLEDGE | = | BEING KNOWLEDGEABLE |

What this means is that, in the spiritual world, when you experience something, you are *Being* that something. You can never separate having and Being in the spiritual realm. Subjectivity is reality. This is Brahman or Self.

It is the realm where subject and object are not separate, rather are One.

When you have any one positive emotion, you simultaneously have any other positive emotion. For how could you feel love, without also feeling joy and peace? And is it not true that truth and honor are also wise?

When you have a negative emotion, these are all split off emotions from the basic and fundamental emotion of fear. Fear is the derivative of all negative emotions. All negative emotions manifest in a physical world. Negative emotions cannot exist in a purely spiritual world because in the spiritual world, there is no fear, no pain, no suffering. If you were Pure Spirit and every other Soul were Pure Spirit, what would you have to fear?

Whether you wish to operate at the ego level or the Soul level will depend upon how you utilize your free will. Every moment, you have the free will to choose between the Will *toward* Goodness and the Will *away* from Goodness. This inner, subjective world is the world that you are. It is the only reality because it is the only state of Beingness. When you open your eyes, you cannot help but see the phenomenal world of physical things all around you. The ego sees the phenomenal world and is obsessed with analyzing the physical world. It is so under its spell that the ego thinks that the physical world is real. That which appears to be real is what we value. That which we value is what appears to be real. In this circular false reality of *samsara*, the ego would have you believe forever that physical things, in and of themselves, are real and are what constitute the highest reality. This is the false state of being which is what Advaitans refer to as "lower knowledge" or *apara vidya.* It is also *avidya,* or ignorance, because it is the mind deceiving itself that what is not real and not-Self is, instead, real and is the Self. The Advaitans speak of the concept of superimposition which is what the ego does when it attempts to superimpose reality onto that which is not reality. That which can never be a content of experience is not ultimate reality, therefore, since you can never experience BEing a diamond, fur coat or Mercedez Benz; those physical things are not *ultimately* real. To an Advaitan, these physical things are of the world of appearance or illusion because they can never be a content of experience within your consciousness. You can only experience the joy that these physical things give you; therefore, the joy is the ultimate reality, not the physical thing itself. So this process of superimposition where you falsely place an attribute onto something that it can never have is the cause of *avidya* or ignorance and is the cause of much suffering in the world. It is the belief that sense perceptions are real when they are not. If you close your eyes, you realize that the only thing you can ever BE is subjectivity. Let me be specific. If you open your eyes and reach for a diamond ring, the ego deceives you into thinking that the diamond ring, in and of itself, is what makes you happy. The ego deceives you into thinking that material things, in and of themselves, translate into happiness. And so you get caught up in the vicious cycle of things and more things in order to have a simple feeling of BEING joyous. If you close your eyes and hold the same diamond, what are you BEING? You are NOT being a diamond. You can only forever BE joyous. Another example is when you smell a rose. The ego would have you believe that you are smelling the scent of rose because one of your senses—smell—certainly seems to indicate that you are. If you close your eyes and just simply BE, you realize that the only experience you can ever have is the BEINGNESS of joy. This subjectivity is all you can ever BE forever and ever throughout eternity. You cannot BE anything physical or material, therefore, the phenomenal world is, in that sense, illusory and false because it attempts to deceive you that you are something that you are not.

Now you may ask "When I experience negative emotions, aren't they real?" Certainly, in a material world, we are all subject to negative emotions at the lower level of consciousness, the ego consciousness, which perceives a split world because it "sees" through a radically different "lens" than does the Higher Self or Soul. Negative emotions only manifest in a physical, material world. The physical, material world is illusory, symbol, representational of that which you ARE and, in that sense, negative emotions are not real. That which is real is forever and ever and there is never a time when it does not exist. Negative emotions only exist in a material world. The higher knowledge, *para vidya*, understood by Advaitans is the Higher Self or Soul consciousness and it is a radically different way of "seeing" the world because it only "sees" that which is forever, that which is eternal, that which never changes, that which is real. It only knows Reality which is to say that it comes to know that subjectivity "is" the Higher Self and it is the only reality which exists forever although the ego would have you superimpose a false reality over that which is truly real. William Indich, in *Consciousness in Advaita Vedanta,* refers to the difference between *para vidaya* and *apara vidya* as the difference between "the knowledge by which the immutable, everlasting, all-pervading and imperishable, i.e., Brahman, is realized, and the 'knowledge of the world—of objects, events, means, ends, virtues and vices.' Thus, higher knowledge is knowledge of reality, while lower knowledge has as its object the created world, phenomenal appearance." Indich further says that:

"higher knowledge is a fully autonomous state of being in which the identity of the all-pervading consciousness underlying the apparently distinct subject, object and means of knowledge is realized....higher knowledge is strictly speaking not subjective knowledge of reality as object. Instead, it is the awareness of the identity of the knowing subject as reality itself...in higher knowledge, the essence of the knowing subject is realized to be identical with the essence of the objective world. Here, knowledge and reality, epistemology and metaphysics merge in non-duality. When the essence of the knowing subject, the Self (Atman) is known, all reality is known. 'That which is the finest essence— this whole world has that as its soul. That is Reality. That is Atman. Thou art that.'"

Ignorance (*avidya*) exists when there is a failure to discriminate between the illusoriness of the phenomenal world (which is seen through the eyes of the ego consciousness) and Brahman, Higher Self, the world beyond and above ego, the eternally real world, the transcendental ground of existence, that which is lord and governor forever. Suffering exists at the ego consciousness level because the ego cannot "see" reality, it cannot see itSelf, it cannot see its own Beingness, it does not recognize its own Soul, its own eternality, that which is lord and governor for eternity. It is in this sense that the ego can never truly BE. For BEING is a state of loving knowingness and only the Higher Self knows this. The ego, in truth, knows nothing since it is ignorant of its True and Authentic Self, its whole, indivisible, infinite, one Self.

The ego *has* nothing because it *is* nothing because it believes that which is nothing is something! The ego grasps and hoards what, in reality, is nothing—material things---living under the false belief that what you see with your physical eyes is ultimately real. The ego is forever empty because only Spirit can ever fill. The ego, forever living in a delusional world of lack, separation and difference, is in a perpetual state of perceiving, judging, discriminating, hoarding, defending and deceiving. All current world systems led by the immature masculine are funded by the ego because the current world systems divide, separate, disempower and hoard for the ego. Politics, business, finance, religion, education, science, medicine, psychology and all systems today are founded upon the principle of the ego. Capitalism and communism are simply two world systems which are two sides of the same coin. Make no mistake, the ego is operating in this world when only 1% of the world controls 97% of the world's wealth. Capitalism, on the surface, appears to be far superior to communism. However, in looking closer and deeper into its structure, we can see that with a median income in the United States of approximately $20,000 while 1% of the people control 97% of the wealth, its sinister leader—the ego—is operative and in control. The ego wants everything for itself and wishes to share with no one because the ego sees a world of superiority/inferiority, separation, difference and lack. This world is not meant for 1% of the population to control 97% of the world wealth and your Higher Self knows this truth. Something is grievously wrong with the leaders of the political and financial world systems when we can see that the ratio between the median income in the United States and the highest income of the wealthiest person in the world is approximately 1:500,000,000,000. Something is grievously wrong in communism when the masses own nothing and have little and are at the mercy of those who are in power who own the masses and have all the wealth. The masses are in prison and the few in power are free. Capitalism is a system that works through competition; therefore, it stimulates and fosters deceit, greed and corruption. It enthrones individualism at the expense of the collective community. Those who have the wealth are free while those who have little are at the mercy of those who have everything at their disposal. Communism is worse because it vilifies the individual and approbates the group. Capitalism and communism are but two sides of the same coin unless the Soul is operative. You might say that the evolutionary maturation of political systems advances from communism to capitalism to socialism although if the ego is operative in the leadership in any of these systems, there will not be an optimal political state. The ego is forever hoarding things for itself. In a world where the ego consciousness rules, capitalism fosters social castes (superiority/inferiority) and devalues a sense of community and sharing of resources. Until those who are operating in the Soul Consciousness are in leadership positions in this world, the ego will continue to rule and there will forever be a gross and gaping schism between the "haves" and the "have nots." Until that time, the masses will be at the mercy of a few leaders whose egos will not allow sharing and empowerment.

In a capitalist society, we say that "opportunity abounds." This is delusional hypocrisy, at best, and outright deceit, at worst, when the white males who are in virtually every position of power in virtually all world systems on this planet have an explicit or implicit belief that females and minorities are inferior to them. When less than 1% of the CEOs in America are female, it is a stark reminder of white male supremacy. It is unknown what percentage of CEOs are minorities, but likely the figure is so negligible that, statistically speaking, it becomes non-existent. This translates into legislation and forced respect which is what occurred when women at the turn-of-the-century and African Americans largely under Martin Luther King, Jr. revolted from oppression, prejudice and discrimination. To say that opportunity abounds for every person under capitalism is laughable when the white males who are in power have, for 3,000 years, abused, oppressed and otherwise denied females and minorities positions of leadership under the egotistical and lame excuse that "females aren't aggressive enough" and "minorities aren't savvy enough." Let's be honest. Most male leaders on this planet operate under the immature masculine consciousness. It is that simple. Since males have committed heinous atrocities against females and minorities for hundreds of years, I don't believe the cold candor of my statement could ever match the harshness and abusiveness of what females and minorities have historically been forced to endure in bitter silence.

Medical science is built upon a foundation of disease. Disease exists because the mind cannot regain its natural essence of wholeness. Wholeness can only come from Goodness. Goodness can only come from love. Love is the only thing which fills, therefore, medical science is built upon a foundation which looks everywhere other than where the answers lie. The ego searches and hunts forever in a world of complexity as it seeks to find answers in a world of matter. Answers to every problem in the world lie within your Soul and the natural laws of Goodness. Diet, pollution, chemicals, pesticides, stress, tension, deceit, greed, envy, jealousy, sadness, shame, guilt, fear and anger are the causes of all disease whether it is in this incarnation or negative karma from a previous incarnation. When medical science finally sheds its ego and learns to seek for answers from the Soul, it will make great strides in finding the simple answers to disease and illness. Until then, the ego will attempt to make things as complex as it can in order to hide the simple truths from the masses. The truth is that all disease is caused by us through our wrong thoughts, wrong emotions and wrong actions whether in this lifetime or a previous one. You are the cause of disease and you can be the healer of disease. No one can take this power away from you unless you elect to give it away. Only you can be deceived into thinking that someone other than yourself caused your disease and someone other than yourself can heal yourself. At the core, separation from the Higher Self is the cause of all disease. Reunion with our Souls is the reawakening of healing and wholeness since this is the state of love. There are essentially only two emotions: love and fear. The Soul yearns for the wholeness of love. The ego is the cause of all fear. It is from this basic truth that disease, illness and psychological unrest manifests.

Psychology has spent 125 years studying the ego and all the illusions of its false belief system. We now have voluminous writings on the complexity of the ego yet we still have growing numbers of people with mental illnesses and disorders filling psychiatric units, homeless shelters, abuse shelters and therapists' offices. The truth is that medical science still doesn't know the etiology of schizophrenia any more today than it did 100 years ago. We simply have developed a drug which better "manages" the client population, drugs them and sedates them to the point that they suffer less and are less of a burden on the population. We still spend billions of dollars treating schizophrenics, bipolar and major depressives by medicating them all. We continue to medicate the symptoms, but the disease is still there. Not only are drugs administered for the illnesses, but more and more drugs are needed to combat the side effects from the drugs which are taken to combat the illness! We have found the harmful long-term side effects of anti-psychotics; when are we going to conduct the research to discover the long-term negative side effects of anti-depressants? The pharmaceutical companies are making billions of dollars medicating this population with no incentive to cure the diseases. After all, if a cure is found, there is no more money spent on drugs. What does that tell us? All these fancy, intellectual, high brow terms written about the ego, its defense mechanisms and its pathologies make up countless academic books, yet humankind is no more mentally healthy today than 125 years ago. In fact, some may argue the world is sicker. What has happened is that drug companies are making obscene amounts of money with research dollars going into more drugs, not cures, for illnesses. Medical science still relies heavily on synthetic, expensive drugs to find answers. Medical science continues to de-emphasize natural, self-healing treatments which offer much promise for mild to moderate illnesses and disorders. It is now time for medical science and psychology to focus on the Soul and all that heals and restores wholeness to humankind. The time is ripe to allocate some of these billions of dollars to studying ways that humankind is restored to wholeness instead of spending billions of dollars on studying illness and disease. This won't be easy. The ego will fight it every step of the way because the ego is greedy to maintain its sole position of worldly power, influence and wealth. This means a radical transformation in the vision of these two fields and a mass change in consciousness away from the immature masculine ego and toward the Goodness of the Soul. The ego seeks answers through complexity because that is where it hides. The Soul seeks answers through the simplicity of nature all around us and through its own Goodness.

Religion has its egoistic leaders as well. Certainly, history is strewn with religious "holy wars" which is a contradiction in and of itself. Nothing holy is ever at war and no one who is at war is ever holy. They are mutually exclusive. Where there is war, the ego reigns supreme. We have a wicked history of man's inhumanity against man where males in power perpetuate war and violence against both man and woman. Every war that has ever been waged has been the result of the destructive energy of the masculine ego consciousness even when the figurehead was a female. The masculine ego consciousness of destruction is still the culprit behind war. And yet somehow the world is supposed to believe the myth perpetuated by men that females are irrational and inferior? Catholics killing Protestants, Protestants killing Catholics, Protestants killing Jews, Muslims killing Jews, Jews killing Muslims. All of these atrocities between us are nothing but the ego consciousness fighting to be supreme. Were the end result not death, it, too, would be laughable, but lives have been lost and in unimaginably brutal ways such as mass extinctions in ovens, hangings and physical torture. Men promulgating the edict that females are "irrational" in light of the horrors that the immature masculine has been responsible for seems, at best, the height of hypocrisy and, at worst, blatant abuse. The ego defends its own insanity and attempts to construe what is insane as rational and logical.

What you experience within is what you are and you have the choice to experience this inner world in Goodness or not. The ego would have you believe that you do not have power over your thoughts, your feelings and your actions. For sure, the ego is dedicated to ensuring that you not think about your thoughts, think about your feelings or think about your actions because, in so doing, is the first step toward the elimination of the ego. The ego deludes itself into thinking it has real power, but it does not and never will. It does have power, but its power is false and illusory because the ego is responsible for all destruction and refuses to utilize the authentic power of the unifying Will toward Goodness. Real power is that which is shared and multiplied.

In the spiritual realm, when you give love to another person, that love grows and multiplies. Sharing a spiritual fruit causes that fruit to grow and multiply. In the physical world, when you share a material item, that item does not grow. If you give your partner a watch for his birthday, the watch does not grow. What can grow is the love, the spiritual fruit, which is an outcome of giving the physical gift. If you give your parents their favorite wine for their birthday, the wine does not grow. Only the love and kindness with which the gift is given can multiply. This is one of the reasons that we refer to the spiritual realm as having authentic and eternal power. Nothing in the physical world can grow or multiply without the invisible spiritual realm of the Will activating knowledge, creativity, love and wisdom. This is true power because it is that which brings all things into existence.

The Soul consciousness is an attainable state of mind for every human being, but it requires awakening to it and then assisting others as well. It is not attainable by obtaining college degrees, material wealth, executive job titles, social positions, political or religious status. A person with a high school diploma may have the Soul consciousness while a person with a doctorate in theology may not. An individual who is a commoner may awaken to their Great Soul while the royal monarchy may be left in total unawareness and ignorance of the Soul consciousness. A person may have little money in their bank account yet be full of Soulfulness, while those who are spoken of frequently in *Fortune* magazine are in spiritual bankruptcy. There may be someone who never attends church services who is full of Soul consciousness while those sitting in church pews or standing in the pulpit preaching the spiritual message have no consciousness of the Great Soul. World positions and titles mean nothing to the Soul unless these are used in service to the spiritual realm where Goodness abounds.

We must awaken to this Being experience as an experience that is Real. That which you cannot Be, is not. Only that which you can Be, is Real. It is Real because it is a conscious state of the Soul which merges thinking (the masculine) with the feeling (the feminine) in an *equal unity.* Both the masculine and the feminine are equal and require their integration within the individual if we are to rise to the next plateau in this long journey toward returning to the integration of the One Divine Self.

*If you want to eliminate the suffering in the world, then eliminate all that is dark and negative in yourself. Truly, the greatest gift you have to give is that of your own self-transformation.*
—Lao Tzu

*Look Within, Approach with all Devotion, Stay as Heart.*
—Sri H.W.L. Poonja

# XVI. THE FOUR-FOLD PROCESS OF NATURE OR FOUR OPERANTS OF THE SOUL

The soul, just like the body, has certain dynamics which operate to maintain and sustain it. One could say that these are operants in the sense that they are processes which produce certain qualities in our lives or certain effects. We can, therefore, call them the four operants, or we can also call them the four-fold process of nature itself. These four operants exist whether we are operating within the ego consciousness or whether we are operating within the Soul consciousness. It should be understood that these operants are part of nature itself and it is how we utilize these operants which determines the quality of our consciousness and create a certain quality of our human existence. These four operants are:

cycles (time)
patterns (space)
devotion (mass)
rituals (frequency)

Cycles are inherent within everything that exists in all kingdoms, i.e., mineral, plant, animal, human and spiritual kingdoms. At the ego level, these may be thought of as that which is the opposite operating within the unity. At the Soul level, it is understood that cycles are simply part of the eternal circle of life. The ego thinks of cycles as stages from beginning to end. One might say the ego, in a perceiving world of separation and difference, thinks in terms of Point A to Point B. Point A starts here and Point B stops over there, but they are perceived as separate from each other and having a clear beginning and end. The Soul knows cycles to be eternally circular with no beginning and no end. You could say that the Soul views these cycles as the eternal and sacred geometric circle. Where does a circle begin and where does it end?

There are cycles all around us in the visible world such as the cycles of the four seasons; the cycle of life and death; and the cycle of ecological equilibrium. All fields of study in some way or another seek to understand the cycles which relate to that field of study. Astrologists seek to understand the cycles of the heavenly bodies; medical science seeks to understand the cycles of the anatomy; psychology pursues understanding the cycles of the mind; physics seeks to understand the cycles inherent within physical matter. At the ego level, these cycles are perceived in terms of the passage of time since the ego perceives beginnings and endings as it relates to physical matter. At the Soul level, these cycles are known to be eternal moments of "now" since the Soul sees the illusoriness of physical matter and the eternity of the spiritual realm with a merging of alpha and omega.

The primary cycle from which all other cycles unfold is the eternal cycle from spirit to matter, then back to spirit. A crude, but not dissimilar, example is the cycle with which the chemist is familiar where the gases descend into liquid which, in turn, descends into solids. Then the ascent back to gases begins. We can relate this to the eternal cycle of consciousness which never began and never will end. Having examined the evolution of consciousness, we understand that our next step in the process is proximately somewhere in the middle of a cycle. As the Soul consciousness takes over, we are, in essence, turning the tide and returning our focus again on Spirit. Having reached the depth of our descent in the ego consciousness of the material world, humankind may now turn its gaze and attention back to the Spiritual world of its origin.

At the Soul level, there are four (4) basic cycles from which all other lower cycles manifest:

—change and changelessness (time) (knowledge and truth)

—separateness and togetherness (space) (love and goodness)

—sameness and difference (mass) (creativity and beauty)

—activity and rest (frequency) (wisdom and will)

Ultimate truth is changeless. Ultimate goodness is oneness. Ultimate beauty is sameness. Ultimate will is at rest. This refers to the highest or spiritual realm where nothing is relative and all things are whole.

In the physical world, we perceive cycles in terms of time, although in the spiritual world, time does not exist. Think of the eternal, never beginning and never ending waves of Light when you think of spiritual cycles. Music also has cycles and patterns within it. Where would you place the beginning of a wave and where the end? Spirit only knows "now" since there are no boundaries and limits to impose the concept of time. If we take the four seasons of the weather as an example, on the physical plane, we perceive four separate and distinct times for these seasons and each follows the other. In the spiritual world, these are understood to be one "now" moment after another. If there is no beginning or no end, where can you possibly place "yesterday" or "tomorrow"?

The quality of your human existence is impacted based upon the cycles which you choose to implement on a daily, weekly, monthly and yearly basis. For instance, you have no choice as to whether you proceed through the cycle of birth through death. That is a process of nature. But how you proceed through it and what you concentrate on during that process will be one factor in determining the quality of your human existence. For example, the ego consciousness focuses on the cycle of birth to death as largely a matter of physicality, gaining material possessions and assets, obtaining socioeconomic status and ensuring that the legacy that is left to posterity is one of amassed wealth. The quality that results from this focus on material wealth is different from the Soul's quality. The Soul will use this cycle of life through death as a means whereby it can garner spiritual knowledge, seek itSelf in all its spiritual fullness, obtain spiritual fruits and share these fruits with others. Any seeking of material wealth is considered *secondary* to the primary focus of spiritual wealth. The quality of life experienced by this Soul consciousness will be substantially different than the quality of life which the ego consciousness experiences. We all have free will and in that choice, we have the liberty to choose how we move through this cycle and the quality of how we experience life.

Patterns are also inherent within all that exists both in the physical world and in the spiritual world. In the spiritual world, think of the particles and the waves of light as forming patterns. Patterns are inextricably tied to cycles, but are somewhat different from cycles in the respect that cycles represent a kind of coming and going or a kind of ascending, descending or a kind of proceeding and receding. Think of cycles as the smooth ebb and flow of the ocean where the water moves closer to shore and moves away from shore in an eternal cycle of movement. Patterns may not have the smooth "to and fro" of cycles. The four basic geometrical patterns at the Soul level are the circle, the triangle, the square and the unification of two triangles which is the hexagram or star of David.

Patterns are also the combining of opposites. As an example, you may have a cycle of getting up in the morning, going to work, exercising after work, going home, reading a book, going to sleep and then awakening to do it all over again. Think of this as a circle. A pattern may or may not move in smooth, round circles. In fact, your patterns may be more spontaneous and sporadic. For instance, you may have a pattern in your life where sometimes when you receive a salary increase at work, you go out and splurge on yourself. Or you may experience some romantic personal rejections by retreating into a depression. Or maybe when you and your spouse have a heated argument, you get angry and project your anger onto your kids. Maybe whenever you hear of a person who has won the lottery, you get annoyed and jealous. Like cycles, patterns are inherently psychological which manifest in a physical way.

Just as with cycles, fields of study pursue an understanding of the inherent, relevant patterns. Psychology studies the patterns of the human mind and human behavior; medical science studies the patterns of the anatomy; astrology studies the patterns of the heavenly bodies; physics studies the patterns within the visible world. Not surprisingly, there are universal patterns which are behind and within the visible world. It is the cycles and patterns which allow us to make sense of the unseen order in the universe.

The patterns of the ego consciousness will always be fueled by fear. The patterns of the Soul consciousness will always be a result of love. When you have a pattern of kicking the proverbial dog every time you have stress at work or yelling at your kids because your work day was particularly stressful, your ego is responding. The ego, in and of itself, must defend itself because it knows that its existence is predicated upon bolstering itself at the expense of others. On the other hand, the Soul consciousness develops patterns which are based on love and kindness. The Soul forever seeks to extend itSelf to others and to find itSelf in others and through others, therefore, defense mechanisms of denial and suppression and making others feel inferior so it can feel superior are unnecessary. The Soul is Goodness and seeks Goodness in others and seeks to extend Goodness to Self and others, therefore, what about Goodness needs to be defended?

Devotion is an operant which can also be understood as *focus, attention, intention or direction of the Will.* The devotion, or attention, of the Soul is always toward Goodness, always toward spiritual fruits and their dissemination to the Whole. The devotion, or attention, of the ego is always toward the primary focus of the material world.

The ego is devoted to separation and division; therefore, it must defend itself from others. Defense and attack are critical psychological components of the ego. The ego is devoted to the ways of the material world and cannot understand the Soul's devotion to equality and Goodness. The ego consciousness will defend its existence by attacking the Soul consciousness since the ego cannot survive if the Soul is unfettered. The ego is addicted to chaos, conflict, separation, difference, inequality and all negative emotions because these sustain it. Every perception of the ego consciousness is to defend that which supports it. The ego consciousness can never understand the consciousness of the Soul. If it sought to imbue the Soul consciousness, the ego would be no more. Therefore, the patterns of the ego consciousness will always be those patterns which maintain and sustain conflict, separation, difference, inequality and superiority/inferiority. Goodness, Truth and Unity are the only superiority and these are energies within every human being. All humans are capable of this consciousness and it is inevitable that Spirit will reign supreme because it is the unification of all opposites into the One.

Devotion is a critical part in the ascent of human consciousness since it requires moving one's attention and focus of the Will in order for the Soul to be brought back into awareness of the spiritual realm. The Soul is always devoted to that which inspires and motivates the spiritual realm. The Soul is that energic force which recalls the spiritual realm and reminds us of its existence. Since some art and music moves our Being toward some Goodness, i.e., beauty, peace, joy, etc., then in this sense they are tools by which the

Soul experiences the spiritual realm and all that is invisible to the naked eye. There is an inherent harmony within all beauty, so if the harmony is not captured by the viewer when the art is seen or the music is heard, the beauty is not felt either. Further, the lower levels of human consciousness may not grasp the beauty and harmony in art and music.

Rituals are those repeated concentrations of the Will. The essence of ritual is repetition which gives the Will power. When performing rituals, a person is reminded over and over of the focus and intention behind the ritual. In this way of concentration, rituals are a way of reminding us of what is valuable and important. Many historians talk of the rituals of ancient civilizations and how they worshiped "many gods." Many ancient civilizations were merely focusing their attention on either creativity, knowledge, love, wisdom or some manifestation thereof. They had not disconnected from the spiritual truth that *all physical things are symbols of spirit*. It was their way to truly stay connected to the spiritual realm where these "gods" of the spiritual realm were deified.

For the ego, rituals serve to inflate its sense of grandiosity. For instance, the corporate executive who already has millions, but wants billions so he can feel more omnipotent, has daily rituals of business phone calls, business meetings, making deals on the golf course, wining and dining clients which will temporarily satiate an ultimately insatiable desire. Feeding and sustaining ego with little or no interest in genuinely helping others is a ritual of excessive self-involvement.

This is why meditation is so very important in bringing the Soul back into our everyday experience. Meditation is really the energy of attention, focus and concentration. Eastern mystics and eastern religions have understood the importance of concentration and focus and have taught the value of this important ritual of Soul unfoldment and alignment. Historically, Western medical science, which projects the ego consciousness, has dismissed this practice and considered meditation as ineffective. Only since the 21st century has Western medical science and psychology begun to seriously consider and study the effects of meditation. The next step is for Western medical science and psychology to study the functioning of the energy fields and chakras of the body so as to prevent disease and disorders.

Rituals of the ego are those events, situations, processes and activities which reinforce the material world over the spiritual world. When the ego thwarts the Soul, humankind is prevented from advancing toward psychological peace. Rituals of the Soul are those activities and processes which reinforce the primacy of spirituality over the secondary concern of the material world. Soul rituals are spiritually cleansing and reinforcing and include meditation, prayer, silent retreats, assisting those in need, daily walks in nature, committing to random acts of kindness every day and extending general Goodwill to humankind and the animal kingdom. These are Soul rituals which reinforce universal responsibility and universal virtue. It is what connects humanity with the spiritual realm because virtue "is" the spiritual realm. When these activities and processes become rituals, they become habits which have profound effects deep within our individual Being and the collective consciousness of the whole of the planet.

When we go over the four-fold process of nature, we are examining the four operants of nature. These four operants are utilized by either the ego or the Soul. Let's take a hypothetical example of how the ego dominates and uses the four operants.

Ken is a corporate executive who is CEO of a large health insurance company. He has a combined annual income of $2.6 million dollars. His immediate family consists of a wife and two children. His mental focus is devoted to amassing large sums of money, accumulating substantial wealth and assuming very powerful business roles in the community. He hides behind a facade of "providing well for his family," but his real motivators are material gain and worldly power. His entire ethos is based upon this goal and whatever means he takes to achieve this end is justified. We have established that his psychological devotion, through the ego, is material wealth. Now let's examine what rituals, cycles and patterns exist in his life because these are the "fruits" that he bears which point to the incongruency between his verbalized goal and his internal motivations.

Ken wakes up every morning at 4:30 a.m. His personal cook makes his favorite breakfast, his personal assistant ensures that he reads the *Wall Street Journal* and is informed of all business meetings that day and his personal chauffeur is there to pick him up promptly at 6:30 a.m. so he can arrive at work by 7:15 a.m. Ken's Executive Assistant makes sure that Ken has a hot cup of coffee, the *New York Times*, *The Wall Street Journal*, a copy of his investment transactions over the last week from his personal broker and any urgent and important phone messages. Ken has received a phone call from one of the corporate hired Washington lobbyists and wishes to meet with him at 10:00 a.m. The senatorial election is two months away and the lobbyist is uncertain about whether the incumbent (favored by the corporation) will win the election. The corporation had provided $20,000 in campaign money for this Senator because the latter is in favor of legislation which will allow corporations to continue disparate payments between medical and mental health benefits. Even though Ken's wife suffers from clinical depression, Ken's allegiance is to "the business." From 8 am. to 10 a.m., Ken has a meeting with his direct reports to go over the upcoming corporate reorganization which will involve layoffs of 1,000 employees in three cities and substantial realignment of three business units. Ken's son-in-law, head of the marketing department of one business unit, which will be hit hard by the downsizing, will retain his position. All other marketing employees at this same business unit location will be laid off.

At 10:00 a.m., Ken meets with the lobbyist and the decision is made to provide more money for the campaign. At 10:30 a.m., Ken gets a phone call from the CFO requesting a meeting regarding the upcoming quarterly earnings report scheduled to be released in two days. At the meeting, the CFO informs Ken that the SEC is requiring that their company, along with many others, sign a legal document certifying that their past two quarterly earnings statements are accurate and comply with all standard accounting rules and practices. Ken and the CFO are cognizant of over $3,000,000 in overstated earnings for those two periods, so they contact their legal counsel for legal advice. Legal counsel advises the company to make a public announcement instead of signing the document for the SEC. The CFO also recommends that the company make a donation to some charity because the tax write-off is needed.

At 11:15 a.m., Ken receives two phone calls. One is an urgent phone call from his wife's physician stating that his wife needs to be admitted to the hospital for clinical depression and alcoholism. This is her third admission in eight years. Due to Ken's anxiety regarding his public image, he reminds the doctor of his obligation to ensure that her identity is kept confidential. The other phone call is from the second largest client (a technology company) requesting that they meet at the country club at 1:00 p.m. to discuss some concerns the client is having with the service of Ken's company. This client has expressed his concern twice over the past four months, so Ken decides to meet the client. They meet that afternoon and Ken agrees to purchase $200,000 in software upgrades from them and to fix the service problem. The client asks Ken to dinner and relays that it has been arranged that there will be two call girls to "entertain" them during their dinner at the strip joint. At 6:00 p.m., they meet for dinner. Ken calls his wife at the hospital, but the nurse relays that she is unable to take phone calls.

Ken spends his evening with the client and the "call girl" and arrives home at 10:00 p.m. He calls his office to check for phone messages and has one from his personal broker. Ken calls his personal broker at 10:40 p.m. Since Ken's personal wealth is estimated at over $92,000,000, the personal broker makes himself available to Ken during off-hours. The personal broker advises Ken to sell certain shares of stock and invest them in a safer investment vehicle due to the current economy. Ken approves the transaction and also tells the personal broker to sell 100,000 shares of stock from his own company and approves the broker to buy 20,000 shares of another company. Ken then retires for the evening at 11:30 p.m. At 4:30 a.m., he awakens and begins a new cycle.

Ken is the stereotypical ego masculine consciousness focused on self-gain and the material world. Every cycle, every pattern, every ritual is a conscious alignment with this goal. The fact that Ken makes money does not, in and of itself, make Ken a "bad person." Money is what humans have chosen to value and trade with, therefore, it is a necessary component in the world and in every society today. That makes it a *potentially* very good thing! However, the lesson that human beings fail to learn is that *it is how we use money and assets that determines the level of peace or chaos we experience in our lives.* Virtually every civilization has been powered by the corrupt, greedy ego masculine consciousness. Hoarding money and material wealth without also using a portion of that wealth to assist others has not given us the peace that we desire.

Ken could just as easily be Sally, but the harsh fact is that corporate senior executives are mostly males. As we look critically at the human condition, what can we deduce based on mere logic and reason? The immature masculine ego controls our planet. It leads politics. It leads business. It leads finance. It leads academia. It leads law. It leads religious institutions. If something does not work after thousands of years, is it not common sense that another way must be determined and tried?

John Adams once said that it is the duty of the government to provide an education for every person. Thomas Jefferson said "he who expects to be ignorant and free, expects what never was, nor never will be." Worldly education is essential for building a civilization and cultivating culture and critical thinking. As research by social psychologists indicates, worldly education can allow for the broadening of one's perspectives and a greater respect and tolerance for thought, opinions and cultures which differ from our own. A certain amount of worldly education is important if the world wishes to enjoy a more peaceful existence. But worldly education without spiritual education is insufficient in addressing the needs of the Soul.

Admittedly, not every leader or person in the world is a Ken type of person. We have a continuum of people from those who give selflessly without thinking of themselves to those who think only of themselves and never consider others. Surely the Greek, Indian and Chinese philosophers had it right when they claimed that the "middle way" is the right way. Neither end of the spectrum is conducive to peace and happiness. For on the left end of the spectrum, the "other" is happy, but the "self" is not. At the other end, the "self" is happy, but not the "other." To love self and other *equally* seems to be the harmonious way of the Soul. Certainly, the Christ admonished us in this direction and the Buddha actually admonished us to embark on the Middle Path as well. It seems that the balance of the masculine and the feminine, would, indeed, be the Middle Path.

If we are to establish cycles, patterns, devotions and rituals which recognize and honor the Soul, we must begin re-examining our priorities, goals and daily activities. Whatever we concentrate on is what will occupy our minds and dictate our actions. Here again, social psychologists who study the influence of the media, tell us there is a correlation between what we visually examine on a ritual basis and our mental attitude. It's no coincidence that most Eastern religions advocate meditation as a means whereby we can concentrate on Goodness. For in concentrating on Goodness and making this a daily ritual, we learn to listen to our Souls and to incorporate its expressions into our lives.

There are physical, mental, emotional and spiritual cycles, patterns, devotions and rituals. Those related to the physical are those which have to do with your body such as work, play, sleeping, eating, fasting, drinking, exercising and sex. In the world of ego consciousness, most of our physical operants are what govern our mental and emotional outcomes because the world values our physical aspects more than our mental and emotional aspects.

The Soul is devoted to Spirit of pure Goodness. This is the nourishment of the Soul. Rituals related to the Soul would be those mental, emotional and physical rituals and activities which promote truth, wisdom, love, kindness, beauty, compassion, justice and the like. The Soul will always retreat behind the veil of the ego when the ego consciousness dominates and overpowers as the ego seeks and tolerates deceit, greed, cruelty, injustice, shame, guilt, anger, destruction, war, violence and conflict. A ritual which brings harmony, peace and joy will nourish the Soul and, consequently, allow the Soul to emerge and unfold. Some of these rituals might be:

—incorporating a daily ritual of walking in nature every morning or every
    evening
—reading a spiritual book every week
—listening to classical or instrumental music every day
—volunteering with a local charity once a month
—meditating every morning or evening
—gardening

This is certainly a small list, but it gives you a sense of the types of rituals which nourish the Soul. Without a doubt, those rituals which involve working with the outdoors is Soul enhancing, but also working with animals can provide a strong connection with your Psyche. By first devoting yourself to a spiritual practice in your daily routine and then developing rituals which enhance the power of the Soul, you can incorporate into your cycles and patterns a Soulful balance.

*Only through the bringing together of head and heart—intelligence and goodness—shall man rise to a fulfillment of his true nature.*
—Martin Luther King, Jr.

*When male and female combine, all things achieve harmony.*
—Lao Tzu

# XVII. THE MEDIUM OF THE SOUL

The world of spiritual fruits, i.e., knowledge, creativity, love, wisdom, joy, etc., has a "substance" within which they function. The "substance" of spiritual fruits is pure light. Think of it this way. Your thoughts and emotions "float" on and within light. Light, so to speak, "carries" thoughts and emotions. Because Aristotle said that light is not a substance, there would be virtually no study of the nature of light until Kepler in the late 16th century and Newton and Huygens in the 17th century, some 1,500 years after Aristotle. This is indicative of how difficult it is to introduce a new thought, concept or theory which goes against an established theory, especially when the author of the older, established theory has achieved world-wide fame. History is replete with the difficulties which people had to surmount when their new ideas or theories challenged the accepted thought which preceded it.

Newton believed light was composed of particles and his followers were called atomists; Huygens postulated that light was composed of waves. Largely because of Newton's reputation, Huygens' idea didn't catch on at the time. It would take another two hundred years, in 1905, when the little known 26-year-old Albert Einstein would write four prolific theoretical papers in the span of nine months that would change the face of physics forever. His first paper, which eventually earned him a Nobel Prize, postulated a theory of light quanta and showed that light has a *dual, paradoxical nature of both particle and wave.* Let's mention some paradoxical scientific truths related to light in order to—pardon the pun—shed some light on the subject! We owe these paradoxical truths to physicists.

Light is constant. It travels at the constant speed of 186,000 miles per second. Time is relative. The closer you approach the speed of light, the more time slows down. Indeed, time stops at the speed of light and the length of an object shrinks to zero at the speed of light. These are important implications to Einstein's famous third paper on the theory of special relativity which he wrote in about two months. Initially, few physicists paid attention to this theory. What is remarkable about this theory is not only its novelty and uniqueness, but that this paper was published without reference to any previous sources—unheard of within the scientific community because all scientific papers always referred to other scientists in the field. Because his idea was such a radical departure from mainstream scientific thought, Einstein wasn't taken seriously. Important to academia elitists, he had not received his doctorate yet. Also important to scientists and academicians, his paper appeared too simplistic to be valid. Last, it offered very little math which was highly uncommon. Certainly Einstein, an unknown person without a doctorate, must have challenged the arrogance of established authorities since our world lives under the false perception that Truth can *only* be derived by those who have advanced academic degrees, who have spent years in research and who are graying in the temple area, a concept embedded in the law which states that tradition and authority are ultimate holders of truth. One would think Einstein would have been awarded several Nobel Prizes, but he was only awarded one. The paper outlining his special theory of relativity did not meet specific criteria at that time established by the Nobel committee such as having lots of mathematics and having abundant references to so-called "established authorities"!

Another paradox regarding the nature of light is that you can never observe a particle as both a particle and a wave at the same time. If you observe a particle of light, you cannot also observe the wave property. If you observe the wave of light, you cannot simultaneously observe the particle of light. Yet both particle and wave are necessary in order to fully understand the nature of light. This brings us to the Uncertainty Principle developed by Heisenberg which states that you can never measure a substance at the subatomic level without disturbing it. Simply stated, if you observe at that level, you disturb it. That means that any attempt to quantify the subatomic level is impossible. You can never know the exact location of an electron. So what are particles doing when we aren't observing them since observing them disturbs them?

We now move to an even more baffling paradox by mentioning the famous double-slit experiment by Thomas Young. Light is shone onto a surface with a small hole cut into it and passes onto the second surface which has two holes cut into it. This light then spreads out from these two holes onto a third surface making a pattern of light and dark called an interference pattern. It is a series of overlapping waves. Oddly, the brightest light appears halfway between the two holes instead of directly behind the holes. The intensity of light decreases as you move away from each successive patch of light forming a classical wave pattern. Common sense tells us that, if light were particles, we would expect to see two blobs of light behind each hole, yet what has formed is a wave pattern, thus, if we see a wave pattern, light must be traveling as a wave. If we now take single particles, we assume that particles will pass through one of the two holes. However, as more spots appear and build up, the pattern that emerges is the classical wave pattern for waves passing through two holes at once. These electrons seem to have an intelligence, an awareness of where they should land since they form a perfect wave pattern instead of randomly appearing on the screen. It is as though the particles have cognition and an awareness of past and future! Let's get even crazier and set up a detector at each hole so it can watch exactly which hole each particle goes through. The detector will observe just one particle going through one hole at a time and the result is two blobs of light! Take away the detector and the interference pattern appears. So how can particles seem to know when they are being observed?

This now takes us to Bohr's Copenhagen interpretation, which states that it is meaningless to determine what particles are doing when they are not being observed. If we integrate the double-slit experiment with the Copenhagen interpretation, we arrive at the unthinkable concept that the electron really only exists when it is observed. Reality seems to be created by the observer! This has resulted in some physicists believing that consciousness is a vital part of the concept of reality in the Copenhagen interpretation. Even though Bohr and Einstein respected each other professionally, the two would be at odds with each other over this interpretation for the remainder of Einstein's life. A famous quote of Einstein's, "God doesn't play dice with the world," relates to his unstinted belief that the universe is not based on probability and uncertainty. Einstein died attempting to find the elusive Theory of Everything that would reconcile his theories with Bohr's.

Pretty interesting and amazing stuff, right? So what does all this have to do with consciousness? As mentioned above, some physicists think that these experiments are pointing to consciousness as an underlying substratum or principle. Within the Soul Consciousness theoretical model, light is the "substance" upon which all spiritual fruits lie. It is difficult to speak of light as a substance, but humankind has such an embedded belief in matter, that it is best to present light as a "substance" in the beginning to slowly move consciousness in the direction of spiritual Truths. All this paradoxical logic in physics and paradoxical logic in understanding the Soul has some relation. It is this relationship which is a beginning bridge between physics and the Soul, since light is the "substance" of the Soul.

Remember, Einstein stated that *everything is energy*. Matter is dense light (dense vibrational energy). Invisible light is pure light (high vibrational energy). Both are light because there is nothing that exists except light in some form or another for all eternity because everything functions at a vibrational level and everything derives from waves and particles (atoms). This is the essence of all that "is."

Light is simultaneously *both* particle (atoms) and wave, therefore, everything at the spiritual level is paradoxical logic. As we have stated, Aristotelian logic can only exist at the physical, material level. Intellectualization is an outcome of Aristotelian logic and reasoning and is the level of functioning in which the current world functions as humankind is obsessively preoccupied with intellect, logic and reasoning. An example of Aristotelian logic is: A is A, but cannot be both A and not-A. Paradoxical logic, dominant in Chinese and Indian thought and first introduced formally in the West by the pre-Socratic Greek philosopher, Heraclitus, is the logic of the spiritual realm where all opposites converge. Heraclitus spoke of paradoxical concepts such as unity within diversity and the Many within the One. Lao Tzu's words which form Taoist philosophy and epistemology are pervasively paradoxical. Indeed, in Timothy Freke's translation of *Lao Tzu's Tao Te Ching*, Lao Tzu states "The Truth is paradoxical." Intuition is a higher level of functioning and is the higher noetic Truth which allows one to make sense of paradoxical logic. It is only through paradoxical logic that physicists will arrive at the ever elusive Theory of Everything (TOE) because Absolute Truth and Absolute Reality lie within the realm of paradoxical logic where, in an Advaitan sense, all dualities seem to converge and harmonize.

Everything that exists does so through the properties and nature of light. Your body lives, and is animated by, the electrical currents which run through it. Air, water, heat and earth are the four essential elements of your body. Air runs throughout your entire body system. Your body is comprised of approximately 80% water. The normal temperature of your body is 98.6. And, of course, your dense body returns to earthly dust upon its decomposition. There is an electrical system which operates in your body at all times and it is the animating principle of your entire physical body. Without this electrical current, your body would not be alive. Hence, it is essentially light energy which gives your body life.

Consciousness runs through and within and on this electrical current. Put another way, your thoughts run through and within and on this electric current. Thoughts and light are inseparable. Think of the radio waves and how we are able to receive a message from one place to another place far away and you will begin to form a concept of how your thoughts are carried throughout the Universe. When you pray for someone or meditate on a subject, your thoughts are carried along by light. Your thoughts have different vibrational frequencies such that there are higher thought frequencies and lower thought frequencies. Higher thought frequencies are those which are pure Goodness such as love, kindness, compassion, truth, honor, justice. These vibrational frequencies result in certain molecular and cellular level changes in your body over time. Lower thought frequencies are negative emotive thoughts such as deception, anger, hate, greed, shame, guilt, sadness, prejudice. These lower thought frequencies also result in certain molecular and cellular level changes in your body, specifically, diseases and illnesses. Lower thought frequencies create a gravitational pull toward the material world because lower thought frequencies are a result of valuing the material world over the spiritual world. That which you value is what will manifest around you on a physical level. If the world were to begin to elevate its consciousness to the Higher Self, the Soul consciousness, more people would begin to develop healthier minds and bodies and the intuitive capabilities of consciousness would grow. The intuitive capabilities of the Soul would grow over generations and this would simply become a normal way of living.

Knowledge, creativity, love, wisdom and will are spiritual energies which are responsible for all form including your body form. What can possibly *be* without these energies? The Soul is the mediating principle, or second principle, in the eternal expression and various manifestations of the one Source—Light. Astrologers have studied light since antiquity and attempted to remain connected to the spirit principle—light—which is the eternal and ubiquitous "medium" or "substance" of all that exists and ever will exist. Light is omnipresent. There is nowhere that light does not exist. Knowledge, creativity, love, wisdom and will flow forever within light itself and are responsible for all form. Black holes are misunderstood by some to be a place that is void of light. Actually, black holes are vortexes of such large masses of light that no light can escape them.

The primal urge within every individual is to Know Self. It must be understood here that to "Know Self" means returning to the Pure Knowing consciousness that exists within the spiritual realm. The Soul consciousness is not the highest state of consciousness for humankind and is a stepping stone after the ego consciousness, but before the Spirit or Pure Knowing consciousness. There is the ego, Soul and Spirit consciousness for humankind just as there are the solid, liquid and gaseous states within the chemical world. Every physical thing is a symbol for something in the spiritual world. Eternally, there is a back and forth cycle between these three stages. This is forever and it will never end being the Alpha and Omega repeated constantly and eternally.

The ego consciousness has three stages, the Soul consciousness has three stages and the Spirit consciousness has three stages. There are a lower, middle and higher stage within the ego, Soul and Spirit stages. This is representative of the eternal and ubiquitous cycle of the light wave which eternally goes from the highest point of the wave to the lowest point of the wave and back to the highest, repeating this cycle eternally.

Another eternal cycle is that of frequency. The ego consciousness is the lowest human thought frequency and dense light (matter) is a result of this low frequency. The Soul consciousness, an even higher frequency than the ego consciousness, begins to manifest at a higher frequency than does the ego because it is the mediating principle which is responsible for recalling and reminding the individual of the true lord and governor, Spirit. The Soul consciousness recognizes matter as another form of light, but an inferior form of light since it is dense light. The Spirit consciousness which is understood to be the highest frequency of consciousness since it is the state of Pure Light, Pure Knowing, has freed itSelf from the chains of the physical body and functions and operates only within the world of Pure Light. Pure Light is eternal, omnipresent, omniscient and has no boundaries being everywhere at the same time. There is nowhere in which Light does not exist.

During the "descent of man" from the spiritual realm of Pure Knowing to the material form (the physical body), man has moved further and further away from the one true, eternal source and, as a result of scientism and intellectualization, has come to ignorantly believe that all answers to creation can only be answered through something that can be seen with the physical eye. This process of moving away from the Truth is referred to in the theological and religious circles as the "fall of man." Adam and Eve are symbolic of the descent of humankind away from the spiritual source—Light—where all Truth, Beauty and Goodness exist and toward matter, where all blind confusion and ignorance manifests. The yin (feminine) and the yang (masculine) co-exist peacefully within the Pure Light realm because they are the contraction/expansion, passive/active principles of Light. With the "fall of man," these principles split. When there is a reawakening of the Soul consciousness or the Higher Self, the Truth of the Will toward spiritual Goodness surfaces. Actually, the term "spiritual Goodness" is redundant because Goodness *is* spiritual and can never be anything other than spirit. Love is spiritual; love is Goodness. Knowledge is spiritual; knowledge is goodness. All combined spiritual fruit is Truth, yet any *one* spiritual fruit is Truth. All spiritual fruit is Goodness; yet any *one* spiritual fruit is Goodness. Love is true. Creativity is true. They are both cause and effect. Love as a cause produces love as an effect. Nothing in the spiritual realm can ever be divided. To speak of one spiritual fruit is to simultaneously know all other spiritual fruit. What about love, kindness, compassion, truth, knowledge, creativity, wisdom, honor and justice could ever be quantified? To quantify anything assumes the existence of boundaries which, in turn, assumes limits. No boundary can ever be put around a spiritual fruit; therefore, scientific study of spiritual fruits must be derived not from studying the spiritual fruit, rather from studying *the effects of the spiritual fruits on humankind.*

Science and religion split because each thought that they cornered the market on truth. The immature masculine was at the head of these disciplines. From religion, philosophy split off and then psychology split off from philosophy; all thinking they held the truth and truth could only be found by dividing and analyzing. The ego was in charge. From science, we have split off into various fields like math, geometry, chemistry, physics, anthropology and astronomy. Due to the separating, dividing and conquering ego, these fields have refused to acknowledge the spiritual realm and have refused to cooperate and collaborate with each other. Their competitive and warring nature of the ego has prevented them from having the humility and wisdom to collaborate and unify their works. It is this very dividing and conquering nature of the ego which sustains the ego. For if these disciplines were to begin collaborating and finding the similarities and commonalities in their various fields of study, the ego would be at risk because they would all move closer to the Truth. The Truth is that all of these fields carry one piece of a spiritual puzzle and it is only when these leaders integrate the feminine aspect of collaboration and cooperation within their Self that the Truth, in all its beauty, will become apparent.

Fundamentally, there is only one question that ever needs to be asked and answered. There is no discipline that exists which does not, in some way or another, seek to answer this question. Who am I and where is my origin? The answer to this question stands in front of us every moment of every day waiting for us to unleash the veil of the ego and know the spiritual realm of spiritual fruits. One could say that, every day, we miss the forest by concentrating so heavily upon the trees. Or another way to put it is that we search for truth and yet we finally discover that our essence is Truth. Frantic in our search for Truth, we forget that Truth is there for us to experience every moment of our lives. Science has erroneously taught us that only the complex is real. Science tries over and over to study truth and reality as though it were an object. But Truth is never an object. Truth is eternally and always subject. This is why chi-square, ANOVA, covariance and statistical significance and every other kind of scientific measurement become a moot issue when Ultimate Truth is discovered. What about that which is Whole Being could ever be subject to measurement? Scientism, in its ego consciousness, dismisses the intuitive capacity in humankind which is the very tool and pathway by which the Soul can know Truth. One can say that science, as a study, is truly cold and heartless focusing only on intellectual thinking, only on matter, the visible to find truth. Science objectifies everything studying only particulars which divide. Modern science, with its focus on Aristotelian logic, will only find answers at the mundane and profane level and never at the spiritual level because the spiritual level is a world of paradox. Only in a world of reconciliation of opposites (the masculine and the feminine), can science arrive at Ultimate Truth. Only in studying the invisible within the visible, can Truth be found. Perhaps the height of irony lies in the fact that science studies the properties and nature of physical Light, yet is unable to lift the veil of the ego to see the spiritual Light! In this sense, science remains heartless and Soulless.

It is the next evolutionary step for humankind to "ascend" from the ego consciousness of concentrating on matter (dense light) to the Soul consciousness which recognizes and honors the reality of the spiritual domain. Victor Frankl stated in his book, *The Will To Meaning*, "human existence is not authentic unless it is lived in terms of self-transcendence" which means that humankind must transcend the ego. By its narrow, spit ego thinking, humankind remains in a quagmire of stagnant consciousness. Plato and Plotinus spoke of the spiritual realm as pure Ideas and knew them to be the only thing that has been and forever will be. These Ideas were, to them, as much of a Being than anything they knew because they knew that to have love is to *be* love. To have any spiritual fruit is to *be* that spiritual fruit. That is a state of *Being*. The ego expresses itself through the five senses of sight, hearing, touch, smell and taste. The Soul expresses itSelf in matter through these five senses, but as the Soul is nourished more frequently, its memory of the spiritual realm is activated primarily with the sixth sense of intuition. Ultimately, in the spiritual realm, illumination (the third and highest realm of knowing), Pure Knowing is reached. This is *nirguna* Brahman.

Only when physics and psychology begin to embrace paradoxical logic will there be a discovery of highest truths because Highest Truth *is* the world of paradox. You will return to your essence, your Highest Self, the realm of Pure Knowing, Pure Light. In the spiritual realm, as you move toward expansion of knowledge, you are simultaneously moving toward contraction, the Center of Self. Psychologists and philosophers banter about whether life has meaning or not. Both are true in the highest sense. Human life has no meaning in the sense that the world of illusion or maya is meaningless, yet human life does have meaning in the sense that we are always moving toward true meaning which is to return to a spiritual awareness of who we are. Psychologists also banter about which kind of therapy is the "best" therapy. There is no "best" therapy in the sense that humans evolve forever so we understand that what is "best" therapy today is not "best" therapy in 100 years. There is a "best" therapy in the sense that, at a certain evolutionary stage, there is considered a therapy which will work more effectively than others. Psychologists have had decades of arguments over whether homosexuality and gender are products of nature or nurture. We call it the nature/nurture debate. In the highest sense, both are true. Nature is understood as the biological component, the DNA, which is affected by generations of spiritual depravity or spiritual fullness and, in that sense, people's biological make-up changes at the cellular level due to changes in spiritual consciousness. Nurture, which refers to the relationships between two people, also affects a person's consciousness and the cellular level over generations. Therefore, it is understood that both nature and nurture contribute toward the changes in humankind on all levels. Spirit affects body and mind, but Spirit forever and ever is lord and governor.

Illumination is the highest form of knowledge because it is the knowledge of experiencing the knowing of the highest Truths. This is the realm of paradoxes. Let us think for a moment about the paradoxes that exist within Light. Here are a few:

Light is both particle and wave.

Light is both space (air) and matter (atoms).

Light is both active (moving) and resting (immobile).

Light is both sound and color.

Light is both high and low (being limitless).

Light is both deep and wide (being without boundaries).

Light is both known and not known.

Light is both One and many.

Light is both center and circumference.

Light is both cause and effect.

Light is everywhere and there is nowhere that Light is not. Without Light, your thoughts and emotions could not exist for where could you place them and how could you project them but for the existence of Light? Thought is energy.

Light is your essence. The urge to know your essence is the greatest urge that exists in humankind. It is the urge to know God because God is the realm of Pure Knowing. God knows Self and Other as combining into one infinite, indivisible spiritual Self. This is the One connected, limitless and eternal Self. This is the realm of the individual many rays of light within the indivisible One Light. The paradox of diversity within unity abounds. This is Pure Knowing. And you are guaranteed to reunite with this Pure Knowing essence because this is who you are. Every thought, every moment, every situation, every being strives toward the reconnection with this One Self who is the many Selves within the One eternal Self.

Your Soul remembers this One Self in which you were an individual Highest Divine Self within the One Divine Self of the Universe. Your Soul recalls the divine nature of Self where everything is connected through the spiritual realm of Goodness. The Soul knows that in order to reconnect and reunite with this spiritual realm, the Great Will toward Goodness must be activated and directed toward that sole purpose. When your Soul reawakens to this memory, your Great Soul will begin guiding your life purpose toward that ultimate goal of Pure Knowing. Once this reawakening occurs, it becomes increasingly difficult to direct your Will away from Goodness. This consciousness has been referred to by two psychologists, Abraham Maslow and Carl Jung, as self-actualization and individuation. In Freke's translation of *Lao Tzu's Tao Te Ching*, Lao Tzu states "Natural Goodness is so deep and far-reaching, it leads everything back to an awareness of the Whole."

The Will toward Goodness is like a magnetic energy force which compels you to seek Goodness more and more. The more you direct your Self toward Goodness, the energy of that force becomes greater and the energy of the ego consciousness becomes weaker. The Soul directs this magnetic energy force toward its own essence. Your own essence is, in fact, an energy force or energy field which is magnetic. This is why you will begin to be drawn toward other positive people when your Great Soul is energized and awakened. Knowing that this goal of returning and reuniting with the One Self is attainable and, indeed, is inevitable, the Great Soul will also seek to reawaken others to their Higher Self.

*If you go searching for the Great Creator, you will come back empty-handed. The source of the universe is ultimately unknowable, a great invisible river flowing forever through a vast and fertile valley. All things are brought forth from the subtle realm into the manifest world by the mystical intercourse of yin and yang. The dynamic river yang pushes forward, the still valley yin is receptive, and through their integration things come into existence. This is known as the Great Tai Chi.*
—Lao Tzu

*If there is any such concept as God, it is a subtle spirit, not an image of a man that so many have fixed in their minds.*
—Albert Einstein

# XVIII. THE SPIRITUAL REALM AND LEGION

The Spiritual realm is that realm of Light where Pure Knowing exists. As has been stated, Light is the "substance" of spiritual essence. Light "carries," so to speak, all spiritual fruits of Goodness, i.e, knowledge, love, creativity, wisdom, truth, beauty, etc. Your consciousness lies within Light in both a literal sense and in a metaphorical sense. Consciousness does not derive from the grey matter of your brain. When your physical body dies, your Spirit consciousness, your essence of Being still exists. Lao Tzu says "you need never fear you will cease to exist, even when your body has turned to dust." Awareness never began and will never end. Any psychological theory which fails to acknowledge and incorporate this infinite, ubiquitous, eternal collective unconscious, this spiritual realm, is incomplete and Soulless.

Consciousness is pure energy because it "contains" spiritual essence; physical matter is diluted energy because it is but a symbol of spiritual essence. Pure knowledge, creativity, love and wisdom manifest in this Pure Light of Knowing. The One Divine Self is composed of a legion of many individual Highest Selves. This is the spiritual realm of Souls who do not have physical bodies, rather they are only consciousness and Being. This is the state of bliss. Buddhists refer to this as a state of blissful consciousness called Nirvana and Advaitans refer to this as a blissful consciousness of *saccidananda*. There is no "place" where this state exists because what is spiritual has no limitation or boundary. This spiritual realm is highest reality because spiritual fruits are all that exist here. There is no evil, only Goodness. Every human being came from this conscious state. It is your home and it is where you will ultimately return. You have many, many lifetimes to experience living in a physical body where karma exists, but ultimately every human being will return to this conscious state. Only in a physical world can the duality of good and evil exist because only here can the ego exist. When in the spiritual realm, every conscious Being is pure Will of Goodness for the All. This is referred to as "pure knowing" and "pure bliss". You are no longer a physical body, but you are a Being of love, creativity, beauty, peace, joy, etc. In *Man's Search for Himself*, Rollo May states that "joy is the goal of life, for joy is the emotion which accompanies fulfilling our nature as human beings". This is why the early ancient peoples worshiped many "gods." Joy is a god. Love is a god. Creativity is a god. Beauty is a god. Peace is a god. Health is a god. They are gods because they are whole in and of themselves. They are states of Being, of Being One. These are distinct, yet they are all One and the same. If you know joy, how can you not know peace? If you know love, how can you not know joy? If you know beauty, is this not joy? The pre-Socratic philosophers referred to them as the "many in the One." The analogy of the many rays of the sun is appropriate here.

The spiritual realm is a realm of wholeness for what about Spirit could ever be partial? That which is whole is full of Goodness because Goodness is whole forever. Love is the fullness in which the Higher Self operates. Only love fills, therefore, until psychology becomes focused on that which fills which is the Goodness of love and all its manifestations instead of that which is empty (the ego), psychology will continue to only be the perpetual study of incompleteness and emptiness. In that sense, psychology will only be studying the incomplete, the empty. The mind which studies incompleteness and emptiness "is" the mind of incompleteness. What you focus on is what you become. This is the awesome power of focusing and meditating.

All answers to all problems lie in the Higher Self because this is where all truth and knowledge lie. The ego has no solutions to any ultimate problems since the ego is forever split, not recognizing its spiritual wholeness. Truth is whole forever and ever and there is no Truth that will ever be found in an incomplete system of thought.

Western mainstream psychology dismisses spirituality and a spiritual realm as it relates to a healthy Psyche because Western mainstream psychology (specifically, psychoanalytic, cognitive and behavioral models) are atheistic models which refute spirituality. Jung abandoned writing for the academic world the last decade of his life because academic psychology refused to recognize any psychological model which espoused spirituality. Instead, in those later years, Jung wrote almost exclusively on spiritual matters in relation to the Psyche.

The Brahman consciousness has always been and will forever be. As William James said, there is a stream of consciousness that never ends. When psychology recognizes that there is a spiritual realm, we will begin to have a better understanding of why small children and perhaps people with addictions have greater difficulty adjusting to the physical world than do others. It is my hypothesis that alcoholics, drug addicts and children who are generally unable to overcome trauma had great difficulty incarnating into this lifetime and have great difficulty living in a world dominated by a lack of wholeness and fullness. They likely had karmic debts to work through and could not reconcile those spiritual debts. In the future, when psychology accepts that Souls transmigrate and once large groups of people begin re-connecting to their past lives and the karma generated from those past lives, we will have a clearer understanding of many of the inexplicable, unresolved problems and issues which manifest. Humankind was never meant to be disconnected from the spiritual realm. This is a manifestation of being disconnected from the spiritual whole to which we all belong and will one day return even if it takes a trillion aeons to do it.

If you close your eyes and imagine that you are a spiritual Being with no physical body, but are a bundle of pure, flowing energy or pure light, then you can begin to have a small grasp of what it is like to be in the spiritual world. There are no clear boundaries between you and other spiritual Beings for how can spirit be segregated? Those Souls existing within the spiritual realm have a higher Truth and know Truth. Anyone who does not accept the fact that there are higher states of consciousness is simply ignorant. Higher states of consciousness are better states of consciousness because they are expanded states of consciousness where peace lies. In lower states of consciousness, peace does not exist, therefore, it is understood that, in higher states of consciousness, we experience qualitatively a more optimal state of Being. To avoid the elitist attitude, it is important to remember that we all return to these higher states of consciousness. It is only a matter of the Will.

In the spiritual realm, there is a knowing consciousness that everything physical is an image or a symbol of that which is in the spiritual, invisible realm. All things which are visible to the physical eye, are images, symbols and representations of some spiritual truth, some spiritual fruit. What has happened is that Spirit has taken itSelf and created itSelf in yet another form. An equivalent example would be where water is transformed into steam when it is heated or when water changes to ice when it is frozen. Steam and water are the same things, yet they are different forms. Ice and water are the same things, but they are different forms. The natural world was created by the Boundless Infinite changing itSelf into yet another form, yet still Being Boundless Infinite. Physical form is an image created in order to please the Infinite Oneness to which we all belong. It is a creation of joy to bring joy. It is an extension of that which forever "is."

Within the spiritual realm, there exists a lower order of spiritual beings called angels and a higher order of spiritual beings called archangels. In Brian Walker's book, *Hua Hu Ching: The Unknown Teachings of Lao Tzu*, he translates the *Tao Te Ching* and says this about the angelic realm:

> "*If you wish to become a divine immortal angel, then restore the angelic qualities of your being through virtue and service. This is the only way to gain the attention of the immortals who teach the methods of energy enhancement and integration that are necessary to reach the divine realm. These angelic teachers cannot be sought out; it is they who seek out the student. When you succeed in connecting your energy with the divine realm through high awareness and the practice of undiscriminating virtue, the transmission of the ultimate subtle truths will follow. This is the path that all angels take to the divine realm.*"

Like in the physical world, lower should not be misinterpreted to mean that the lower beings are of lesser importance. Lower and higher refers to the fact that there are some beings who have moved closer to Pure Knowing but it is understood that all beings have the potential to reach the highest realms *and will do so in time*. And so we come to understand a hierarchy of Knowing although this refers to spiritual knowledge, not worldly knowledge. Worldly knowledge is subordinate to spiritual knowledge. While worldly knowledge is neither inherently good nor bad, it can be used for either purpose. It is valued as good if it is used for purposes of Good. Worldly knowledge is bad if it is wielded for purposes away from Goodness. Spiritual knowledge, however, is only that knowledge which is Good and furthers Goodness and is accomplished by a certain way of "seeing" the Oneness in all that exists. "Seeing" in this sense does not refer to visual sight of physical things and objects, rather to *a way of knowing* which, in turn, *affects how one relates to everything*. For Jesus, the Buddha and Lao Tzu, each of these three individuals were able to achieve a way of "seeing" or a way of knowing which profoundly affected the way they related to others. Specifically, this way of "seeing" or knowing resulted in intrapsychic peace and interpersonal compassion. Metaphorically speaking, one could say they found a pair of lens through which they saw the world in a unified and special way which, in turn, allowed them to relate to others with love, peace and joy. Being this Higher Self was their essential core Self and they only projected that which the Higher Self is: love, peace and joy. This is why they had a stance of *non-defense* and a wholly loving, kind, compassionate way of relating. That which is whole, complete and full needs no defense. It simply *"is."*

Just as you have chosen to incarnate into a physical body, there is a legion of other spiritual Beings who have elected not to do so. Either they have chosen not to incarnate at all or they have already incarnated and do not wish to do so again. This spiritual cavalry is called the angelic realm. It is less important what you call them than it is to know that they exist and they watch over us while we live a human existence. Jesus the Christ and the Buddha are spiritual Beings who elected to incarnate, but are now within the spiritual realm. We do not see them with our physical eyes, but they do exist nonetheless. Their consciousness is "alive."

There is an entire and infinite spiritual cosmos that assists us daily though many people are unaware. Your Soul knows they exist and, in fact, your Soul communicates with these Souls while you are sleeping which is why it is so important to recall and journal your dreams. Some people communicate with the spiritual beings while they meditate which is a deep trance-like state. This is not a psychotic state where "evil voices" talk, rather is an altered state of peaceful consciousness.

In this world of matter where unrest, turmoil, violence and destruction reign, your Soul is not at home. It is much like a prisoner of war facing the daily combat of the human existence. In this world of matter, the ego reigns and is strengthened as Western science and modern psychiatry and psychology continue to promote the false belief that matter is real. As long as psychology fosters the construction of a strong ego, humankind will never move beyond the pathology of the ego and never experience the transcendent or the numinous.

Children are born into this world with a natural connection to the numinous, but most adults cause this spiritual connection to be broken by telling the child that their imaginary playmates are not real. Being full of faith and innocence, it comes quite naturally for children to interact with the spiritual world. Children who speak of angels or guardian angels are experiencing their connection with the spiritual legion. But because the adult does not have the capacity to spiritually "see" the playmate, the adult will ridicule and scold the child. This, in most instances, causes the child to choose between the spiritual world and the physical world. And in most instances, the child will choose the physical world where the biological mother and father exist and where the social norms created by society and every world system have taught that communicating with spiritual beings is a sign of psychosis. Losing the faith and belief in the spiritual world, or quite simply being afraid of being chastised and neglected by the parents, the child shuts off the contact with the spiritual beings. Because spiritual beings do not interfere with a person's free will, when the child shuts off that vibrational frequency, the child is no longer intimately connected to the spirit world.

The spiritual legion is awaiting all human Souls to awaken to their next potential—the recognition of the supremacy of the Soul over the ego and the need to rediscover and nurture the Great Soul. When this disconnection has been healed, we will begin to see the slow dawning of a heaven on earth.

*Do not go about worshipping deities and religious institutions as the source of the subtle truth. To do so is to place intermediaries between yourself and the divine, and to make of yourself a beggar who looks outside for a treasure that is hidden inside his own breast.*
—Lao Tzu

*Chanting is no more holy than listening to the murmur of a stream, counting prayer beads no more sacred than simply breathing, religious robes no more spiritual than work clothes. If you wish to attain oneness with the Tao, don't get caught up in spiritual superficialities. Instead, live a quiet and simple life, free of ideas and concepts. Find contentment in the practice of undiscriminating virtue, the only true power.*
—Lao Tzu

# XIX. UNCONSCIOUSNESS VERSUS CONSCIOUSNESS

The spiritual realm is the realm of Pure Knowing. This is the realm of Pure Spirit and Light. All things are known here because deceit and ignorance can only exist in a material world. All knowledge is consciously held within the collected Mind of all who dwell in the spiritual realm. One could say that there is only full and absolute consciousness and full and absolute awareness there. There is no sleeping in the spiritual realm, therefore, what could be unconscious? Unconsciousness can exist only in a world of physical matter because a "split" consciousness can only exist in the world of matter.

Today, psychologists refer to "consciousness" as the physical awakened state. There is no reference or acknowledgement to a transcendent or "awakened consciousness" in mainstream psychology. The field states that, because we are not asleep, we must, therefore, be conscious. To a person who is connected to their Soul, she/he understands that, just because a human being is not sleeping, does not mean they are necessarily spiritually conscious. Indeed, to the person whose Soul unfolds, she/he comes to deeply understand the true difference between worldly consciousness and spiritual consciousness. Just because every human being on this planet is walking around in a state of worldly consciousness, does not translate into a world full of spiritually conscious human beings. Spiritual consciousness is a state of mind that is broader than worldly consciousness. Spiritual consciousness may be thought of as a more "awakened" state of mind or an illumined state. It is that state whereby the Soul turns toward Spirit and begins its ascent back to the knowledge of the infinitely connected Whole of existence. To the Soul, the ego consciousness is asleep and unconscious! The ego is considered to be in a dream world of illusions where the ego thinks that what is unreal is real and what is real is unreal. The spiritual Self or Full Self is incarnated within a symbol of Goodness, the physical body. When you were physically born into this world, you disconnected from your Full Self because you have incarnated into *a symbol of who you are*. It is the state of consciousness whereby you have lost your divine identity of Godness, of the Goodness, of the spiritual fruits from whence you came and in which your entire Soul is made. This is why it is largely futile to argue with the ego consciousness because it does not understand, comprehend or grasp Soul consciousness. The ego consciousness will always reject any mindset which embraces, empowers, includes and unifies human beings because the very act of unifying is the beginning of the end of the ego. The ego does not have the Fullness of Being that the Higher Self has, but all the ego has to do is remember its essence and it will then remember that it has everything it thinks it is missing! When the ego does this, it transforms into the Higher Self! Loving-kindness unifies, therefore, the ego must reject it. Compassion unifies, therefore, the ego must reject it. Concepts of equality for all human beings will be rejected by the ego consciousness because the ego cannot exist in a world of equality.

What psychologists refer to today as the unconscious becomes fully conscious when we return to the spiritual realm. There is no split since everything is fully awake at all times. In the spiritual realm, consciousness is

One. Though there is difference between Souls in the spiritual realm, there is an interconnectedness that can never be broken. What about two rays of light could ever be split?

Dreams are an essential form of communication from the spiritual realm. Paying attention to your dreams is to pay attention to symbols which will guide your daily life. Sigmund Freud hypothesized and believed that dreams were a central repository for all unconscious desires, wishes and fears. For him, along with many today in mainstream psychology and psychiatry, this state of mind is a dark, dim world ruled by pathology. The Soul experiences it differently, however.

The Soul, whose language is silence, knows that dreams are more than fears and desires. Dreams are the mental and spiritual world of visual symbols and the meanings behind those symbols. These symbols serve as guideposts. Erich Fromm, in his 1951 book, *The Forgotten Language: An Introduction to the Understanding of Dreams, Fairy Tales and Myths*, was prescient in his knowledge of the future use of dreams as it relates to the understanding of the Higher Self. He states:

> "The study of myths and dreams is still in its infancy. It suffers from various limitations. One is a certain dogmatism and rigidity that has resulted from the claims of various psychoanalytic schools, each insisting that it has the only true understanding of symbolic language. Thus we lose sight of the many-sidedness of symbolic language and try to force it into.....one kind of meaning. Another limitation is that interpretation of dreams is still considered legitimate only when employed by the psychiatrist.....On the contrary, I believe that symbolic language is the one foreign language that each of us must learn. Its understanding brings us in touch with one of the most significant sources of wisdom...The Talmud says, 'Dreams which are not interpreted are like letters which have not been opened'....Indeed, both dreams and myths are important communications from ourselves to ourselves. If we do not understand the language in which they are written, we miss a great deal of what we know and tell ourselves in those hours when we are not busy manipulating the outside world."

Rollo May, in *Man's Search for Himself*, refers to dreams as "sources of wisdom, guidance and insight" which have been interpreted since ancient times, however, mainstream society has disconnected from the significance of our dream world which, according to May, "results in the cutting off of an exceedingly great and significant portion of the self. We are then no longer able to use much of the wisdom and power of the unconscious."

Jungian analysts and transpersonal psychologists are most noted for their emphasis on dream analysis in the therapy setting. These two psychotherapists consider dreams as psychic gold to be mined which can provide the client with profound insights and, in turn, can lead to positive changes.

There are generally five kinds of dreams: 1) dreams which reveal events from our past incarnations, 2) dreams which provide us with current explanations and directions in our present incarnation, 3) dreams which foretell future events in our current incarnation, 4) astral traveling and 5) dreams which, in the psychoanalytic tradition, symbolize wishes and desires. It is not uncommon to have recurring dreams of the first type, i.e., dreams of your past incarnations. When you identify them, you will often be able to explain otherwise inexplicable fears such as fear of heights, fear of driving over bridges, fear of black cats, etc. Dreams which are "now" related have that sense of "nowness" when you attempt to interpret it. As you become more adept at interpreting dreams, you naturally begin to intuitively have a sense of which type of dream you are dreaming.

The fourth type of dream, astral traveling, is when your Soul (while you are physically sleeping) travels to other places and observes. Remember that your "substance" is light, therefore, your consciousness "travels," so to speak, in the spiritual realm. You have no physical body and there is no such thing as space and time. If you ever have dreams where you have a sense of flying above the ground, these can be astral travel dreams. It may also be a symbolic dream indicating some meaning that needs identifying. Jung was perhaps the first major figure in psychology to utilize dreams as a tool of spiritual guidance for the client. Believing the unconscious to be the archetypal realm, his clinical practice was heavily focused on the client's unconscious, her/his dreams and the valid and useful interpretation of those dreams as a spiritual guidepost.

There are universal symbols in dreams. For instance, when you dream, typically things to your left symbolize the past; things to your right symbolize the future. Water represents emotions. If the water is clear and peaceful, this may symbolize a peaceful, calm state. If the water is muddy and choppy, this probably represents a confused, emotional state. Hair represents understanding or thinking. Eyes and glasses represent coming into a realization. Shoulders represent burdens. Feet represent movement or action. Snakes symbolize temptation or the lower ego consciousness. Jung believed that wind, fire and birds represent the Holy Spirit. Ultimately, every person must go within to ask what the meaning of something is for them. While there are some universal symbols within dreams, each person must interpret her/his own dream life. Not all of our dream life is comprehensible or recalled, but every person dreams whether they have a memory of it or not. The more you nurture your Soul and develop a rich spiritual life, the better you are able to remember your dreams.

In the unconscious world, you may literally be replaying some past life event. As the Soul reincarnates into a new body, the Soul still has vestiges of prior lives. Many people have certain fears which are inexplicable because they are not based upon any recalled traumatic situation in this life. For example, for years, I have had a lifelong fear of traveling over bridges with large bodies of water underneath. There is no event which has taken place in this life that would give a plausible or rational explanation for this excessive fear which always causes me to panic. Finally, in my late thirties, I began meditating and asking my Higher Self and the spiritual realm to allow me to receive the knowledge of my intense fear of traveling over bridges. After several months, I had a dream which I believe removed the mystery of this fear. In my dream, there was a young woman driving a car with her two young sons in the back seat. The boys were around ages six and ten. Just as the woman is driving the car across a bridge with water underneath, one of the children throws a blanket over the mother's face. She loses control of the car, careens to the left and drives the car off the bridge and into the water. I am convinced this was an actual event which occurred in a past incarnation and this incredible fear has carried over into this incarnation.

Ever since I was a young adolescent girl, I had a recurring dream of being chased by a bald man who had an axe or a knife in his hand. The dreams never seemed to go further until finally I had a dream in my late thirties which I believe was a fuller, more understandable picture of what occurred in a past life. Once again, I started specifically meditating and asking to receive an answer to the mystery of these recurring dreams. The result was this dream. I was an adolescent girl, roughly around age seventeen, running from two men, one with black, wavy hair and one who was bald. I ran to a house, opened the door and no furniture was in the house. The room had hard wood floors and the window had a sheer valance blowing in the slightly cool wind. There were dying leaves blowing on the floor so I knew it was fall. All of a sudden, a black cat screeched and ran across the wooden floor.

I looked to my left at a staircase and ran up it to hide in the dark hallway. As I looked down, the two men came in and began slowly walking up the stairs toward me. The dark-haired man had a small axe in his right hand. The dream ended at this point. I knew upon awakening that this had been a life when I had been murdered at a young age. This gave me an answer as to why in my current incarnation I had always had some subconscious fear of dying young and I also have always hated and feared black cats. This was a recurring dream throughout my adolescence and young adult years, so I knew it carried particular meaning. In this instance, it was a past life, however, some recurring dreams can be portentous. You should always pay close attention to any recurring dreams. I have had many dreams which have warned me of future happenings so that I am able to prepare for them.

A few dreams have been actual images from future events in this life. For instance, I had a dream that a friend of mine went on a job interview at a law firm. I saw her very clearly being greeted by a young, good looking man in a dark business suit and he was escorting her and walking ahead of her up a slightly curved stair case. Almost one year later, this friend of mine described the actual interview which took place and, just as my dream indicated, a young man in a business suit had greeted her and escorted her from the lobby up a slightly curved stair case.

In the dream world, you have spiritual guides who are attempting to provide you with answers which will serve as a weathervane for you in this life. Dreams will often have content that will give you directions when making choices in the physical world. Spiritual guides are not angels, but are Souls who have incarnated into physical form, but are now back in the spiritual world. Oftentimes, your spiritual guides have been family members or friends whom you knew in one or more physical incarnations. Since your spiritual guides know how difficult it is to live in a world full of fear, they assist you in finding answers to your daily life.

Angels are Beings of a very high energy frequency and who may never have incarnated in physical form or may have incarnated only once or a few times. They seek to protect you and steer you to a higher purpose that is spiritual and serve humankind in some way. Through religions, we learn that there are different angels. Some of the well known archangels are Michael, Gabriel, and Raphael, but there are many others. These archangels are, and represent or symbolize, energy. Michael is the energy which combats evil. Gabriel is the energy which is a messenger or deliverer of Goodness. Raphael is said to be the archangel who imbues the energy of creativity.

It is not necessary that you know angels by name, rather it is only important that you know they are there in multitudes beyond any number you can imagine and that they protect and help you. Sometimes they will appear in dreams; sometimes during meditation. When you meditate and are able to reach a deep meditative state, you can begin to dialogue with angels. All you need do is inquire and ask an angel to reveal their name and speak to you. Some of my spiritual Masters are Elohim, Joachim and Srinatha and one of my Spirit Guides is Lenora. They seem to address different types of issues when I appeal to them. Angels do not have audible voices, but are commonly referred to as voices that silently speak. (Watch that paradox again!) This may take many meditative practices before you are able to connect with the angelic realm, but the more you meditate, the greater your likelihood that your energy frequency will vibrate at a high enough level for them to silently talk with you.

When you dream of famous figures, it is important to determine first what that person represents to you. For instance, if you have a dream of John Wayne, determine the characteristics by which you identify him. He may represent courage, strength, honor, integrity and truth. If he appears, for example, as your fiancé walking down the wedding aisle with you on his arm, perhaps your dream is telling you that your future partner will have these same qualities. If you dream of riding a bicycle next to a graveyard full of headstones, it could be a warning of some ending or loss ahead, especially if the graveyard appears to the right.

It is important to know that dreams are not a mere wasteland of negative psychic garbage or just happenstance thoughts as some psychologists would have you believe. Many have meaning and contain symbols of your history and future. Thus, it is essential to the Soulful life to be attentive to dreams and trace them. Maintain a journal of your dreams and follow them over the course of time. After you determine that you want to establish a practice of this, you will find yourself recalling dreams more frequently. Sometimes, you may awaken and have the memory just barely outside your reach. When that happens, lying in bed for a few more minutes and working to recall one figure in the dream will oftentimes bring back larger portions of the dream. Always remember that others can assist you in analyzing their meaning, but in the end, your Soul is the only one that can accurately interpret your dreams.

*Humanity grows more and more intelligent, yet there is clearly more trouble and less happiness daily. How can this be so? It is because intelligence is not the same thing as wisdom.*
—Lao Tzu

# XX. FREE WILL

For thousands of years theologians and philosophers have debated whether or not free will exists, as opposed to whether creation is predestined as though both cannot paradoxically exist together.

We have said that, at the Soul level, paradox is the fabric of existence, therefore, both free will and predestination exist. You have the free will to be and do as you please, yet the spiritual laws are inviolable and they will guarantee the final "outcome" of your actions. In this sense, you have both free will and yet there is an overall predestined outcome. As for free will, every human forever retains free will. Every person has the choice every minute of every day to choose to move toward Goodness or away from it. In this sense, you have free will. If you choose Goodness, you have automatically chosen one or more spiritual fruits from the spiritual realm. If you choose to move away from Goodness, there is a different result which surfaces and you have total free will to determine how long you wish to suffer! The end result of either Goodness or the absence of Goodness is always the same although the details along the way are different. The predestination of every human being is immortality no matter what choices they make in their physical incarnation. Goodwill speeds up the return to the Light; evil slows it down. But everyone returns to the immortal state of Pure Knowing. If every person on this planet were to awaken today, begin to only perform acts of Goodness and to manifest higher levels of consciousness, the end result would be a return to the Highest Self. If every person on this planet does not awaken today and perform acts of Goodness, the end result will eventually be a return to the Highest Self. What am I trying to say? That the return to the Highest Self is guaranteed, it is predestined although you have control (free will) over whether you want to suffer or be in peace while you are a human being. In Reality, the journey from communion with Higher Self and the fall away from Higher Self and the eventual return to the Higher Self is the journey from Point A to Point A and no real distance or time has lapsed since there is no time or space in the spiritual realm. Only in the dream world of material things which appear to be separate and different do we think that a journey is one of distance and time.

Good always overcomes evil and this is a spiritual law. It is inviolable. So you have evil will and you have Goodwill. And you're free every moment to choose which you wish to manifest. Will, in and of itself, is neutral. Which direction you wish to move it in is your choice. The entire premise of the Soul Consciousness is that only Goodwill to Self and others is that which will bring joy and peace. Indeed, Assagioli, in his book, *The Act of Will*, says that "good will is joyous!" He spoke often of the Transpersonal Self or Higher Self which I call the Soul Consciousness. He states in *The Act of Will*:

> "The realization of the Transpersonal Will, the expression of the Transpersonal Self, is so intensely joyous that it can be called blissful. Here we have the joy of the harmonious union between the personal and the Transpersonal Will; the joy of the harmony between one's Transpersonal Will and those of others; and, highest and foremost, the bliss of the identification with the Universal Will."

If we continue to operate with the ego consciousness, the extinction of the entire human race will be its eventual outcome. If that is what we choose with our free will, the annihilation of the human race means that there is a karmic debt that must be fulfilled. It would have to be satisfied by reincarnating until humankind "gets it right" which is to say that, until human kind learns the lesson of Goodness, the cycle of incarnation into a world of chaos, war and suffering will continue. Somewhere along the way, which may mean it takes 99,000,000,000,000,000,000,000 more years for humankind to "get it," we all return to our essence—Pure Light. How quickly we return is left to us because the Highest Divine One Self does not control or condemn. Only the ego controls and condemns which is to say that our lower selves control and condemn each other which, in turn, prevent us from rising to the next highest level of consciousness where forgiveness becomes a more frequent way of relating.

Evil is the absence of Goodness. Using free will to choose to ignore and deny love, truth, kindness, honor, justice, compassion, etc. will result in deception, injustice, dishonor, hate, anger, greed, shame, guilt and intolerance. This brings us to an important point of what to do when someone has wronged you. The ego consciousness projects the same energy back onto the person. In other words, if you're driving in traffic and someone gets angry because you're not driving fast enough so they shout an angry indecency at you, you have the free will to choose how to respond. You can choose to project back onto that person exactly what they projected onto you. Or you can choose not to do that. You have total free will which energy you wish to project because that is the power of the Mind.

When we choose to return the shadow ego consciousness with its projections, we are sure to experience chaos and discord. And due to the law of cause and effect, each cause *must* have a corresponding effect. All negative emotions manifest on a physical level from the ego which is ruled by fear. In its actions, the ego responds with some negative emotion when it is threatened. If the ego perceives its worldly power will be diminished, it may react with greed and anger. If the ego perceives its worldly wealth may be lessened, it may react with greed or sadness. If the ego perceives that its beauty may be decreased, it may react with jealousy and shame. If the ego projects these onto another person, that other person may, in turn, project the same or similar negative emotions back onto the originator and even onto other innocent people. This creates what is referred to in many Eastern religions as negative karma. In simple terms, it is a debt which must be repaid. Only when a person fails to project back the negative emotion can the cycle of karma be broken. In this case, the originator has the choice of either to ask for forgiveness or to continue to project the negative emotion even if it is only held within. Since every emotion is energy, we can think of negative emotions much like electricity. When you project a negative emotion onto another person, that negative energy returns to you. It is a destructive energy. Positive energy operates differently and more like a magnet because when you project a spiritual fruit such as love, kindness or joy, this tends to draw similar energy to it and this energy then magnifies. This is a creative energy because it multiplies and creates. There is nothing in this physical world that multiplies when you give it away. If you give a diamond ring to your girlfriend, more diamond rings do not appear. If you give your father a new tennis racket, more tennis rackets do not surface. Only in the spiritual realm of love, kindness, joy, peace, truth, honor, etc. does giving away something actually make it more abundant. When you give away love and kindness, it is amazing how it grows and grows!

It is only when we, as a society, begin to project the Soul consciousness outwardly that we will begin to experience harmony between groups. The Soul is tolerant and accepting of all people whose Will is activated toward Goodness. Worldly differences are not the barometer by which the Soul projects judgment. The Soul wishes forever to experience itSelf which is to say it wishes forever to experience spiritual fruits. It always seeks higher levels of experience because it knows that spirit is the lord over matter. Love, knowledge, creativity and wisdom and the Will toward Goodness are lord over matter. This is so forever and ever. As humans, we can be lost to this spiritual truth only for a time. When we awaken to the Soul consciousness, it could be said that we begin to awaken to the Truth of who we are and what we can be. Free will plays a critical role in what we are today and what we will become tomorrow. Whether we choose the limiting, separative, destructive ego or utilize our free will to choose to manifest the fullness of the Soul is always our choice. And it is in that choice that we choose heaven or hell on earth.

*According to the doctrine of karma, everyone is conditioned and determined by his conduct, as this is enacted over a period of innumerable births, deaths and rebirths.*
—Eliot Deutsch

# XXI. REINCARNATION AND KARMA

Virtually all Eastern psychologies and philosophies take the concepts of reincarnation and karma as tacitly factual. While academically discussed by scholars of Eastern philosophy and psychology, it simply is not something whose existence is questioned because, to those cultures, it is rather like debating whether air exists. Western consciousness, however, vociferously rejects the concept. As Deutsch states in *Advaita Vedanta: A Philosophical Reconstruction*:

> "There is perhaps no other basic doctrine in Indian philosophy which has had such a hold upon the popular thinking and practical religion in India and which, in spite of Plato's *Republic* and *Phaedo*, has met with as much resistance among Western philosophers, as the doctrine of karma."

Certainly the majority of ancient Greek philosophers believed in the transmigration of souls. Pythagoras, Socrates and Plato are noted for their belief in reincarnation. No Western psychological model explicitly recognizes reincarnation or karma. With the Soul Consciousness model, it is assumed that the Soul incarnates and reincarnates into the human body in order to experience itSelf in and through matter and that karmic debts are manifestations of deeds performed.

Karma is a sort of spiritual debt which is subject to the law of cause and effect and builds based upon either virtuous deeds or deeds of ill will. We mostly think of karma in terms of a person who commits some wrong, therefore, it has mostly unfavorable connotations. Every injustice committed that is not healed during an incarnation must be repaid, so to speak. Karma is transmuted by the originator of the negative energy by having an authentic energy of forgiveness or when the individual "receives" back that same negative karmic energy which she/he "sent" to another person or persons. These are the only ways a person can rid themselves of negative karma. Every cause must have an effect regardless of how long it takes for that effect to be felt. This is an inviolable spiritual law. The energy that you transmit must return to you. Since negative emotions only manifest on a physical level, then a person can only build up negative karma while in a physical incarnation. There is no such thing as karma in the spiritual realm of Pure Knowing because there is no negative energy in the spiritual realm. There is no negative energy in the spiritual realm because there is no fear there. Where there is no fear, there is no pain and suffering. Where there is no pain and suffering, there is no negativity. Total peace, serenity and absolute love are all that exist in the spiritual realm. Hell can only exist in a material world where the ego manifests.

When a person does not receive back the negative energy that they gave to a person, they must return in another incarnation to repay the debt and receive that negative energy and learn the lesson. This is why religions mention the "sins of the fathers" being visited upon the children. It is referring to the fact that a person must somehow pay off that debt or account for that debt in the "spiritual ledger." If it's not repaid so that the transaction is balanced out, the person has to return in another incarnation until the debt is repaid and the lesson is learned. The ultimate and highest lesson is really that what you give to others is what comes back to you. This is why the Christ said that you have to treat your neighbor as yourself. If you don't, it reflects back on you quite literally. Some of these "lessons" come back to us as diseases and illnesses so the eradication of disease and illness is not solely a matter of eating the proper foods, drinking plenty of pure water, surrounding ourselves in a clean ecological environment and eliminating negative stress. It is this, but more than this. It is also a matter of treating other people as we treat ourselves.

Many religious people in the Judeo-Christian belief systems do not believe in reincarnation and assume the Soul only lives once in a physical body. If the soul incarnates once into the physical body, why is it not plausible that it can *re*incarnate? Why is one incarnation accepted within mainstream religion, yet it is unacceptable to conceive of a soul reincarnating again and again? The belief in karma and reincarnation naturally implies that we humans have responsibility for our actions and that there is a universal spiritual law of justice to which we are all held accountable.

Negative karma is an unbalanced, unhealthy energy account opened by the ego consciousness. Thinking of it in accounting terms, it means owing someone something. The way to avoid negative karma is to turn the other cheek when someone wrongs you. That literally means to ignore a negative person if you are able. It does not mean, for example, to allow someone to continue to abuse you or take advantage of you. It means that you should move and turn away from that person, but don't return their negative energy with more negative energy. Ask for justice when you have been wronged instead of giving back negative energy. In this way, you are avoiding repaying a wrong with another wrong; you are asking for the other person to right their wrong to you. If you have wronged another person, you have already created a liability and you have a spiritual debt to pay. Only by having an authentic heart of forgiveness or by receiving back that same negative energy can you wipe that debt clean. The former is preferable, but either way, the slate has to be made clean.

The ego returns a negative emotion with a negative emotion. The ego lives through fear. What does it fear? It fears that it is lacking, so it wants what the "other" is or has. In this sense, the ego forever wishes it were something other than it is. Why? Because the ego always perceives the world through the lens of lack. The ego fears because the other is different, separate, and special. This thinking breeds all kinds of unfavorable behaviors as it is constantly defending itself in order to gain something it perceives is lacking. This, in turn, creates a host of negative feelings and behaviors such as prejudice, discrimination, hate, anger, greed, envy, jealousy, violence, shame, guilt, sadness and anxiety.

All physical and mental diseases, illnesses and disorders are, ultimately, the result of not obeying spiritual laws of harmony and balance. There is nothing that happens to you that you did not bring out either in this lifetime or some past incarnation through actions which violate spiritual laws. No disease, illness or disorder manifests in your mind or body during your current incarnation which is not directly caused by your actions which occurred either in your current lifetime or a previous incarnation. Either you have assumed karmic debt in this lifetime and are reaping the consequences or you have a karmic debt from a previous lifetime and are repaying it in this incarnation. A person may also elect to assume a disease or illness in order to achieve personal Soul growth or to benefit a Higher Purpose for others. This is not to say that people who are diagnosed with diseases and illnesses should simply abandon efforts to increase health and well-being. Sometimes an unhealthy decision or choice during a current lifetime is the root cause of a disease or illness manifesting and moving toward positive change will ameliorate or eradicate the illness. All physical and mental maladies do have a reason for manifesting and, ultimately, they do arise because of the person's own actions, choices or decisions, regardless of which lifetime that decision was made or action was taken. Spiritual debts must be paid and that is simply an inviolable law. People are the ultimate cause of their own illnesses regardless of whether the cause initiated in this lifetime or a previous one. Chance doesn't play a role here.

Modern Western medicine has convinced most of us that diseases and disorders are "genetic" or caused by "environment" or "viruses." This is yet another escapist attitude which ignores and dismisses spiritual laws and allows us to falsely believe that somebody else is the cause of our ills and problems. Make no mistake, the quantity and quality of what you eat and drink, the vitamins and minerals in your body, internal and external stress, the quality of the air you breathe, whether your thoughts and emotions are predominantly positive or negative, whether you have negative or positive people surrounding you and how you treat others are all factors which determine whether mental or physical illnesses, diseases and disorders manifest in your body. This may sound uncompassionate because few people want to be told that they are responsible for their own illness or disease, but we are all self-responsible. You can only draw an illness or disease to yourself if you allow it and it is either because of something you have done or failed to do during your current incarnation or it is because, prior to incarnating on a physical level, you agreed to experience that in your physical body. A person may have stayed with an abusive husband for so long that the negative feelings of fear, shame and guilt build up in their body and they develop an illness. Or someone may maintain an unhealthy diet and poor exercise for too many years which causes a physical illness. An individual may abuse drugs and alcohol and remain in an unsatisfying career, all which causes that person to stay wallowing in negative emotions of fear, hate, envy and sadness for year after year, ultimately drawing mental and physical illness to them. Or someone may be the kind of person who keeps giving and giving to others and never asking anything from anyone else which fosters a kind of "poor me" victim attitude which, in turn, creates ambivalent feelings of fear, guilt and anger. Not having the awareness that they have actually given others' permission to take advantage of them, this person fails to realize that they have volunteered being a victim and there was no real victimization in the sense that victim literally means no options. All choices were their own, given freely, with no gun at their head and they could have set boundaries with people at any time, but failed to do so. Built up over time, those negative feelings create physical changes in their body and finally draw disease and illness to them.

All negative feelings and thoughts must manifest on a physical level. It does pain us to hear the unkind words "you caused your own cancer because you allowed negative emotions and thoughts to overwhelm your life" or "you caused alcoholism because you carried too much shame and guilt inside for too long" or "you caused your heart attack because of the corrupt and deceitful lifestyle you led" or "you caused mental illness because you agreed to assume that as an experience before incarnating into your current lifetime." It's much easier and simpler to buy into the Western myth that something or someone other than self is responsible for our disease and illness. The belief in this myth has put billions of dollars in the bank accounts of pharmaceutical companies. Harsh as this may sound, until we begin to take responsibility for avoiding drugs and alcohol, avoiding toxic people, creating healthy lifestyle choices, improving our diet, decreasing or eliminating negative, unhealthy environments and until we become accountable for how we treat ourselves and how we treat others, rampant disease and illness will be the norm.

It is with great sadness that I am reminded of a very dear friend of mine who died recently. He had been married over twenty years when his wife was diagnosed with cancer in 2001. Seven years prior to his wife's diagnosis, my friend had discussed divorce with her and had initiated a brief marital separation. She became very emotional and reminded him of his parental obligations to their teenage daughter, his professional responsibilities as a successful psychologist and corporate consultant in the community and threatened the loss of financial and personal assets should he proceed with the divorce. He remained in the marriage because of these parental, professional and financial obligations and responsibilities. Having divorced his first wife to marry his current wife, an acrimonious relationship had ensued between himself and his ex-wife which never really healed. More importantly, his first daughter, who was age four at the time of the divorce, never forgave him for abandoning her. In fact, as an adult in her early twenties, she entered psychotherapy, took her father into therapy with her and told him how much she hated him for leaving her. Burdened with the guilt of leaving his first daughter and facing the potential emotional turmoil from his second daughter should he divorce a second time, my friend shared with me that the guilt would be overwhelming if he created the same karma with his second wife and second daughter that he had created when exiting his first marriage. In addition, my friend, at age seventeen, fathered a son by a girl whom he refused to marry and, in his adult years, his guilt and his failure to acknowledge it to anyone other than his mother began weighing on him. By the time his current wife was diagnosed with cancer, he was considerably unhappy, had been in psychotherapy with several therapists and had also been taking anti-depressants and opiates for quite a number of years to numb his emotional pain. He was literally self-medicating in order to avoid the pain of living an inauthentic existence which was incongruent with the yearnings of his Soul. With the marriage having reached a state of substantial conflict and discord for both of them and with no mutual exchange of authentic, consistent emotional nurturance essential for a spiritual-based marriage, they both attempted to hide the marital discord from the social and professional community. Unaware of the inner world of this man, many in the community blamed him for his wife's fatal illness. He died with few people understanding the scope and breadth of the profound unhappiness, depression and intrapsychic world of this man.

This is one poignant and tragic example of the outcome of living an inauthentic existence and living one's life based on obligation and duty, rather than love and wisdom. It is a timeless story to which countless people fall victim: failing to follow one's inner Wisdom of the Soul. Physical and mental disease and illness are predictable outcomes when you live an existence based upon sacrificing your own self and your own happiness in order to make others happy. Make no mistake---no one can cast an illness or disease upon you. Not your parents, spouse, friends, children or any other person. You have to give permission *within yourself* to allow illness or disease to manifest and you give permission for illness to manifest inside you when you are in a chronic state of negative thoughts and emotions such as fear, hate, anger, guilt, shame, sadness, jealousy and envy. When referring to my friend, you might say that neither he nor his wife made choices from seeking the wise counsel of their Great Souls. You could say that my friend's failure was his overpowering guilt and shame around his inability to follow his inner Soul's direction and live an authentic life while his wife's death could best be understood as overwhelming fear, sadness and anger because of an inability to honorably and nobly accept an ending to her relationship. In the end, both paid the ultimate price. How many unhealthy relationships exist year after year solely because of financial, professional and parental obligations and duties? If the physical and mental illnesses and diseases could be qualitatively measured of the couples who remain for years in abusive or neglectful relationships, what would the cumulative health price tag be?

Karma is a powerful force and we allow good and bad situations to come to us through either our deeds or through forgiveness. If we forgive ourselves and others, we may avert negative karma. If we cannot forgive ourselves and others, negative karma will manifest in our lives and we certainly can draw illnesses and diseases to us, some of which are fatal. At first blush, the doctrine of karma appears callous and cold-hearted. But the truth is that karma just "is." It merely is the boomerang energy and effect. Karma, in and of itself, is a neutral energy whose outcome depends solely upon your negative or positive deeds and thoughts. What a person reaps, she/he will surely sow. It is a spiritual fact that exists for eternity. It explains why seemingly bad things happen to otherwise "good" people. "Good" people must have done "bad" things, if even in a prior lifetime. It's the only explanation for these otherwise inexplicable happenings. What you do in this lifetime will carry over into another lifetime. What you reap is what you will sow, regardless of how many incarnations it takes to sow it. Until this spiritual fact sinks into the human consciousness, we will keep on creating escapist theories which never arrive at the real problem and, thus, never allow us to create *real solutions*. Until we accept responsibility for our own diseases, disorders and illnesses, the solution will forever escape us all.

The Soul consciousness recognizes the harmful ripple effects of revenge and vengeance and avoids it. Knowing that every cause creates an equal effect, the Soul will respond to these scenarios differently than the ego. The Soul demands justice or truth. In this way, the Soul prevents the electric current of back-and-forth negative energy, thus, preventing negative karma.

When having been wronged, seeking justice, not revenge, is the Soul's course of action. On a practical level, when we receive injustice, we must argue and ask for justice, not return injustice for injustice. By asking for justice instead of returning the negative energy, we prevent accruing a negative karmic debt. Ghandi, Martin Luther King, Jr., Jesus the Christ and Buddha are examples of humans who have learned the important law of cause and effect. All they did was imbue goodness. The ego, being fearful, attacked them.

As long as humankind continues to manifest injustices against each other, humankind will continue to incarnate on a physical plane. Buddhists refer to this cycle of birth, death and rebirth as *samsara* and the liberation from this karmic cycle as *moksa.* It is understood that *moksa* can only be achieved when the person achieves a state of *saguna* Brahman, that Being state of Soul Consciousness which Jesus the Christ, the Buddha and Lao Tzu achieved.

When the recognition of Soul Consciousness is achieved fully, there no longer is a fear of death because the Soul knows that it is immortal. Immortality exists in the spiritual realm because this is all there is and ever will be. Everything else is but a dream or an illusion, mere morphic projections from the One Mind. Physical death is but a transformation from one form of energy to another, from a physical body back to your spiritual essence. Spirit is forever and ever and this kingdom has no end.

In the future, as the consciousness of humanity rises, more people will be able to achieve deeper states of consciousness in which they can access some memories of prior incarnations. When this occurs, people will have opportunities to heal those unresolved conflicts and be *proactive in avoiding* physical and mental illnesses, diseases and disorders. Today, masses of people ignore this critical piece and, as a result, are baffled as to why they develop disease and illness. Disease and illness are a result of a build up of negative energy from this lifetime or prior incarnations. Balance and harmonious right relations is the solution. Were the planet to function on the Soul Consciousness level, disease and illness would virtually not exist. Health and well-being would be a common way of life.

The Will is a most powerful energy and exerts itself either with Goodness or evil as its object of desire. Arthur Schopenhauer, Rollo May, Viktor Frankl and Roberto Assagioli wrote about it and, indeed, the latter attempted to elevate it to a regal, focal psychic energy within his psychological theory of personal and spiritual psychosynthesis as explained in his books, *Psychosynthesis* and *The Act of Will.* The energy of the Will is another aspect ignored by mainstream psychology and medicine although psychology has given an adumbrated version of it in the area of "motivation". The Will is understood to be completely neutral and is really just power. It is controlled, so to speak, by the ego or the Soul in terms of whether the Will is used toward Goodness or away from Goodness. The Will is, in a sense, the psychological horsepower behind and within mind, feelings and actions. At higher levels of consciousness, a psychological merging of sorts occurs such that there is no discernable difference between Goodwill and thought, feelings and actions. Depending upon where your focus, concentration and intention are aimed, the Will is the "power" which causes all things to be brought about. When a politician takes gifts from corporate lobbyists and votes on legislation which is not in the long-term best interest of the constituents, the Will is at the disposal of the ego. The Will is at the mercy of the ego when a thief robs a bank or when an abusive husband beats his wife.

The Soul assumes the Divine Will which is to say that the Will is used in service of Goodness, Fullness of Being, Higher Self, Spirit, Brahman. When the Divine Will is activated, it has a transformative power and it is for this reason we see miracles of healing occur. With greater numbers of people activating the Divine Will toward Goodness, more healings on the planet will take place.

*The ego is entranced by all the names and ideas, but the subtle truth is that the world and particle are the same....Everything is equal to every other thing. Names and concepts only block your perception of this Great Oneness.*
—Lao Tzu

# XXII. THE TEN FUNDAMENTAL LIES OF THE EGO

The ego can only perceive and can never *know* because it is the self that is empty. Thus, the ego is a lie and an illusion since your true nature is the fullness of Being. The ego is split, therefore, it does not know the Oneness behind everything. As long as the ego continues to have an obsession for splitting everything, analyzing and separating everything out to find the answer, it will never find Truth or Reality. The Soul knows Truth and Reality because it forever looks upon it and forever seeks it. The ego has a vested interest in neglecting the Soul because as long as the Soul is neglected, the ego goes on and on separating and dividing everything out. As long as everything is allowed to be separated and divided and as long as we have superior/inferior projections onto others, the ego is guaranteed survival. Once you begin to have the veils of darkness removed from your eyes, the ego starts getting really nervous because it is going to be threatened when the Truth is known. The Truth is that the Holy Trinity is the lord and governor over all and there is nothing, in its essence, that is separate and different and lacking. So what are these common lies that the ego wishes us to carry forward into each generation so as to ensure its legacy? We will examine them one by one:

The Social Lie: Some people are superior; others are inferior.
The Educational Lie: Worldly knowledge is authentic power.
The Religious Lie: You can never be divine *and* human.
The Political Lie: Self-governance is impossible.
The Business Lie: Business is no place for the Soul.
The Medical Lie: Disease is caused by the body.
The Scientific Lie: Reality is only that which is observable.
The Judicial Lie: Only worldly authority can determine truth.
The Philosophical Lie: Aristotelian logic is supreme.
The Artistic Lie: Creativity only comes from genius.

Let us take one untruth at a time. As for the social lie that some people are superior and others are inferior, this can be stated as a truth if your belief system tells you that spiritual Goodness is invalid, untrue, meaningless or not as important as worldly truths. You have free will to believe anything you want while you are living in this lifetime, but your belief system will translate into a certain mode and manner of living. For a world which is obsessed with social position and prominence, projecting superiority and inferiority will inevitably be a way of life. What will also be a result of this will be a world full of unfulfilled, unhappy and empty people. It is our choice which we choose.

As for worldly knowledge, it certainly can give a person power. But the question isn't so much whether it gives power as it is what kind of power it imbues and what results this kind of power creates. Once again, we live on a planet that is dominated by the immature masculine ego which has, by and large, abused worldly knowledge and power for thousands of years. Worldly knowledge and intellectual prowess have become an obsession of the world consciousness and yet its outcome does not result in substantial numbers of happy and fulfilled people. The world has seen its share of intellectual fools, genius greed-mongerers and brilliant despots. It has brought us technological advances to be sure. But intellect (masculine energy) without love and wisdom (feminine energy) has never, nor will it ever, bring peace and harmony. Our obsession with, and bias toward, intellect has not solved the ubiquitous human dilemma: why do we experience pain and suffering? It should be evident that intellect and worldly knowledge *alone* are not, nor never will be, the saviors of the world. It is not masculine analysis that will save humanity, but feminine synthesis.

Your essence is that you are god-like, therefore, it is not only possible, but it is divinely inevitable that one day you will remember your god-like essence which is to say that you will remember your Goodness and you will return to this conscious state of Being. Steer away from any theologian, psychologist, psychiatrist, teacher or human being who denies that you have an innate potential to return to a divine conscious state of Being. There are ten thousand paths to this state of Being and each person chooses their own path, but it is destiny that every person will return to this spiritual essence even if it takes a thousand incarnations to do so. Any person who steers you away from Divine Goodness is afraid of reclaiming their own Divine Goodness and you should simply know that they are not at an evolutionary point in their consciousness to accept this ultimate truth. There is no judgment about our journey to return to our Divine Essence. Each person will hear the Divine Echo from within at their own pace and in their own way. Concentrate on yourself and reconnecting with and re-owning Goodness for yourself and others. The Goodness you give to yourself and to others is the greatest gift you can give yourself and others. This is authentic sanity and psychological health. It is the world's only hope for salvation from an insane world ruled by an insane ego.

Self-governance is possible. Humankind may find that conscious state tomorrow or it may take 100 trillion more aeons of envying, hating and killing one another to finally arrive at a remembrance of our Divine Essence. But it is certain that we will return to it because the energy of Goodness is that for which everything yearns. Even people who are evil are seeking to feel good about what they have done, so in some warped and twisted way, the ego is still seeking Goodness even though it doesn't know it. When humankind is able to carry the Soul Consciousness, there will no longer be a need for political structures as we know them today. Leaders will manifest, but no one person will be perceived by the masses as "the" leader, rather many leaders for different aspects of daily living will arise. You may say that shared leadership will become a way of daily life. Monarchies, despots and dictators will be perceived as an archaic life which was necessary when humankind was controlled by the ego consciousness. With the Soul Consciousness, the person knows Good, therefore, does Good in a Platonic sense. When this consciousness is embodied for Self and others, self-governance is a natural consequence flowing from this state of Being.

To say that our world is ruled by corrupt and greedy business leaders today is to state a rather pathetic and obvious truth. It seems safe to state that the immature masculine ego dominates the business arena and Wall Street and is responsible for the greed, corruption, inequality and overall ethical abuse rampant in today's corporations and politics. Perhaps nowhere else more than in the business, financial and political empires is the Soul needed today. There seem to be no visible examples of male leaders who imbue Soul Consciousness in business leadership, yet if humankind is to elevate to the next level of consciousness, the Soul must unfold in how we conduct business. Making excuse after excuse as to why females and minorities are not capable of assuming leadership positions, the immature masculine ego clings to a consciousness whereby male executives greedily use their company and position to accumulate masses of wealth with little, or no, regard for employees; live duplicitous lives by having a spouse at home and paramours on business trips; tacitly promote other white males into the "old boys network" so as to maintain male dominance in the political, financial and social systems; and reap the benefits from the myth of masculine supremacy. If Soul does not enter into the highest echelon of the business and financial worlds, it will crumble. It is only a matter of when.

Spirit animates the body. The body is the temple for the Soul and the Soul resides within this temple. The same life force which turns an acorn into an oak tree is the same force which animates your body. There are different physical properties, to be sure, between the two, but there is only one life force and this life force is spirit. This consciousness pervades every living thing and even those things which most do not consider alive such as rocks and hills and mountains. Dis-ease results from a lack of harmonious existence. Pythagoras spoke of how the body and soul must be in harmony much as a musical instrument is in harmony. "To know Good is to do the Good" has an implicit idea that harmony and peace flow from this place of Goodness and virtue. Western medicine has been teaching partial truths for several hundred years and this is slowly being dispelled by medical and mental health professionals who adopt an integrative ideal and are attempting to re-focus humankind on spiritual truths as comprising the core of our health and well-being. Your spiritual essence is health, therefore, you have the means to heal yourself naturally. Pharmaceutical companies do not publish every research finding, rather only the ones which benefit their interests. They will have you believe that you must have medications for every illness that you have and that you must take them for long periods of time. Make no mistake, the world is over-medicated and it need not be so if humankind elevated its consciousness. Certainly, synthetic medications have a purpose and it is unrealistic to assume we can eliminate them entirely. Some diseases require them for long-term use and some acute illnesses require their administration short-term. However, millions of people take synthetic drugs when natural, less expensive methods would achieve the same goal and untold numbers of people use some drugs for long-term use when short-term use, followed by implementation of natural, self-healing modalities would create a more optimal effect, particularly since pharmaceutical companies are not invested in doing research and informing the public on the long-term negative effects which can occur.

Humankind has turned so far away from its spiritual essence that disease and illness is becoming the norm and good health is considered an anomaly. It would take many generations of a mass group of people expressing the Soul Consciousness in order to turn the tide of disease and illness. Disease and illness did not manifest in an hour, so it will not take an hour to eradicate it from the face of the earth. It took generation after generation to build up negative energy fields which have, in turn, negatively affected our minds and bodies. With a common sense approach to medicine, humankind can utilize the best of modern treatments with a balance of returning to a more basic, natural way of healing ourselves. The pharmaceutical companies which are ruled by the immature masculine ego will want you to put all your faith and trust in drugs as *the* answer to maintaining your health. The size of their bank account depends upon whether that myth is believed by large numbers of people. Until humankind learns to live what Aristotle calls "the Good Life," there will be rampant disease and illness. Overall, good health is a daily way of Being including proper and balanced nutrition, proper exercise, pollution-free environment, foods absent of chemicals and pesticides, absence of negative stress, eliminating toxic people, avoiding illegal drugs and alcohol abuse and treating others as you would like to be treated.

We have written previously about the scientific myth that matter, the observable, is real and spirit, the unseen, is not. The truth is that only that which is eternal and changeless is real. All else is illusion. Until humankind gets this right, no world peace will be found.

Spiritual Truth lies within the mind and heart of every human being. This spiritual Truth is the return of knowing who you are within your deepest essence; therefore, it is impossible for you not to recall it. Worldly authority is important, but it is not lord and supreme. Worldly authority is not primary because it is predicated upon the physical world. Only spiritual Truth is primary because only it is eternal.

The immature masculine ego would have you believe that logic and intellect are supreme since the immature masculine ego survives as long as we believe that logic and intellect having supremacy over love and wisdom. Virtually all Eastern philosophies teach that intuition and illumination are higher forms of noetic truths than are logic and intellect, yet in Western culture, we cling stubbornly and ignorantly to a lower form of knowing. Certainly it takes intellect and logic to survive in this world, so to eschew them would be utmost folly. But intellect will never lead a person to the Higher Self and the Soul Consciousness as it takes more than that. Only a return to the value of intuitive truths will lead us to higher Truths and ultimately to spiritual illumination. This is the rediscovering of the equality of the feminine and the masculine energies.

Creativity is a natural state of the Soul. The creative energy is eternal and every human being has this natural energy within. The key is to rediscover that energy and channel it toward some Goodness. Whether it is gardening, singing, painting, scientific research, building houses, teaching or starting a business, every person has some creative gift to offer themselves and the world. Find your creative energy, imbue that energy and express it with love and joy. When you find that, you will be finding your Full Self.

*When soul is neglected, it doesn't just go away; it appears symptomatically in obsessions, addictions, violence, and loss of meaning. Out temptation is to isolate these symptoms or to try to eradicate them one by one; but the root problem is that we have lost our wisdom about the soul, even our interest in it.*
—Thomas Moore

# XXIII. NEGLECTING THE SOUL

You can say that whenever you devalue, discard or distort Truth, you are neglecting the natural, free-flowing expression of your Soul. Whenever you have the opportunity to create Beauty and, instead you decide to destroy or abuse it, your Soul is being dismissed and ignored. If you have a chance to love Goodness, but you choose to turn away from it, you have bound your Soul from its essential, freely flowing energy. If you are given the option to use your Will to choose wisely and you do otherwise, your Soul has metaphorically been chained and imprisoned against its noble, flowing energies. The ego consciousness is the mind which cannot fully know virtue because it imprisons the natural Goodness of the Soul. This neglect is the cause of all emptiness in the world.

Adults are typically so inculcated and indoctrinated into adopting the ego consciousness, that they don't even realize to what extent their own Great Souls are being fettered. That still, small inner Voice is so muffled that it seems inaudible amidst the cacophony of everyday life. Nor do many adults have a substantial awareness of how they shackle and imprison their children's Souls. In many ways, little ones come into this world more spiritually advanced than adults. Overall, little children have insatiable desires to know, a quenchless need to create and a guileless manner in loving. You can see this in the ways children prefer to spend their time. They find immense joy in creating sandcastles, snowmen, clay sculptures, structures made of blocks, mudcakes, houses made of blankets. Little ones thirst to know. Their inquisitiveness is so much a part of their little natures that we come to speak of kids being "little sponges," soaking up as much knowledge as they can. The sheer innocence of love shines through as we see a little child run pick a wildflower and bring it back to another little one who strikes their fancy. It seems to be done for no other reason than out of the pure joy of Being and giving. Wee little ones seem not to be highly concerned with their playmates' skin color, race, ethnicity, social or economic level unless a parent has intervened to influence them. To be sure, wee little ones have no concept of religious preference and political affiliations. It is not until the parents begin the fettering process of telling the child that other children with different skin color are inferior or other children who don't go to the same church or synagogue are inferior or the parents do not belong to a certain work class that the child begins to learn to place values upon differences and judge those differences. Instead of simply teaching children to accept and appreciate differences in others, the parents' devaluing system is learned by the child. In addition, some parents adamantly push children into educational paths and professions that meet the parents' needs while the child's Soul is screaming to choose something else. Having their own Souls imprisoned, adults continue the cycle with their own children.

Your Soul and every other Great Soul is crying out to be unfettered by the fear, anger, violence, greed, corruption, deceit, destruction, hate, foolishness, envy, jealousy, sadness, shame and guilt that the ego would have us hold onto. There are ten thousand ways that the Soul can manifest Truth, Beauty and Goodness. There are no necessary religious affiliations, social or financial status, worldly titles or educational levels required to re-awaken and acknowledge your Great Soul. But for the world to restore its wholeness, all must eventually awaken to this state of Being consciousness. It is a state of consciousness that focuses on Universal Principles, not the particulars of a person's beliefs or values. Are both the process and the outcome one of the Universal Principles such as truth, love, kindness or goodness? This is the litmus test of Being. Then will an authentic psychology have achieved its goal.

Where abuse and neglect of the Soul exist, ego is lurking somewhere in the vicinity. Abuse and neglect are actions derived from fear; therefore, ego is always the author where this occurs. There are hundreds of ways to neglect or abuse the Soul, but perhaps the most descriptive way is to violate the Golden Rule, "Do unto others as you would have them do unto you," and dismiss the admonition, "Love others as yourself." While the latter is taken specifically from the Christian religion, some form of it exists in other major religions as well. There is some truth in all religions. The Golden Rule, a secular phrase, is also synonymous with another secular phrase, "what you give out, comes back to you" and other religious rules such as "Whatsoever ye reap, that shall you also sew" and the belief that many eastern religions share of the cycle of karma. These are ubiquitous spiritual laws that are embedded in many religions and throughout secular thought.

The Golden Rule covers a broad array of actions. The Soul does not condone lying, deceiving, cheating, stealing, killing, violence, abuse, hate, greed, envy, jealousy, failing to take responsibility for one's actions and a host of other negative actions and emotions driven by the ego. Every Soul on this great planet intuitively is disgusted with the upper management of corporations whose entire life is led by possessing more and more wealth and power at thousands of percentages above those in the lowest ranks because the Soul knows that, ultimately, all things are shared equally in the spiritual realm. Universal Soul already, in its deepest Being, knows this is true. Every Soul intuitively shrinks in disgust when a politician stands plastically poised to the world and espouses policies which generate untold amounts of wealth for corporations at the heavy expense of the common people. There is no Great Soul who is not intuitively repulsed when the mention of war is made because the Soul knows that violence is the ultimate aggrandizement of the ego, which seeks to have power and control.

The Soul does not condone killing. Buddhists, who believe in the reincarnation of the Soul, do not even condone killing insects since they are a form of life. According to Buddhists, by killing another life form, this subjects a person to bad karma and to the bondage of repeated reincarnations. Buddhists do not believe in war or violence of any kind. In this sense, Buddhists are in touch with the Soul since it eternally seeks Goodness. Killing is a reaction coming from the ego. People who kill animals merely for the sport of the kill are not expressing from the Soul since the Soul finds nothing sporting or engaging about any kind of killing. To love to kill is a response from the ego which is simply blind and ignorant to the spiritual oneness behind all existence. To kill another person "in the name of God" is the ultimate ignorance and irony because Godness is Goodness. Killing another person is, in essence, a definitive statement of the lack of Goodness. This is an example of how the ego is insane and untruthful and convinces some that what is untrue is true. To believe something as insane and contradictory as "holy war" and "it is good to kill in the name of God" is to be operating from an insane ego consciousness.

We live in a world where we have come to erroneously believe that power can only be garnered through avarice and aggression. Authentic power lies only within that which unites, therefore, greed and aggression are illusive powers because they divide and separate. Authentic power is that of Love which eternally seeks to unite. Kindness is an outcome of love and it unites and, as such, is far more powerful than is hate, anger, greed and aggression. The ego consciousness has led us down many primrose paths which lead to a cliff and this is certainly one of them. We have few leaders who imbue the gentle, but powerful energy of kindness. Rudeness, sarcasm, cruelty, unkindness and an overall defensive, attacking consciousness seem to pervade most societies. In 2002, an organization called Public Agenda conducted a survey about rudeness in America. Eighty percent (80%) of the people surveyed said "a lack of respect and courtesy in American society is a serious problem" and 61% believe that the situation has worsened. More than 50% of the entire population surveyed stated they had walked out of a business due to poor customer service. A lack of kindness seems so pervasive that one wonders if we will become so complacent that one day we simply accept unkindness as a *de facto* symbol of American culture. It seems we have taken beloved virtues such as kindness and generosity and have sadly and erroneously come to believe they are an indication of weakness or even cognitive deficits. We have sadly come to associate generosity with being simple minded. What does this say about our ability to construct a belief system? What does this say about the human condition? Once the Soul Consciousness manifests, the eternal power of loving-kindness will return to the planet because this is the only power that heals and unites.

When we lie, deceive and cheat others, we not only abuse our Soul, but others as well. With the recent and unexpected demise of the largest oil company in the world, the public reads of the apparent greed, deception and nefarious business deals which have left so many investors with little more than a feeling of numbness. Even the judicial system appears to be showing signs of straining under the pressure of greed, worldly power and control. As the shock of systemic sexual abuse within the Catholic religious institutions hit the newspapers, people began questioning how pervasive the abusive patriarchy is amongst the clergy and whether or not the 2,000 year history of secrecy, vanity and defensiveness of the Catholic Church will ever end. There seems to be a dearth of virtues remaining in humankind and the price a person pays when they exhibit them, i.e., being considered weird or stupid, being ostracized or ridiculed, losing their job, has become so high, that many people lack the courage to oppose the strong tide of the majority. Yet, there is always a price we pay when we fail to heed what is virtuous and Good. More and more people are reacting to the stresses caused by fettering the Soul as we see higher levels of chronic mental, emotional and physical fatigue and illness. People are exhausted with the corruption of our systems and there seems to be no end to ego inflation. Before we allow ourselves to be overcome with greed and corruption, we must rise and take a stand. The Soul would compel us to take proactive stands such as writing to our congressmen and congresswomen to express our interests. When corporate organizations make products which are unfriendly and harmful to the natural environment, it is the Soul which nudges us to take action by not purchasing products and services from these kinds of economic entities. If every person were to say "I'm just one person and I can't change the world," we would never succeed. But if every person were to say "I'm one more person who cares about changing the world and I do make a difference," then the positive energies of the Soul would overpower the negative energies of the ego. Change would happen. But it takes the courage to listen to your Soul.

Neglecting the Soul means that you fail to hear that still, small voice from within which always pulls you toward that which is good, true, honorable and just. Abuse of the Soul results when we allow ego to neglect that which we intuitively know is Good for Self and others. These abuses are more power to the ego. As a human race, we must stop neglecting and abusing our Souls and reach for all that reawakens and revives the divine and sacred.

*Meditation has a good chance of eventually becoming one of the leading therapeutic techniques....the orientation is synthetic rather than analytic.*
—Roberto Assagioli

*Music can indeed be a powerful healing agent...the magic of sound, scientifically applied, will contribute in ever greater measure to the relief of human suffering, to a higher development and a richer integration of the human personality.*
—Roberto Assagioli

*... 'cold' and subdued colors have a quieting effect, and 'warm', vivid, and bright colors have a stimulating and exciting influence...the influence of color as a therapeutic agent...opens up great possibilities...much scientific experiment and accurate differentiation is needed, but the beneficial results will justify further research.*
—Roberto Assagioli

# XXIV. AUTHENTIC THERAPY FOR THE SOUL

The Soul's fundamental and essential drive is to reconnect with itSelf and the Universal Soul Consciousness where other Souls exist so that the Soul can remember and reunite with its wholeness, with its essence. The

Soul is non-physical energy and seeks to reconnect with, and become consciously aware of, spiritual energy because that is its essence.

The Soul expresses itSelf in order to seek and restore itSelf so that Higher Self may know itSelf. To know itSelf is simultaneously to know the Goodness of the All and, therefore, everything on the earth including plants, animals and other human beings are a beautiful expression of the All. As such, the Soul knows this and, thus, the "self" with a small "s" or the narcissistic "ego" (as understood by Assagioli, Jung and Buddhists) no longer exists to wreak havoc on the world.

The Soul knows that it is part of a cosmological All of existence and cannot be separated from this Wholeness, this Allness. When the Higher Self is subjectively, ontologically known, the Soul has unfolded and its energic expressions are balanced. Ultimately, the Soul wills itSelf *toward* its essence by *means of* its essence: knowledge, creativity, love and wisdom. It is in this sense that subject, object and means become One. When the Great Soul expresses itSelf, it is nourishing and replenishing itSelf. There is no need for "others" to fill, rather this is done within Higher Self. This is the state of abundance or "fullness of Being" referred to by Advaitans. When the Soul is nourished, the outcome will be truth, justice, peace, love, joy, compassion and loving-kindness. One may say that by seeking itSelf, the Soul finds peace. Where peace is, there must also be truth, justice, love, joy, compassion and beauty. This is all Goodness. Soul wills itSelf toward all things good. In a circular causality, its will toward good engenders more goodwill. Some religions refer to these "fruits of the spirit" although you need not belong to any particular religion in order to manifest these spiritual energies. This implies that when you are in touch with your divine spirit, you will bear these sacred fruits. To seek them is to have them. To give them away is to own them. To have them is to *be* them. You are the spiritual gifts you give to others.

Since the Soul is a merging of thinking and feeling which, in turn, enhances behavior in positive outcomes, it should be understood that the optimal psychotherapy is a therapeutic strategy *which **simultaneously** merges both the thinking and the feeling aspects within the client* so as to decrease the rambling nature of thoughts and, thus, to decrease intrapsychic conflict. The psychotherapeutic goal of Soul unfoldment is not the examination of thoughts, rather it is the elimination of thoughts. The ego is full of divided thoughts because analytic thought divides; the Soul moves beyond analysis toward wholeness of consciousness which is a synthesis. The ego is the consciousness of intrapsychic conflict because the ego is forever split; the Soul is the consciousness of peace because it is forever whole and full.

When there is a split between thinking and feeling, you are not full. You are experiencing the world through the empty ego. Merging of thinking and feeling is a state of higher Being and this state of Being does not exist except in higher states of consciousness than the ego consciousness. Remember that "higher" means "more inclusive". A state of Being cannot co-exist with the ego consciousness. Either you are in a state of ego consciousness or you are in a state of Being consciousness. As Jesus the Christ said, you cannot serve both worlds—the physical world and the spiritual world. Either you will serve the physical world or you will serve the spiritual world. The physical world is the world of emptiness because it derives from a split consciousness. The spiritual world is the world of fullness because it derives from a consciousness of wholeness and Oneness. You cannot live in the ego consciousness at the same time you are living in the Soul Consciousness. You cannot be *both split* in thought and feeling *and simultaneously merged* in thought and feeling.

Merging thought and feeling can be achieved through the path of meditation and this is why virtually all ancient seers, mystics and gurus teach this path. They have reached the consciousness of merging. At the current time, humankind is living in a state of UNconsciousness in the sense that humanity is UNconscious and UNaware of the Higher level of Being. Another way of saying this is that humankind is mostly living in a limited, partial, exclusive, unwhole consciousness. The Soul Consciousness is UNconscious today. The goal is to bring the Soul Consciousness into Consciousness and into full awareness. Another way of saying this is that the next goal is to move toward a more inclusive consciousness. When this is achieved, thinking and feeling will be merged and this Consciousness will be "carried" on a daily basis by the mass consciousness. This is a true state of Being because the Soul will have unfolded. Jesus the Christ, the Buddha and Lao Tzu were enlightened because they consciously were aware of this merging consciousness and they brought what is UNconscious into their full state of Consciousness and lived it every day. Ultimately, this is a state of consciousness where words are inadequate and unnecessary since Being is a phenomenological and ontological state. Being is not an intellectual consciousness because intellect analyzes and divides. Being is a way of "seeing" the world that is radically different than the "seeing" of the ego. The ego literally sees the physical world which does, indeed, appear to be real with all its separateness and difference. The Soul moves up into a higher way of "seeing" through spiritual eyes because the Soul sees that it is that which is BEHIND the physical world that is real. In an earlier chapter, I talked about reaching for physical things like diamonds, yachts, fur coats and gold. Recall that I said it is NOT the actual physical thing that every human being truly seeks, rather it is the JOY, BEAUTY, LOVE which is BEHIND and WITHIN the physical object for which we reach. If everybody picked up diamonds and they made everyone sick, we would NEVER reach for them. Instead, diamonds give us JOY when we behold them. Yachts, mansions, gold, fur coats and all this "stuff" are but symbols, images, representations for the JOY we desire. It is in that sense, that physical things are illusions and not ultimately real because you can never BE a diamond. You can only BE JOY! You can never BE a yacht, but you can BE JOY! The ego has forgotten this simple, profound truth and, instead, the ego grabs and hoards physical things because it focuses on the physical thing instead of the spiritual essence behind and within the thing. This is why there is so much greed. The ego sees lack and thinks it must get in order to have. You do have to get "things" in order to have them. But you need only HAVE JOY in order to BE JOY. As you become more and more awakened to this truth, you will realize that ALL THAT EXISTS IS BEINGNESS. This is the only reality. For you can never BE anything physical. You can collect every diamond in every diamond mine on this planet, but you can never, ever BE a diamond. You can only BE a spiritual fruit such as joy and peace.

All current psychotherapies are "either/or" therapies because they are *either* directing the client toward thinking (insight, redirected thoughts, cognitive reframing) *or* they are directing the client to access feelings (sadness, depression, loneliness, anger, shame, guilt, jealousy, envy, fear). In truth, there are really only two core emotions: love and fear. All negative emotions arise out of fear. Fear is the landscape of the ego because it is incomplete, empty and split. Being or Soul Consciousness can never hold negativity because negative thoughts and negative feelings divide and separate. Only joy and love unite, therefore, to arrive at a Being or Soul Consciousness, you can only be in a state of joy, love, bliss and peace. Rehashing negative thoughts and feelings over and over will not get the client to a Being state because rehashing negative feelings and thoughts "is" the ego consciousness.

Another point to be made about differences in clients' cognitive and relational styles is that each psychological theory has a gender bias inherent within that model. Not the clinical practitioner of the model, but *the theory and techniques themselves have an implicit gender predisposition.* Psychoanalytic, cognitive and behavioral are predominately masculine models of treatment because they focus heavily on thinking patterns and/or cognitive insight. Indeed, it is a fact that many males who are intellectually based and not highly in touch with their emotions (their feminine side), gravitate toward the cognitive and/or behavioral models whereas, humanistic-existential therapy is a predominately feminine therapy because it focuses largely upon a client's emotions and females resonate toward it.

The Soul Consciousness model operates within an androgynous framework since it pursues change beginning at the unconscious level and the treatment modalities focus on reconciling the opposites of thinking and feeling. One could say that it moves the client toward an integration of the feminine and masculine energies. It is understood that, at higher levels of psychological maturity (what Jung refers to as *individuation* and what Maslow refers to as *self-actualization*), the individual is better able to express a balance between the feminine and masculine energies.

Psychoanalytical/psychodynamic and cognitive-behavioral therapies are primarily thinking therapies. The therapist primarily concentrates the session on your thoughts. Humanistic-existential therapies have the noble *goal* of attempting to guide the client to an ontological state (a Being state), but it is not an optimal therapeutic strategy for Soul unfoldment because the focus of therapy is on expressing emotions. Since clients arrive at a therapist's door because of negative situations or events and not positive ones, this means the client is invested in expressing negative feelings such as sadness, guilt, loneliness, anger, shame, guilt, jealousy, envy and fear. There is no therapeutic strategy to have the client merge thinking and feeling. The client is either thinking about thinking or thinking about feeling. Merging of thinking and feeling can only occur in the realm of the quiet, Silent Voice within, therefore, only meditation, music therapy, chromatherapy, aromatherapy and these types of self-in-relation-to-Self modalities can provide the optimal therapeutic milieu for the Soul Consciousness to emerge and unfold.

The core issue of every human being who arrives in a psychotherapist's office or on a psychiatric unit is the struggle between the split ego consciousness (emptiness or the empty self) and the Soul or Being Consciousness (fullness or the Full Self or Full Being). Moving through, and purging, the toxins of the Soul is the most important and essential struggle any client will engage in. There are no exceptions to this regardless of what the client articulates as the "presenting problem". This issue is the core issue to tackle and everything else that is mentioned is ancillary to it. The central struggle in this lifetime and every human incarnation is the battle to return to your essence, your Great Soulfulness, essential Beingness, the world of Spirit where all is whole, full and peaceful.

Psychotherapists and psychologists from all theoretical orientations have been preaching the importance of the client "working through" their problems by "talking it over." "Working through" and "talking over" issues *ad nauseum* is the ego consciousness leading to yet another path within the ego consciousness! It's analogous to an illusion going from one mirror to another trying to see itself. The ego consciousness dwells on the negative because it cannot rise above to merge thinking and feeling into a state of Higher Self where Being is felt. The ego consciousness is not sane. Ego consciousness is not sane because it is not whole. It is not whole because it does not "see" with spiritual eyes the wholeness and Oneness of all there is. It is not whole because it is not full. It is not full because it sees a world of separation and difference. Seeing a world of separation and difference is living in a consciousness of insanity because that which is not full can never know peace. And that which is not at peace is neither stable nor sane.

Clients don't make appointments with therapists in order to spend an hour talking about their joy, bliss, peace, love, hope, certainty, creativity, wisdom, etc. Clients arrive at the clinician's office because they are experiencing a lack of these energies or, better said, a lack of Fullness. One or more of these energic expressions is missing in their life. Furthermore, the client doesn't know where to find them and subconsciously thinks the therapist has them somewhere or has the map to find them and can point to the hidden treasure chest where they all are. Some clients give thousands of dollars to a therapist thinking that one day that magical map is going to appear that will point them to where all those missing energies are or the therapist is going to say some magical word or phrase that will point the client in the right direction to where all that treasure of Fullness lies. This lack of Fullness is the result of the ego consciousness. Fullness can only be an experience of knowingness, of subjectivity; it can never be an object to reach for in another person. Fullness can only ever be known within the spiritual realm because this is the only reality where peace lies.

The most effective means by which Fullness is achieved is by approaching the client's unconscious mind because that is where the Great Soul is today— in the unconscious with a veil over it. The goal, as we have said, is to bring the Soul into Consciousness, into full awareness, into a state of full Being, the Full Self. Since the Soul is unconscious in most of humankind today, it is understood that the optimal approach to the Soul is through the realm of the unconscious. As we have said, at the conscious level, the ego consciousness is either thinking about emotions or thinking about thinking. Richard Bandler and John Grinder are practitioners of Neuro Linguistic Programming (NLP) which is a therapeutic technique that utilizes the client's unconscious in order to induce change of behavior. Bandler and Grinder say in their book, *Frogs into Princes*, that "learning and change take place at the unconscious level" and that the unconscious mind is "that part of your functioning which is responsible for about ninety-five percent (95%) of your learning and skill."

Following Bandler and Grinder's thinking, Soul consciousness is brought about best by reaching the client's unconscious mind. Spending years dialoguing with a psychoanalytical therapist may yield the client important insights, but, since this therapeutic approach focuses primarily on only one aspect of the Soul energy (thinking by cognitive insights), it is highly unlikely that it will induce ego transcendence and a reconnection with the Soul consciousness. Furthermore, the focus is primarily on the client's past. Indeed, most psychoanalytic therapists spend months, if not years, allowing the client to regurgitate past material, so time is an important piece of psychoanalysis. Time and space are irrelevant in the spiritual realm where only an ongoing experience of eternal "now" moments exist. You can only BE in the moment. If you think about the way you were yesterday, you cannot BE yesterday. You can only BE in the now. Forever and ever, you can only BE now, therefore, your past does not determine your future unless you delude yourself into thinking it can. That is the power of your mind. Hence, psychoanalytic theory, as such, and its psychotherapeutic interventions focus on ego integration and are not relevant to the Soul.

Following the admonishment of a cognitive-behavioral therapist, the therapeutic work is usually only going to work with the client's conscious mind. In simplistic terms, a cognitive-behavioral therapist has the goal of either motivating you to change your thinking or motivating you to change your behavior. Stop an old behavior and replace it with a new one. Stop old thoughts and replace them with new ones. It may yield short term behavioral change, but developing deep insights and long-term behavioral changes may not ensue. It is also unlikely that a reconnection with the Soul will develop because cognitive-behavioral therapy is like winding a clock instead of working with a human being. It is highly mechanistic and does not reach your unconscious immediately. Having a cognitive therapist tell you to stop your irrational thoughts may be productive in decreasing fear and anxiety for the moment, but it is not working directly with your unconscious nor is it honoring your emotions. In fact, many males find this type of therapy appealing, while many females find it dismissive of their emotional needs because it focuses so heavily on cognition. The only genuine Soul therapy within this model are the creative visualization and meditation work that are essentially taken from ancient Eastern philosophical thought. Cognitive-behaviorists latched onto these modalities in the late 90s because they saw that neuropsychologists were doing research in this area and were seeing some substantial efficacy in assuaging anxiety. Certainly Skinner, Beck and Ellis, the founders of cognitive behavioral theory and therapy never talked about the Eastern technique of meditation as a psychotherapeutic tool when they developed their original theories in mid-20th century. It seems more plausible that, since meditation began growing in popularity with the masses, cognitive behavioral therapists wanted to grab a brass ring when they saw it and tout it as being their own technique. Whether you elect to place meditation under the rubric of cognitive behavioral therapy or not is really unimportant. Meditation is a more effective means of developing Soul consciousness than are traditional CBT techniques.

The humanistic-existential therapist focuses largely on feelings and it is mostly because of this that clients with much feminine energy find this type of therapy appealing. It focuses less on cognition and behavior, however, like cognitive-behavioralists, it does not work directly with the unconscious. The humanistic-existential therapist comes closer to reaching the ontological state of the client because it emphasizes what the client is currently subjectively experiencing (*process* instead of *content*), but traditionally does so only through the client's conscious mind. In this sense, these therapeutic techniques do not arrive at the door of the unconscious which is where the Soul is waiting to unfold and manifest.

Also, psychoanalytic, cognitive, behavioral, humanistic and existential techniques require the therapist to have certain skills, competencies and abilities in order to competently treat the client. While humanistic and existential *theories* presuppose that all humans have an innate drive to move self toward a healthier level of functioning, even these two theories offer vague, nebulous and multiple hermeneutical directions and interventions that therapists may use. It is not highly evident what specifically Frankl means by "logotherapy" and "healing through meaning" or exactly what therapeutic techniques are to be used. Much debate still exists among person-centered therapists over what Rogers means when he says that the psychotherapeutic process of "non-directiveness" is the most effective way to approach the client so that the client can move toward "authenticity." Maslow gives no clear-cut, universal ways for the therapist to attend to the client, rather Maslow's goal was to create an atmosphere where the client's growth is facilitated. Concepts such as "focus on process, not content," "being with the client," "being present with the client," "empathy," and "unconditional positive regard" are common among humanistic-existential practitioners. These have meaning to veteran humanistic-existential therapists, but novice therapists are expected to either simply know how to "be present with the client" so that growth can be facilitated or a recent graduate is expected to be supervised with another "competent" therapist. The focus of process and not content is a clear directive, in and of itself, however the simple fact is that a therapist must possess excellent intuitive skills to be highly effective within this treatment modality. The processes and methods are highly nebulous so a novice therapist is left with little clear direction on how to treat a client. Additionally, there is virtually little way to empirically study and find high reliability and validity regarding these treatment modalities. Let me say that for the highly intuitive therapist, these modalities can be highly effective in ego integration. However, the truth is that many therapists are not highly intuitive and, even if they are, the point is that the practical *goals of the actual techniques are inconsistent with the goal of the actual theory that it proposes.* Simply put, *humanistic-existential theory advocates Fullness of Being, but humanistic-existential therapeutic techniques are really only useful for ego integration.* Some other treatment modalities are necessary for Soul Consciousness.

Who is to say what defines a "competent" therapist? Ask 10 psychotherapists and you'll get 10 different answers even if they vary slightly. You would likely get more common answers if the question was to give the definition of an "incompetent" therapist. When intuition plays such a large role in effectively treating clients and there are literally dozens of different perceptions held by so-called "skilled and competent" therapists, is it any wonder that society, at large, has such an unfavorable perception of psychotherapy? Additionally, one "highly skilled, competent" therapist will differ in his/her techniques and approaches from another "highly skilled, competent" therapist even though both supposedly adhere to the same theoretical model.

While there are many competent therapists who practice psychotherapy and give the profession respectability, the truth is that there are also some who are technically and/or intuitively incompetent, are a gross embarrassment to the field and who, thus, form much of the basis whereby society looks askance at the field. There are therapists who are poor listeners and even those who fall asleep in therapy sessions. Some lack adequate empathic responsiveness and intuition; some fail to utilize occasional therapist self-disclosures which can be used to enhance the client's perception of an emotionally safe milieu or to allow a client to feel less isolated in their experience. Still other therapists are judgmental, give advice to clients based upon their own moral values and guide the client to move in the direction of action which is most congruent with the ethos of the psychotherapist as opposed to the cultural, moral, ethical and spiritual fabric of the client. Notwithstanding the fact that certain presenting problems such as physical, sexual and emotional abuse are considered as primary etiologies of mental illness and the therapist should engage the client in a way that the client will move toward the amelioration or complete cessation of these abuses, there are other situations which are far less clear such as clients who come into therapy because they have been unhappy in their marriage for many years. It is unknown how many clients, after years of marital discord, come into therapy with a need for an "expert of psychological health" to give them implicit or explicit permission to end a relationship, only for the therapist to dissuade the client and, instead, encourage (through either verbal or nonverbal communication) the client to remain in the partnership mostly due to an unconscious or conscious personal or moral belief of the therapist. Without question, successful marriages require mental work and emotional investment and it is unwise to abandon marital effort quickly. However, to be sure, the pervasive moral law that one should stay married no matter what psychological or physical toll is paid sounds like the admonishment of an ignorant fool.

Some psychotherapists perform silent analytical surgery of a client's spiritual ethos such that the client's spiritual anatomy is dissected, or at worst, devalued or ignored. While this is slowly changing, until the 1990s, psychoanalytic therapists and cognitive-behaviorists were well-known within the field for considering spirituality a pathological projection. Freud, Skinner and Ellis have all voiced their atheist comments which speak of their disgust of spirituality and religion. While I have mentioned some of Freud's thoughts regarding the subjects, Ellis has called psycho-spiritual beliefs "bullshit" and Skinner's thoughts are very similar to Ellis'.

Then there are those therapists who are really burned out, but keep on providing services to clients. Psychologists and counselors know this to be a threat to the client's growth. It is a very real concern. Even the very best psychologists and therapists have "bad" days or weeks where they are barely able to listen to what the client has to say much less process the content and feeling. It is unknown to what extent the client is aware of this state of being "tuned out" although I'm confident highly intuitive clients sense it. It's a real turn off. Yet who on this planet has not had a bad day or a bad week where they've still had to show up for work?

Another serious erosion to the field of psychology are those psychotherapists who project their own issues into the therapy session and their own counter-transference either harms the client or prevents the client from moving beyond a phase. One of my professors in the doctoral program where I am enrolled is originally from the Deep South and she moved to the Northeast many years ago. When she initially moved to the Northeast, she spent several years seeing a so-called "highly respected psychologist in the local community." This "highly respected psychologist" coached my professor for years on how to get rid of her Southern accent, a deep part of this professor's Being. Years later, the therapist confessed that she had failed to identify her own counter-transference and, as a result, should never have guided this client to become something other than who she was! This is such a testimony to the fact that just because someone is considered a so-called "very respected therapist," doesn't mean they are below making critical errors in judgment. Further, this was a prime example of just how difficult it is to simply allow someone to Be who they are. "Respectable, competent" psychologists are no exception.

There are many reasons why psychology has failed to garner large, wide-spread respect and support for its profession. Certainly, all the reasons I've mentioned contribute to that lack of public support, but I suspect that, added to that, not everyone in the psychological community has agreed that different clients have different relational and cognitive styles and that, based upon those differences, certain clients will be drawn to certain therapies and repelled by others. Largely until the 1990s, many clinicians would try to fit every client within one particular treatment modality assuming a one-size-fits-all type of treatment process. Specifically, the psychoanalytical, cognitive and behavioral schools of thought were adamant that every client could be approached and effectively treated by their particular modality. Finally, when the sobering 1995 article from *Consumer Reports* was published which articulated that no specific modality of psychotherapy has proven to be more effective than any other, a growing number of clinicians began to humbly accept that clients have different needs, styles and preferences and that what works best for one client will not necessarily work most effectively for another. Clinicians within all models have been humbled to realize that no one particular therapy can "fix" all client populations. The exclusivity of the "my modality is the best modality" which existed prior to the 1990s has now largely been replaced by a more realistic and accepting approach to a wide variety of interventions. It seems logical that, out of that conclusion, we can deduce that each psychotherapeutic model applies to only certain client populations and there is no exhaustive and complete list of factors to guide therapists in determining which modality best suits a certain, unique individual. As such, one must admit that effective treatment depends, to a large degree, upon the skill, expertise, clinical judgment *and* intuition of the therapist. Some therapeutic strategies do, indeed, require empirical data, skill, education and clinical judgment, however, we cannot deny that there are many occasions where just the right intervention was used at just the right time and its impetus can be attributed to nothing other than intuition.

Could it be that some practitioners are not well trained or simply do not possess the inherent skills and qualities that are necessary to assist a person through the difficult process of achieving a healthier state of psychological well-being? There seems to be an unspoken dictum amongst those in the field of psychology that years of experience and education level do not necessarily translate into effectiveness (as the story of my professor's therapist above indicates), yet the research that is conducted always operates under the assumption that the therapists that are part of the research are, indeed, "skilled and competent." Who claims to be the arbiter of what constitutes "skilled and competent therapy" when intuition plays such a substantial role in the overall movement and process of therapy? Yes, there are certain techniques that are inherent within each modality, however, techniques alone would render therapy no more than a robotic dialogue. Indeed, Rollo May would say that techniques, *per se*, should not be the focus of therapy.

An important issue that is impossible to screen for and monitor is the level of psychological maturity of the therapist. All current psychological models tacitly presume that the therapist is functioning at a fairly high level of psychological maturity and well-being, yet there is no gauge by which universities and training programs can definitively measure this. Some therapists' *overall* psychological maturity is only *equal to* the clients' level of maturity. To be sure, some of our historically famous psychiatrists were prejudiced against females; some therapists are not empathic, have narcissistic tendencies, are overly skeptical and tend to be suspicious and mistrusting of others.

Another point about psychoanalytic and humanistic-existential models is that they focus on "the Pink Elephant." You're saying "What in the world do you mean by that?" If I say to you: "DON'T think about a Pink Elephant!" what are you going to think about? THE PINK ELEPHANT, of course! I have given you the unfavorable image by speaking the words. I have failed to give you the alternative, favored image to conjure up. If I really don't want you to think about the Pink Elephant, then I *should simply tell you what it is I want you to think about.* I should say: "Think about red roses" or "Think about a picnic on a sunny, breezy day sitting in a green, lush meadow." It is in this sense that Ericksonian hypnosis and guided imagery are advantageous in providing the client with the kinds of thoughts that are healing, namely positive thoughts. Ericksonian hypnosis and guided imagery avoid having the client dwell on the Pink Elephant! Instead, it allows the client to fill her/his unconscious with positive thoughts much like the "Rewind" feature on a tape recorder. The client pushes "Rewind" to erase the negative energy and pushes "Play" to fill the unconscious with positive energy. As a human race, we have filled our unconscious with negative thoughts and pictures from horror movies; daily news of local or national murders and rapes; parental verbal abuse and neglect; societal "norms" which sometimes are antithetical to the Soul's natural ebb and flow; the dictum of many educational curriculums which are elitist and focus heavily on intellect (the masculine) at the expense of the heart (the feminine); and the greed and corruption of two "masculine" systems in politics and business. Is it any wonder that our unconscious is filled with garbage when we feed it such horrendous food? So what does it take to empty it and replace it with positive energy? Certainly, not obsessing about the Pink Elephant! That's what the ego does—obsess about the Pink Elephant. We've obsessed on the negative for thousands of years and it's gotten us deeper and deeper into a landfill of psychological garbage. It seems simple that, if something hasn't worked for thousands of years, TRY SOMETHING ELSE!

The techniques of psychoanalytic and humanistic-existential therapies are inherently Pink Elephant image therapies. At least in this sense, cognitive-behavioral therapy diverts the client *away from* the Pink Elephant! Every time you go into the office of a psychoanalytic or humanistic-existential therapist, you are encouraged to concentrate on every frustration that is consuming you. They are therapies that allow you to dwell on all the negative energies in your life as, week after week, the therapist gives you free reign to create various images of the Pink Elephant. Each session of psychoanalysis you may speak openly about the negative things in your past which have contributed to the problems in your current life. Each session in humanistic-existential therapy, you are encouraged to express the angst, anxiety, loneliness, depression, fear, shame, guilt, jealousy and anger you are currently experiencing.

If negative issues are your focus, this is where you will likely remain session after session. Concentrating on, articulating, analyzing and debating about the Pink Elephant is one way to move through your issues, but the road will cost you substantially more money in therapist fees and substantially more time away from home than will developing a meditation practice in your own home. Your mind is a very powerful force. *Whatever your Mind focuses on is what will constellate for you.* Where you place your focus will directly affect your subjective experience and what you experience subjectively is what you will focus on!!! While these mainstream psychotherapies are valuable for ego integration, specifically for clients who have experienced substantial environmental threats such as physical, sexual and emotional abuse, there is no inherent goal within the therapeutic techniques which guide the client to emphasize the will toward hope, courage, optimism, love, joy, peace, creativity, truth, wisdom, beauty or faith. The theories imply that by focusing over and over again on the negative, somehow the positive will manifest. In fact, psychoanalytic theory doesn't even recognize an intrinsic human will toward psychological wholeness, therefore, it does not hypothesize that humankind has the will and intention to move beyond pathology or neurosis to a transcendent consciousness. Humanistic-existentialists do believe in an innate human potential toward psychological growth but the techniques utilized by the therapist contraindicate Soul growth because the goal of therapy is to allow the patient to "stay present in the moment" which, for clients who seek out therapists, are usually having some very difficult, negative moments in their lives at that time. Humanistic-existential therapists assume that "allowing the client to just simply be" is a good thing. I agree with that in terms of ego integration. But many clients who go to humanistic-existential therapists already have reached the middle level, if not the higher level, of ego consciousness, thus, spending months in the ego consciousness could be better spent teaching a client to meditate.

While the Soul Consciousness model recognizes that all human beings suffer psychologically, the theoretical model also has as its fundamental premise that one of the primary reasons that human beings suffer is that we dwell on toxic energy. Based on that assumption, we understand that clients who are already functioning at the middle or higher levels of ego integrations are not optimally benefitted by rehashing negative thoughts and feelings, certainly not for months or years. For these clients, spending months or years in a therapist's office dwelling on negative aspects and energies are not harmful, but they are not providing the least expensive, most natural, self-healing method toward higher levels of consciousness. John Diamond, M.D., best-selling author and psychiatrist, writes about current psychotherapeutic techniques in *Your Body Doesn't Lie*:

> "You may come out of therapy with a better understanding of your problems, but the end result will be a diminution of your Life Energy. But you say, isn't that what psychotherapy should be—discussing what's wrong so that it can be relieved? Yes, by all means, mention what is wrong, but not to have it discussed and analyzed and 'worked through.' Bring up your negative emotions and change them into positive ones instantly, then and there."

The therapeutic focus of the future is this: *spend minimal time talking about lemons; spend the bulk of your life turning lemons into lemonade.* Transforming the negative unconscious into a positive consciousness. Do negative emotions exist? Yes, they exist, but they manifest because of the ego and they continue to exist because of the ego! So how do we transcend the ego? We do so by increasing what Diamond calls "the Life Energy". This energy within us is what the Chinese call *Chi* and the Hindus call *Prana*. It matters not so much what we call it, but rather that we all begin to have a general concept of it and collaboratively agree that this is the central energy that psychology and medicine should be focusing on. So how do we manifest this balance of energy? We do so by techniques such as meditation, guided imagery, music therapy, sound therapy, color therapy, aromatherapy, Tai Chi, Qigong, nutritional attention and other means whereby the client is able to utilize natural modalities to re-program the unconscious from its current negative energic contents to positive energic contents and to, ultimately, be in control of their own healing process instead of giving away that power to a therapist. These natural, self-healing interventions allow the client to merge thinking and feeling, are potentially less expensive than traditional forms of psychotherapy and, after learned by a trained practitioner, can be practiced within the client's home. They lead to stress and anxiety reduction and enhanced states of well-being. When performed as ritual and devotional processes, in time, the client will move closer and closer to the positive energies of the Soul Consciousness. In the Soul Consciousness model, the therapist is truly teaching the client to *self-heal.* I am reminded of the Chinese proverb "Give a man a fish, he eats for a day. Teach a man to fish, he eats for a lifetime." Psychoanalytic, cognitive, behavioral and humanistic-existential models are truly useful in that they are giving the client a fish to heal for a day or a week. In that sense, I applaud them. They have been valuable in moving psychology to where it is today. But they are not modalities in which the client learns to self-heal for a lifetime and, in fact, they can create client dependencies upon the therapist for counsel. Meditation, color therapy, music therapy, sound therapy, aromatherapy and other energy-based techniques such as Qigong and Tai Chi are direct methods of self-healing, therefore, they are understood to be more optimal therapies in transcending the ego and attaining higher (more inclusive) states of psychological well-being.

With the psychotherapeutic modalities of meditation, music therapy, chromatherapy, sound therapy and aromatherapy, the concerns regarding the therapist become all but moot because the therapist is no longer burdened with having to be "on queue" and *in sync* with the client for one hour every time the client shows up. With these cutting edge psychotherapies (which are really ancient treatment modalities), the client is relating to Higher Self, not the therapist. Thus, the client-therapist relationship becomes peripheral while the client's relationship with Higher Self becomes central.

As these reasons are listed and I advocate for the field of psychology to move forward and adopt a new paradigm in treatment modalities, it is likely that some people are saying: "But we can never move away from 'talking' psychotherapy because everybody wants to be listened to!" I certainly agree with the part about everybody wanting to be listened to. Indeed, every human being wants to be heard. Everybody has an innate need to be understood. However, today, while most of us function within the ego consciousness, we understand that truism *only in relation to the ego consciousness* which does seek to be heard, listened to and understood from "the other." In truth, at the deepest level, every person really wants to hear the Silent Voice within because this is the voice of Ultimate and Absolute Truth. This is the Silent Voice of your Higher Self which, when deeply connected with it, will allow you to seek your own counsel for problems and issues which arise. It is the Divine Beloved which forever is the Divine Echo of Truth, Beauty and Goodness. So it is true that every person has a deep need to be heard, listened to and understood, but that yearning to be heard by "the other" is the yearning of the ego which only seeks outside itself because it is empty within. The ego is empty because it is focusing on illusions, not reality, so it seeks to be filled by "the other," either "other" people or by "other" physical, material things. So the deepest Truth is that every client who reaches the doorway of a therapist is not really seeking to be heard, listened to and understood by "the other" (the therapist), rather the deepest Truth is that this person is seeking to find, hear and know their own Full Self within, the Transcendent Self, the Divine Soul who expresses itSelf naturally. The Full Self is whole, complete and full and does not have an empty feeling which prompts it to constantly seek outside since the Full Self, the Soul, knows that all Fullness is from within itSelf and the collective, Universal Soul. This is the domain of the silent world of color and music which is the essence or "substance" of the Soul.

Any wise therapist must confess that each client is different and, thus, drawn to a certain type of therapist based upon cognitive, emotional, and expressive styles. These unresearched areas of lack of high intuition in the therapist and the personal mismatch between client and therapist are likely a significant contributor to the lack of high public trust and respect for the field of psychology as a whole. Behind this lies the truth that the field of psychology is still highly divisive within its own corridors as each model seems to still vie to be supreme. There is still no collaborative effort between therapists of all modalities to band together to seek out a unified theory of consciousness most likely because of the culprit of the ego. For all these reasons, it is even further necessary for psychotherapeutic techniques to move away from verbal dialogue as a core technique to self-reflective techniques placing the emphasis on direct modes of self-healing.

It is understood that, at higher levels of psychological maturity, the individual is better able to express a balance between the feminine and masculine energies. In light of this, as a client moves toward higher levels of ego integration and certainly toward the transpersonal realm, the psychoanalytic, cognitive, behavioral and humanistic-existential therapies are no longer considered highly or optimally relevant to the higher functioning client. This is not an indictment on any one of these therapies *per se* because, viewed in isolation, each theory offers something of value to a person functioning at a certain level of consciousness. Rather, the point is to say that, as a person moves toward the higher end of the spectrum of consciousness, these therapies become less and less relevant in terms of continuing to assist the person toward an ever higher level of consciousness. These current therapies only take humankind to the twelfth grade. We now need treatment modalities which take clients through collegiate level. A person who is already functioning fairly high on Maslow's hierarchy who seeks traditional forms of psychotherapy is analogous to a person who continually repeats the 12th grade. Given an average level of cognitive functioning, with each repeat of the grade, its efficacy diminishes. The person's level of knowledge and psychological growth has exceeded the course level. So for these clients, moving toward natural, self-healing modalities as core therapies will become the norm.

With greater and greater numbers of people evolving in consciousness, there will be an ever *de*creasing number of people whose psychological needs require psychoanalytic, cognitive, behavioral or humanistic-existential techniques. Even beleaguered modern medicine recognizes that psychoanalysis has reached its apogee in usefulness as Dr. Paul McHugh, professor of psychiatry at Johns Hopkins University School of Medicine stated in the November 2002 issue of the *Harvard Mental Health Letter*, states that: "…psychiatry is in crisis. It is surrounded by vigorous and growing fields of knowledge but does not know how to make use of them or contribute to them…..psychoanalysis no longer provides an overall guide for reasoning about mental disorders…."

We can say that it is has taken roughly 100 years for classical psychoanalysis to have become outdated and largely irrelevant, therefore, we can hypothesize that, at some point, psychodynamic, cognitive-behavioral and humanistic-existential techniques will, by and large, reach their apogee of value and usefulness as well. In light of this, the field of psychology must be ever vigilant in arriving at, and agreeing upon, a cohesive evolutionary theory of consciousness. This, in turn, will challenge psychology to generate visionary thinking as to what types of treatment modalities will best serve various client populations so that psychological research can be ahead of, not behind, the needs of people. *The field will be left behind if the current trend of the knowledge level of the client/patient population about alternative therapies exceeds the knowledge level of the healthcare provider.* Already begun in the 1990s, is a groundswell of consciousness that has begun to question conventional modern medicine and focus on what many people consider to be self-healing techniques and forms of medicine. This consciousness of "I can heal myself" is expected to burgeon, not diminish, hence, psychology must be in step with this movement. This should result in a general agreement between clinicians about what types of therapy work optimally with which client population and, finally, what are the most relevant and effective treatment modalities in which psychologists must be trained. Calling for a collaboration within the field, Wilber states that "the problem is to discern a semblance of order and a synthesizing structure for this vast complexity of different and frequently contradictory psychological systems." Without this collaboration and synthesis, psychology risks becoming irrelevant.

Therapy to bring about Soul consciousness must work with the client's unconscious mind since humankind has disconnected with what Maslow refers to as the "transcendent values." As we have said, today the Soul is relegated to the realm of the unconscious. Jung refers to this as the "unconscious Deity." The way to manifest the Soul Consciousness is not through consciousness, but through reaching into the individual unconscious and this must be achieved through self-reflective psychotherapeutic techniques such as meditation, not through behavioral and cognitive techniques which only address the client's conscious awareness. Erich Fromm recognized this decades before meditation was even seriously looked at. He was truly ahead of his time. In his book, *The Art of Being*, he states "from the practice of concentration, a direct path leads to one of the basic preparations for learning the art of being: to meditate." Also, Ken Wilber has been stating for 25 years that it is an "ethical imperative" for psychotherapists to recommend and teach their clients meditative techniques.

The Soul Consciousness model moves beyond Carl Rogers' premise that the goal of therapy is the verbal dialogue—the relationship between therapist and client. Rather *the goal of Soul Consciousness therapy is for the client to reconnect with Higher Self.* This is the self-in-relation-to-Self modality, not the self-in-relation-to-other technique of psychoanalysis, cognitive, behavioral, humanistic and existential theories where the client is always in relation to the therapist, the "other". May, in his book *The Discovery of Being*, points the way toward this self-in-relation-to-Self mode as he speaks of *Eigenwelt,* the highest mode of "knowing" one's self:

> "What does it mean to say 'the self in relation to itself'?...What does the 'self knowing itself' mean?...This mode of the self in relation to itself was the aspect of experience which Freud never really saw, and it is doubtful whether any school has as yet achieved a basis for adequately dealing with it. *Eigenwelt* is certainly the hardest mode to grasp in the face of our Western technological preoccupations. It may well be that the mode of *Eigenwelt* will be the area in which most clarification will occur in the next decades.....*Eigenwelt* cannot be omitted in the

understanding of love."

The therapist does *not* have ultimate answers for a client; only the Higher Self does. Deepok Chopra, Andrew Weil and John Diamond are just three medical doctors who have written books about the mind-body connection and the innate ability for every human being to heal Self. This innate healing power comes from the Higher Self. They are visionary leaders who, over twenty years ago, began courageously leading the march toward reawakening the human consciousness to ancient truths which have been buried by modern medical science and pharmaceutical companies. *These ancient truths lie within your Higher Self and you need only remember them.* Western medical science has no incentive or vested interest in you awakening to ancient truths because, in so doing, modern Western medical science will lose economic power and will be forced to *share knowledge and power* with Eastern medicine. Neither do pharmaceutical companies have any incentive or vested interest in you awakening to ancient truths because, by doing so, these companies lose their economic vise and, hence, worldly power.

If you awaken to ancient wisdom, your Higher Self will direct you to natural, self-healing methods as a primary way to maintain health and avoid disease. Only an individual's Higher Self has all ultimate answers, not the "other." It is through reconnecting with the Soul, the Higher Self, the Ground of Being, that the individual reconnects with authenticity and higher psychological health and well-being. This is understood by the transpersonal therapist as "ultimate states" of consciousness which transcend the psychoanalytical, cognitive-behavioral and humanistic-existential states of integrated, self-actualized, individuated ego.

Having said this, it should be understood that many people on the planet still function at the lower and, mostly, middle levels of ego consciousness and, therefore, we cannot throw the baby out with the bath water. I agree with Wilber that ego level therapies will continue to be in vogue, albeit with an ever *decreasing* demand, throughout the first half of the 21st century. At the lower level of ego consciousness and with clients functioning in the bottom two tiers of Maslow's hierarchy, it is likely that behavioral and cognitive techniques which are highly directive will continue to be necessary in the short-term for those clients who have drug and alcohol abuse issues and for clients who have a past of serious sexual, physical and emotional abuse. At least until the public sees the wide-spread application and efficacy of other natural, self-healing remedies such as meditation, music therapy, chromatherapy, aromatherapy, Qigong, Tai Chi, Yoga and nutritional therapy, these self-in-relation-to-other therapies will exist.

At the middle and upper level of ego functioning, these clients become ever increasingly appropriate for natural, self-healing modalities. Talk therapy and pharmacological intervention will not cease to exist, but the need for them *as long-term treatments* will decrease over time as people gravitate toward integrative healing as a form of preventive maintenance. Pharmacological intervention is an effective, expedient, potent way to de-escalate a psychological crisis such as suicidal ideation, severe depression, extreme anxiety and mania or to address active psychosis. It is logical to expect that drugs will continue to be a critical and necessary intervention during psychological crisis states, but pharmacological intervention, as a sole or primary intervention, for long-term anxiety and depression will eventually be replaced by preventive health regiments which include alternative and natural methods. Humankind's epidemic dismissal of daily inconvenience and its addictive reliance on expedient healing is both a symptom and mirror of the equally insidious and pathological need to speed up life to a dangerously unhealthy NASCAR pace. Gandhi's comment, "there is more to life than increasing its speed," seems frighteningly appropriate today.

Behavioral and cognitive therapeutic techniques as an adjunct with short-term pharmacological intervention will likely remain important with this client population until the integration of ego is achieved. Clearly, it must be stated that the eradication of all verbal dialogue and all pharmacological interventions is *not the goal*, particularly, as was mentioned before, with psychotic patients, with patients who are in psychological crisis such as those who are suicidal, or patients who have unresolved issues around sexual, physical and emotional childhood abuse. To be sure, there is a greater need for talk therapy by those clients who have experienced serious environmental insults during childhood and adolescence since it is commonly known in the psychological field that children, and most adults, who have suffered serious environmental insults had no voice whereby they could expose their abuser. Indeed, many of these tragic victims who did attempt to voice their abuse were angrily silenced. Hence, it is critical that these abuse victims be given a voice in psychotherapy so they may tell their painful story of suffering and perhaps move toward a cathartic healing through this process of revelation. With non-psychotic patients and with patients who are not in a psychological crisis, however, talk therapy is likely to eventually evolve over the next several decades as being useful only for the initial phases of the psychotherapeutic process or during strategic, brief intermittent phases when meditation, color therapy, music therapy, Qigong, Tai Chi, Yoga and aromatherapy cause sudden emotional needs to emerge or unresolved traumas from the past to surface. Talk therapy may prove useful for, say, three to twelve sessions in the beginning of treatment and perhaps for multiple sessions at some later point if past, buried trauma resurfaces. But as these natural, self-healing treatment modalities increase in use and effectiveness, there will be a decline in the *long-term* use of talk therapy interventions. There will be fewer people seeing a therapist for years at a time as the new paradigm of treatment emerges. It is, therefore, probable that the old paradigm of long-term talk therapy will be replaced by a new paradigm of self-in-relation-to-Self techniques (meditation, chromatherapy, music therapy, Tai Chi, Qigong, Yoga and aromatherapy), especially as these modalities are proven to be more effective through longitudinal scientific studies over the next several decades.

As the individual integrates the ego and moves toward the higher levels of ego functioning, these Western techniques become less effective in offering a facilitative milieu for the manifestation of the Soul Consciousness. As the Soul begins to manifest on a conscious level more and more, then the client's unconscious world will change as well. This follows both Jungian theory and Advaitic thought. It is most likely that the severe split between conscious and unconscious will be healed as humankind reaches higher levels of consciousness such that there will be a free and open exchange made between the unconscious and the conscious realms. Today, because we ignore and dismiss the Soul, this split is a huge chasm and the result is a substantial ignorance of what exactly the unconscious is and what role it plays in the human condition. Much research still needs to be done to better understand this largely unknown realm.

We return to Sigmund Freud's hypothesis that the unconscious is, primarily, a vast wasteland of sexual and aggressive desires and unfulfilled wishes. Freud with his deterministic view of humankind likely felt that the unconscious never changes. Once full of garbage, always full of garbage. Only in the sense that Freud believed the goal of psychoanalysis was to make the unconscious conscious is this theory considered relevant to the Soul. Since Freud considered ego integration as the apogee of mental health and because the Soul Consciousness believes overcoming and transcending the ego is the central goal of the Soul, we can say Freud got to first base, but he never made it to home base. Freud posited that simply knowing subconscious wishes and drives would be sufficient to work through one's issues. This is what led to insight which, in turn, led to change. By its very nature, it is a masculine model of thinking. Freud was in many ways the exemplar of the ego consciousness as he considered the feminine to be "irrational," refused to entertain any ideas outside his own theoretical model and would arrogantly cast out of his enclave any person who dissented from the Freudian world view.

With the ego consciousness pervasive within the human experience, it is logical that we would feel that the unconscious never changes. However, as the field of psychology begins to turn its focus, and spend research dollars on, the healthy and optimally functioning human being as the guiding consciousness, psychology and medical science will move closer to understanding optimal mental health and what benefit this conscious state of mind will have on the human condition. We saw one substantial move in the right direction as the Dali Lama publicly met with psychologists, neuroscientists and Buddhist scholar-practitioners at MIT in September 2003 to dialogue about the efficacy of meditation as a means of achieving calmer, more peaceful and sustained states of consciousness. Research in this area is increasing and the results are consistently reflecting that meditation practice causes substantial changes in brain wave patterns from alpha (aroused) waves to theta (deep relaxation) waves. In the August 4, 2003 issue of *Time* magazine, the article, "The Science of Meditation," exposes a number of research projects on meditation since the 1960s and their favorable results on mental health.

It is through a blending of East and West that science and psychology will make the next quantum leap forward in efficacy and, ultimately, in respectability. First and foremost, meditation must become considered within mainstream psychology as quintessential and core psychotherapy. Indeed, Wilber states in *Up from Eden: A transpersonal view of human evolution*, that "meditation....becomes an absolute ethical imperative...if we are to contribute to evolution." Further, he says in a 1995 issue of *Journal of Transpersonal Psychology* that:

> "The subjective and introspective approach...does not attempt to prove the existence of Spirit by deduction from empirical or natural events, but rather turns the light of consciousness directly onto the interior domain itself—the only domain of direct data---and looks for Spirit in the disclosures of that data. Meditation and contemplation become the paradigm, the exemplar, the actual practice upon which all theorizing must be based. The God within, not the God without, becomes the beacon call."

We recall in an earlier chapter the Dalai Lama saying that meditation is the only path to enlightenment and the only method whereby we transform our minds. Lama Chogyam Trungpa Tulku Rinpoche spoke to the Association for Humanistic Psychology in 1971 about "An Approach to Meditation." He states in the *Journal of Transpersonal Psychology* that "meditation seems to be the basic theme of spiritual practice.....the only way to relate to the present situation of spirituality...is by meditation." In referring to the ego, he says:

"Since the whole structure of the ego is so well fortified against attack, an external invasion is not going to destroy the ego at all. In fact, it is going to reinforce the whole structure because the ego is being given more material with which to work. Meditation practice is based on an undoing, unlearning process. It is an infiltration into this well-fortified structure of the ego... Fundamentally the idea of enlightenment—the notion or term 'enlightenment' or 'Buddha' or 'awakened one'—implies tremendous sharpness and precision along with a sense of spaciousness. We can experience this; it is not myth at all."

May points to the importance of meditation in *Discovery of Being* saying that "self-awareness....brings back into the picture the quieter kinds of aliveness—the arts of contemplation and meditation which the Western world, to its peril, has all but lost."

Meditation, a practice of concentration and contemplation commonly thought to bring about higher states of consciousness, has been a practice utilized for over two thousand years by the Chinese, Asian Indians and Mayans. Even though research began in the 1960s, it has only been since the 1980s that a serious and increased research effort began. Meditation, along with music therapy, chromatherapy and aromatherapy, is based on the knowledge of the body and mind as being an *interconnected* energy system. Your mind and body (the mind-body connection) are energies which, when balanced and in harmony, are in a state of psychological and physiological health. To study the body separately from the mind is folly because the mind has a direct effect on the physiological state. This falls in tandem with the two primary ancient medical models which are based upon the same basic knowledge: Ayurvedic medicine and Traditional Chinese Medicine (TCM). In proposing a new paradigm of psychotherapeutic treatment modalities, it is important to acknowledge these two oldest known forms of natural medicines. Because meditation, music therapy, chromatherapy and aromatherapy are so intertwined with the energy principles of Ayurvedic medicine and TCM, I pause here to provide a basic understanding to those readers who are unfamiliar with these age old forms of healing.

Ayurvedic medicine derives from ancient writings called the *Vedas*. *Veda* literally means "knowledge." There are four primary *Vedas* with the first known Veda, the *Rg Veda*, written during the Vedic Period between 2,500 and 600 B.C. and the last known Veda written during the Scholastic Period culminating in the end of the Vedas around 1700 A.D. Each Veda has four parts: *Mantras, Brahmanas, Aranyakas* and *Upinasads*. The Mantras are hymns and are considered the beginning of Indian philosophy, the Brahmanas are religious documents, the Aranyakas speak of meditation and the Upanishads are philosophical texts. The *Bhagavad-Gita*, which is considered as one of the three most authoritative texts in Indian philosophical literature along with the *Brahma Sutras* and the *Upanishads*, was written during the second period of Indian philosophical development, the Epic Period, between 600 B.C. and A.D. 200. It was during this period that Buddhism arose with direct and indirect realism schools belonging to the Hinayana thought and the idealism and relativism belonging to the Mahayana line of thought. Buddhism is based on Indian philosophy from the Upanishads. When Buddhism formed, there was not an initial motive of creating an entirely separate system of thought, rather it was more to take existing philosophical Indian texts and create a new way of explaining the metaphysical so that it would be more in line with current thought.

The most widely accepted philosophical system of thought in India today is *Advaita Vedanta* (*Advaita* means "non-duality"; *Vedanta* means "end of the Vedas") which is taken from the original Brahma Sutras written during the third period, the Sutra Period, roughly around the time of early Christian thought. Vedantins presume the existence of a Soul which transmigrates and assume the existence and attainment of enlightenment, also known as Absolute Reality, Truth or Knowledge or *nirguna* Brahman, through intellect and intuition which are two faculties considered indispensable in the attainment of enlightenment. Most of early Indian thought promulgates meditation as the direct path to this state of consciousness. Spiritual, mental, emotional, physical and environmental harmony is a central tenet. In *Indian Philosophy*, author Jadunath Sinha speaks of seven central tenets across all Indian philosophical thought:

Indian philosophy concentrates on the spiritual.

Indian philosophy believes philosophy and life are intimately intertwined.

Indian philosophy has in inherently introspective approach to reality.

Introspection leads to idealism in most Indian philosophies.

Indian philosophy makes unquestioned and extensive use of reason (intellectual knowledge), but intuition is accepted as the only method through which the ultimate can be known.

Indian philosophy accepts the authority of the intuitive insights of the ancient seers of Absolute Truth.

Indian philosophy is characterized by a synthetic approach such that true religion is a combination of all religions, i.e., "God is one but men call him by many names."

Ayurvedic medicine was developed mostly from the *Rg Veda* and the *Atharva Veda* (the fourth major Veda) which contained references to maintaining health and preventing illnesses. The systemization of this knowledge became known as the fifth Veda, *Ayurveda,* and was compiled within three classical texts between the 6$^{th}$ century B.C. and 1000 A.D. by three men who practiced and taught Ayurvedic medicine.

Ayurveda is Sanskrit and literally means "the science of life." It is a combination of science, philosophy and spirituality. Two primary assumptions of Ayurvedic medicine is that it focuses on the prevention of disease and it empowers the individual to assume responsibility for her/his health. Unlike modern Western medicine, Ayurvedic medicine takes a holistic approach and considers the harmonious balance between spiritual, emotional, mental, behavioral, physical, familial, social, environmental and universal dimensions as determinants of overall good health. Balance translates into good health. Imbalance translates into ill health. Unlike Western medicine, Ayurvedic medicine concentrates primarily on maintaining balance first and only secondarily on preventing disease. Ayurveda stresses relaxation, management of stress and proper nutrition with food, herbs and minerals. Meditation, music and aromatherapy are three ways to manage stress. In *Secrets of Ayurveda,* there are seven conditions present in a state of good health:

All three doshas (vata, pitta, and kapha) are perfectly balanced,

The five senses are functioning naturally,

the body, mind and spirit are in harmony,

all the tissues of the body are functioning properly,

the three malas (urine, feces and sweat) are produced and naturally e
liminated,

the energy channels (marma points) of the body are unblocked and flowing

with energy,
the digestive fire (metabolism in Western terms) is healthy and the appetite
is working normally.

The three doshas are the three constitutional types of your body and mind.
The seven chakras, while not specifically identified in ancient Ayurvedic
medicine, are recognized by ancient Indian thought and are critical energy
centers located through the middle of your body down the spinal column. The
major marma points in Ayurvedic medicine correspond to the seven chakras.

In Eastern religions, the seven chakras in the human body are spiritual
centers which, if balanced, create mental and physical homeostasis. As you
allow the energic expressions of the Soul to balance and activate, these seven
chakras will be functioning at optimal levels. Chakras are balanced through
sound and color. Each chakra has a vibrational frequency and a corresponding
sound and color frequency. They are outlined below:

I.    *Root chakra*:    pelvis bone, uterus, ovary, fallopian tube,
urinal track, vagina, penis, testicles, prostate gland,
rectum, bladder, legs, knees, calves, ankles and feet. This
is the chakra which is responsible for all physical energy.
*Corresponding color*: ruby red
*Color meaning*: passion, excitement, energy
*Corresponding sound*: HE

2.    *Spleen chakra*:  spleen, gall bladder, hip bones, small
and large intestine or colon and that part of the spinal
column. All negative emotions tend to drift and collect
in this area.
*Corresponding color*: orange
*Color meaning*: clarity
*Corresponding sound*: HO

3.    *Solar plexus chakra*: stomach, liver, pancreas, upper
parts of large and small intestines, kidney and that part
of the spinal column. This area energizes learning and
creating through stronger intellectual interest.
*Corresponding color*: yellow
*Color meaning*: courage, boldness, strength
*Corresponding sound*: SA

4.   *Heart chakra*: heart, arms, shoulders, hands, lungs, thymus gland, ribs, bronchial tubes, spinal column in that section. All positive emotions of love, peace, joy, etc. can be magnified here.
*Corresponding color*: emerald green
*Color meaning*: growth, healing
*Corresponding sound*: KA

5.   *Throat chakra*:  thyroid gland, tonsils, larynx, top of spinal column. This is a large creative center in your body. Words that you speak have a vibrational energy and will draw similar vibrations to you. Negative words will draw negative things to you. Positive words will draw positive things to you.
*Corresponding color*: sky blue
*Color meaning*: creativity, collaboration
*Corresponding sound*: RE

6.   *Third eye chakra*: eyes, ears, nose, sinuses, teeth, jawbones, pineal gland (some call this the psychic gland). Discernment and wisdom are found here.
*Corresponding color*: royal blue
*Color meaning*: wisdom, good judgment
*Corresponding sound*: MA

7.   *Crown chakra*:  brain, beginning of nerve system, hair on the head. This is the center for reaching the highest spiritual truth and knowledge.
*Corresponding color*: violet
*Color meaning*: power, spiritual truth, knowledge and understanding
*Corresponding sound*: RA

Once Western medicine discovers these spiritual centers and their connections with the physical centers in the body, science and spirituality will be merging and humankind will be on its way toward a faster amelioration of human suffering.

Think of chakras as either expressing or blocking energy. When the Soul is cared for and nurtured consistently, these chakras are balanced and are expressing energies toward Goodness. Each chakra's energic center will move in a clockwise direction and, if completely balanced, an energy strand much like the DNA strand will be created. These energy centers are blocked if the ego is governing actions. Fear, anger, sadness, guilt, shame, envy, jealousy and greed will block the Soul's energies from their natural, free expression.

When these energy centers are clear and unblocked, good health exists. Meditation is a practice which can unblock and balance these major energy centers. While there are many different kinds of meditations, when meditating, it is good to concentrate on each point, starting with the lowest chakra and proceeding to the highest, and imagine each corresponding color emanating from the energy center. Your mind, through focus and concentration, is able to profoundly affect this energy flow.

Hopefully, you will see that the core philosophy of Ayurveda consists of a balance of soul, mental and physical energies which are affected by multiple internal and external factors. The soul is subtle energy, your essence, and is transcendental in nature. This tri-fold energy system is controlled by the individual, therefore, it is the individual, not the doctor or therapist, who heals self. The power of healing is not given away to "the other," rather is held within Self. This is simply an introduction to Ayurvedic medicine as space does not permit a lengthier exposition. For beginners, you may read *Secrets of Ayurveda* by Gopi Warrier, Dr. Harish Verma and Karen Sullivan or *A Beginner's Introduction to Ayurvedic Medicine: The science of natural healing and prevention through individualized therapies* by Vivek Shanbhag, M.D., N.D. For those interested in reading more about Indian philosophy, you may read *Indian Philosophy* by Sarvepalli Radhakrishnan and Charles Moore. For the reader who wishes to explore, in depth, Indian philosophy and psychology, you may read *Indian Philosophy* in three volumes by Jadunath Sinha and *Indian Psychology, Volume 1: Cognition, Volume 2: Emotion and Will and Volume 3: Epistemology of Perception* by the same author. Sinha provides an extremely broad and in-depth exploration of Indian thought, so it is recommended that these are read only after gaining a fundamental knowledge of Indian philosophy and psychology. For those interested in gaining a basic knowledge of *Advaita Vedanta*, Eliot Deutsch's previously mentioned book is an excellent start followed by William Indich's *Consciousness in Advaita Vedanta*. They are all worth the read.

Traditional Chinese Medicine (TCM) has many different names and particulars from Ayurvedic medicine, however, it is important to understand that both have the same overarching concepts: 1) the body-mind-spirit is an integrated whole and cannot be separated, 2) the balance of internal and external factors must be considered in maintaining harmony and health, and 3) it is imbalance of the internal energies and an imbalance in relation to one's environment which results in disease. The earliest Chinese medical text is the *Yellow Emperor's Inner Classic* written in eighteen volumes over several Chinese dynasties. It is the earliest complete book on TCM and speaks of the intimate relationship between human beings and nature, one of the central tenets of TCM. The philosophy of Taoism begun by Lao Tzu is thought to have influenced the development of TCM, therefore, just as is inherent within Indian thought, philosophy, psychology, spirituality, religion and ethics are considered to be intertwined and inseparable. Key foci in TCM are acupuncture, first practiced over 2,000 years ago by a physician named Bian Que, and herbal remedies. It is believed that a physician in the 2nd century A.D. by the name of Hua To is the first to perform surgery using anesthesia made from herbs. The body exercises he created form the basis of Tai Chi, a set of body movements used in physical and mental fitness and which has gained some popularity in the United States over the past decade. In the 2nd century and 3rd century, respectively, Zhang Zhong-jing wrote texts related to infectious diseases and Wang Shu-he was the first expert on pulse diagnosis. From the 6th to the 10th century A.D., more works were written including the first pharmacopoeia sponsored by the Chinese government, *Classified Materia Medica for Emergencies.* Four leading doctors between the 12th and 16th centuries worked in the area of hot and cold diseases, purgatives and diaphoretics, spleen and stomach functions and herbal remedies. The classic text, *Compendium of Materia Medica,* published in 1578 is an encyclopedia of herbs and lists 1,892 drugs and 10,000 prescriptions. As with Ayurvedic medicine, TCM is best used when combined with Western medicine as no one system is considered to be a catch-all for every known illness or disease.

Two basic principles of TCM are Yin and Yang which are the feminine and masculine principles found throughout the universe and the five elements—fire, water, earth, wood and metal. The human being is comprised of both yin and yang and the five elements. When these are in balance, health and harmony result. When these are out of balance, disease and illness persist.

Yin and yang can be understood as opposite energies which co-exist throughout nature. Some common yin and yang energies are night and day, cold and hot, wet and dry, resting and active, yielding and forceful, slow and rapid, heavy and light. In Chinese philosophy, Qi or Chi, the life force, emerges from the tension of the opposites of yin and yang. Yin and yang are co-dependent and, paradoxically, are opposite, yet perfectly complement, each other. It is impossible for either to cease to exist. When yin or yang is either in excess or in deficiency, there is disharmony resulting in ill health. Simple examples would be when you have an excess of heat, you have fever or when you have a deficiency of water, you are dehydrated. Another simple example is when you have an excess of sugar intake, you are susceptible to diabetes and when you have a deficiency of calcium, you are susceptible to osteoporosis. Two last simple examples would be when you drink alcohol excessively, your liver is susceptible to disease or when you have a deficiency of rest, your body becomes susceptible to all kinds of stressors. When these elements or energies are operating harmonically, they form a circular whole and good health exists. When the Chi or Qi is blocked, it is because of an imbalance in the yin and yang flow of energies and the result is disorder in the human mind and/or body. Since Qi is viewed as the élan vital or life force, one can understand the significance of balance. In terms of physics, you may think of yin as the light wave, yang as the light particles and Qi as that which exists between the wave and the particles. Said another way, you may think of the feminine (feeling) as the wave, the masculine (thinking) as the particles and the Will as that neutral void, or ether, in between.

The five elements are literally all around us and can best be understood by the lay person in terms of qualities or patterns in the human. Fire (growth), Wood (germination), Earth (nourishment), Water (decay), and Metal (ripening) symbolize an eternal cycle in nature and in the human. The five elements give a framework of understanding the dynamics of not only the substances and organs in the human body, but also emotional and mental states. In TCM, the organs are the core of the human body and are the central points in maintaining life. All disease is categorized as either exogenous (outside) or endogenous (inside). Chinese medicine considers the harmonic relationship between man and nature as core to good health so that a broken arm, a snake bite and even weather changes are considered to be outside factors. Some inside factors include poor diet and overwork which contribute to physiological imbalances and psychological stress.

TCM believes that the five elements are linked with the five dynamic substances which form the human body—Qi (metal), Blood (wood), Essence (water), Spirit (fire) and Fluids (earth)—and they all have a supporting function with each other. Viewing these interactions as a balance between body and mind, diseases are viewed as a function of the relationship between these substances and not as a single disease or illness. Similarly, good health is seen as a function of the harmonic relationship between these vital energies.

Qi or Chi is considered the most important substance and the other four elements are manifestations of Qi energy. Qi is not air although it is a life force which circulates, warms, protects and animates the body. Without Qi, the human body cannot exist. Its order in movements and transformations rely on this life force energy. Qi is taken from three sources: 1) from parents, 2) from food and liquids, and 3) from the vital portion of air through breathing.

The five emotions which TCM recognizes are: fear (kidney), worry (spleen), anger (liver), sadness (lung) and joy (heart). Emotional imbalance results in disorders in the organs, therefore, all inside and outside factors must be considered when these organs lack health. Mental and physical overwork is endemic in the world and is a common etiology of disease. Make no mistake, the greed inherent in the business world is a direct contributor to ill health as corporations and businesses demand unreasonable physical, mental and emotional expectations from their employees. Balance between work and play is essential if we are to maintain good health, so excess or deficiency in these areas is a trigger for illness. Sexual activity, diet, and trauma are other areas in which a TCM practitioner would focus.

Like Ayurvedic medicine, TCM refers to energy centers in the body and calls them the Meridian System. There are twelve Regular Meridians and eight Extraordinary Vessels that are of primary importance. The twelve Regular Meridians connect to the organs and to the surface of the skin and are distributed bi-laterally through the body. Divided equally between yin and yang energies, the twelve Meridians correspond to an organ and are subdivided based upon whether they flow to the hand or to the foot. The Qi in yin Meridians flows from the ground upward; Qi in yang Meridians flows from top toward the feet. Qi travels in a fixed direction. Yin Meridians meet in the chest (feminine energy of the heart) while yang Meridians meet in the head (masculine energy of the mind). At the extremities is where both yin and yang Meridians join. The flow takes twelve hours to make one cycle. Each organ has a peak level of vitality.

The eight Extraordinary Vessels are receptacles for the Regular Meridians. Think of the Meridians as pathways and the Vessels as repositories for Qi energy. The Vessels are responsible for the regulation of the yang Meridians, embryonic development and the regulation of the twelve Regular Meridians and Blood. It is along these Meridians and Vessels in the body that acupuncture and massage are used to manipulate and restore these energy pathways and reservoirs to a balanced energy state. There are a total of 2,000 points which can be used in acupuncture, but it is a usual 200 points which are used by the acupuncturist. Between one and twenty needles are used in this usually painless procedure, depending upon which energy points are selected. The average session lasts thirty minutes. Last, it should be noted that, as was previously mentioned, herbs (not synthetic drugs) are a primary pharmacological intervention for the treatment of illness and disease in both TCM and Ayurvedic medicine. If the illness does not dissipate through the use of herbal remedies or if the illness is considered to be too far progressed, non-herbal remedies may be recommended. Typically both acupuncture and herbal remedies are utilized as preventative measures or before a health condition becomes acute. You can *generally* consider Ayurvedic medicine and TCM as preventative medicine and to be used in the treatment of mild and moderate illnesses and diseases whereas we would turn to Western medicine for acute or terminal cases. There have been people, however, with serious illnesses such as cancer who have used alternative medicine as an adjunct to Western medicine. Perhaps with increased time and medical studies, this will become more accepted.

Consciousness is explicit within Indian philosophy whereas Chinese medicine uses the concept of Spirit (one of the five substances) to interpret consciousness. Spirit is located in the heart. According to Chinese thought, there are three Spiritual souls and seven Animal Souls. Operating as a polarity, the two Soul groups decide the fate of an individual after physical death. As you can see, the concept of a Soul is intrinsic in ancient Chinese and Indian thought. Hopefully, you can walk away with the key understanding of how TCM and Ayurvedic medicine do not draw sharp lines between the mind and the body as does Western medicine. Emotions and mental states are understood to be direct causes of physiological illnesses such that work, family, social environment, natural environment and diet become direct correlates in sustaining good physical, emotional, mental and spiritual health.

For those interested in a basic understanding of TCM, you are referred to *Tao and Dharma* by Robert Svoboda and Arnie Lade. For more in-depth reading, you may read *The Basis of Traditional Chinese Medicine* by Shen Ziyin and Chen Zelin and *The Clinical Practice of Complementary, Alternative, and Western Medicine* by W. John Diamond, M.D.

## MEDITATION

Let us return to the topic of meditation. Remember that we are referring to ancient healing methods, but because of the epidemic reliance on pharmaceutical drugs and technology, ancient healing methods have not received attention or research funding from the Western medical community. Much of the future of healing is going to involve the return to these ancient, natural, self-healing methods as they are utilized in tandem with modern technology. The theoretical base will remain while advanced tools and equipment will be used to bring these ancient, yet "cutting edge," healing treatments to the forefront of medical science and psychology. This, in turn, will allow science to perfect the techniques and methodologies. It is, for sure, an auspicious time when we are able to combine ancient wisdom and knowledge with the best of the modern science in order to make substantial advances in physical and mental health and healing.

Substantial research is lacking and mainstream psychology overlooks meditation as a viable core psychotherapeutic technique, even though some studies suggest that meditation (especially long-term) results in more peaceful mental states. Certainly, most ancient Eastern philosophies and psychologies have pointed to meditation as the primary path and indispensable path toward illumination, enlightenment and transcendence of the ego. Jesus the Christ and the Buddha reached the Higher level of consciousness through meditation, not through psychotherapy sessions. They were not trying to find Truth through "the other," rather had an intuitive sense that Truth is within. Indeed, Jesus the Christ said "the Kingdom of Heaven is within." Eliot Deutsch states in, *Advaita Vedanta: A Philosophical Reconstruction*:

> "the actual experiential attainment of *moksa*, of self-knowledge and wisdom, for most Advaitans, is the work of the third stage which is that of 'constant meditation'......He must meditate, he must maintain an intense concentration on the identity of his self with Reality....dissociating himself from the phenomenal play of his surface life, he must become a witness to it. Through detachment he turns away from all egoism, from fear and sense-distraction."

*Moksa* refers to liberation or freedom from karma, freedom from *samsara* (the cycle of birth, death and rebirth). According to Deutsch, *moksa* refers to:

> "attaining a state of 'at-one-ment' with the depth and quiescence of Reality and with the power of its creative becoming. Spiritual freedom means the full realization of the potentialities of man as a spiritual being. It means the attaining of insight into oneself; it means self-knowledge and joy of being."

In this way, we can think of Being or Soul or Higher Self as that Being which has attained spiritual freedom.

The Soul is the landscape of silent solitude, therefore, in order for the Soul to manifest, it needs silence or sedating music, not chatter. To be sure, meditation and soothing music are elixirs for the Soul. The Soul knows silence; the ego knows cacophony. The Higher Self is found in solitude and through stillness, quietness and serenity, not through a cacophony of talking or noise. This is why psychotherapy of the distant future will not consist of a therapist sitting across from the client dialoguing year after year. Certainly, people say things that give us insights and we can say that talk psychotherapy has been of benefit to people who are within the three lower tiers of Maslow's hierarchy. Talk therapy is a necessary therapy for certain populations and for a limited time, but it is only a paradigm. It is not a lasting paradigm and it is not the future of psychotherapy. The Soul is deep within you at the unconscious level, therefore, finding your Higher Self or your Soul is found by going within to the sacred, silent center of your Soul who knows the Ground of Being.

Soul Consciousness is brought about by moving beyond the ego, thus, the reason for the term "transpersonal" meaning "beyond the personal" or "beyond the ego." Current psychotherapeutic modalities seek to *integrate* the ego and the ego consciousness; therefore, they are insufficient and inadequate therapies to bring about a *transcendence of the ego* and to move *beyond the ego*. The future psychotherapeutic techniques must be transpersonal techniques which seek to transcend the ego consciousness and reach the transcendent, Higher Self, the Whole Psyche, the realm of Soul Consciousness. This is achieved only through a self-in-relation-to-Self model of therapy. The current client-therapist "talk therapy" modality is one in which the client is likely (consciously or unconsciously) relating to, or comparing themselves to, the "other," the therapist. When transcending the ego, the client must reconnect with the inner, transcendent, Higher Self. It is this Higher Self who has the wisdom necessary to make life decisions when faced with the existential dilemmas that are an inherent part of being human.

Transpersonal therapies are also understood to mirror, and be parallel with, the process of becoming more "self-responsible," which is an inherent characteristic of the Higher Self. It is this Higher Self, with its Universal commonality of seeking to know Truth, to create Beauty, to love Goodness and to be wise about the Will of the All, which also differs in the particulars of the *ways of* seeking to know, to create, to love and to be wise. Said another way, your Higher Self shares the same Universal desire with every other human being as it seeks to know, seeks to create, seeks to love and seeks to be wise as a means to bring Goodness to both Self and to others; however, your Higher Self differs from everybody else in terms of the particular means and methods utilized in order to express these Universal energies. Consider it as what the Buddhists refer to as the ten thousand paths to Nirvana or, in this model, to Soul or Higher Self. In this sense, we can now begin to develop some agreement about process and results because the *process* of therapy and the *results* of therapy become merged. You are unable to separate process from results because *the process of the Soul* is to know Truth of who you are (your "I"), to create Beauty of the It (symbols of who you are), to love Goodness between each other (We), and to be wise about the All, the Divine Will. *The results of the Soul* are the same as the process of the Soul: to know Truth (I), create Beauty (It), love Goodness (We) and be wise about the All, the Divine Will. It should be clearer that, in order to rise to the next level of consciousness, all theoretical models and treatment modalities must be integrative. They must spread across a spectrum, to use Wilberian terms. They must ultimately reach a merging of thinking and feeling. They must create a merging experience of body/mind/soul/spirit. The Higher Self will intuitively move toward the necessary therapeutic process which will bring one closer to the Soul Consciousness. Within the Soul Consciousness model, it is understood that the Higher Self is the reconnection you need to make in order to manifest Soul Consciousness.

I realize this is a radical departure from current psychotherapeutic interventions and this will likely cause the defensive, if not vituperative, ego consciousness to surface since this theory threatens an economic power base of not only practitioners, but also pharmaceutical companies whose billions of dollars is made primarily by *treating* disease and illness, *not in curing it*. Many will initially dig their heels into their old way of operating instead of openly considering another alternative and researching its efficacy. While I have spent considerable time articulating reasons that psychology must move away from "talking" modalities, I realize that we cannot simply wave a magic wand and "poof" these modalities instantly out of existence. First of all, as has been stated before, talk therapy serves a purpose for a specific clientele today. Second, no one can be forced to transcend or move toward enlightenment. The ego is, after all, well entrenched and, as has been previously reiterated, has a defense fortress around it to ensure its on-going survival. Without question, there will be people who vehemently and adamantly revel in ego consciousness and any mention of moving to a higher state will only rally the defensive ego to its own preservation. There will also be those who are so intellectually inclined and are so lacking in intuition that they fail to perceive the correlation between the Higher Self and a more peaceful state of mind. Both are ego looking through different telescopes, but from the same elevation. To that, we simply say *that is where that person is developmentally functioning*. Nothing more and nothing less. No judgment is necessary since we all will arrive at the Soul developmental stage in our own time and in our own way even if it takes hundreds of incarnations. Having said this, it is unethical to force someone to seek a higher consciousness. Quite simply, force is antithetical to the Soul who is gentle and transforming. The Soul doesn't force. It simply guides, compels and inspires. So force and control is not in the realm of Soul Consciousness. It is understood that, once exhausted by the pain and suffering caused by the ego, sooner or later everyone activates the Divine Will toward the peace of the Great Soul.

Thus, some clients will continue to have a need for cognitive and behavioral therapy because they are functioning at that level of need. But there are other clients functioning at a higher ego level who are currently pursuing these types of therapies who would potentially benefit more from transpersonal treatment modalities. In spite of this, some professionals will do everything they can to cling to the familiar way of operating. It is likely that mostly those who follow the Jungian and transpersonal theories (and a portion of the humanistic-existential therapists who are really transpersonal therapists deep down and believe ego transcendence is a goal of therapy), along with those psychotherapists with knowledge of, and training in, Eastern psychologies and philosophies will be the vanguards of Soul Consciousness therapy. They will be open-minded enough to enthusiastically look toward a new vision of psychological healing as entailing self-reflective techniques. Those clinging to the old paradigm will eschew self-healing techniques; those embracing the new paradigm will learn new psychotherapeutic modalities and weave these into their practices.

Through Eastern techniques such as guided meditations with positive affirmations; color therapy with color baths; sound or cymatic therapy with instruments such as tuning forks; music therapy including various ethnic and cultural melodies, drumming, and chants; and aromatherapy with various oils and scents, the client's body *and Soul* will be the focus. These psychotherapeutic techniques will be combined with treatments such as Qigong, Tai Chi, Kundalini Yoga, nutritional therapy, acupuncture, homeopathy and herbal therapy in order to address the physical, mental, emotional and spiritual essences of the client. By combining the best of the West and the East both in medicine and in psychotherapy, the field of psychology in the future will not only manifest a cornucopia of psychological treatments for clients suffering from mental illnesses and disorders along a continuum from mild to severe, but will develop a collaborative bridge between medicine, psychology and philosophy in the treatment of clients.

Let us not forget the critical component in healing: the Will to heal Self. There already exists research within the social psychological field of the Pygmalion effect. This study by Rosenthal done several decades ago established a strong relationship between positive expectations set by the teacher and performance among the school children they taught. It is as if what is expected is what manifests. Additionally, pharmaceutical companies have much to lose if the truth about the placebo effect becomes widespread knowledge by lay people.

A paucity of research exists today concerning the relationship between positive thoughts and the cellular make-up of the body, however, this research will burgeon in the future by neuropsychologists and scientists. Literally, there is a gold mine awaiting discovery by Eastern and Western psychologists, therapists and medical professionals if only they can awaken to a new vision, revision the way we do things and unite, then collaborate with each other on their research and their findings.

In these aforementioned treatment modalities, it is understood that the client can have a merging experience of both thinking and feeling which, in turn, has a direct effect on behavior. This is why meditation is promoted. It is the realm of the Silent Soul. Remember that the Soul's language is not through verbal language. When you are meditating, your goal is to move away from thoughts into the landscape of infinitely merged Mind and Heart and you have potential to have a merging experience of Being. This is the landscape and home of the Soul and it should be understood that this is the primary method by which a client is able to manifest Soulfulness. The role of the therapist is to assist the client in the unfolding of the Soul and Soul consciousness from a strictly unconscious state. One may think of it as the unification or merging of consciousness and unconsciousness.

While it may be optimally effective for the psychotherapist to begin with 2-5 sessions with a client in dialogue around presenting problems and current issues that are creating intrapsychic conflict and/or interpersonal problems, it is understood within the Soul Consciousness model that the client must be provided a quiet, still ambiance in solitude. As has been stated, the best that current mainstream psychotherapies can do is *integrate* ego. The ceiling of effectiveness is reached when that is achieved. Intellectualization, logic, reasoning, developing insight, behavioral change and addressing emotions is not, *in and of itself,* adequate or sufficient to develop Soul Consciousness and will not lead to the highest energic expressions of Soulfulness. And without manifestation of the Soul Consciousness or the Higher Self, large-scale psychological health will not manifest on this planet. The Soul's language is silence and symbols, therefore, talking with another person would be counterproductive and counterintuitive to the unfolding of the Higher Self and Soul Consciousness. Intuition is the noetic knowledge which the Soul utilizes. Any psychological model whose primary psychotherapeutic technique is constant verbal dialogue between therapist and client will not result in the client's highest knowledge of their Higher Self and, far into the future, this type of psychotherapy is destined to be largely irrelevant and become outdated when a growing mass consciousness reaches the upper-middle to highest levels of the ego consciousness.

## Color Therapy

Color therapy represents the next phase of natural, self-healing vibrational medicine to become widely recognized by both medical science and psychology. It just needs more exposure and research dollars. Color can be considered the visionary elixir of the Soul. The therapeutic use of color and light for healing purposes goes back to ancient Egyptian times when healings were performed in temples. Color has an effect on each of us. Light flows through us and affects us emotionally and hormonally and, at the deepest level, affects us at the cellular level.

We have already briefly discussed the electromagnetic energy field around the body which is sometimes referred to as the *aura*. You can think of this field as a "subtle body" as opposed to your physical body which is a "gross body" meaning it is denser energy than your subtle body. As we said before, your subtle body is a protective sheath around your denser, physical body. When this protective sheath is unbalanced long enough, your physical body and/or emotions will ultimately be affected.

Everything in the Universe is energy and nothing is excluded from this. Anyone who is a physicist can hardly deny this. Max Planck said that matter is really imprisoned light. Einstein's theories point in the same direction. It seems that ancient wisdom and modern physics are just about to agree that we are all, essentially, beings of light. It seems that there are dozens of intellectual giants who have come to this general conclusion, yet still seem reluctant to boldly state what everything in their research findings is pointing towards. All esoteric, ancient wisdom teachings say the same thing: No other person can tell you about your path to truth; you have to discover your own path. Each person has to access their own inner wisdom, their own Higher Self in order to discover their own Truth.

Trees, flowers, light, dirt, minerals, animals, humans, gold, diamonds, water, fire, clothing, cars, houses, furniture all have a certain vibrational frequency because all of it is energy in different forms. The sooner we begin to reference inanimate things and animated life as being and having energy, the closer we will be to newer and advanced discoveries. The ancient Chinese and Indians have known about energy and incorporated that into their medicines.

We all learned in high school biology class that plants cannot live without light yet we forget about the importance of light in relation to human life. It's so easy to forget and take for granted something that permeates our lives. No one can live without the energy of light and, in fact, Seasonal Affective Disorder (SAD) is a condition whereby some people become seriously depressed during the winter months because of the lack of adequate sunlight. Over the past decade, there has been a growing amount of research in this area and it has finally been recognized as a legitimate disorder due to light deficiency. We now recognize light as an effective treatment for people with SAD. Light has definite biochemical effects on us ranging from emotional and mental to physiological. Humans obtain Vitamin D through exposure to sunlight. Vitamin D enables you to absorb calcium in the body which, in turn, helps in the building and maintenance of bones, teeth and nerves. Vitamin D also assists in the immune system with the production of white blood cells. So your body definitely needs sunlight! This is not fanciful or mythological. It is fact. If we don't get enough sunlight and stay tucked away inside dark rooms or even rooms with fluorescent lighting, many of us become moody. This is no coincidence. The body literally needs light and the Soul yearns for Light because this is its free-flowing essence.

Roberto Assagioli, the Italian psychiatrist who developed psychosynthesis, a transpersonal psychological model, stated in his book, *Psychosynthesis: A Collection of Basic Writings*:

> "It is generally admitted that each color has a distinct psychological quality of its own, and consequently a definite effect....further investigation and experiments are needed to give more light on this fascinating subject...it is now generally accepted that co-called 'cold' and subdued colors have a quieting effect, and that 'warm,' vivid, and bright colors have a stimulating or exciting influence. Certain shades of blue are usually considered as having a soothing, harmonizing effect; light green is refreshing; red and bright yellow are usually stimulating, while pink suggests serenity and happiness....The influence of color as a therapeutic agent is also becoming increasingly recognized. I think in this respect it opens up great possibilities, but as a science it is still in its infancy.....much scientific experiment and accurate differentiation is needed, but the beneficial results will justify further research."

Humans have multi-colored auras and your aura changes colors depending upon your diet and the emotional and mental state which you are in at the time. Predominately blue auras are exhibited by people who are calm and have inner peace. White is a sign of purity and, as previously mentioned, is the color of Jesus the Christ's halo. Gold is the God consciousness. Green symbolizes healing and growth. Yellow is a sign of courage. Orange is a symbol for clarity. Red represents passion.

Admittedly, there have been charlatans associated with color therapy at the turn of the century, so the field has suffered setbacks from these spurious individuals whose knowledge was not grounded in scientific facts. To be sure, scientific research has found that light and color indubitably affect the body functions and emotions. Blood pressure and respiratory rate increase under the color red and both decrease under the color blue. It has been shown that eye blinks increase under red light and decrease under blue light. Muscles seem to activate under warmer colors of red and orange than under cool colors such as blue and indigo. These are consistent findings through scientific research and are not myth, fantasy or the dubious pronouncements by charlatans.

Each color found in the visible light spectrum has a specific wavelength and its own vibrational frequency which produces a certain energic effect in your mental, emotional and physical bodies. With the use of all colors in the color spectrum and relating these to the seven (7) chakras in the body, your body will be "tuned" to its natural, healthy vibrational frequencies. It is through stress, poor diet, ecological distress and negative thoughts and emotions that each of the chakras become unbalanced or blocked which lead to unhealthy vibrational frequencies. Chromatherapy is a treatment modality which uses color to restore balance and harmony in the vibrational frequencies in the chakras within the body and in the auric field around the body. It assists in restoring your body's natural vibrational energy frequency. Color therapy, just like modern medicine, cannot heal everything, but its restorative, healing power is currently being overlooked.

Color has been of interest to great men for centuries including Aristotle, Newton, Goethe, Hegel, Schopenhauer, Einstein and Schrodinger. Interestingly, it has been stated that Einstein, though considered an intellectual genius, used mostly intuition to guide him toward his discoveries. Although ancient civilizations as early as the Egyptians used colors in healing, it was not until Dr. Edwin Babbitt, also compelled by intuition, began research on color and its effect on psychological well-being that the concept of color as medicine emerged in modern times. Babbitt wrote about Chromo-Therapeutics in *The Principles of Light and Color* in 1878 and it created a stir amongst the medical community. He established a relationship between color and emotional and mental states. Most notably, he found that red has a stimulating, exciting effect while blue has a calming, sedating effect. He knew about the electromagnetic field and believed that every object (inanimate and animate) emanates its own light and color. He further associated colors with minerals and elements. Babbitt devised three instruments called the Chromo-lume, Chromo-Disc and Chromo-Lens. The first two instruments were used to treat topically while the latter was used for both topical and internal treatment.

Since colors have varying "charges" or "frequencies" as do organs of the body, the energy field and area of the body where the instruments were placed would absorb the color energy necessary in order to balance out the excess and deficiency of energy. He saw results from both the Chromo-Disc and the Chromo-Lens. His method of using sun-charged water with the use of colors (an ancient healing method) is something that should instigate a plethora of research today. In his book, Babbitt had this to say about the power of color:

"Many of our scientists…grasp with all their souls after the grosser elements of nature, writing long treatises on a bug, a worm, a mineral, or a skeleton, but when marvelous facts are revealed with regard to these more beautiful essences of being, these lightnings of power without which the whole universe would be but a formless and lifeless mass of debris, they utterly fail to receive the glad tidings with philosophical candor, commence persecuting the discoverer as though he was an enemy, and return to the corpses and bones of the dissecting-room in preference to the radiant forms of the world of life."

Next, Dr. Dinshah Pshadi Ghadiali, a medical doctor from India who held numerous doctorate degrees, further developed color healing basing his research on three principles: 1) the human body reacts to light, 2) colors relate to physiological function and 3) color tonation aids bodily function. Through his research, he arrived at a knowledge of certain physiological and emotional states per each color in the spectrum. Through his research, he arrived at a complete system of color medicine. He arrived at an anatomical chart for tonation, a technique of exposing specific colors to certain designated body areas. Dinshah worked with twelve colors with the three primary colors of Red, Green and Violet. Red (warm) is the lowest color located near the Infrared end of the light spectrum. Violet (cool) is the highest and located nearest the Ultraviolet end of the light spectrum and Green is the middle, neutral color in the color spectrum. Secondary colors were Yellow, Blue and Magenta which, when combined with the three primary colors, produced the tertiary colors of Orange, Lemon, Turquoise, Indigo, Purple and Scarlet. Warm colors are Red, Orange, Yellow and Lemon. Cool colors are Turquoise, Blue, Indigo and Violet. The neutral color is Green. Purple, Magenta and Scarlet draw from vibrations of both the warm and cool spectrum.

Dinshah's vibrational rates of each color are listed below with the seven chakra colors highlighted:

**Red** vibrates at 436 trillion times per second

**Orange** vibrates at 473 trillion times per second

**Yellow** vibrates at 510 trillion times per second

**Lemon** vibrates at 547 trillion times per second

**Scarlet** (combination of Red and Blue) vibrates at 547 trillion times per second

**Green** vibrates at 584 trillion times per second

**Magenta** (combination of Red and Violet) vibrates at 584 trillion times per second

**Turquoise** vibrates at 621 trillion times per second

**Purple** (combination of Violet and Yellow) vibrates at 621 trillion times per second

**Blue** vibrates at 658 trillion times per second

**Indigo** vibrates at 695 trillion times per second

**Violet** vibrates at 731 trillion times per second

If you look at the mathematical proportions, you will find that Violet is the same vibrational distance from Green as is Red. Indigo is the same vibrational distance from Violet as Orange is from Red and so forth.

Dinshah arrived at a summary of color attributes which are summarized below:

**Scarlet** (combination of red and blue) is a kidney and adrenal stimulant; also increases blood pressure, heart rate and emotions.

**Red** should never be used for the relief of stress, fevers or inflammations since red has an exciting and stimulating effect. It stimulates the sensory nervous system; is a liver builder and stimulant; increases blood count and circulation.

**Orange** is a stimulant as well and raises the pulse rate, but not usually the blood pressure. It builds the lungs, thyroid, bones; stimulates tissue and respiration; is a parathyroid depressant and a decongestant. It can be used, along with yellow, to lift depression, sadness or apathy.

**Yellow** is a stimulant for the senses and is also a cleanser of toxins from the digestive tract; is a stimulant of the motor nervous system; nerve builder; stimulates both the intestinal tract and the lymphatic system.

**Lemon** (combination of yellow and green) is considered a master cleanser of toxins, nourishes and repairs cells and is used to lift depression as well. It dissolves blood clots, is a bone builder and brain stimulant, a thymus builder and stimulant, an expectorant and a mild digestive system stimulant.

**Green** is the neutral color and is in the middle of the color spectrum. It is the color of the pituitary gland. Green is a cerebral equilibrator and pituitary stimulant and equilibrator. It also stimulates the rebuilding of tissues and muscles.

**Turquoise** (combination of green and blue) is a brain depressant and assists in healing skin burns.

**Blue** is used to treat burns, to reduce fever, pain and inflammation and has a sedating, calming effect on a person's emotions. It is the color of the pineal gland.

**Indigo** is a respiratory depressant; parathyroid builder and stimulant; thyroid depressant and is a sedative. It can be used to reduce inflammation.

**Violet** decreases muscular activity; is a spleen builder and stimulant; a lymphatic gland and pancreas depressant; promotes the production of leukocytes and is a tranquilizer.

**Purple** is excellent for meditation as it induces deep relaxation and sleep; is a kidney and adrenal depressant; lowers blood pressure, heart rate and body temperature.

**Magenta** (combination of red and violet) is also an emotional equilibrator.

The two major physiological systems we refer to for psychological purposes are the sympathetic and parasympathetic nervous systems. Red has been used in many research settings and would be the color to use if the goal was to stimulate the sympathetic nervous system, in other words, to cause excitement or stimulation, that "fight or flight" part of our system. It is the stress producing part of the nervous system. Yellow could be thought of as an anti-depressant. Blue has been used in many research settings to stimulate the parasympathetic nervous system or that part of the nervous system which calms and restores. Blue is considered the most useful in combating anxiety although turquoise, indigo and violet have calming effects too.

Kate Baldwin, a medical doctor and Chief Surgeon at a Philadelphia hospital at the turn of the twentieth century, was a student of Dinshah. Baldwin used light substantially in her private practice and in her practice at the hospital and, in 1926, had this to say about colors:

> "After nearly thirty-seven years of active hospital and private practice in medicine and surgery, I can produce quicker and more accurate results with colors than with any or all other methods combined, and with less strain on the patient. In many cases the functions have been restored after the classical remedies have failed. Of course, surgery is necessary in some cases, but the results will be quicker and better if color is used before and after operations."

Harry Riley Spitler, a medical doctor and optometrist, wrote the book, *The Syntonic Principle,* after years of research and was able to find relationships between light, cell and tissue growth, the immune system, the sympathetic (the stress-producing part) and parasympathetic (the maintenance and restorative part) nervous systems, the perception of pain and hormonal production. Syntonic is a Greek word meaning "to bring balance." Like Babbitt and Dinshah who used light to heal, Spitler also proved the healing effects of light. However, unlike Babbitt and Dinshah who used color and light directly on the body, Spitler used light through the eyes. He concluded that the imbalance of either the parasympathetic or sympathetic nervous systems caused physiological or emotional problems. His work proved that balance of the autonomic nervous system could be achieved through administration of light through the eyes. Through his research and work, he arrived at nineteen Syntonic Principles which are listed in the last chapter of his book and outlined below:

There exists a closely predictable relationship between light frequency, incident into the eyes, and response.

There exists a relationship between light frequency and the rate of growth of cells and tissues and their rate of cell division.

There exists a relationship between the light in the environment and the physical development of the individual.

There exists a relationship between light frequency in the eyes and the mass body potentials.

There exists a relationship between the light frequency of the environment and the development of the Biotype, modifying the hereditary tendency.

There exists a relationship between light and light frequency and the action current leaving the eye toward the brain.

There exists a relationship between the light frequency incident into the eye and the power of the pituitary gland.

There exists a relationship between the reproductive cycle and the light frequency environment with respect to the number of individuals of any species.

There exists a relationship between the light frequency environment and the dynamic tension present between the two divisions of the autonomic nervous system.

There exists a relationship between the light frequency environment and the secretion of hormones by all of the co-acting as well as antagonistic endocrine glands, with the pituitary as the master gland.

There exists a relationship which is largely predictable between light frequency environment and the restoration of health following departures from the normal, which are still within physiologic limits, particularly those departures which may be directly influenced by the autonomic or the endocrines toward health.

There exists a relationship between light frequency into the eye and the degree of nerve cell irritability, thus modifying reflexes.

There exists a relationship between light frequency into the eye and bodily health.

There exists a relationship between nerve impulses from the eye, due to incident light frequency, and the state of tension in the autonomic nervous system.

There exists a relationship between light frequency into the eye in either its vitamin A content or the degree of its adaptation to low degrees of illumination.

There exists a relationship between light frequency into the eye and the perception of pain.

There exists a relationship between light frequency into the eye and the relative responses of both striated and smooth muscle.

Syntony of the autonomic nervous system may be produced by light frequency into the eye.

The ability to continue to live depends upon syntony of the autonomic in both acute and chronic illnesses, and this attainment of syntony may be aided by light frequency into the eye.

Robert Gerard, a medical doctor and student/colleague of Roberto Assagioli, also pursued a doctorate and he completed his dissertation in 1958 by conducting research to determine the effects of the colors red and blue on physiological and psychological states. His findings are highly suggestive and support prior research which indicates a relationship between color and psychological well-being, along with improved physiological indicators such as blood pressure and pulse.

Peter Mandel is a German naturopathic and chiropractic physician and acupuncturist noted for founding colorpuncture. The Mandel Institute for Esogetic Medicine is located in Bruchsal, Germany where he practices colorpuncture and engages in ongoing research in this area. Having studied acupuncture in Hong Kong and India, he has been able to formulate Esogetic Medicine. Colorpuncture is a technique where acupuncture points from TCM are used to transmit light through the meridian system. Like TCM and ayurvedic medicine, colorpuncture assumes there is a balanced flow of energy through the meridians which result in good health. Acupuncture uses fine needles to move Chi (life force) throughout the body; colorpuncture uses different frequencies of colored light. As color hits the skin, vibrational impulses occur at the molecular level which travel along the meridians to the brain. This results in the balancing of the entire energy system including both the meridians and the electromagnetic field around the body.

Esogetics is Mandel's healing system and includes colorpuncture, Energy Emission Analysis and the color and sound therapies. It is a unification of ancient Greek and Egyptian systems of healing along with principles of TCM. Colorpuncture is based on Goethe's original theory of colors and Mandel uses the seven basic colors associated with the chakras to add or decrease energy to the meridians and energy field surrounding the body. The Soul-Spirit Colors are turquoise, crimson, light green and rose and are considered to facilitate the awareness of the deeper layers of the psyche and spirit. Mandel believes these can provide a more intense therapeutic effect which goes deeper into the various levels of consciousness and precipitate insights and feelings of well-being.

Mandel has developed his color/sound therapies after becoming interested in whether it would be possible to influence energy flow in the meridians with sound and music. Working with music educators, Mandel developed the Esogetic Sound Pattern Tapes. These tapes hold sound patterns that have frequencies that are equivalent to the vibrational patterns of the various colorpuncture treatments. Certain frequencies, patterns and modulations are associated with areas within the brain. The brainwave activity between the two cerebral hemispheres is harmonized so that states of profound relaxation can be achieved.

Mandel says this about disease:

"Any kind of disease should be considered as an alarm signal for disharmonies in spirit and soul...We have to turn away from our suffering and sickness because they are the hindrances on our path towards the inner. We have to bid farewell to those frustrations and fears which prevent us from progressing and from coming into contact with our higher selves."

Today, Jacob Liberman, O.D., Ph.D., John Downing, O.D., Ph.D., Norman Shealy, M.D. Ph.D., Gabriel Cousins, M.D., Elson Haas, M.D., Mary Bolles, B.A., Steven Vazquez, Ph.D., Robert Dubin, D.C., Akhila Dass, O.M.D., L.Ac., Manohar Croke, B.A., Lee Hartley, Ed.D., Brian Breiling, Psy.D. and Samuel Pesner, O.D. are a handful of professionals recognized as experts in the field of chromatherapy. They have been utilizing chromatherapy with their clients for up to three decades, have been witness to amazing therapeutic effects and believe light is one of the most potent tools for mind-body healing. These are respected medical doctors, optometrists and psychologists who, at the beginning, had an intuitive sense that color therapy was a natural way to self-heal so they pursued the knowledge and then began using it in their profession. All of these professionals follow an integrative approach in their practices combining the best of ancient, natural healing methods with newer technologies. While they realize that no medicine is a healer of all, each one of them have witnessed healing through chromatherapy and believe it is a core rehabilitative technique for the future. Each of them have contributed a chapter to the book, *Light Years Ahead: The Illustrated Guide to Full Spectrum and Colored Light in Mind-body Healing*, so I'll simply allow each of these competent professionals to speak for themselves. I encourage anyone to read the entire book because it is a fascinating account of these medical professional's work and research and is truly a beacon of light (pardon the pun) for medical science and psychology in terms of the vast potential waiting to be explored.

Gabriel Cousins, M.D. is a holistic physician, psychiatrist, homeopath, family therapist, Essene minister, Reike master, meditation teacher, international peace activist. He has published several books and numerous articles in biochemistry, school health, clinical pharmacology, and Alzheimer's. He uses nutrition, homeopathy, acupuncture, psychiatry and family therapy, crystal healing and meditation in his practice:

"Nutrition all comes from God and is nourished by God or the cosmic force. The cosmic energy…..is the basic nutrient for our bodies. In this context, all levels of energy available to us are considered nutrients—this includes sunlight. Once we understand that various densities of energy are the essential nutrients to all life processes, it allows us to appreciate a paradigm of nutrition which sees material food as just one level of energy density in the context of a larger spectrum of nutrients that aid our healing and spiritual development. Consciousness is the essence of food that we digest……Our ability to both absorb and radiate light directly leads to spiritual development and health.

"We are human photocells whose ultimate biological nutrient is light. Food, through the process of photosynthesis, brings sunlight energy in the form of resonating electrically active carbon-

carbon bonds and electron clouds on double-bonded structures into our physical bodies. This light is then released into our systems as electrical energy."

Elson Haas, M.D. specializes in nutrition, herbology, Chinese medicine, acupuncture, bodywork and the use of guided imagery into a general medical practice. He has published three books and is director of Preventive Medical Center of Marin in California:

"Since sound and light are primary energies, they will play an increasingly important role in the future of medicine.....Light and sound are the primordial energies from which life evolved—the essence of nothingness into somethingness. We, too, are an expression of this energy—light, color and sound. Color and sound are vibration and affect all other vibrations. The human body is energy/vibration...Although we live on air, water, and food as nourishment, we are energy and light, and we are affected and nourished by light. The more open, aware, and sensitive to light vibrations we are, the more we can be influenced and healed by the basic light of nature....Light is energy. Each color is a vibration, a frequency of vibrating energy that intermingles with other life energies....Light, color and sound are vibrations of energy that are based on wavelengths and cycles per second of electromagnetic vibration....We are vibration; all forms of energy affect us...The chakras can be conceptualized as a subtle energy nervous system and correspond to major nerve plexi from the pelvis to the top of the head...As a medical doctor, I believe phototherapy affects the human energetic system at the level of core energy...Reflecting back on all the patients who received colored light phototherapy in my practice, the best results happened when light therapy and psychotherapy were combined."

Mary Bolles, B.A. is an expert in the area of Ocular Light Therapy on learning disabilities such as dyslexia. She specializes in Whole Brain Accelerated Learning, Sensory Integration, Natural Vision Improvement and Auditory Integration Training. She has a private practice in Colorado and uses light, sound and motion to enhance learning and eyesight:

"The journey into light and color is really to 'know thyself', and the end of this quote, actually is 'to be divine.' An emotional tone scale that I discovered in my training is that the emotion of the pineal gland is enthusiasm. Enthusiasm means literally, 'the act of bringing God within.'

"What I see most consistently in clients of all ages is that after the light, sound and motion treatments they have less fear. Fear may actually be the learning problem. Fear actually causes a breakdown in the connections between the various brain centers. Thus, the major change I've witnessed in most people after light therapy is a lessening of fear and an accompanying increase of peace within that person.

"I'm working with really difficult children and I know that this synergy is a lot easier on the children than working with one modality alone......had I used sound earlier with some of the children rather than only light, I would have been able to have a greater impact on them...In our daily life we've got light, sound and motion going on all the time, and to separate it out makes it more difficult to use as an enhancement tool. It makes sense that we should keep it all together."

Brian Breiling, Psy.D. is a body-centered Marriage and Family Therapist specializing in depression, anxiety, phobias, PTSD, chemical dependency and adults recovering from abuse. He is certified to practice massage therapy, Reiki, hypnosis, biofeedback and school psychology. He received his doctorate from the California Institute of Integral Studies and has a private practice in Tiburon, California:

"Quantum physics is one hundred years ahead of much of medical science. Its descriptions of reality on the subatomic level and at the level of galaxies are all quite similar; these are views of reality that even have a mystical quality. Interestingly, the reality described by quantum physicists is strikingly similar to the world view and energetic concepts of traditional Chinese medicine and traditional Hindu medicine known as ayurveda, concepts which are thousands of years old. I believe light and phototherapy are the fulcrum of this interface between mind-body medicine and subtle energy healing......light is one of the most potent tools for mindbody healing. Light, comprised of both electric and magnetic energy, may also be the conceptual 'missing link' between materialistic medicine and the emerging conceptualizations of quantum healing and subtle energy medicine. The future theory and practice of light medicine could serve to bridge the science of current mindbody medical disciplines such as psychoneuroimmunology with alternative and traditional medical practices such as homeopathy, acupuncture and ayurveda."

Lee Hartley, Ed.D. is a licensed Marriage, Family and Child Therapist and a pioneer in the combination of clinical hypnosis and light therapy. She has extensive experience working with clients with Premenstrual Syndrome (PMS) and Seasonal Affective Disorder (SAD) and those who have an abuse history:

"In my practice, I often do psychotherapy using hypnosis and the Lumatron concurrently and I find that some of this information eventually surfaces. In session we will usually cover these incidents, and at the same time I will suggest that they work with the light at home on a daily basis. I find that these two different light treatment approaches are a wonderful combination. I've always appreciated using hypnosis, because it speeds up the therapeutic process."

Jacob Liberman, O.D., Ph.D., F.C.S.O. is Director of The Aspen Center for Energy Medicine and is a pioneer in the use of light and color. His methods have proven effective for thousands of individuals from business executives to Olympic athletes. He has published two books and holds a Doctor of Optometry degree from Southern College of Optometry and a Ph.D. in Vision Sciences:

"We are living photocells. The body gives off light, and not only white light, but different colors of light. I didn't understand this until I had a direct experience of it, and presently I've been experiencing this for almost twenty years…..Our relationship to light is very crucial to our evolution…..We're in a very important time historically; there are a lot of paradigms that are melting, and crumbling, and the paradigm of how vision works also needs to crumble….the pineal gland is the body's 'light meter,' it is the body's regular of regulators. It regulates everything that's happening in the body, and it's the only part of our being that doesn't receive information from any higher neurological centers. What that means to me is that it's the part of us that's connected to God—higher energy, energy itself, whoever or whatever that is…..since the pineal gland is the body's light meter, it receives information from the environment about light and darkness and spectral characteristics by way of the eyes; it also receives information about the earth's electromagnetic field…..it is a part of our being that is receptive to information from the heavens above us…and from the earth beneath our feet….the pineal gland is the connecting rod between the grounding forces and the heavenly energies….the pineal gland creates a very interesting hormone called melatonin, which is the only hormone in the body that we know of right now that can do anything it wants, anytime it wants, anywhere it wants….it is a very powerful hormone that comes into creation from the pineal's relationship with light and darkness, and it is also released because of light and darkness….the pineal is basically being told what is happening outside, whether it is light or dark, what time of the year it is, what time of the day it is. The individual cells then use this information to orchestrate their internal function and synchronize themselves with Mother Nature….In other words, the pineal is the part of our being that lays the basic foundation for relationship….everything that happens is a function of relationship.

"I began working in my office, treating a lot of children who had learning difficulties, discovering some very interesting things about these children who supposedly had difficulties in school. What I noticed was that they really didn't have that many difficulties, but they were just frightened to be in school…..One of the things I know about children is, they know more than we know. You see, they're the next generation and they're a bit more advanced and evolved than we are. They keep trying to tell us things, but we don't listen because we want to be in control. I noticed that when many children are put into—or incarcerated in—what we refer to as learning institutions, which may have very little to do with learning for the most part—a lot of stress develops….we notice that children who are highly stressed in an academic setting have a visual field which is very tiny….I noticed early on that light, administered by way of the eyes, seemed to create miraculous enhancement in these situations; it would open up the field of vision. When it did, children would have positive personality changes, physical changes, academic changes, and performance changes. After a while, one of the mothers of a child I was treating said, 'Well, if you did that with Johnny, how about my migraines?' I treated her, and three or four weeks later her migraines, which she had had for seventeen years, began to dissipate.

"...the Egyptians looked not only into the sun, but at colors as well. They said it would not only heal the body, but it would open up the past memory banks of the observer, almost like a homeopathic remedy.....I utilize light as a way of bringing to the surface old unresolved, unexpressed emotional traumas, which I feel are the roots of the weed we call disease...What I am beginning to find is that all disease is the end result of a breakdown in relationship, whether it is relationship within ourselves, between us, with the environment, with the cosmos, or whatever. It is a direct function of the way that we utilize our minds. If the breakdown is within the harmonious, functional relationship, then the cure is to re-create the relationship.

"Tools, techniques, and mental constructs are just ways to return our consciousness to the lost parts of ourselves."

John Downing, O.D., Ph.D., F.C.S.O. is an optometrist in California who has conducted over 25 years of neuro-science research and clinical practice in the area of Ocular Light Therapy. He created the first modern light therapy device called The Lumatron Ocular Light Stimulator for which he received a U.S. Patent in 1990. He has doctorates in optometry and vision science and teaches his method of light therapy to practitioners in over 20 countries:

"Sam, age 28, was one of my first cases to have a before and after recording of the brain's electrical pattern, called a brain wave pattern of an electroencephalogram (EEG). Sam had epilepsy and was having a grand mal seizure every two weeks. He was developing brain damage from his numerous seizure-caused falls which produced severe blows to his head. After examining Sam, I classified him as a neurologically slow type with a correspondingly slow brain wave pattern. For this type of patient, I usually suggest Ocular Stimulation with the red side of the spectrum, and that is what I used in this case. I started him on a series of twenty, 20-minute sessions of Lumatron red light stimulation through the eyes. He then received one month off, followed by a second series of twenty, 20-minute Lumatron orange light stimulation. After Sam completed light therapy, he was still having seizures. However, instead of every two weeks, they were every two months. Then they decreased to three months, and after that it was a year before he had another one. The last time

I saw him was seven years after light therapy, and he was having much milder seizures and only once every nine months. His success with light therapy not only saved him from most of the future brain damage that he would have incurred, but he reported functioning much better both mentally and emotionally, with a significant reduction in the slurring of his speech.

"I have developed a Constitutional Profile that gives me a starting color and I give a certain weight to the problem and the person....The patients are the ultimate determiners to the practitioner as to what color they're going to need.....It's far better not to say you're going to cure something, but to just focus on optimizing the patient's ability to take in photocurrent. Let's balance their hypothalamus with light!"

Norman Shealy, M.D., Ph.D. is the Founder and Director of the Shealy Institute in Missouri and is a pioneer in the use of holistic treatment modalities for chronic pain, depression and stress-related disorders. He has developed a number of techniques and is currently researching the effects of Ocular Light Stimulation on neuro-chemical responses in the brain. He received his medical training at Duke University, has written many articles that appear in professional journals and is the author of several books including one written with Caroline Myss, *The Creation of Health:*

"Ultimately attitude is the only thing there is. Attitude is the basic cause, and I believe at this moment in time, the ultimate primary cause of most disease.

"Light, the amount of light, the quality of light, the color of light, or the frequency of light, influences everything in your brain and, consequently, everything underneath that....Our attitude of encouragement, of relating, of getting people back into living, seems to be more important than the individual treatments that we do....It does not matter what you do. It is your attitude, your intent, the thought field you create around you that helps trigger the healing process in the individual....Only when your intent is right and the patient is willing to cooperate with you is healing allowed to happen.

"For the last twenty-two years I have dealt almost exclusively with chronic pain sufferers and I soon recognized that what I was actually dealing with was chronic stress. I believe that, basically, all of us who are in the so-called 'health profession'—which really are the 'disease professions'—are dealing with one illness. There's only one major illness, and it's called depression.....Actually, there is only one basic emotional problem, and that is fear, that's all there is. There's fear and there's joy, the two primary emotions. There are a very limited number of reactions to fear. The natural reaction to fear is to be angry; that is normal and healthy and it should lead to action. If it doesn't lead to action, it will lead to depression. Sometimes it leads to guilt, because people then blame themselves. And occasionally, not infrequently, people don't want to admit fear, so they call it anxiety. That's al there is. Every other emotional reaction is a synonym of fear. Anxiety, guilt, anger or depression are also reactions to fear, resulting primarily form either this feeling of abandonment or of abuse or of being wronged....The goal of our work with individuals is to teach them to live the transcendent will, the will of the soul, that is, detachment from all that you cannot or choose not to change and have no need to know why. It's non-judgmentalism, being at peace and having a desire to do good to others, which is the only definition of love that fits every situation. Everything perceived as lacking, which is desire, has nothing to do with love. Now, if one could live from this transcendent will 100% of the time and could do this from early on in life, my suspicion is that there would be almost no illness...The causes of disease occur when we move away from this principle and we know that we are not living our life in harmony with our own basic inner rightedness."

Dr. Shealy believes there are four basic types of people: 1) depressed, 2) both angry and depressed, 3) self-actualized, and 4) angry and blaming. He believes there are five basic fears: 1) fear of death, 2) fear of illness or being an invalid, 3) fear of abandonment, 4) fear of poverty and 5) fear of abuse. He believes the seven most important neurotransmitters are: 1) melatonin, 2) norepinephrine, 3) tyrosine, 4) phenylalanine, 5) beta endorphin, 6) serotonin and 7) acetylcholine. His research indicates that of all the depressed clients that he has seen in his clinic, 92% were deficient or excessive in one to seven of these neurochemicals. He uses Downing's Lumatron and the Shealy Relax Mate which is a set of portable goggles which produce light stimulation primarily for depression and anxiety. In his clinic, he says that he treats "the worst of the worst", in other words, people who have not responded to psychopharmacological interventions or psychotherapy. He uses any combination of autogenic training, biofeedback, self-regulation skills, Vibrating Music Beds, the Lumatron, the Shealy Relax Mate, information about fear and the transcendent will and the chakras in order to get rid of "unfinished business". Music has become an important adjunct and is used as a technique to enhance intuition and relaxation. His work reflects that, within one week, 90% of these patients overcome depression. Shealy believes that the primary cause of disease is attitude; there is only one major illness (depression); there is only one basic emotional problem (fear); and healing is ultimately triggered when the individual personality allows the light of the soul fully into being.

I've attempted to provide the reader with the actual voices of some of these bold, innovative leaders in the field of chromatherapy so you can see that this is no longer a field mistaken as being led by charlatans. These are competent, bright, compassionate and well-respected professionals who are opening the door to natural, self-healing techniques which will be core medicine for the unfolding of the Soul Consciousness. They are, quite literally, ahead of their time.

Once again, chromatherapy is dismissed by medical science and mainstream psychology, however, the paucity of research literature that exists is overwhelmingly suggestive that there is a vast goldmine of research awaiting the field of psychology and medicine to either dispel or validate chromatherapy as an adjunctive treatment modality for psychological and physiological health and well-being.

Practitioners of Feng Shui are knowledgeable about the psychological effects of colors and choose different colors when designing and decorating homes and offices. Jenny Liu received her BA in Environmental Design from UC at Berkeley and her MA in Architecture from UCLA. She did a Master's Thesis on Feng Shui. In her words, "our body absorbs color energy through the seven (7) energy centers or vortexes in the body….Color energy is ubiquitous and we absorb it through food, vitamins, herbs, sound, minerals, clothing and aromatherapy."

Cloth wraps or color baths from a color-filtered light source will become a highly utilized psychotherapeutic technique in the future and will become one of the four primary psychotherapeutic techniques alongside meditation, music/sound therapy and aromatherapy. Chromatherapy combined with music therapy is considered optimally effective as the vibrational frequency of colors are thought to correspond with certain musical notes. Color is a higher frequency within the light spectrum with sound being directly behind it. The integration of color and sound and other treatment modalities such as aromatherapy can be combined to enhance the treatment.

What I call the "hard-core intellectuals" will likely dismiss this modality because hard-core intellectuals have no interest in building their intuitive capabilities and are uninformed as it relates to the Soul and Spirit. It's a waste of time to even engage in conversation with a hard-core intellectual because it's like trying to convince a narcissist that he has a problem. What's tragic about hard-core intellectuals is that they think IQ is going to solve all the problems of the world when, in actuality, it is a roadblock to psychological wholeness if not equally balanced with heart energies from the Soul. Intellect alone will never solve the problems of the world because it is only a partial energic expression of the Soul.

## MUSIC THERAPY

It has been said that music is the language of the Soul. The basic thought behind sound therapy is the same as that of light therapy—everything is operating at a constant vibrational rate. If we follow this thought, then all the cells of your body are constantly vibrating at a certain frequency such that sound and color can either enhance or prevent relaxation. Sound therapy can be used to reduce muscle pain, back pain, headaches and inflammation. Using either Tibetan or crystal bowls or tuning forks, these sounds produce varying vibrational frequencies thought to enhance the frequency of each chakra. Also utilizing tapes that have the sounds of nature such as the ocean, seagulls, wind, rain, birds and crickets can be highly effective in producing relaxed mental states.

Music therapy is the only "nonconventional" therapy that is being utilized today by mainstream psychologists, thus, the paradigm is shifting and it is slowly changing to a conventional modality. Pythagoras utilized music as a therapeutic tool with his students. Music is understood to produce certain vibrational frequencies in the body and mind and research has shown there is a positive relationship between music and enhanced psychological well-being. Utilizing the sounds of nature such as birds, crickets, the ocean, and rain mixed with classical or instrumental easy-listening music can enhance relaxation and alleviate some physiological symptoms such as high blood pressure.

Don Campbell, in *The Mozart Effect*, tells us that music can "take us back to the self-generated healing systems." As a form of healing, he integrates imagery and music and has this to say about music:

masks unpleasant sounds and feelings.

can slow down and equalize brain waves.

affects respiration.

affects the heartbeat, pulse rate and blood pressure.

reduces muscle tension and improves body movement.

affects body temperature.

can increase endorphin levels.

can regulate stress-related hormones.

can boost the immune function.

changes our perception of space.

changes our perception of time.

can strengthen memory and learning.

can boost productivity.

enhances romance and sexuality.

stimulates digestion.

fosters endurance.

enhances unconscious receptivity to symbolism.

can generate a sense of safety and well-being.

Campbell has been studying the effects of imagery and music for more than a decade and concludes that music is medicine which will continue to grow in use as more people come to realize its natural power to heal.

Jonathan Goldman, in his book, *Healing Sounds: the Power of Harmonics*, tells us that "the universe is nothing, more or less, than an endless number of vibrations and rhythms." Using a simple formula for healing: Frequency + Intention = Healing, he believes that it is not only the frequency of the sound or music being heard, but equally important is the person's intention to be healed. Goldman says this about his formula:

"A more advanced understanding of intent involves what may be understood as alignment with the purpose of our higher selves, or the 'Divine Will'. It is that aspect of consciousness that is able to align with the sacred energy of sound. It is 'Thy will', not 'my will'. When we have reached this level, our intent is to become a vehicle for sacred sound and we are able to by-pass the lesser aspects of the self which may be out of balance.......The intention of the person working with the sound is as important as the frequency which is being projected at a person to create resonant frequency healing. Since the concept of intention is, at present, a scientifically immeasurable quality, it is extremely difficult for many in the medical community to understand it. Nevertheless, I am convinced that this formula is correct and that without the aspect of intention, working with pure frequency alone is not the answer."

Goldman has spent twenty years working with harmonics to produce healing and believes that sound is what carries consciousness. He is particularly interested in the use of mantras to balance and align the seven chakras in the human body, a practice used in Ayurvedic medicine. 'Mantra' is Sanskrit meaning "the thought that liberates and protects". Hindus and Buddhists are well-known for the use of mantras and chants as they are considered to change the consciousness of the person reciting them. Generally speaking, each chakra resonates to a different vowel sound and the individual can use these vowels in a chanting process in order to clear the chakras. Goldman's seven chakras are:

EEE: Crown
AYE: Third Eye
EYE: Throat
AH: Heart
OH: Solar Plexus
OOO: Spleen
UH: Root

In an earlier chapter, I mentioned author John Beaulieu who uses meditation, music, tuning forks, mantras and toning in his work. Tuning forks are a simple way to "tune" the chakras and create physiological and psychological harmony. Like Goldman, Beaulieu believes intention is key to healing. In the use of healing forks in healing and meditation, he describes three components: extension, intention and reception. Extension involves learning the method by which the tuning forks actually produce sound and has to do with tuning them to the Pythagorean intervals. Intention is the focus of the individual and receptivity is the ability of the individual to actually receive what is intended. Guided imagery can be useful in focusing intention and receiving that which is being willed.

There is an abundance of various ethnic or cultural music such as Native American, African American, Sikh, Muslim, Hindu, Tibetan, Christian or

Jewish choral music, chants or affirmations a therapist might use with the client. Most clients will intuitively be drawn toward one or more specific types of music and it is important to honor whatever musical tastes the client has as long as the type of music is considered therapeutic. Positive affirmations can be very powerful since we believe that which we are told over and over again. Just as a child who is repeatedly told over and over that they are "bad" or "stupid" will eventually develop a self-concept of bad and stupid, so can an adult re-learn negative and self-defeating thoughts that have become embedded deep inside the unconscious mind. Positive affirmations are effective adjuncts to meditation and, along with color, music and aroma, combine to create a potentially powerful psychotherapeutic intervention.

Between meditation, music therapy, color therapy and aromatherapy, without question, music therapy has aroused the most interest and has received the most funding for research over the past twenty-five years. Music therapy now has a solid beginning base of over two decades of research. Twenty-five years ago, music therapy was dismissed by psychologists, but after a fair amount of research, its efficacy has been, more or less, proven in certain areas.

Today, research is being carried out by countries all over the world including London, Scotland, Japan, India, Australia, China, Canada and the United States just to name a few. The research is carried out in hospitals, group and individual therapy settings, universities and nursing homes. Client populations which have been shown to benefit from the therapeutic effects of music therapy are mothers during the childbirth process, prison inmates, autistic children, cancer patients, mentally retarded, AIDs patients, persons with generalized anxiety, patients with high blood pressure, adolescents, dementia patients and the elderly population in general. Pregnant women who have had music therapy during the labor process have experienced more relaxed states than those who did not have music therapy. Music therapy is a growing modality with the autistic population as research has shown that autistic persons demonstrate enhanced learning when music therapy is a part of their learning curriculum. The research suggests that cancer patients who have music therapy as an adjunct to chemotherapy and radiation therapy report a higher quality of life throughout this painful process and some evidence suggests that it has a positive affect on the immune system. In 2001, the *Chinese Mental Health Journal* documents two research projects conducted with cancer patients in a hospital setting. In both experiments, cancer patients were divided into two groups. One group would receive music therapy and the other would not. In one of the research projects, not only was music therapy provided, but also inner image relaxation techniques. In both projects, those cancer patients who received the music therapy experienced less psychosomatic symptoms, greater muscle relaxation, less depression and anxiety and an overall enhanced quality of life as self-reported on a Quality of Life Scale. Enhancing the quality of life of cancer patients continues to be a dominant theme in oncology.

A more commonly known effect of music is the favorable impact on a person's heart rate, blood pressure and subjective anxiety. The *Journal of Music Therapy* is a popular academic journal which publishes research in this area. One research project published in 2001 by a university Psychology Department in Australia resulted in findings which support the common body of literature. A group of 87 students were asked to prepare for an oral presentation listening to Pachelbel's Canon in D major or in silence. Those students who listened to Pachelbel reported less subjective anxiety than did those who prepared for the oral presentation in silence.

Perhaps an even more intriguing area of research is the use of music therapy with the seriously mentally ill, i.e., those who have been diagnosed with schizophrenia, schizoaffective disorder, bipolar/manic depression and major depression. In 2001, the Tokyo Institute of Psychiatry conducted research with a group of 63 female chronic schizophrenic patients in the Tokyo Metropolitan Matsuzawa Hospital in Tokyo, Japan. Patients were divided into two groups and administered music therapy for one hour once per week for four (4) months. Tests were provided to assess for symptomatology, quality of life and musical experience. Results showed improvement in communication, motivation, interpersonal relationships, socialization, empathy and an improved adjustment to hospital life, although improvement declined after the four month treatment process. In another project conducted by the Tokyo Institute of Psychiatry in 2002, two groups of female patients in a ward for long-stay were selected. One group received 15 group music therapy sessions over four months while the other group subjects were to wait until the course was completed before receiving the music therapy. Comparisons of the groups indicated significant advantages in the group which received the music therapy in terms of personal relations although, like in the previous study, the follow-up reports reflected that the gains were not durable.

The Brookdale National Group Respite Program in Berkeley, California believes that music therapy is an effective treatment modality for a wide range of the elderly including persons with Alzheimer's, vascular dementia, HIV, meningitis and Jakob-Creutzfeldt disease. There is an increase in community programs utilizing music therapy to address the needs of the growing elderly population in general, and specifically those patients who are diagnosed with diseases which sometimes have concomitant behavioral problems such as dementia. While the overall research has not shown substantial increases in concentration, it does suggest that music therapy with the elderly results in more stable communication and some improvement in cognition during the therapy.

In spite of the research, mainstream medicine and psychology still fail to embrace it as a core rehabilitative treatment and it tends to be utilized only by therapists who are personally interested in that modality.

## AROMATHERAPY

Aromatherapy is simply the process whereby essential oils are used for their therapeutic and healing effects. We have evidence of juniper berries around Neanderthal cave sites, so it is likely that prehistoric man knew of the healing properties of some herbs and spices. Black pepper is noted in ancient Chinese and Sanskrit texts around 2000 B.C. Herbs, spices and oils were pervasively used as early as 1,500 B.C. by the Egyptians who considered some to be as valuable as gold. Egyptians used these natural products for religious rituals, physical healing, embalming, skin beauty, fragrance and emotional and mental well-being. We know that the Greeks were using essential oils for fragrances and incense around the 8th century B.C. Frankincense was valued equal to gold by King Nebuchadnezzar of Babylon and the Greek physician, Hippocrates, used certain herbs for health purposes. The herbs and spices used in aromatherapy are also some of those used in Ayurvedic and Chinese medicine. Aromatherapy is best considered as an adjunct with meditation, chromatherapy and music therapy and not as a core therapeutic modality.

Essential oils made a come-back in the 12th century when the Persian physician, Avicenna, discovered the process of distillation. Western society did not take any substantial notice in modern times until, in 1910, when Rene Gattefosse, a French perfumer and chemist, accidentally burned his hand in the laboratory. His immediate reaction was to stick his hand in a vat of water which turned out to be lavender oil. He purportedly suffered no pain, swelling or blistering which prompted him to begin investigating the properties of essential oils. For decades now, the French have been using certain extracts in hospitals against airborne bacteria and fungi. Dr. Jean Valnet, a physician during the Indochina War, used essential oils with success on certain medical and psychiatric conditions. An Austrian biochemist, Marguerite Maury, began using essential oils in cosmetics and massage and wrote the seminal text, *The Secret of Life and Youth*. She set up the first aromatherapy clinics in Switzerland, France and Great Britain. Her book, along with Robert Tisserand's, *The Art of Aromatherapy*, established the guiding principles that holistic aromatherapists use today.

There are two different types of oils in aromatherapy: essential oils and carrier (or base) oils. The essential oils which come from flowers, roots, herbs, spices, bark and fruit peelings are those concentrated oils which are considered as having the essential, core healing property, while the carrier oils are the base oils used for dilution of the essential oils. Because essential oils are concentrated, they are rarely used directly on the skin. Generally speaking, there are 3 drops of essential oil to every teaspoon of carrier oil. Carrier oils are vegetable, seed or nut oils and some common ones are sweet almond, avocado, jojoba, wheat germ and grapeseed oil. Essential oils are kept in small, dark glass bottles so as to lengthen their shelf-life which is generally about two years after extraction although Patchouli is said to actually get better with age while a few have a shelf-life of around six months. Some people keep essential oils in the refrigerator.

Massage therapy is typically a favorite way to use essential oils although you can use oils any number of ways. You can use oils while bathing, with vaporizers such as light bulb rings or in a boiling pot on the stove, as a room spray, to make your own perfume. Putting a few drops of oil in a sink of hot water, then placing a towel over your head to trap the steam inside and inhaling the scent for 5-10 minutes as the steam rises is yet another way to relax.

Aromatherapists usually blend essential oils together so there is a balance of base, middle and top notes. No more than three or four essential oils mixed together is recommended. Base notes are those which are deeper, richer and last longer. Middle notes are those which are usually fruity and their scents do not last as long as base note scents. Top notes are typically light and refreshing like the citrus fruits and their scent evaporates quicker than base and middle note scents. When you are shopping for perfumes and colognes, you should ask the salesperson which fragrances have predominate base notes as these are the scents that will last the longest although they are also usually the most expensive. Perfumes with mostly top notes do not last long, therefore, they are usually cheaper. The common base note essential oils are sandalwood, patchouli, vetivert, frankincense, myrrh, balsam peru and cedarwood.

Essential oils such as Bergamot are used in perfumes, others in skin care products such as creams and soaps for their purported anti-aging properties and simply for their fragrance. Some of the essential oils used in aromatherapy are also used for medicinal purposes such as anti-bacterial, anti-inflammatory, anti-rheumatic, anti-spasmodic and anti-viral properties. Tea tree oil is an ancient remedy and was used as an antiseptic during World War II. Oils have been used for thousands of years for many things such as emotional stress, skin disorders, the immune system, muscular pain, reproductive system, respiratory system, digestive system and circulation. Common uses are for depression, anxiety, stress, acne, asthma, bronchitis, muscle tension, colds, fatigue, fever, headaches, hypertension, insomnia, menstrual cramps, PMS, menopause and burns. Oils are contraindicated for pregnant mothers and for persons with epilepsy and it is generally understood that less oil is required with children than with adults.

Since the focus of this book is on *mental* health and well-being, aromatherapy utilized for physical healing falls outside the scope of this book. This book will focus on those essential oils which are commonly used for depression and anxiety since most people who seek psychotherapy have one or the other in either a mild, moderate or severe form. It is recognized that anxiety and depression will commonly cause some physical ailment such as headaches, fatigue, muscle tension, mood swings, loss of appetite, digestive problems and back pain, so it is important to learn those essential oils which are commonly used to treat these physical symptoms.

The essential oils commonly used as anxiolytics are bergamot, lavender, geranium, frankincense, roman chamomile, cypress, ylang ylang, melissa and jasmine. Common essential oils used as antidepressants are cinnamon, angelica root, niaouli, mimosa, bergamot, lavender, clary sage, neroli, cypress, chamomile, ylang ylang, melissa, jasmine, cedarwood, myrtle, rose, vetiver and geranium. Spikenard was used in biblical times and can be used to combat mood swings. Lavender is considered as one of the most versatile and useful aromas and Rose Absolute is considered as the Queen of oils.

As with music selection, a client will likely be drawn to certain scents and less drawn by others. This is understood as the client being subconsciously aware of what aromas are necessary to enhance well-being, just as the client will, in many instances, intuitively know what color and music vibrations are necessary for the type of healing that is needed at that particular time. No client should be forced to inhale aromas which they consider unpleasant.

Some of the current clinical research published in professional journals has to do with the effects of aromatherapy with HIV/AIDS patients and the elderly with dementia, but also to generally healthy populations who are suffering from anxiety, depression, agitation and lack of concentration. In the *Journal of Clinical Psychiatry*, July 2002, a group of seventy-two people residing in healthcare service facilities in Great Britain who had clinically significant agitation with severe dementia were randomly assigned to aromatherapy with Melissa essential oil or with a placebo. The oil or the placebo treatment was applied twice a day to the patients' faces and arms. Over a four week period, no significant side effects were observed and sixty percent of the group who received Melissa saw overall improvement in agitation while fourteen percent of the placebo group saw improvement.

There seems to be a paucity of research in this area and the research seems to be inconsistent with some studies indicating little or no effectiveness while others indicate statistically significant results. Most of the research that is published to date appears to be using only aromatherapy as the core treatment and not as an adjunct with meditation, music therapy or color therapy. Publications indicate that research is occurring in Japan, Germany, Great Britain and the U.S. or, minimally, these are the countries which have an interest in publishing their findings. It is likely that aromatherapy, used as an adjunct with the aforementioned therapies, will prove to be an effective and useful adjunctive modality in the enhancement of mental health and well-being. While these therapies are not intended to completely render conventional Western modalities obsolete, it is expected they will burgeon in use and efficacy in the coming decades. To the extent that ever growing numbers of people are listening to their inner voices which compel them to pursue natural, self-healing remedies for mental and physical health, these modalities seem to be next-in-line treatments for a world seeking Soul.


## NUTRITIONAL THERAPY

Nutritional therapy is currently accepted by Western medicine as a means of developing and maintaining physical health and as an indirect way to achieve better mental health, although most people struggle with maintaining a proper nutritional diet because of the overwhelming discipline it takes. Generally, the research which points overwhelmingly to natural, organic foods is not prolific because of the serious economic threat that would be posed if people no longer spent their money on food products which have been brought to market through the use of pesticides, chemicals and preservatives. Most of the research in this area is coming from people and organizations who are motivated by the Soul to find those foods and healing methods that are in abundance in nature, since the evidence seems to keep pointing to man-made chemicals, preservatives, pesticides, pills and products as posing the most serious long-term threat to the health of humankind. While these man-made products are marketed by their makers as providing great benefit to people, time and again, after several decades, research findings conclude that the long-term side effects are more deleterious than the short-term gains to be found. For instance, research dollars are currently being spent to determine if long-term use of anti-depressants causes higher incidences of cancer. Medicine is fighting a serious uphill battle with many diseases and they always assume that a genetic or physical flaw is the cause of many of them. Who is to say that the *combination* of man-made pesticides, preservatives, chemicals that we use in our food, clothing, carpet, hairspray, cleaning products, house paint and a myriad of other products, along with long-term use of man-made pills, our poor diet, chemically treated water, second-hand cigarette smoke, the negative emotions we hold onto because of the overwhelming stress in our lives and the way these deleterious agents are expressing onto some vulnerable gene in our body are not major contributing factors to the ever-growing numbers of people with Alzheimer's, Parkinson's, autistic spectrum disorder, cancer and other diseases whose causes have yet to be determined? Medicine seems to always want to assume immediately a genetic or physiological cause of illness and disease. While physiological and genetic deficits do appear in most disease and illnesses, medicine cannot state whether they are cause or effect. In other words, medicine cannot state with 100% confidence that other external factors are not manifesting physical disease such as the chemicals and pesticides in the environment, the physiological expression of stress and the physiological expression of negative emotions actually act on the body which, in turn, manifests as physical diseases. Logically, the answer to the etiology of some disorders and illnesses must be a combination of psychological, physiological, genetic and environmental influences even though medicine and science, in general, seem historically predisposed to finding the physiological deficit and theorizing that it was the cause. The interesting question becomes to what degree do negative emotions caused from emotional, physical and sexual abuse and stress, poor diet, man-made chemicals, pills and products used long-term, along with poorly filtered water, inadequate vitamins, diet and second-hand smoke, act upon the body and contribute to the cause of the expression of some diseases and illnesses?

Because modern Western medicine was largely dismissive in the 20th century of meditation, color therapy, sound therapy and aromatherapy, these areas offer the entire field of psychology a wealth of research opportunities waiting to be plumbed. What little research does exist seems to indicate that some clients do exhibit improved mental states, therefore, these therapies potentially offer a gold mine of opportunity to heal. Also needed are professional standards and training institutions which would bring some validity, reliability and respectability to those who practice these techniques. Having said this, we understand that there will always be people who do not heal, no matter what type of treatment you give them because of karma from a prior incarnation or a lack of Will. In the future, people will be able to develop insight into their past karma so they will have conscious opportunities in the current incarnation to "wipe the slate clean," so to speak. There is a current hypnotherapeutic method called *past life regression* which can be used to bring past lives to the conscious mind of the client, but that, too, is dismissed by mainstream psychology and medical science today.

Current medical research is still unable to explain the "Placebo effect," an effect which occurs in research studies where the patient who receives the inactive pill (the placebo) exhibits as much improvement as do the patients who receive the active drug. Furthermore, some patients who take the placebo also exhibit the side effects of the active drug! Irving Kirsh is a medical doctor who, along with his colleagues, published a meta-analysis in 2002 of placebo-controlled clinical trials of antidepressants. The report covered six (6) commonly prescribed antidepressants: Prozac, Paxil, Zoloft, Effexor, Serzone and Celexa. Results from this study found that as much as 80% of the positive response to these antidepressants may be a placebo effect. In other words, many patients who were in this study who had taken the placebo pill got better on their own and statistical analysis determined it was too great to be attributed to chance. The outcome of this highly controversial study is that, essentially, antidepressants may have no universally meaningful pharmacological effect. It could be the patient's will to be better or some other factor other than the drug which brings about enhanced psychological well-being. Without negating the very real need for some patients to benefit from pharmacological intervention such as those who are in crisis, are suicidal or actively psychotic, the significance of this study cannot be overstated and the findings seem to suggest that the power of the human will has been long underestimated as it pertains to psychological health and well-being. Minimally, to many, it exposes the economic interests of pharmaceutical companies and their need to defend the efficacy of antidepressants.

The power of belief and positive intention as it relates to good health is beginning to gain some interest by mainstream medical scientists and psychologists although few research dollars are allocated to this. Assagioli in *Psychosynthesis* refers to the Will as the "unknown and neglected factor in modern psychology, psychotherapy, and in education." Even though psychological research, based on today's psychotherapeutic techniques within cognitive, behavioral and psychoanalytical therapies, indicate that having no therapy is *equally as effective* as having cognitive, behavioral or psychoanalytical therapy, the field, as a whole, does not commit money and resources to research the power of the Will to get better and how it relates to improved mental and physical health. Until the field of psychology is willing to invest time and money into researching the power of the Will, a vast untapped psychotherapeutic domain will continue to lie idle.

These reflect only a handful of studies in the growing body of research in the relationship that music, meditation, color and aroma have with psychological and physical health. It is expected that this research will proliferate in the next three decades as the demands of managed care create searches for less expensive treatments and as society, in general, continues to respond to an inner wisdom that beckons toward self-healing, natural modalities. It has been said that the public interest in natural, alternative self-healing methods currently exceeds the knowledge and interest within Western medicine which is, today, still depending upon the pharmaceutical companies for primary interventions. Additionally, it has been said that the Food and Drug Administration is heavily influenced by the multi-billion dollar pharmaceutical industry. If true, the FDA has no vested economic interest in focusing on alternative or integrative approaches to healing because alternative medicine and interventions, by their very nature, diminish the value of pharmaceuticals as it pertains to the long-term treatment of many illnesses and disorders.

Hospitals of the future will incorporate some, or all, of these modalities into their treatment plans. Particularly with patients diagnosed with depression, depression mixed with anxiety and bipolar disorder, meditation, color therapy, light therapy and music therapy offer hope. These modalities are less expensive than the outrageous prices that pharmaceutical companies charge for drugs in the U.S. today. Research opportunities abound in this area. Major potential also lies in the area of research to establish whether these modalities have a positive impact on certain physiological diseases. Mental disorders and physical diseases cost the world billions of dollars each year, so insurance companies would likely be interested in a world-wide effort to study these treatment modalities. Since implicit in these future researches is the use of intuition on the healing process, a more mature psychological make-up will be required of leaders and researchers, both male and female.

Indeed, the Soul Consciousness model is a provocative theoretical model today. Virtually all theoretical models are radical when first introduced. From a scientific standpoint, it is a dictum that theoretical models are primarily judged not by their accuracy or empirical proof, but instead *whether or not the theory generates new thought and research opportunities* for its respective field or other relevant fields of study. Freud's theory will likely become subsumed by a broader theory which encompasses evolution, therefore, his model—*as a stand-alone model*—will become outdated and will receive only footnote attention in academic courses well before the 22nd century arrives. It will only become useful when viewed within the context of an evolutionary model of consciousness. Already psychoanalysis is considered outdated and irrelevant in most circles. However, it is inarguable that Freud's theoretical model generated an abundance of new ideas, thoughts and studies so, when viewed from that angle, Freud's legacy is a crucial piece in understanding the immature ego before it matures into a fuller, more whole expression of the Soul, the Full Self.

The psychotherapeutic settings of the future will be radically different from today's setting. Psychotherapy will be offered in clinics which offer meditation, chromatherapy, music therapy, sound therapy, hypnotherapy, aromatherapy and nutritional therapy as treatment modalities. These clinics will collaborate with Ayurvedic and TCM practitioners and Western medical doctors, however, it seems likely that, far into the future, both psychotherapeutic and medical practitioners will be working side-by-side in the same clinic. This will necessitate no less than a genuine collaboration between psychologists, therapists and medical doctors in treating clients as the collective consciousness is transformed into a collaborative consciousness. Long-term pharmacological interventions (for mental health issues) will become far less commonplace as these newer, cutting-edge therapies reflect broader and more long-term results with the client population. Additionally, psychotherapies of the future will begin to be utilized increasingly as *preventive* interventions. Today, under the current medical model, we take an individual who is diseased or disordered and help them resume a stable existence. There is no widespread focus on authentic optimal health maintenance because medical science and pharmaceutical companies don't maintain their power status when people begin to practice healthy living on a daily basis. The old Western medical model presumes the doctor is a god and the patient is at the mercy of this god and never the twain will meet. In this model, patients constantly give away their own power to the treating clinician. We have not evolved to a mass consciousness of disease and disorder *prevention,* nor have we evolved to understanding that most diseases and illnesses are caused by our own inability to maintain homeostasis. We have not learned that self is ultimately responsible for disease and illness and no one outside of us is ultimately responsible. The self is still looking everywhere other than the self for both the cause and for the cure. With this psychological pattern, people allow their bodies and minds to be diseased which causes them to seek help from a doctor or psychotherapist whom they think has the power to correct the problem. In the future, psychotherapeutic and medicinal modalities will be utilized so we do not become as diseased and ill as we are today. In other words, psychology and medicine will have a major paradigm shift from focusing *only* on disease and disorder to focusing *primarily on prevention of disease and disorder* and secondarily on healing. Psychology will cease its obsessional focus on the defenses of the ego and, instead, begin focusing on the energic expressions of the Soul. That which the mind focuses on is what becomes its reality. The focus will become maintaining and accentuating good health.

Martin Seligman, a recent past president of the American Psychological Association and professor at the University of Pennsylvania, is one such proponent of a more positive model of psychology that focuses on optimism and hope. He has coined a phrase "learned optimism" and conducted research on it. In the January 2000 issue of *American Psychologist,* Seligman states that "if psychologists wish to improve the human condition, it is not enough to help those who suffer. The majority of 'normal' people also need examples and advice to reach a richer and more fulfilling existence." He recommends a "change in the focus of psychology from preoccupation only with repairing the worst of things in life to also building positive qualities." In the same journal article, Mihaly Csikszentmihalyi, a psychology professor at Claremont Graduate University has this to say about the transformation of psychology:

"What psychologists have learned over 50 years is that the disease model does not move psychology closer to the prevention of these serious problems....psychology is not just the study of pathology, weakness, and damage; it is also the study of strength and virtue. Treatment is not just fixing what is broken; it is nurturing what is best. Psychology is not just a branch of medicine concerned with illness or health; it is much larger. It is about work, education, insight, love, growth, and play."

John Diamond is a medical doctor in New York who has been practicing psychiatry for forty years. He is a Fellow of the Royal Australian and New Zealand College of Psychiatry, a Foundation Member of the Royal College of Psychiatrists (UK), and is a Fellow and past President of the International Academy of Preventive Medicine (US). His focus is on complementary medicine and holistic healing which integrate body, mind and spirit and has founded the Institute for Music and Health and The Arts-Health Institute to train people how to utilize the arts as a therapeutic modality. Having authored several books, I love how he speaks freely and passionately from his Soul about his desire to guide clients to self-healing. Below are several quotes from his book, *Facets of a Diamond: Reflections of a Healer:*

"I am no longer a psychiatrist. I renounce it. I renounce psychiatry because I believe cruelty is at the core of the profession. In my early days in psychiatry the head psychiatrist of a hospital took me aside, placed his arm around me paternally, and offered to teach me the first lesson of private-practice psychiatry. 'John....do what I do. Put them in a private hospital for a couple of weeks and give them shock treatment. If they are not better by then, certify them to a mental hospital. That way you will have no trouble, and by then you'll have got most of the money you are going to get out of them anyway'......Psychiatry should be at the forefront of all the therapies, pioneering, blazing a trail for all of them to follow. It, most of all, should recognize that our suffering is really in our souls. It, most of all, should be teaching love. Love rarely, if ever, appears in any index of a psychiatric text; it is not medical enough for the profession. If it proclaimed the supreme importance of love as the greatest therapy, then the profession could not tolerate cruelty in it and furthermore would attract a different type of doctor to enter into it....I will come back to psychiatry---gladly---when it speaks of the soul, of the spirit---of Love. When these are major topics in its learned journals.

"There is a most important difference between treatment and therapy...Treatment can only ever be through the application of the medical model: find specifically what is wrong and then act on it in the prescribed way. Handling the case, managing it, by the application of an external influence, a prescription in one form or another. In contradistinction to this, *therapy* comes from the Greek word meaning 'inclined to serve, to attend on, to be obedient to'. Rather than being the manager, as is the treater, the therapist is the servant, the attendant. He does not impose his power, but rather acts as a servant for the healing power that is within the sufferer. He places himself at the service of what Hippocrates called the *vis medicatric naturae,* the Healing Power of Nature, which we all possess. So chemotherapy is a complete misnomer, it is really chemotreatment. And so is nearly all of orthodox medicine. And psychiatry too, which is primarily dedicated to imposing power of one form or another on the patient so as to control or in some other way modify his disquieting behavior......Today there are so many procedures called therapies of one kind of another. But how many of them are really therapeutic?

"The True Therapist, the Healer, never diagnoses any disease. He is not interested in this *per se*, but in the diminution and disturbance of the Life Energy, the Spiritual malaise that is the basic cause of all suffering. Nor, therefore, does he prescribe treatment for any disease. For apart from not being concerned with the disease as such, he is not a treater but a therapist. And for this reason any recommendations to the sufferer are directed toward enhancing the sufferer's own Life Energy, for only then can there ever be Healing.

"I do not see myself as being a doctor of medicine in the usual sense. I do not diagnose, treat, or prescribe for any particular disease—although my role is certainly concerned with 'the restoration and preservation of health'. Not the treatment of disease per se, but rather the achievement of positive health by activation of the Life Energy, the true Healing Power which we all possess. All of my efforts are directed toward activating this

Power, rather than, in the more medical sense, imposing external ones. That is to say, seeing suffering as an internal problem, not an assault by a foreign enemy. Seeing suffering as being the result of an imbalance and a diminution of the Life Energy."

Mind, body and spirit cannot be separated any longer. Cartesian thought which separates mind and body must be transcended. The techniques of acupuncture, Ayurvedic medicine, Qigong, Tai Chi, Kundalini Yoga, music and sound therapy, color therapy, aromatherapy which have existed since ancient days must surface as vast potentials of research for psychologists and medicine. In one sense, this is the future. Yet in another way, it is a return to the past of natural healing. Only we now have advanced tools and equipment and better knowledge which will make the blending of natural healing with our advances even better! It is the hope of health.

Therapy in the future will be focused primarily on prevention and secondarily on restoration. Instead of psychotherapists specializing in behavioral, cognitive or psychoanalytical therapeutic verbal techniques who spend hours talking through client issues, the psychotherapist of the future will be a specialist with knowledge of one or more of the modalities mentioned above. Clinics which offer a multiplicity of these treatment modalities will be highest in demand by the public. The clinics will have these various professional therapists available to consult with the client and advise the client throughout the therapeutic treatment process. Instead of psychotherapy between one therapist and one client, the treatment of the future will consist of a client being assessed by a team of therapists knowledgeable in one or more of the cutting-edge modalities and, if necessary, a medical doctor of homeopathy, acupuncture or other relevant medical professional. Knowledge of the energy centers in the body and their relationship to poor health and good health will become a basic and fundamental knowledge of all therapists who have these clinics because light, sound, aroma, nutrition and stress have direct relationships to these energy vortexes in the human body. These future psychotherapies will result in a decreased need for the client to have a gender preference in the therapist, a decreased need for the therapist to be knowledgeable about specific ethnic or cultural nuances unique to a client and there will be less importance placed on the match between therapist style and client. Future psychotherapies dealing with color, light, music, sound and aroma substantially decrease the issue of client/therapist "match" and allow the client to customize (in collaboration with a clinical team of therapists) a treatment process to meet her/his needs. In tandem with the premise of the Soul Consciousness, the future psychotherapies will inherently have a highly collaborative element to them as client and clinical team work together toward providing the most optimal psychotherapeutic milieu for the client. In this sense, the Soul Consciousness model offers the client the broadest amount of *self-responsibility* and *self-directedness* toward healing than all prior psychological models.

Since it is understood within the Soul Consciousness model that each person (as long as they are not in a state of psychological crisis) has an intuitive sense of what their needs are and what it takes to move to the next level of functioning, many clients will become adept at selecting a particular color to work with, a particular musical sound and a specific aroma to breathe. For those clients who have not developed their intuitive sense, the healer will initially play a larger role in the decision of the color, music and aroma to use.

A virtual panorama of opportunity exists for psychologists to begin a serious, systematic study of the effects of these treatment modalities for the treatment of general anxiety, major depression, schizophrenia, schizoaffective disorder, bipolar/manic-depression, ADD and other pervasive disorders. In my prior job on the psychiatric unit of a local hospital, I came to believe that, even with all the advances made in the study of schizophrenia, bipolar/manic depression and major depression, the Western medical community still, by and large, only recognizes two forms of treatment for these populations—drugs and cognitive-behavioral therapy. Certainly, medical doctors do their best to address the patients' needs, but based upon my daily observations in a hospital setting, most doctors really just manage the drug regiment and monitor side effects for psychiatric patients. Little, if any, substantive psychotherapy occurs in an in-patient setting for a couple of valid reasons. First and foremost, psychotherapy is usually not highly effective in cases of psychological crisis simply because the client is in such a heightened state of depression, anxiety and/or disorganized thoughts such that memory, attention, concentration, insight and judgment are radically impaired. Thus, any kind of discussion with a psychiatrist or psychotherapist has minimal value for the client because her/his thinking and emotions are irrational and unstable. It is much more effective to allow the drugs to take effect first and recommend the patient seek psychotherapy on an out-patient basis later when the client's thoughts and emotions are more stable. Second, the goal of current acute in-hospital psychiatric settings is to move the patient to a *minimal* level of stability and then to discharge, therefore, it falls to an outpatient provider to provide psychotherapy. Gone are the days when insurance companies approved long-term in-patient hospital stays of 30 and 60 days so that the patient would have sufficient time in the hospital to return to a much more stable psychological level of functioning and to take advantage of psychotherapy while in the hospital.

It is not my desire to denigrate medical doctors because I'm convinced that many are operating within a less-than-optimal managed care environment where the insurance company dictates to the doctor how long a patient can stay in treatment and what types and kinds of treatment will be paid for. For hospitalization, if the insurance company approves only a three day hospital stay, but the doctor really would prefer the patient stay for five days, the doctor is left in a most unenviable position. In fact, some patients blame the doctors for early discharges when, in fact, it has been the insurance company which dictated the discharge. Were doctors to allow an extra day or two of unpaid in-patient hospitalization for every patient whom they feel would benefit with an extra day or two in the hospital, few hospitals would exist. My point is not to say that these people don't, in truth, need these additional days. Rather the point is to say that now the insurance companies, not the medical community, wield the most power and control as it pertains to the management of health. I'm convinced that some medical doctors would be favorably disposed toward complementary types of treatment, however, because insurance companies do not currently fund them, the doctors' hands are tied. As with all things, the pendulum has swung too far to the other side. Which speaks to my point: there is little heart and soul in Western medicine. Notwithstanding this current managed care environment, some doctors still operate within the old paradigm of the conventional medical model and have little or no desire to view their patients within a wholistic or spiritual framework. They see bodies and no soul or spirit. To them, bodies are only one level above a machine to fix and stabilize. These scenarios create a schema where the patient is relegated to little more than a medical chart with a DSM diagnosis. The patient is objectified and is no more than a pathological label. There is no Soul in this kind of treatment because there is no heart (feminine) in it, rather only intellect (masculine). With the exception of feminine energy from nurses, there has really been little feminine energy in modern Western medicine.

Some consistent complaints I heard from psychiatric patients is that they are extremely tired and fatigued or they are extremely bored with not enough activity to occupy their time. Some of this frustration is directly related to the disorder or illness for which they are being treated, but perhaps not all in every person's case. Many told me they wished they could go outside which speaks to their innate need for sunlight and fresh air. Luckily for patients at this hospital, there is an enclosed outdoor patio where patients are allowed to go for several brief breaks. While the hospital is considered the Mercedes Benz of psychiatric clinics in my local area and while the nurses are highly competent and compassionate, the unit, like most others, is still largely held visage under the rules of managed care—medicate, monitor and discharge. The good news for this psychiatric unit is that psychiatrists allow the more stable patients to use their CDs and radios to listen to music, there are a piano and guitar available for those patients who are musically inclined and are safe to use them, there is a competent recreational therapist who occasionally teaches Tai Chi to patients and the unit has a very competent and compassionate art therapist who is excellent with utilizing creative expression as a therapeutic tool. It is an effective effort to incorporate more creative, natural modalities within the narrow, restricted confines of a managed care system. Within the recent past, research has been conducted and books published about the relationship between creativity and bipolar disorder. Research suggests there is a high correlation between the two. This suggests a greater need for art and music therapy for this client population. I often wonder how in-patient psychiatric patients, in general, would respond to frequent, consistent daily alternative treatments such as color therapy, music and sound therapy, aromatherapy, Tai Chi, Qigong and yoga.

We have already said that the Soul's language is not verbal. It is a symbolic language; therefore, therapeutic strategies are challenged, in the future, to develop a translinguistic and psychosymbolic approach. Since the Soul communicates in symbols, we need to find those nonlinguistic symbols which are ubiquitous in nature and to which the Soul gravitates. There are three universal symbols in nature: light (color), sound and aroma. Thus, therapy for the Soul would include these modalities.

Not surprisingly, the Soul is stirred by the harmony of music and the peacefulness of the sounds of nature. Some clients will intuitively gravitate toward the sounds of birds and crickets in nature, while others will be drawn to a certain type of music such as Native American, African, Indo, Celtic, choral, classical or instrumental. It is understood that certain types of music are simply not conducive to an elevation of energy frequency such as rap, heavy metal and heavy rock music and are not part of the therapeutic process. Matter operates at a very low vibrational frequency and the goal is to elevate the body to a higher vibrational frequency. The vibrational frequency of rap, heavy metal and heavy rock music is low so it is not utilized as a healing intervention. Harmony in nature or in music are considered an integral part of evoking the Soul, therefore, it cannot be overemphasized as a key component of a successful therapeutic intervention.

Certainly, relaxation techniques, guided imagery, visual reframing or a hypnotic trance may be induced to create a connection with the unconscious mind. Even discussing dreams and recanting positive mantras can be a positive part of the therapeutic process, along with utilizing color, music and aroma.

Connecting with the unconscious is a type of meditative experience whereby the client silently makes contact with the Soul and energizes its frequency. Meditation, as a form of pure contemplation, should be recommended to the client as a daily practice which can be accomplished in the client's home. Meditation, when done properly, transmutes negativity because it is not analytical, rather it is a synthesis. If you meditate successfully for 20 minutes or more, you feel a sense of peace and calm which, in turn, affects your behavior in the world around you. The peace and calm you feel inside directly affects what you project into the outside world. The more devoted you become in your practice of meditation, the more you learn since most of your learning is done at the unconscious level. It takes practice since most of us have been indoctrinated for twenty, thirty, forty or more years into the ego consciousness of separation, divisiveness, lack, prejudice and judgment. We did not learn the ego consciousness in one day, nor will we unlearn it in one meditation session.

Also, in the future, children and adolescents will be introduced to these self-reflective techniques at younger ages. Today, a small number of places are recognizing the potential that meditation holds for children. Today, few parents make teaching spiritual truths and wisdom a focused, structured, but fun endeavor. Yet this is so crucial in the development of the Whole Psyche of a child. All the worldly knowledge combined to fill the largest library in the world will not compare to the knowledge of the Soul or Spirit because it teaches the wisdom of love which transmutes negativity and unites humankind in a communion with Higher Good. The Soul desires to be unrestrained and unfettered in all its glorious expressions which is why religious dogma and doctrines; politics and greed within business organizations; human, animal and environmental abuse; political corruption; elitist attitudes; gross socioeconomic inequality; and placing the importance of intellect over love are all anathema to the Soul. The future of optimal parenting will be based on these core teachings to children who are truly our future.

In an earlier chapter we learned that our essence is Light, so we must examine the nature of light in order to use it to raise our vibrational frequency and, hence, our level of consciousness. Raising the level of consciousness from the ego to the Soul consciousness should have a positive affect on our minds which, in turn, will have affects on our behavior. *You have the innate power to heal yourself.* Ultimately, no other person can heal you unless you tap into this inner health. When you give others all power to heal you, you have given your inner power away. The Soul knows this. The ego consciousness is fed by fear, greed and jealousy, so its existence depends upon keeping humankind in the dark about this truth. By maintaining ignorance, the ego lives. By deception, the ego continues to breed. By fostering the erroneous belief that you cannot heal yourself, the greed of the ego consciousness stays alive and feeds the coffers of companies who will only make billions if disease and illness thrive. Yes, pharmaceutical companies spend research dollars developing products which purportedly heal. The pharmaceutical companies have much wealth to lose if humankind returned to its ancient remedies that are all around us in Mother Nature. **Man-made drugs offer long-term *treatment* which translates into long-term *income* for pharmaceutical companies**. Remember, your body is made of water and minerals and is animated by electricity which takes heat and air. When you deplete or have an excess of something or when your electrical system is not working optimally, your mental and physical health go awry. In order to maintain the physical system, you must pay close attention to the water intake and the mineral levels in your body in addition to ensuring that the electrical system is maintained which means you must ensure that the energy centers in your body are operating in harmony. Your body is energy.

As has been said earlier, you cannot feed the Soul with material things. Any contemplation, activity or repose which is guided by goodwill toward knowledge, creativity, love and wisdom can be considered nourishment for the Soul. If these energic expressions are stirred in you and you equally honor these expressions in others, then you are being guided by Soul.

## Gaining and Sharing Knowledge

Earlier in the book I outlined two types of knowledge: worldly knowledge and spiritual knowledge or higher knowledge as *para vidya* and the lower knowledge as *apara vidya*. Higher knowledge is knowledge of the Absolute or of Reality (Brahman); lower knowledge is worldly knowledge of things, events, situations, objects. Both are to be honored and respected, but spiritual knowledge is ultimate and absolute whereas worldly knowledge is relative and has less value. You can measure how much worldly knowledge you have, but you can never measure how much spiritual knowledge because spiritual knowledge is infinite and unlimited. Your Great Soul already has spiritual knowledge. All that is necessary is for you to recall it. It is a matter of whether you listen to your Soul and rediscover these ancient truths or whether you elect to respond to ego and ignore spiritual truths. Every moment of your human life, you have that choice to make. In that choice, you choose peace or chaos.

Before the mid-twentieth century, gaining worldly knowledge was primarily considered a masculine privilege and duty while men sought aggressively and maliciously to exclude females and minorities from obtaining it. Men obtained and held power and control by promulgating the belief that men should learn medicine, science, law, philosophy, business, etc. while women should be preoccupied with learning menial or domesticated tasks. In every century, men have been allowed to define what society values. In recent decades, women are challenging false man-made beliefs and social constructs as women have begun to recognize their own inner power and are gaining a foothold in changing that tide by voicing and establishing their rights.

The ego seeks worldly knowledge in order to sustain its superior position to others as it perceives worldly knowledge as a vehicle for power and control. The Soul, in its eternal quest to know, may also seek worldly knowledge, but will never use worldly knowledge as a means to coerce, control, abuse, deceive or separate. Instead, when Soul obtains worldly knowledge, it has a desire to embrace, share and disseminate knowledge so others may share in the experience of the joy and freedom of knowledge.

Certainly, knowledge of medicine, science, law, math, literature, art, music, etc. allows us to improve ourselves and others and to, hopefully, bring us greater experiences of pleasure and happiness. Without them, we could not flourish and grow intellectually as a human species. We must honor all of these types of knowledge and respect what it gives us. But these types of knowledge will only bring us fleeting moments of pleasure, not peace of mind. Thus, we must refocus our priorities on that knowledge which the Soul expresses—spiritual knowledge—and honor worldly knowledge as a secondary value.

Those who obtain higher levels of worldly knowledge are best able to teach those who have not yet gained worldly knowledge and so we should honor those who teach others. However, many people who gain worldly knowledge misunderstand and misinterpret its importance in the grand scheme of things. Worldly knowledge without spiritual knowledge will never bring humankind peace because, ultimately, a world without spiritual knowledge is a world without peace, purpose and meaning. It is a world where people are still asking the question: Who am I? This is the state of our world today.

So that we may all experience serenity, each one of us, regardless of the level of worldly knowledge, must refocus our values on obtaining spiritual knowledge and using and expressing these truths to improve the human condition. This is what Soul finds sacred. Those who have already obtained much worldly knowledge are challenged to seek and discover spiritual truths so that they may serve as more purposeful teachers.

## Expressing and Appreciating Creativity

Creative energy is expressed in so many wonderful and beneficial ways. Painters, sculptors, musicians, writers, architects, carpenters, bricklayers, mechanics, construction workers, engineers and scientists are just a few of the people who use creative energy. We should honor them all because they are focusing their energies on building and creating something in this world of value. But these are worldly things and, as such, they will not bring us ultimate serenity.

As you may guess, there are two types of creativity: worldly and spiritual creativity. Constructing a house, building an automobile engine or a bridge are worldly creative expressions although we may be in touch with our Soul when we make them. Like worldly knowledge, these creative energies allow us to derive enjoyment and pleasure in our daily lives, but it is spiritual creativity that has higher value.

Spiritual creativity seeks to find beauty, truth, love, compassion, kindness, joy and, ultimately, peace for ourselves and others. The Soul adores these expressions. These sacred energies are eternal and the Soul will always resonate to them much like a magnet to iron. The Soul finds solace in these fruits of the spirit and will forever be drawn toward them because this is the essence of the Soul. So if you are gazing upon Michelangelo's statue of David, the Soul is stirred because it has reacquainted itself with beauty and joy. It is not the statue, rather the eternal expressions of beauty and joy which the Soul values highest. Likewise, if you are hearing the melodious rapture of Handel's *Messiah,* it is the experience of peace, love and joy which stirs your Soul; the actual musical score on the paper is secondary to these stirrings. The Soul always yearns for the energic expression behind matter, so it is the love, joy, peace and beauty behind material things we create which Soul adores.

Just as with knowledge, creativity has historically been designated and defined as a masculine energy and most of our worldly creative endeavors we owe to the male gender. As we keep moving toward equalizing all four energic expressions of the Soul, more women will assume these worldly creative roles.

## Giving and Accepting Love

Since the beginning of time, humankind has defined love as feminine. One of Jesus' primary purposes was to reflect to the world that love is an eternal expression of the Soul and, thus, is to be expressed by both men and women. It is no coincidence that this man's overarching message was to love one another. He wanted us to love ourselves, but also love others as we love ourselves. In a world teetering on spiritual bankruptcy, the simplicity of his message is sacred and healing.

The Buddhists' message of compassion is linked closely with the message of love. Buddhists believe that all human suffering is the result of attachments to worldly things and that humankind's ignorance of this and other basic spiritual truths is what leads to pain and suffering. Not unlike Jesus the Christ, the Buddha also taught his followers the higher spiritual principles which govern us. The Buddha compelled people to have compassion with each other as we struggle in a world of pain and suffering. Without compassion, we will never break the chain of negative thoughts and emotions.

Whether you are a man or a woman matters not to your Soul. Your Soul seeks to give and receive love, loving-kindness and goodwill. It does this eternally whether in spirit or whether incarnated in physical form. Men have historically relegated this energy to females and, as such, have devalued it and dismissed it as unrelated and irrelevant to the functioning of most worldly systems. Due to the casting aside of the mature feminine energy of love and kindness, these systems are abundant with narcissism, corruption, deceit, arrogance, greed and an overall abuse of ego power. In short, the Soul is largely neglected and undernourished throughout institutions where males dominate.

As a species, we must mature psychologically. We must meet the challenge of balancing our energies and honoring and respecting the expressions of love, compassion, kindness and goodwill to All. We must learn to value these expressions as strengths, not weaknesses. Otherwise, we are doomed to war and violence and, ultimately, extinction. We must reevaluate love and kindness and its place in the world systems. By validating it and expressing it more often, we are revering our Souls. This seems like a daunting task, but it must begin with each of us. As men give themselves permission to express loving-kindness and honor this exchange between their brethren, we will move toward a global nourishment of the Soul. Once fathers begin reflecting gentle loving-kindness toward their sons and also giving their sons explicit permission to exhibit kindness and compassion, humankind will begin experiencing the outward manifestation of the mature masculine and we will begin to see a reflection of the Soul all around us. This is the major quest of masculinity in the 21st century.

**Seeking and Teaching Wisdom**

The world gives us one kind of wisdom; the Soul gives us another kind. Worldly wisdom is crucial as it fosters healthier and more productive human relationships and it keeps us from making imprudent decisions that lead us to unsafe, unhealthy or unpleasant outcomes. It is certainly wise not to engage in promiscuity as it could lead to diseases and it is most unwise to yell obscenities to a police officer who stops you for speeding. It is not prudent to go to a job interview unprepared and it would not be in one's best interest to go barefoot in the middle of winter. While these simple wisdoms of the world are necessary, it is spiritual wisdom that gives us the universal principles by which we are all governed.

Spiritual wisdom is the knowledge of the highest principles and laws by which the Soul is governed and the obeying of them. In a phrase, spiritual wisdom seeks that which honors the All. Philosophy is the love of wisdom, therefore, a true philosopher is a lover of wisdom. The Soul eternally seeks wisdom, therefore, it can be said that the Soul seeks to observe and obey all spiritual laws.

The Buddha incarnated in large part to reflect and model spiritual wisdom to a world that was not obeying spiritual laws. When ego or the shadow of the Soul is operating, it is violating spiritual laws. Jesus was referred to as a Counselor because he embodied wisdom. He had knowledge of, and obeyed, spiritual laws. Both these wise men adored the Soul and revered Spirit. This is the consciousness of loving the All as the One.

We commonly refer to wisdom as some indefinable, but enviable trait that develops with age. This need not be so. The Soul or Psyche is not as complex as historians would have us believe. The ego is complex and will never be understood because it is the mind of insanity and who can comprehend insanity? As I have said before, we have the free will to focus our minds and attention on whatever we wish--the disease or the cure, the healthy or the unhealthy. I advocate carefully studying that which makes us healthy and whole. Optimal health will not be reached by dissecting animals, placing cells under a microscope and straining to understand it. These are effects, not causes. How much simpler can it be to explore those things which are healthy since health is what we are seeking?

You can be sure that you will not find wisdom by accumulating wealth. It is certain that, by obtaining multiple college degrees from Ivy League universities, you will not necessarily obtain spiritual wisdom. Nor will you attain the status of wise counsel by merely reading and memorizing verses from the Torah, the Talmud or the Christian Bible. Rest assured that no rabbi, preacher, priest, monk, nun or other person of ecclesiastical association has cornered the market on an awakened consciousness, nor can they sell you boxes which contain pounds of awakened consciousness. You and only you have the ultimate power within yourself. Awakening and rediscovering spiritual essence is open to anyone willing to go within to reconnect and rediscover what can never be lost only forgotten. A human intermediary is not required for you to reach the most important part of your essence--your Great Soul. Any person who tries to tell you that the path to enlightenment must be found by spending money, garnering wealth, getting more college degrees or by saying penance to a priest is looking for enlightenment in the wrong places. Look within yourself. Your Great Soul will tell you all the answers you will ever need to know.

Truth is really very simple and easy to locate. No person holds a patent on Truth as Truth can be found by every human being simply through the adoration of the Soul. Thousands of people in all kinds of professions such as psychology, religion, philosophy, medicine and science make things so difficult for people to understand that it is little wonder we get confused and perplexed looking in a thousand places *outside of ourselves* for all the answers. In truth, all the answers to the most important questions are derived from within your own Soul. Every person is a guide and every religion, philosophy or technique is but a mere roadmap. Even this book you are reading is but a guide. You must find Truth from within. All you really need do is reconnect with your spiritual essence—the Grandeur of your Great Soul.

Jesus and the Buddha did not reach enlightenment by gathering wealth, college degrees or Bible verses. They found it through meditation from within. Wisdom was discovered by finding where it resides in all of us, within every human Being, within the Great Soul. There is no person on this planet who has any greater or lesser capability for finding wisdom than you. Every Soul knows Truth and, in that Truth, is wisdom. All you need do is awaken from your slumber and rediscover your own Great Soul.

There are a number of exercises which you can do to restore and nourish your Soul. The Soul yearns for, seeks and loves freedom balanced with sharing joy. Thriving and flourishing in freedom, the Soul rejects and recoils from all things and people who want to control, dominate and overpower it. Instead, it seeks the solace of quiet solitude or the joy of sharing.

Each person must hear that Divine Echo from within to determine what activity their Soul is seeking. Spirituality in the East has utilized and espoused meditation for three millennia and it is certainly one means by which you may awaken your Soul. There are dozens of books in print which outline various kinds of meditation, so you should know that there is not a 'one and only' way to meditate. Whatever works best for your Soul is exactly what you should do. Having said that, there are some basic principles to follow if you want to gain the most from your meditative experience. The basics are a quiet, private, comfortable space with positively no interruptions and a minimum of approximately 20 minutes. Most Eastern techniques advise sitting positions, but you may elect to lie down. Beyond that, some people meditate in silence while others prefer to have a meditation tape playing. Some people must maintain a yogic stance sitting cross-legged on a mat on the floor while others prefer to sit on a couch with both feet planted on the floor and their hands gently in their laps. Below is one simple meditation which works for me, but the more you meditate, the more you will find your own style. You may try it or you may elect to sign up for a local yoga class to learn a different style. Always remember that, beyond the basics, whatever feels and works best for you is the "right way" to meditate. Your Soul knows.

Go to a quiet, private room where there are no other people or pets or distractions. Begin playing a soft meditation tape. Find a comfortable seat like a couch. Sit with your back straight, but not uncomfortably, and with both feet on the floor or you may cross your legs. Your hands should rest gently on your thighs. Close your eyes and sit there in silence listening to the meditation tape for approximately a minute or until you feel your body is unwinding from the stress of the day. Once you feel your body beginning to limber up, start taking slow, deep breaths. When you breathe in, think of light flowing throughout your entire body through the opening in your nose. Every time you breathe outward, imagine dark clouds of smoke coming out of your nose and dissipating into the air. The light symbolizes peace; the dark symbolizes chaos. You are filling your body with the light of peace and, at the same time, releasing your body of the dark toxins of chaos. Continue to do this for about five minutes or until you can imagine that your body is made of beams of pure light extending outward. The light represents peace, so by the time you have imagined your body to be made entirely of light, you should be experiencing a calm, peacefulness from within. Then you may slow your breathing down to a normal pace. Now begin imagining a tranquil, quiet, serene place. It may be that you are walking in a large field of lush, green grass near a quiet, calm lake on a sunny, breezy spring day. Find an image of a place that calms you. Stay in that scenery of peace and solace for another 15 minutes. During that time, keep pushing away all the thoughts of your daily existence and give yourself permission to stay in this place of peace and solace. Keep returning to this place of peace even though it may be difficult to shut out the internal dialogue and chatter of your everyday worries. Find calming, soothing mantras such as "I deserve to be in a place of peace," "I can find peace whenever I turn my mind toward peace," "I will find peace and give peace to others." By ending your meditation session, you may tell yourself, "I can find peace within and carry peace with me always."

Remember that you may find an exercise enjoyable while your neighbor may find it unpleasant. Just because you resonate toward painting doesn't mean that your best friend does. There are a thousand paths to the Soul, but there is only one goal—Fullness of Being. All in all, when you listen to that still, small voice within, it will tell you whether you're on the right track. There are literally thousands of ways to greet your Soul, but below are some universal ways of caring for your Soul.

Taking a walk in your favorite park

Spending time with your pets

Painting a landscape
Riding horseback
Gardening
Strolling through the woods
Listening to soothing music
Gazing at the stars at night
Adopting an abandoned pet
Surprising your best friend with a gift of thanks
Riding bikes alone or with a friend
Hiking in the mountains with a hiking group
Fishing
Reading a favorite book
Participating in a community cause
Donating your time to Habitat for Humanity
Being kind to someone in need
Picking flowers
Taking a relaxing bath
Holding hands with someone you love

You may notice that some of these Soulful exercises and activities are carried out privately while others include one or more persons. The focus is on an activity that is authentic and genuine and which brings you joy, peace, honor and loving-kindness. You may find fishing and hiking unpleasant, but gardening and painting sheer joy. Follow that silent joy from within. All your answers are there.

*Reality is mere illusion, albeit a persistent one.*
—Albert Einstein

*All reality belongs only to unities.*
—Gottfried Wilhelm von Leibniz

# XXV. SOUL AND REALITY

No psychology will ever be united without answering three fundamental questions within its theoretical framework:

What is reality?

What is optimal consciousness, its construct, its function, its nature and its process?

What is optimal consciousness moving from and what does it seek?

No theoretical model can fully and completely define Self until the question about reality is answered because Self, in its ultimate wholeness, is Reality. Ego, the individual self, is not real. Universal Self, One, the All, Universal Consciousness is Reality. Consciousness *is* Reality. In order to adequately and completely understand Self, we must understand its construction, function and nature and then determine its evolutionary path. When we answer these questions, we can then attempt to move in the direction of a psychology that, instead of being split and fragmented much like the ego consciousness, it can become a cogent, cohesive field of study with a large degree of agreement as it pertains to the Universals.

One reason Western psychology split from Western philosophy in the early days is because philosophy failed to describe the structure, function and nature of the mind. Indian philosophy is more integrally tied to Indian psychology because Eastern thinkers have understood ontology as a higher reality than physical matter, so the split between Western philosophy and Western psychology is more pronounced in the West. Another reason Western psychology split from Western philosophy was because the latter was still asking the question "What is reality: spirit or matter?" Psychology immediately took the materialistic views of the philosophers Comte, Hume, Hobbes, Locke and Mill believing that religion and spirituality are nebulous, abstract and irrelevant and the only reality is that which can be seen with the naked eye. Hence, psychology began with the premise that religion and spirituality have no place in normal human functioning. Only until Jung and the transpersonal psychologists postulated spirituality as a normal, healthy part of the human consciousness did that tide change.

Psychology as a discipline will never mature or arrive at a comprehensive psychological model until it heals two egoic splits:

—the split between the ego (which says the only reality is that which can be seen with the naked eye) and the Soul (which knows the only true reality is that which is invisible to the naked eye), and

—the split between the ego (which desires to separate and divide itself from other disciplines) and the Soul (which knows that each discipline, i.e., psychology, philosophy, religion and science, has a portion of the answer to a comprehensive and accurate picture of the Whole, healthy Psyche, Self).

The ego splits and divides. The Soul unites and heals splits. When you are in the spiritual realm with no physical body, you are both a whole Self and indivisible from all other Souls. If you close your eyes and think of yourself as pure consciousness and pure Light, then you can begin to understand how you would be unable to physically separate yourself from other Souls, but that you would be a whole Soul just like all other Souls who have a consciousness. When you incarnate into the world in physical form, it is because of unresolved spiritual debts (karma) from a previous life. It could be that you were a greedy landowner and you beat your slaves. Or you were a greedy businessman and you cared only for yourself in garnering world wealth and power with little or no compassion for others. It could be that you were a murderer or that you were a prostitute. Perhaps you were an abusive husband to your wife and children. Or it could be that you were a selfish wife who thought worldly possessions were the most important thing so you selfishly took and took from your husband with little or no compassion for him or your children. It could be that you became addicted to drugs or alcohol and used these as means to escape causing your family untold emotional and financial hardships as they attempted to help you overcome your addictions. Because you failed to pay that spiritual debt, i.e., make things right, you had to return again in physical form in order to have another opportunity to wipe the karmic slate clean by obeying the spiritual laws.

When you reincarnate and return to this physical world, from the very beginning of your existence, your family, society and every system that exists teaches you that you are separate and different. This world is so steeped in the ego consciousness of separation and difference that any attempts to reject that worldview is met with scorn, rejection and ridicule. The ego does not believe in any interrelatedness and interdependence between the plant, animal, human and spiritual kingdoms, does not believe in a spiritual realm beyond the physical and does not recognize or obey spiritual laws. If it did, it would be transformed into a higher level of consciousness and, hence, the ego would dissolve. The ego is jealous of the Soul and wants what the Soul has, but it doesn't understand what the Soul has that the ego does not possess. The ego only sees the Soul as a threat to its existence because the ego thinks it is missing something. Therefore, the ego must defend itself and this is why the ego has so many ego defense mechanisms as a way to ensure its survival.

The Higher Self is not split like the ego. Socrates said "Know Thyself." This is the "knowing" of the Higher Self, the Soul. The Higher Self is comprehended as a loving, knowing, creative, wise Self that moves toward itSelf which is to say that it moves toward a consciousness of spiritual knowledge, creativity, love and wisdom which translates into Goodness toward the All, the One. The Higher Self cannot be explained unless it is understood as an ontological and phenomenological Being which is to also say that this Higher Self is a combination of a philosophy in the way it views Self and others; it is spiritual in the respect that it seeks spiritual fruits of love, kindness, truth, justice, honor, etc.; it is psychological from the perspective that the Higher Self can experience mature wholeness, fullness and well-being; and it is scientific from the venue that the ego objectifies reality.

Science alone is inadequate and insufficient to explain the Soul because the Soul cannot be intellectualized, measured and predicted by our traditional scientific methods. It is sure that the egoistic science will reject any theory of the Soul since egoism, in and of itself, forever seeks to split, exclude, dismiss, deny and otherwise ignore anything that is inexplicable in terms of observation. The ego consciousness cannot "see" truth. Anyone denying the existence of the Soul is like the person who says air doesn't exist because they cannot see it. The Soul exists because you experience it phenomenologically and ontologically, not because you intellectually, rationally and logically comprehend it. The Soul's method of knowing is intuition, not intellectualization, therefore, the ego (which intellectualizes) cannot know the Soul. The less predictable and less rational aspect of Soulfulness, specifically, the loving, wise aspect of the Soul, cannot be understood by the ego. Love, the feminine aspect of the Psyche, has always been arrogantly devalued or dismissed by the ego consciousness because of the threat posed to its existence. The numinous energies of love and wisdom toward Self and the whole simply cannot be grasped by the ego consciousness because the ego wants all things for itself, not for the Whole.

The ego consciousness is born when you incarnate into this physical world. It cannot exist in the spiritual realm. The ego "splits" off into dozens of directions when you incarnate. With this false world reality which teaches that there is nothing beyond the visible world and that everything is different and separate, children learn to perceive a false reality of difference and separation. Because the power of the mind is so great, what it believes becomes its perceived reality although it is a false reality. Cut off from the true reality of the spiritual realm, of interrelatedness and interconnectedness between all that exists, the ego thrives as it constantly seeks to find itself and to defend itself. The ego never finds itself because the ego is not real. The ego is a figment of imagination built upon yet another non-reality—physical matter. Those who believe matter is ultimately real will reject the concept of the Soul and the Soul consciousness. The ego must reject the spiritual and the numinous because if it accepted it, the ego would be transformed into the Soul.

Let us restate the definition of Reality. Reality must be eternal. If it's here today and gone tomorrow, it cannot be real. Reality must be True. If Reality is false, then it cannot be real because that which is Real must also be True. Reality must be immutable. If something changes, then it must not be true because what is True never changes. There is nothing that you see with your physical eyes that lasts forever and is immutable, so matter is not ultimately Real.

Goodness is eternal, True and immutable. All things come back around to Goodness for the All regardless of how long we wish to avoid it. That never changes. Goodness is comprised of all the spiritual fruits that we've mentioned in past chapters. Love, wisdom, kindness, knowledge, creativity, justice, truth, beauty, honor. All of these are one ray that emanates from the One Goodness. Goodness is the highest Unity. There is no higher consciousness than Goodness which is the essence of what every religion perceives of God, no matter how God is perceived. It is ultimate and absolute in the spiritual realm of Being and Pure Blissful Knowing.

We understand Soul consciousness as a higher, more inclusive consciousness than the ego consciousness. Soul comes to understand and know itSelf as being part of a greater whole, a greater Good and having manifested out of Highest Good since Good creates out of itSelf forever and ever. Only that which creates out of itSelf is omnipotent and eternal; therefore, the Soul knows the true Reality.

If you want a world of violence, war, conflict, division, separation, difference and lack, all you have to do is to think it, dwell upon it and it will manifest. Fear is behind this kind of world and it is understood that fear is the driving energic force behind the ego. But the ego can only exist in a physical world because in the spiritual realm, you are distinct, but you are never truly separated from other Souls. Difference does not exist as a reality and lack simply cannot exist in a spiritual realm because what could possibly be lacking where everything is One?

If the Soul Consciousness unfolds, it begins to see the world as all interrelated and ultimately inseparable. It understands that the reality that the ego lives under has created all negative emotions and, therefore, has created its own life of psychological and physical life of misery, suffering and pain out of its ignorance to understand and know the Highest Reality— Goodness and Unity.

Social psychologists have done research on the Pygmalion effect and the Hawthorne effect and the power of expectancy. Countless studies support the notion that what you expect comes true. What you believe, becomes your reality. You have been given the free will to create a false reality of separation, difference and lack while you exist in a physical body. What the mass of people believe in the world is a construction of reality until the mass of people change their thinking and, hence, change their construct of reality.

Throughout history, we see how the dominant male majority has created all the rules and the beliefs that the world must buy into. Women have gone along with it until a large enough group of females decided that, just because the male majority made the rule, doesn't mean that the rule is good. This is the power of belief! What you believe, you create.

In light of viewing Reality from Soul Consciousness, we see that all our power can be garnered and used toward Goodness or it can be given away to a majority whose intentions and motivations are anything but Goodness. Power is within us; within our minds and within our hearts. This is the kingdom of heaven and this is where authentic power lies. The Great Self knows this intuitively and all the intellectualization, logic and reason on the planet are inadequate compared to the intuitive power of the Great Soul, the Great Self, to know and discern truth amongst the lie. The evolutionary process from the ego consciousness to the Soul Consciousness must proceed. The Goodness of the Soul must unfold and replace the noxious consciousness of the ego. Our survival depends upon it.

Soul may be defined as: "the unseen, ubiquitous, undivided and eternal divine energy of Being whose structure, function, goal and purpose is to know, to create, to love and to be wise; whose Cause and Effect is Goodness which is Itself; and whose Self is both the Alpha and Omega, the Whole and the Part within the Whole which is Absolute and Ultimate."

Reality may be defined as "the kingdom of the Soul." If the Soul is ubiquitous, then Soul is everywhere and there is nowhere it is not. There are many Souls throughout Reality which is to say there are many Souls throughout the Universe. Some have incarnated into physical bodies; others have elected to stay in the spirit world. Each Soul is interconnected and it is impossible to disconnect. You can only *deceive yourself into believing* something false is true. Soul may be likened unto the ripple on the ocean, both a part of a whole and a whole unto itself. Souls are unseen by the naked eye, but Soul governs life and is the essence of life. The Soul or Psyche, Being perennial, can never be extinguished, but it can be hidden from your consciousness or unknown to you while you live in a physical body.

Let us begin to unravel the untruths that we have been taught since childhood. What is Reality? is perhaps the pivotal question upon which the destiny of humankind hinges. **Reality is that which is true, eternal and immutable.**

The field of psychology can re-examine people with mental illnesses and reconsider them in light of a new model a consciousness of Goodness and of Psyche's struggle to find itSelf again and begin living a life of abundance.

The panorama of Goodness is the landscape of the Soul. It is an eternal universe where consciousness is at peace because it is the universal cosmos of goodwill to the All. What is pure love can only know true peace. And where peace is, optimal mental health is its outcome.

*I have discovered that the highest good is love. This principle is at the center of the cosmos. It is the great unifying force of life. God is love. He who loves has discovered the clue to the meaning of ultimate reality.*
—Martin Luther King, Jr.

*All your talk is worthless when compared to the one whisper of the Beloved.*
—Rumi

# XXVI. THE FOUR DISCIPLINES REVISITED

After having committed ourselves to an overview of the Great Soul, let us now re-examine four disciplines mentioned earlier in the book. We examine philosophy, religion, physics and psychology from a more informed and psychologically mature perspective of Soul consciousness. The professionals within these four disciplines particularly have a major responsibility to the world. They have an opportunity to rethink and revision their fields of study, to broaden the focus and methodologies of research and, ultimately, the most important issue, to be the leaders in changing consciousness, individually and collectively.

As we have stated, from the point of view of science, if something cannot be observed, it is assumed it is not real. Although surveys indicate that most of humanity has some spiritual belief, scientism has no belief in the spiritual realm and no room for faith. Ironically, scientism is a kind of intellectual, dogmatic, narrow consciousness of a fanatical ego. It could be called the valley of the Soulless and faithless. It reduces humankind to physical beings of mechanical and biological processes of the brain, heart and other vital organs. Scientism predetermines humankind's destiny as hopelessly devoid of meaning and purpose beyond that which is our routine, mundane existence. It presupposes there is nothing beyond physical death. It is devoid of Spirit and Soul. One could say that, in its study of life, it is truly spiritually lifeless.

Until the study of quantum physics in the mid twentieth century, most physicists scoffed at the idea of God. However, with the resounding and sobering conclusion that there is nothing between atoms but space, along with the perplexing paradoxical theories posited by Einstein and Bohr, many physicists saw this as compelling evidence that some ruling force governs the Universe. Most of the great physicists—Einstein, Heisenberg, Sir Arthur Eddington, Schroedinger, Planck, de Broglie—studied one or more of the great Greek, Roman, Indian or Chinese philosophers. While most rejected mainstream, fundamental and orthodox religions, some of them were idealists and were deeply spiritual individuals who believed in some governing energy which brought order to the Universe. Louis de Broglie has claimed that "the mechanism demands a mysticism." Erwin Schroedinger studied Hinduism and it is highly unlikely that this had no effect on his scientific outlook. In our professional lives, we are all colored by our beliefs to some degree or another. In that sense, objectivity is relative and subjectivity is real.

Some claim that physicists will, one day, discover Truth and the bridge between science and religion will be built. Others debunk this and see no way for the historical schism to be healed. One thing is certain: the ego consciousness which separates and divides will one day be transformed into the collaborative consciousness of the Soul. When this occurs, all fields will begin to see the interrelatedness of all fields of study and how this historical schism was brought about by the ego consciousness and can only be healed by the Soul Consciousness. Physicists will clearly and without question see the link between science and religion. It is not a matter of whether this will happen or whether it will not; it is a matter of which century. When it does, the scientific community will unite with a transformed religion and the result will be the healing of no less than the human Psyche—the Great Soul. The beginning of this bridge being built will occur, I predict, once the "missing link" is found which will provide an explanation between Einstein's Theory of Relativity and Bohr's Copenhagen interpretation. Heisenberg's Uncertainty Principle which states that the quantum world cannot be measured and any attempts to measure it will, in and of itself, render the measurement unreliable. The outcome of Heisenberg's Uncertainty Principle is that it is impossible to fully predict the behavior of a system at the atomic level and the macrocosmic principle of causality cannot apply here. One may further infer that this is the world of the uncreated and of pure potential, therefore, that which is uncreated cannot be examined and measured. How does one measure the Will or Awareness? When the world of physics begins to see that paradox is a consistent epiphenomenon in the world of quantum physics such that developing a Unifying Theory can only be developed from the acceptance of *paradox or reconciling mutually exclusive positions,* then they, too, may see the light.

In the Western world, we have highly educated and competent medical professionals, yet we still are unable to integrate the best of the Western intellectualization with the best of Eastern mysticism to arrive at an inclusive, collaborative and unifying theory of the optimally mentally and physically healthy person. The Western scientific world is unable to openly and conscientiously embrace the feminine aspects of Eastern mysticism so that a comprehensive theory of health and well being can be developed. To do so compromises ego masculine dominance.

Over the years, surveys have been conducted by psychological and religious groups which consistently reveal that the vast majority of humans, as many as 70%, believe that something numinous, something spiritual, governs the world. Yet, by far, the *minority* who dominate leadership in medical science and psychology continue to ignore spirituality, brush these facts under the rug and consider a spiritual realm a nonreality.

We—the vast majority—have choices every day in the selection of our caretakers. We have a choice in which medical doctor and which psychologist we will place our health and our trust. There is no greater time than now than to begin selecting mental and physical healthcare providers who believe deeply in the human spirit and the Great Soul. The majority of us who have faith that our Souls exist and that it is imperative that the Soul must be nurtured must begin seeking out healthcare professionals who believe as we do. When we ask a friend for a healthcare referral, we must begin asking the question: Whom do you know that will care for my body *and* my Soul? When we are in the selection process of a healthcare professional, we must solicit their answer to the question: Will you seek to heal my Soul as much as you seek to heal my body and mind?

Once the vast majority begins this selection process, we will, over time, make a bold and blatant statement to the medical and psychological community that we demand treatments which nurture, care for and heal the Soul. We must give our power and our money to those professionals who treat us as a whole, spiritual Being who is traveling on this earthly journey in a physical body. This will speak volumes to the medical and psychological communities and, ultimately, the financial resources will begin to be funneled to those healers who resonate toward the healing of the Soul and to researchers who are interested in enhancing, not devaluing, spirituality.

Over the past 100 years, there have emerged four primary theoretical models within the field of psychology. These have been called by some as the "four forces" and can be summarized as:

psychoanalytical
behavioral
humanistic/existential
transpersonal

The earliest widely accepted psychological model posited by Sigmund Freud is the psychoanalytic model. Freud is to be credited, rightly so, as the first person to have the dual desire to conceptualize a comprehensive, systematic theory of the mind *and* develop psychotherapeutic strategies and interventions which had the goal of the amelioration of mental suffering. Ironically, he is the first to also take a serious interest in the mental suffering of females although his theory has a blatant masculine bias in it.

The study of the mind goes back prior to Socrates. Indian philosophy had its beginnings, some believe, as early as 2500 B.C. with its crystallization occurring around 600 B.C. as this is considered the Vedic period of Indian philosophical thought. Buddhist philosophical thought developed somewhat side by side with Indian philosophical thought around the seventh or sixth century B.C. and is usually considered to have developed more or less out of Indian philosophy. It is commonly believed that Taoism developed out of the thinking of a Chinese philosopher by the name of Lao Tzu, but little is known about him as he apparently strove to remain nameless and unknown. Indeed, it is unclear exactly when he lived, but it is considered that he lived anywhere between the sixth and third centuries B.C. In mentioning these philosophies, it is important that we understand just how long humankind's questioning of the human mind has been occurring. Some even refer to a time called "pre-history" as it relates to the possibility of human civilizations that existed prior to what we definitively know through written records. One example of pre-history is the civilization of Atlantis believed to have existed around 10,000 B.C. Plato wrote about it in his works, *The Timaeus* and *The Critias,* although the latter was left incomplete due to Plato's death. Even if we reject the notion of a "pre-historic" human civilization, as does modern science, then we must still admit that civilizations before the dawn of Western civilization were asking questions related to the mind. Psychology is credited with intellectualizing the study of the mind, operationalizing the mind and demanding that the accepted research methods be solely quantitative. Since the field of science is a masculine cognitive thinking style, this style of arriving at answers to questions is what has developed as the mainstream methodology and form of assessment.

It would be Western scientists such as Wundt, Titchener and Galton who would study the mind, but not be very interested in applying that knowledge in a way to decrease mental suffering. You might say they were theorists who were avidly searching for answers which decreased the mystery of the mind, but not clinicians who wanted to take those answers and apply them to people in a clinical setting so as to help them. Not unlike other psychologists, Wundt, Titchener and Galton were influenced by the 17th, 18th and early 19th century philosophers such as Locke, Hume, Comte and Mill who were, by and large, materialists and positivists who considered reality in terms of observable phenomenon. They would emphasize the mechanical nature of human beings and, indeed, some of them referred to the mechanism and movements of the clock to relate its inner workings to the inner workings of human beings.

Freud's psychoanalytic model is extremely complex and dense and the intention is not to expound on it, rather it is to inform enough so that lay people can comprehend it at its highest conceptual level. Arriving on the scene at the beginning of the twentieth century, below are the highlights of psychoanalytical theory:

—provided the first widely accepted psychological theory of the structure and nature of the mind with the id, ego and superego and the psychosexual stages of human development;

—provided the first set of psychotherapeutic techniques (not medical techniques) to be applied with patients who were suffering mentally;

—provided the first systematic patient case studies so as to empirically study the mind, its nature, processes and symptomatologies;

—changed the perception of psychology (as a field of study) to be considered as a true and useful science, rather than as a philosophical idea with no empirical basis and what was considered at the time as no real, practical value to humankind

This model presumes thinking is both the primary route to relieving mental suffering and the therapeutic foundation that leads a patient to change. And so we can think of this model as a "thinking" model. We owe much to Freud, but his theory has many weaknesses which have been pointed out by both female and minority psychologists particularly over the past two decades. Earlier was mentioned the fact that several of his students broke from Freud's inner circle because they saw it is a reductionistic, deterministic theory. Freud's model was built primarily on pathology, not optimal mental health, therefore, the study of love, kindness, joy and any spiritual fruit would not have been part of this model. We have already pointed out that Freud was an atheist and had no belief in a spiritual realm and God.

The behaviorist model, largely built from the works of J. B. Watson and B. F. Skinner begun in the 1930s, was developed, more or less, alongside and as a refutation of the Freudian model and is considered the Second Force of psychology. With Freud, the primary therapeutic techniques of free association (the client talks about anything that comes to mind) and interpreting dreams were utilized. It was believed that all problems derived from childhood and by simply discussing one's childhood in therapy, sometimes for years on the proverbial therapist's couch, would result in the patient gaining the necessary insight that would lead to change which would, ultimately, alleviate mental suffering. The behaviorists came along and said insight alone is insufficient to produce change in a person. Talking for years about one's childhood problems is, essentially, to keep talking about the very thing that is hindering change. If you implore someone to "stop thinking about pink elephants," what are they likely to do? Think about pink elephants! The behaviorists believed that insight is less important than change and that insight usually *follows* change. So their model was built on producing behavioral change first and if the insight followed, that was optimal, although not really essential. Again, their focus was on behavioral change, not arriving at deep psychological insights about one's self. The behaviorist model presumes, unlike psychoanalysis, that behavioral change itself is the primary route to relieving mental anguish and behavioral techniques are the therapeutic foundation which leads a patient to change. One could say this was a "doing" psychological model which largely ignores and dismisses *thinking* and *feeling* believing they are secondary to actual behavioral change. In fact, from a pure behavioral standpoint, feelings are considered irrational and thinking is changed through changing behavior. The behavioral model has a heavily mechanistic view of humans approaching them more like machines than humans. Spirituality is considered a form of irrational thinking. The Nike saying "Just do it" is perhaps a simplistic, although not altogether inaccurate, way to picture this model.

The cognitive model began developing not very long after the behavioral model surfaced because the cognitive therapists knew that part of behavior is, indeed, thinking. Cognitive therapists believe that, essentially, a person's intrapsychic and interpersonal conflict and their maladaptive behaviors arise from faulty thinking. They also believe that people have the power to change their thinking and that, by the very act of changing one's thinking, behavioral changes will follow. Because the patient has a consistent pattern of repeating self-defeating and irrational internal thoughts such as "I'm never going to be worth anything," "Everybody is smarter than I am" and "My partner should be able to read my thoughts," the therapeutic focus should first be to change the irrational thinking and that will automatically result in a positive change in behavior. For this reason, this model came together to form the cognitive/behavioral model that psychologists know today. While this model has merit and some of the client population experiences some success when utilizing these techniques, this model is also highly reductionistic. It focuses on the mind and behavior and is mostly a mechanistic model where humans are perceived as machines that *think* and *do*. This is a highly intellectualized model and little or no emphasis is placed on emotions. Additionally, within this theoretical model, no inherent value or recognition is given to the spiritual component of the patient and, indeed, like the behavioral model, spirituality is considered aberrant. Consider this largely a model of "thinking" and "doing."

In the fifties, sixties and seventies, several famous psychologists and psychiatrists emerged in the landscape of psychology: Victor Frankl, Gordon Allport, Rollo May, Abraham Maslow and Carl Rogers. These theories can be folded under what is termed a humanistic-existential model of psychology, the Third Force of psychology. It was this model which began referring to patients as "clients" which has an implicit inference toward self-healing, instead of "patients" which has an implicit inference that the person is broken and needs fixing. The word "patient" is still the predominate word used in the medical model today and you will find that most medical doctors still refer to their customers as "patients," not "clients." The word "patient" is derived from the scientific, medical model which sees the person as sick and needing to be cured. The doctor is considered the person with the power to heal them. In the humanistic model, therapists perceived humans as largely being capable of their own growth and mental healing with simply the need to be guided toward healing, therefore, these models called their patients "clients." While they recognized the need for medical intervention, the humanists broke away from the concept of the medical doctor and the therapist as being the sole and/or dominant power authority in healing the client. This was yet another huge shift away from the deterministic view of psychoanalysis.

While the humanistic-existential models are far more substantial than is stated here, it can be said that these were amongst the first psychologists and psychiatrists who began with a theoretical foundation and assumption that human beings have the innate potential to become whole. This is inherent within every human being and bestows upon the client a substantial amount of power in the healing process. This model began focusing more on client feelings and their subjective experience, but had a minimal recognition of the spiritual aspect of humankind. Unlike psychoanalytic, cognitive and behavioral models, the humanistic-existentialists would allow a client's spirituality to be used as part of the therapeutic process, if that was what the client felt compelled to introduce within the therapeutic milieu. However, humanistic-existentialists did not initially recognize spirituality as a core premise of a whole and healthy human being. If that aspect was part of the client, the therapist honored it, but the theory itself does not explicitly articulate spirituality as a central energy for psychological wholeness and well-being. The major advantage for the humanistic-existential model was that feelings and subjective experience were validated and placed in the forefront, not the background, of therapy and of healing. Most importantly, unlike psychoanalysts and cognitive/behaviorists, feelings were actually given primacy in the clinical setting.

Frankl had spent three years as a prisoner in Auschwitz and other prisoner camps, during which time he developed his theoretical model called logotherapy. At its core, the will to meaning surfaces. Frankl believed that humankind has an innate need to find meaning and purpose in life. Gordon Allport, perhaps better known as a social psychologist, used the philosophical term "becoming" to exemplify humankind's striving toward a higher potential. Rollo May used the philosophical term "existentialism" which is about the inner, subjective experience and is concerned with ontology, the nature of *being.* This model was moving away from focusing on the objective reality with which some earlier psychologists had identified with, particularly the cognitive/behavioralists. May definitely borrowed from the 19th century Danish philosopher, Kierkegaard, and it is likely that he and Allport were familiar with Greek philosophers such as Heraclitus, who introduced the concept of "Becoming" into the Western world, and Parminedes, who introduced the concept of "Being" into the Western world, both of whom influenced Plato and Plotinus.

May and Allport preferred to use the word *becoming* because it connoted a more fluid process than the word *being* which may be erroneously perceived as static and unchanging. Carl Rogers wrote two books, *On Becoming a Person* and *A Way of Being*, and it is hardly likely that he, like virtually every other psychologist, did not borrow from their earlier brotherhood of Greek philosophers. Carl Rogers has left a substantial legacy to the field of psychology as he postulated the three fundamental therapeutic techniques: 1) empathy for the client, 2) unconditional positive regard for the client and 3) congruence or authenticity within the therapist. Not surprisingly, these are very similar to compassion, non-judgmentalism and sincerity which closely parallel religious concepts. The field of psychology has inherited from Rogers the key concept of the therapist seeing the world from the client's perspective.

Maslow is perhaps best known for his theory of self-actualization which postulates that every person has an intrinsic nature that is neutral or good. By encouraging this development, humans can realize their fullest potential. His seminal work on the hierarchy of human needs was published in 1943 and included the following hierarchy with lower needs on the bottom:

– self-actualization needs
– esteem needs (self-esteem)
– belongingness and love needs
– safety needs (shelter)
– physiological needs (air, food, water)

Maslow said that people move toward self-actualization in a hierarchical fashion. By satisfying the lower needs and moving up the ladder, the human advances toward self-actualization. At the highest level, humans are motivated by goodness, altruism, seeking truth, beauty, justice and order. The important part of Maslow's work was to posit a hierarchy of human needs and to develop a process from lower consciousness to higher consciousness.

Milton Erickson's work in hypnotherapy falls in a category by itself and is not referred to as humanistic-existential in the strict sense of the term, however, his work in hypnotherapy could be considered largely humanistic since the client is believed to have the power to heal self. It is important to acknowledge Erickson because his work was highly effective. He was committed to reaching the subconscious of his clients as he believed that, by far, most learning is done there.

All in all, the humanistic/existential model is a *feeling* model. These theorists did not totally reject the psychoanalytic and cognitive/behavioral models, however, they viewed them as only partially accurate, being one-sided and focusing on only one aspect of the human, not the whole person. The humanistic/existential models presumed there was further work to be done as it pertains to understanding psychological growth and human potential.

It's perhaps appropriate to mention intellectual giant Carl Jung at this time. His model is called Analytical Psychology, although he does not fit within the psychoanalytic model *per se.* Jung believed that there is a spiritual drive to move toward a higher level of consciousness. Some would say he was a transpersonalist although Jung's work is in no way technically identified as such. Jung was one of two famous psychiatrists in the early 20th century noted for their emphasis on spirituality as an essential ingredient of the whole, healthy person. He was a brilliant theoretician and practitioner known best for his introduction of the terms "psychological archetype," "anima" and "animus" and the "collective unconscious." We have spoken earlier of his work with the client's unconscious and dreams. Jung assiduously studied the unconscious and believed in the inherent validity of paranormal activity. Unlike Freud, Jung did not believe his theory was the ultimate truth, rather he believed there was much room for future psychologists to take his theoretical model and expand on it. There is a fairly large cadre of Jungian analysts, but unfortunately his legacy to psychology is left out of most traditional academic psychology programs or, if mentioned, he is spoken as a footnote. This is largely due to mainstream psychology's lack of grasping and understanding of Jungian concepts, their rejection of Jung's emphasis on the numinous and spiritual, and Jung's studies outside of mainstream psychology (such as anthropology, alchemy, philosophy) which are not understood and accepted by mainstream psychology as falling within the acceptable purview of the psychological field.

The last model we mention is one which is much misunderstood and dismissed by the American Psychological Association and mainstream psychology because of its esoteric and spiritual nature and focus and its lack of scientific validity: the transpersonal model. Roberto Assagioli was an Italian psychiatrist who, in the early 20th century, began developing his model which would become the Fourth Force of psychology in the fifties and sixties as it attempted to integrate the best of psychoanalytic, cognitive-behavioral and humanistic-existential theoretical models. Like Jung, Assagioli considered spirituality an essential piece of the mentally healthy and whole person, so he spoke of the Higher Self. The ego was considered the lower self so it was spelled with a small "s." The Higher Self was always spelled with a capital "S" to denote a higher level of consciousness incorporating, essentially, Maslow's self-actualizing and Jung's individuation into one concept. Assagioli was the first psychologist to study the Will and to postulate a theory about the crucial role it plays within optimal mental health and well being. He also used therapeutic techniques which worked with the unconscious such as guided imagery, journaling, reading and dream analysis. Part of his legacy is that he formally considered intuition as a valid and essential mental activity; perceived paranormal activities such as out-of-body experiences as real experiences to be studied; and viewed mystical activities such as shamanism and native rituals as worthwhile mental states to be clinically studied. Assagioli, in his book, *Psychosynthesis*, published in 1965, presaged the efficacy of meditation, color therapy and music therapy as effective future psychotherapeutic treatment modalities.

Ken Wilber is a prominent theorist and genius who has been able to study psychology, philosophy, physics, Eastern mysticism and Western religion in order to take transpersonal psychology three steps forward and form what he refers to as the Integral Approach although he prefers not to speak of his psychology as a "fifth force." Transpersonal psychology synthesizes or forms a whole picture of the individual and its therapeutic techniques attempt to reach all facets of the person from thinking to feeling to behaving to being. Simplistically speaking, Wilber's model does the same but builds on and subsumes the transpersonal model. Wilber states that spirituality is part of the human consciousness and to dismiss it is analogous to dismissing a part of the person. He is perhaps the first theorist to tie the entire range of consciousness into one "Chain of Being" as borrowed from Lovejoy or "Nest of Being" as Wilber more recently has termed it. Transpersonal theorists and Wilber not only believe the human individual can achieve a mental state of Jesus the Christ, the Buddha and Lao Tzu, but these theoretical models believe that it will, indeed, happen as part of the natural evolution of human consciousness. These models do not reject scientism *per se*, but clearly emphasize that scientism without a consideration of spirituality is an incomplete picture of an otherwise whole person. In a nutshell, transpersonal and integral theories believe that to reject spirituality as a part of optimal mental health is reductionistic, incomplete, unhealthy and unsound. Another very important thing to note with the transpersonal and integral psychologies is the fundamental precept that human consciousness evolves and that the ego is *not* the optimal state of consciousness. Psychoanalytic and cognitive/ behavioral theories do not address the evolution of human consciousness nor are any of their therapeutic techniques meant to effectively address this process.

And so we now arrive at a summary of the Four Forces in psychology. These models encompass the entire psychological architecture of *known* human consciousness. Psychoanalytic theory focuses on thinking; cognitive/ behaviorist models focuses on thinking and doing; humanistic/existential emphasizes feeling and being; transpersonal and integral emphasizes a synthesis of thinking, feeling, doing, hence, Being.

It should also be noted that the psychoanalytic and cognitive/behaviorist models are, for the most part, dismissive of other models. Believing that they hold the ultimate truth and the entire picture of the individual, these theories hold a narrow view of human capacity. On the other hand, the humanistic/ existential, transpersonal and integral psychologies do not espouse a narrow, myopic view, therefore, they do not entirely reject the first two models. Much like pieces of a puzzle, the human is viewed as a being who thinks, feels, and acts and inherently strives to reach higher levels of consciousness. Viewed from this angle, the psychoanalytic and cognitive/behavioral models themselves operate from the ego shadow consciousness of dismissiveness while the humanistic/existential, transpersonal and integral psychologies operate from a more inclusive, embracing stance.

Until the last decade of the twentieth century, each of the first three models rejected the others' basic tenets while the transpersonal and integral psychologies have, from their inception, attempted to integrate all four into a broader, more comprehensive view of human consciousness. Today, psychoanalysis in its original form is a victim of the ego itself. It is fast losing its foothold and has largely been replaced by what is referred to as psychodynamic theories. Most therapists over the last decade have begun their own integration of the best of these aforementioned theories into their own clinical practice leaving few clinicians who practice only one strategy to the exclusion of the others. A growing number of therapists are recognizing the numinous and perceiving the evolution of consciousness on a continuum toward a Higher Self. While the Jungian analysts and the transpersonal and integral therapists are not taken seriously by the American Psychological Association (APA), they are a growing number and it is only a matter of time until these more mature psychological theories are valued. As we have seen, the ego consciousness exists in all fields, so there are psychologists embodying the ego consciousness. Yes, psychology and psychologists must evolve too!

In order to move forward as a discipline and a field of study, psychology must expand and include a larger study. A serious turn toward the ontological and phenomenological aspects of psychological health and well being and the unfoldment of the Soul is critical. That love and kindness are ubiquitous and produce such consistently positive effects on both the mind and the physiology of humankind should, in and of itself, be convincing to the leaders of psychology that a serious study of the positive emotions are of great importance.

The history of psychology emphasized the splitting away from its philosophical roots and narrowing down the experience of being human to only that which can be intellectually comprehended, clearly operationalized, defined and measured so as to determine its predictability. When psychology broadens its stance and, in a sense, returns to some of its ancient roots by seeking a study of the Universal aspects of Goodness as it relates to the optimal psychological well being of the whole human being, the field will evolve. Obsessive masculine competition, splintering, exclusivity and denial of the holistic view of health must be replaced with a more balanced feminine perspective that is inclusive and unifying. This will be the acknowledgement of the equality of both feminine and masculine aspects of the Psyche and will also be the introduction of an authentic study of the spectrum of human consciousness. We begin this by embracing intuition, as the Eastern philosophers have for thousands of years, as a viable and vital pathway to understanding higher levels of knowledge and, hence, potentially healthier modes of relating. Historically masculine cognitive styles which are limiting and competitive in their focus must now include more feminine cognitive styles of personal intersubjectivity, ontological relativity and noetic truth which are inclusive and unifying in their direction.

Scientific methodologies of the past with their heavy masculine emphasis on operationalization, definition, measurement and predictability must make way for a larger scope of understanding as we: 1) validate intuition as an authentic relational approach, 2) seek an authentic study of the ontological and phenomenological aspects of Goodness and its resulting psychological

391

outcomes over the construct-functional approach which most males have based their theories on, and 3) pursue a large-scale, serious study of dreams, meditation, yoga, chromatherapy, sound therapy and aromatherapy. An even greater potential benefit would be to consider as a *primary* mission of the field of psychology that of social reform.

Eastern philosophy and psychology and even some Western philosophers and psychologists have long recognized that intellectualization, logic and reason are limiting. Indeed, over the past decade, some psychologists have identified other forms of intelligence, besides the historically and exclusively accepted masculine focused IQ, as having an equal status. Some of these, according to Howard Gardner from Harvard, include language, body-kinesthetic, spatial-temporal, musical, interpersonal and intrapersonal intelligences. Since the 1990s, spiritual intelligence has become a target of interest and study within an ever widening circle of psychologists.

Psychology is being compelled to not just study the mind, but also study the heart aspects. Some interesting findings of modern scientists state that: 1) 95-99% of all species on the planet Earth have gone extinct, 2) five times in the past, the Earth has ridded itself of all species, 3) on average, every 4 million years, a species becomes extinct and 4) the rate of extinction is accelerating. Assuming the rate of wars and levels of conflict, hate, anger, violence, greed and envy which seemingly pervade the planet today, it seems plausible to hypothesize that humankind—if it continues in this same egoistic direction of division, separation, competition, exclusivity, superiority/inferiority—will not exist at some point in the future because it will be unable to peacefully and harmoniously adapt with each other and with the environment.

What my book attempts to do is to reach the broader audience of humanity in hopes that a mass group of people will begin demanding from their healthcare professionals that their Soul be recognized within both the mental health care and the medical profession. Thanks to people like Dr. Andrew Weil and Deepok Chopra, the medical community began in the late 1980s taking more seriously the subject of holistic health. Joseph Campbell's prolific and integrative work on philosophy, religion and anthropology planted much needed seeds for the mental health community, as has Dr. Wayne Dyer's focal work on the power of human consciousness. Eckhart Tolle's beautiful integration of masculine and feminine energies is truly a beacon of light from the Soul. James Hillman, the famous Jungian analyst, ranks high on the list of those who were amongst the first to persuade the psychological community to revision itself and, instead, of concentrating on the science of psychology, to incorporate the artistic or Soul aspect into the field. Wilber's work is so vast and integrative as to place him as perhaps the first major theorist to "come out of the closet" as an authentic surveyor of both the psychological and philosophical landscape of the Soul. More males like these are needed and certainly more females must emerge as leaders into the inquiry of Soul consciousness since it is the mature feminine which has been dismissed as an equal and valid piece within the Psyche of humanity.

The critical task of the field of psychology in the 21$^{st}$ century is to broaden its focus, to shift and transform. This will allow the field to embrace a broader spectrum of human consciousness, to conduct research in broader areas and, most importantly, to become an important, viable leader in the world as it pertains to social reform. Studying the mind is a partial and limited view of the Psyche since mind is only a portion of it. Psychology must explore creative expression and the expressions of love and goodwill. These are Soulful energic expressions currently excluded as a component of any serious mainstream study of mental health although transpersonal, phenomenological and existential psychologies come closest to a holistic study of the Soul. Continuing to focus on the ego is to examine *effects*; to study the Soul is to concentrate on *causes*. Thus, in order to determine causes, not merely effects, of mental health, psychology must undertake a serious study of the Soul which is to say that psychology should contemplate and analyze the whole person and the essence of the person. A balanced, expressed Soul is the cause of optimal mental health; a neglected, abused Soul results in the expression of the dark, shadow of the ego and is a cause of poor mental health.

Psychologists have attempted to create psychological theories based upon the health of the ego which is an oxymoron. Ego is paradoxically, the beginning of the journey towards, and yet is the antithesis of, the Soul. You cannot express ego and Soul simultaneously. They are dependent upon one another, yet are mutually exclusive. As long as psychology and medicine ignore the serious study of the Soul and, instead, focus exclusively on the ego and the body, humankind will not advance toward optimal mental or physical health.

Philosophy is perhaps the quiet sister of wisdom who has continued to sit in solitude for thousands of years while other disciplines have split off although there has been much egoistic division within its own family of philosophy as to who holds the "Truth." It can be considered the least egoistic of the other three disciplines from the standpoint that it just simply continues to be and seems to be, more or less, indifferent about other disciplines. Buddhists differ from Advaitans who differ from Taoists who differ from Plato and neo-Platonists. All this disagreement over who knows Ultimate Truth. Could it be we are all essentially talking about the very same Oneness?

Religion *per se*, with its dogma and doctrine, has suffered endlessly from the same ego consciousness with its exclusivity mindset. For decades people have been leaving religion because of restrictive dogma and doctrine. The belief in an anthropomorphic God has done more harm than all the wars on this planet put together and accounts for more psychological and physical torture and death since time immemorial. It seems so simple to conceive of God as a Universal Energy of Love so that every person would have equal access to this energy rather than to devise some deceptive myth that elevates one section of humankind as superior over other sections. In that sense, religion must be transformed just as the other disciplines must. Transformation is entirely different than destruction since the love of the Soul embraces and transforms and the shadow of the ego divides and destroys.

The Soul never has been, and never will be, matter. So why does man persist in searching exclusively for physical health in the body and mental health in the brain? The physical body is made by Psyche, not the other way around. Consciousness is Supreme and a Universal Mind of Love is Creator of all. The body is a physical vehicle by which Soul may experience and express itself in a nonspiritual world; therefore, it is owed due respect. The brain and heart are vessels by which the expressions of the Soul may exude itself in a nonspiritual world; therefore, we must honor them. But the study of the brain and the heart will only yield results, not core causes. Medical science can continue to dissect rats, cats and monkeys, but our true and ultimate goal is to know what makes us physically and mentally healthy. Psychology can continue to study the ego and its expressions, however, continuing to do so will only result in further examinations of poor mental health. The only study that will produce success in understanding what humans need to do to be physically and mentally healthy is an understanding of the Soul. As we are able to rise to the next level of human existence and return to the care of the Soul, we will begin to eliminate negative karma which manifests itself back into the physical world as poor mental and physical health.

All that we see in the world of matter is but an extension of your inner world of mind. If you have peace, love and joy in your mind and heart, you will extend that outwardly. If you are sad, unkind, jealous, envious, guilty, shameful, frustrated and angry in your inner world, you will extend that to your outer world. All chaos that we experience outside of ourselves is but an outward extension of the chaos that exists in the inner world of humankind. Wars, political corruption, corporate fraud and malfeasance, murder and theft, violence and other crimes all began in people's minds. We are responsible for the world we live in. We create our outer world by what we think and how we treat ourselves and others. We are responsible for peace; we are responsible for chaos. As men and women think and feel, this is who they are.

Soul only knows to share in its likeness and honor the equality of its expressions as it seeks Goodness. The Will of the Divine Soul is toward Goodness forever and ever. Anyone can ignore and deny Truth for as long as they wish, but it does not diminish Truth, nor does it make Truth go away. Truth, like the Soul, is always there, whether we wish to recognize it or not.

And so I now end my book with a brief allegory. It is an ancient story told by sages and mystics throughout the ages. Philosophy, religion, science are all from the same one source although they have been divorced from one another for over 2,000 years. Science, a masculine field, divorced his wife, Religion, the mother of all disciplines, thinking that Science was the only purveyor of Truth. Science wanted to find the Creator of the Universe through creative thinking and knowledge and assumed that Religion, a weak and passive creature that operated on faith in the unseen, would never "see" Truth since Science was convinced Truth was in matter. Setting out to destroy the notion that reality was in the invisible world, Science became a staunch rebel against his prior spouse. Religion violently reacted to this divorce with intense hate and, indeed, caused the brutal execution of many heretics who didn't believe in dogma and doctrine.

Psychology was born from the divorce of this split. Seeing the divorce of the parents, Psychology followed suit. Separating from his sister, Philosophy, Psychology thought he had far more intellect to find the Truth than his sister's soft, yet unyielding pursuit of Truth through wisdom. Knowing true wisdom is silent, Philosophy merely quietly moved forward while Psychology arrogantly relegated Philosophy to an inferior realm believing that the pursuit of wisdom could never yield any substantial results in finding the Truth. Psychology just knew Truth had to be found through the exclusive study of the brain, intellect and behavior. All this writing about wisdom and love and Being wasn't logical, rational and intellectual enough. Such is the story of a split Psyche as exampled through the splits in disciplines.

Truth is not found in divisiveness, but in unity. It should be apparent that psychology is missing the ancient wisdom of his sister, philosophy, and desperately needs to reconcile this split between brother (masculine) and sister (feminine). It is imperative if psychology is to avoid becoming obsolete. Similarly, religion must be transformed from its historically hypocritical moralizer into the true, loving, nonjudgmental field that its very words purport to be the saviors of humankind. Science must openly confess to religion that the physical universe is not Creator. Only then can science and religion begin a slow process of healing their split. The mother and father need each other and the son and daughter need their parents. Apart, they stumble blindly, but together, the community of wholeness and oneness is restored.

Now is the time for a remarriage and communion between these four important disciplines which are, essentially, on the same journey attempting to find the answer to the same question. Who got off track and who is responsible is the subject of much of this book---the ego consciousness. How humankind gets back on track and who must assume responsibility is the Ultimate subject of this book---the Soul Consciousness or Higher Self.

The story of Psyche (Soul) and Eros (Love) is the ancient, timeless story of the reunification of the feminine and the masculine and the transcendence of humankind. For those of you who perhaps do not know the story well, it is the allegory of the split mind (ego) which suffers and the eternally seeking Psyche which is yearning for a return to wholeness and fullness of Being. The female in the story is Psyche because it is the feminine energy which forever and eternally seeks to reunite. It is only love, not intellect, which has this mysterious power of union. The male in the story is Eros because it is the immature masculine which has throughout history pushed away from the feminine and denied itself the integration of the feminine energies of love, wisdom, kindness and compassion. Therefore, it is only when the male gender integrates these feminine energies into himself that there will be an authentic reunion of the Whole Psyche or Soul. In the allegory, Eros (the male) is continually running away from Psyche which is symbolic of males shunning, eschewing and refusing to embody the feminine. This has resulted in a split Psyche or what psychologists refer to as "ego" or "self" with a lower case "s." Finally, Psyche does reunite itSelf with Eros and they are able to ascend to "heaven," their rightful inheritance and home with heaven not as a physical place, rather as a consciousness of peace, a psychological resting place, a sense of Oneness and well-being. This is the Highest Self, the Beloved psychological union written about by Rumi, the 13th century Persian mystic. It is the Adored Beloved within, the Soul in its Fullness of Bliss. It is the story of Psyche knowing the absolute beauty and awe of Eros and knowing that her fulfillment lies only in her reunion with her Beloved. We could say that this division is the "the Fall" of humankind from heaven. It is the oldest and most tragic psychological division since time began. It began when Adam, the immature masculine, coveted the material world more than the spiritual world and when Adam split from love and wisdom. The reunion of the feminine and the masculine and the blossoming of mature Soul consciousness must occur before humankind will move beyond the chaos and confusion in which the split ego would have us remain.

Male writers have, for centuries, thought of the Soul as purely feminine which comes as no surprise because these males have so dis-identified with the feminine energy that, when they first perceive the Soul energy, they feel flooded with the feminine which has been lost to them through the false admonishments of an ignorant, abusive patriarchy.

The story about Psyche and Eros is a story far more glorious than the feminine alone and, indeed, is the ancient, yet modern, story of the immature masculine which is slumbering in ignorance and keeps doing the very thing that denies him peace and wholeness. He adamantly refuses to merge with the feminine and reintegrate the feminine into himself so that masculine and feminine share power equally in the world. Even more tragic, he is vested in ensuring that the feminine remains in a subjugated, devalued and inferior position in relation to him and his psychologically immature self. In the allegory, the immature masculine is asleep, unconscious and ignorant. He is ignorant, but the feminine sees him and knows intuitively that Love is meant to reunite with Psyche. Psyche stops at nothing and suffers untold tortures in her journey to reunite with Love because she knows that it is only when Love is reunited with Psyche that the Soul is, once again, made whole, full and complete. The male attempts time and time again to evade Psyche, but the Soul must seek the reunion in order to merge with its Beloved. This is the eternal search of the Soul to find itSelf and to restore and know its Wholeness and Fullness. The ending of the story is their blissful union in which they immediately assume a higher, more peaceful consciousness which is symbolically referred to as "heaven." The ego is transcended, the Beloved is discovered and peace reigns again with the Soul.

Many males throughout history, including most philosophers and including the eminent psychologist, Carl Jung, have mistaken Psyche for solely or primarily a feminine energy. Since the masculine split from his equal partner, the feminine, these male scholars, philosophers, academicians and theologians would perceive and describe the Soul as feminine since the entire male gender bid adieu from her when time on earth began. Psychologically speaking, these males are unconsciously seeking to reintegrate their own feminine nature within their own Great Souls and, reading of the Soul, would appear as feminine to a male who has dis-identified from the feminine. The allegory of Psyche and Eros is the ancient story of the masculine asleep and ignorant of his lack of wholeness, lack of Love and Wisdom. It is no less than pure tragic irony that, in spite of his emphasis on intellect, logic and reasoning, the immature masculine is a fool lacking Wisdom until he can merge with the Beloved. He must come to know the Soul, the Psyche, as the mature psychological balance of the feminine and the masculine so that we, females and males, can move forward and rediscover the Mature Beloved, the sacred, the sublime from which we all came.

All particulars are found in exclusion; all Universals are found in unity and collaboration. Through the masculine energy which makes everything complex because it analyzes and breaks everything down further and further, we have studied particulars *ad nauseum.* This was simply a natural flow of the masculine and was destined to be so. It has served its useful purpose. Let us honor it for what it has given us. However, the intellect of the masculine will not reunite us with the Soul. Certainly after thousands of years of masculinity at the helm of leadership and still no closer to peace than we are, we can see this truism. Only the collaboration of the mind and heart of the Soul can do this. It is now time to allow the sacred feminine to reunite us all. The equality of the feminine and the masculine and equality between the Self and Other is where heaven on earth begins.

If psychology can heal itself and bring itself into harmony with the Soul, there awaits vast opportunities to transform the field into not only a deeper and more challenging field of study, but also a field which encompasses human and societal transformation. This larger and more significant vision and mission is no less than the hope for the field and the future of humankind. Many of the humanistic-existential, Jungian and transpersonal psychologists have a wonderful opportunity to lead in this new charter. Can psychology succeed in its own evolution and transformation?

It is time for psychologists to also become philosophers and philosophers to become psychologists. It is time for scientists to cross the bridge, shake hands with their religious mates and it is time for theologians to honor the sacred discoveries that science is making which will one day only serve to finally validate Soul and Spirit. For the study of the Full Self, the Great Soul, the Higher Self is a scientific study of Light, a philosophy of life, a psychological rediscovery and a spiritual reawakening. *And this is indivisible*. All disciplines must honor each other, commune with one another and develop a truly generative spirit of collaboration unprecedented in the history of humankind. It is truly an auspicious opportunity. The Soul is awaiting to be unfettered and unchained from the ego who would have it imprisoned forever. The Great Soul waits in all its shining glory to manifest, transform and restore community in the world. This is not a mythical tale. It is our true inheritance. It is the inheritance of the All. The Divine Echo within each of us speaks to us of abundance overflowing. It is time to heed the call. All that is needed is the adoration of the Soul and its Will to know and love.

# REFERENCES

Aronson, E. (1999). *The Social Animal*. New York, NY: Worth Publishers.

Assagioli, Roberto. (1965). *Psychosynthesis: A Collection of Basic Writings*. New York, NY: The Viking Press.

Assagioli, Roberto. (1973). *The Act of Will*. New York, NY: Penguin Books.

Babbitt, Edwin D. (1980). (Editor: Faber Birren) *Principles of Light and Color: The Healing Power of Color*. Kensington Publishing, Inc.

Balibar, Francoise. (2001). *Einstein: Decoding the Universe*. (Translator: Harry N. Abrams) New York, NY: Harry N. Abrams, Inc.

Ballard, C. G. O'Brien, J.T. Reichelt, K., & Perry, E.K. (2002). Aromatherapy as a safe and effective treatment for the management of agitation in severe dementia: The results of a double-blind, placebo-controlled trial with Melissa. *Journal of Clinical Psychiatry*, 63 (7), 553-558.

Bandler, R. & Grinder, J. (1979). *Frogs into Princes*. Moab, UT: Real People Press.

Beaulieu, John. (1987). *Music and Sound in the Healing Arts: An Energy Approach*. Barrytown, NY: Station Hill Press.

Birren, Faber. (1989). *Color Psychology and Color Therapy*. Secaucus, NJ: Carol Publishing Group.

Birren, Faber. (1997). *Color and Human Response: Aspects of Light and Color Bearing on the Reactions of Living Things and the Welfare of Human Beings*. London, England: John Wiley & Sons.

Breiling, Brian J. (1996). (Ed.). *Light Years Ahead: The Illustrated Guide to Full Spectrum and Colored Light in Mindbody Healing*. Berkeley, CA: Celestial Arts.

Burnet, John. (1960). *Greek Philosophy: Thales to Plato*. New York, NY: Macmillan & Company, Ltd.

Buber, Martin. (1958). *I and Thou*. New York, NY: Charles Scribner's Sons.

Byron, Thomas. (1989). (Translator). *The Heart of Awareness: A Translation of the Ashtavakra Gita*. New York, NY: Shambhala Publications.

Campbell, Don. (2001). *The Mozart Effect: Tapping the Power of Music to Heal the Body, Strengthen the Mind and Unlock the Creative Spirit*. New York, NY: Harper Collins Publishers.

Capra, Fritjof. (2000). *The Tao of Physics*. Boston, MA: Shambhala Press.

Coppleston, S. J. Frederick. (1993). *A History of Philosophy: Volume I*. New York, NY: Bantam Doubleday Del Publishing Group, Inc.

Corvo, J. & Verner-Bonds, L. (1998). *Healing with Color Zone Therapy*. Freedom, CA: The Crossing Press.

De Broglie, Louis. (1937). *Matter and Light: The New Physics*. New York, NY: W. W. Norton & Company, Inc.

Deutsch, Eliot. (1969). *Advaita Vedanta: A Philosophical Reconstruction*. Honolulu, HI: Honolulu Press.

Diamond, W. John. (1979). *Your Body Doesn't Lie*. New York, NY: Warner Books.

Diamond, W. John. (1990). *Life Energy: Using the Meridians to Unlock the Hidden Power of Your Emotions*. St. Paul, MN: Paragon House.

Diamond, W. John. (2000). *The Clinical Practice of Complementary, Alternative and Western Medicine*. Boca Raton, FL: CRC Press.

Dinnerstein, Dorothy. (1976). *The Mermaid and the Minotaur: Sexual Arrangements and Human Malaise*. New York, NY: Other Press.

Dinshah, Darius. (2001). *Let There Be Light*. Malaga, NJ: Dinshah Health Society.

Edinger, Edward. (1985). *Anatomy of the Psyche: Alchemical Symbolism in Psychotherapy*. La Salle, IL: Open Court Publishing Company.

Edinger, Edward. (1987). *The Christian Archetype: A Jungian Commentary on the Life of Christ*. Toronto, Canada: Inner City Books.

Edinger, Edward. (1994). *The Mystery of The Coniunctio: Alchemical Image of Individuation*. Toronto, Canada: Inner City Books.

Edinger, Edward. (1995). *The Mysterium Lectures: A Journey through C.*

*G. Jung's Mysterium Coniunctionis.* Toronto, Canada: Inner City Books.

Edinger, Edward. (1996). *The Aion Lectures: Exploring the Self in C. G. Jung's Aion.* Toronto, Canada: Inner City Books.

Edinger, Edward. (1996). *The New God Image: A Study of Jung's Key Letters Concerning The Evolution of the Western God-Image.* Wilmette, IL: Chiron Publications.

Edinger, Edward. (2002.) *Science of the Soul: A Jungian Perspective.* Ontario, Canada: Inner City Books.

Einstein, Albert. (1954). *Ideas and Opinions.* (Translator: Sonja Bargmann). New York, NY: Crown Publishers.

Einstein, Albert. (1956). *The World As I See It.* (Translator: Alan Harris). New York, NY: Citadel Press.

Elkins, David. (1998). *Beyond Religion.* Wheaton, IL: The Theosophical Publishing House.

Ferrucci, Piero. (1982). *What We May Be: Techniques for Psychological and Spiritual Growth Through Psychosynthesis.* New York, NY: Jeremy P. Tarcher/Putnam Book.

Freke, Timothy. (1995). (Translator). *Lao Tzu's Tao Te Ching.* London, England: Judy Piatkus Publishers, Ltd.

Freud, Sigmund. (1961). *The Future of an Illusion.* (Translator: James Strachey). New York, NY: W. W. Norton & Company.

Freud, Sigmund. (1961). *Civilization and Its Discontents.* (Translator: James Strachey). New York, NY: W. W. Norton & Company.

Fromm, Erich. (1959). *Sigmund Freud's Mission.* New York, NY: Grove Press, Inc.

Fromm, Erich. (1961). *Marx's Concept of Man.* New York, NY: Frederick Ungar Publishing Company.

Fromm, Erich. (1962). *Beyond the Chains of Illusion: My Encounter with Marx and Freud.* New York, NY: Pocket Books, Inc.

Fromm, Erich. (1999). *The Essential Fromm: Life Between Having and Being.* New York, NY: The Continuum Publishing Company.

Fromm, Erich. (2002). *The Art of Being.* New York, NY: The Continuum Publishing Company.

Fromm, Erich, Suzuki, D. T., & De Martino, R. (1960). *Zen Buddhism and Psychoanalysis.* New York, NY: Harper & Row Publishers.

Frankl, Victor. (1963). *Man's Search for Meaning: An Introduction to Logotherapy.* New York, NY: Washington Square Press.

Frankl, Victor. (1969). *The Will to Meaning.* New York, NY: The New

American Library, Inc.

Frankl, Victor. (1973). *The Doctor and the Soul: From Psychotherapy to Logotherapy.* New York, NY: Random House.

Gerard, Robert M. (1958). Differential Effects of Colored Lights on Psycho-physiological Functions. (Doctoral dissertation, University of California, Los Angeles.)

Goethe, Johann Wolfgang von. (2000). *Theory of Colors.* Boston, MA: MIT Press.

Goldman, Jonathan. (2002). *Healing Sounds and the Power of Harmonics.* Rochester, VT: Inner Traditions International.

Hall, Calvin & Nordby, Vernon. (1973). *A Primer of Jungian Psychology.* New York, NY: Penguin Books.

Hayashi, N., et al. (2002). Effects of group musical therapy on inpatients with chronic psychoses: A controlled study. *Psychiatry and Clinical Neurosciences,* 56 (2), 187-193.

Hayashi, N., et al. (2002). Effectiveness of group musical therapy on chronic schizophrenic patients: A controlled study. *Seishin Igaku Clinical Psychiatry,* 43 (10), 1141-1147.

Indich, William. (1980). *Consciousness in Advaita Vedanta.* New Delhi, India: Indological Publishers & Booksellers.

James, William. (1961). *Varieties of Religious Experience: A Study in Human Nature.* New York, NY: Macmillan Publishing Co., Inc.

Jaspers, Karl. (1962). *Plato and Augustine.* New York, NY: Harcourt Brace & Company.

Jaspers, Karl. (1962*). Socrates, Buddha, Confucius, Jesus: The Great Philosophers, Volume* I. New York, NY: Harcourt Brace Jovanovich Publishers.

Jaspers, Karl. (1966). *Anaximander, Heraclitus, Parmenides, Plotinus, Lao-Tzu, Nagarjuna: The Great Philosophers, Volume II.* New York, NY: Harcourt Brace Javanovich.

Jenkins, N. (2002). *Aromatherapy: An introductory guide to the healing power of scent.* Bath, UK: Parragon Publishing.

Jolivet, Regis. (1946). *Introduction to Kierkegaard.* (Translator: W. H. Barber) New York, NY: E. P. Dutton & Company, Inc.

Jung, C. G. (1933). *Modern Man in Search of a Soul.* San Diego, CA: Harcourt Brace Jovanovich.

Jung, C. G. (1938). *Psychology and Religion.* Binghamton, NY: The Vail-Ballou Press, Inc.

Jung, C. G. Jung. (1957). *The Undiscovered Self.* (Translator: R. F. Hull). New York, NY: Penguin Putnam, Inc.

Jung, C. G. (1959). *Aion: Researches into the Phenomenology of the Self.* (Translator: R. F. Hull). Princeton, NJ: Princeton University Press.

Jung, C. G. (1982). *Aspects of the Feminine.* Princeton, NJ: Princeton University Press.

Jung, C. G. (1989). *Aspects of the Masculine.* Princeton, NJ: Princeton University Press.

Kernberg, O., Selzer, M., Koenigsberg, H., Carr, A. & Appelbaum, A. (1989). *Psychodynamic Psychotherapy of Borderline Patients.* New York, NY: Basic Books, Inc.

Khalsa, Shakta Kaur. (2001). *Kundalini Yoga: Unlock Your Inner Potential Through Life-Changing Exercises.* New York, NY: Dorling Kindersley Publishing, Inc.

Kierkegaard, Soren (1938). *Purity of Heart is to Will One Thing.* New York, NY: Harper & Row.

Kierkegaard, Soren. (1954). *Fear and Trembling.* Princeton, NJ: Princeton University Press.

Kierkegaard, Soren. (1954). *Sickness Unto Death.* Princeton, NJ: Princeton University Press.

Kirsch, Irving, et al. (2002). The Emperor's New Drugs: An Analysis of Antidepressant Medication Data Submitted to the U.S. Food and Drug Administration. *Prevention and Treatment*, 5, Article 23.

Klotsche, Charles. *Color Medicine: The Secrets of Color/Vibrational Healing.* Sedona, AZ: Light Technology Publishing.

Knight, W. & Rickard, N. (2002). Relaxing music prevents stress-induced increases in subjective anxiety, systolic blood pressure, and heart rate in healthy males and females. *Journal of Music Therapy*, 38 (4), 254-272.

Lachkar, J. (1992). *The Narcissistic/Borderline Couple: A Psychoanalytic Perspective on Marital Treatment.* New York, NY: Brunner/Mazel, Inc.

Livingstone, Sir Richard. (1938). *Portrait of Socrates.* New York, NY: Oxford University Press.

Lombardo, Stanley. (1979). (Translator). *Parmenides and Empedocles: The Fragments in Verse Translation.* San Francisco, CA: Grey Fox Press.

Lundy, Miranda. (2001). *Sacred Geometry.* New York, NY: Walker Publishing Company, Inc.

Maharshi, Sri Ramana. (2000). *Talks with Ramana Maharshi: On Realizing Abiding Peace and Happiness.* Carlsbad, CA: Inner Directions

Publishing.

Mandel, Peter. (1995). *The Pharmacy of Light*. Bruschal, Germany: Mandel-Institute for Esogetic Medicine.

Marx, Karl. (1956). *Karl Marx: Selected Writings in Sociology & Social Philosophy.* (Translator: T. B. Bottomore). New York, NY: McGraw-Hill Book Company.

Maslow, Abraham. (1962). *Toward a Psychology of Being*. New York, NY: D. Van Nostrand Company, Inc.

Maslow, Abraham. (1971). *The Farther Reaches of Human Nature*. New York, NY: The Viking Press

May, Rollo. (1953). *Man's Search for Himself.* New York, NY: W. W. Norton & Company, Inc.

May, Rollo. (1969). *Love and Will*. New York, NY: W. W. Norton & Company, Inc.

May, Rollo. (1983). *The Discovery of Being*. Ontario, Canada: Penguin Books.

McHugh, Paul. (2002). Classifying psychiatric disorders: An alternative approach. *The Harvard Mental Health Letter*, 19 (5), 7-8.

Miller, Melvin E., Cook-Greuter, Susanne R., (Eds.) (1994). *Transcendence and Mature Thought in Adulthood: The Further Reaches of Adult Development.* Lanham, MD: Rowman & Littlefield Publishers, Inc.

Mitchell, Stephen. (1988). (Translator) *Tao Te Ching*. New York, NY: Harper Collins Publishers.

Moore, Robert & Gillette, Douglas. (1990). *King, Warrior, Magician, Lover: Rediscovering the Archetypes of the Mature Masculine.* San Francisco, CA: Harper Collins Publishers.

Moore, Robert, (1991). *Healing the Masculine*. (Tape recording at the C.G. Jung Institute of Chicago)

Moring, Gary. (2000). *The Complete Idiot's Guide to Understanding Einstein.* Indianapolis, IN: Alpha Books.

Neumann, Eric. (1956). (Translator) *Amor and Psyche*. Princeton, NJ: Princeton University Press.

O'Meara, Dominic J. (1993). *Plotinus: An Introduction to the Enneads.* New York, NY: Oxford University Press.

Plotinus. (1988). (Translator: A. H. Armstrong) *The Enneads, Volumes 1-7.* Cambridge, MA: Harvard University Press.

Pollack, William. (1995). Deconstructing dis-identification: Rethinking Psychoanalytic concepts of male development. *Psychoanalysis/*

*Psychotherapy/Psychology of Men*, 12 (1), 30-44.

Poonja, Sri H.W.L. (2000). *The Truth Is.* York Beach, ME: Samuel Weiser, Inc.

Prabhavananda, Swami, & Isherwood, Christopher, (Translators). (1954). *The Song of God: Bhagavad-Gita.* New York, NY: Penguin Press.

Prabhavananda, Swami & Manchester, Frederick. (2002). (Translators) *The Upanishads: Breath of the Eternal. The Wisdom of the Hindu Mystics.* New York, NY: Penguin Putnum.

Radhakrishnan, S. & Moore, C. (Ed.) (1957). A Sourcebook in Indian Philosophy. Princeton, NJ: Princeton University Press.

Rinpoche, Lama Chogyam Trungpa. (1973). An Approach to Meditation. *Journal of Transpersonal Psychology*, 1, 62-74.

Robinson, John M. (1968). *An Introduction to Early Greek Philosophy.* Boston, MA: Houghton Mifflin Company.

Rogers, Carl. (1961*). On Becoming a Person: A Therapists' View of Psychotherapy.* New York, NY: Houghton Mifflin Company.

Rogers, Carl. (1980). *A Way of Being.* New York, NY: Houghton Mifflin Company

Rose, S. (2002). *Essential Oils: An introductory guide to the healing power of essential oils.* Bath, UK: Parragon Publishing.

Sankaranarayanan, P. (1988). *What is Advaita?* Bombay, India: Associated Advertisers & Printers.

Schrodinger, Erwin. (1944). *What is Life?* Cambridge, UK: University Press.

Scotton, B., Chinen, A., & Battista, J. (1996). *Textbook of Transpersonal Psychiatry and Psychology.* New York, NY: The Perseus Books Group.

Seligman, Martin & Csikszentmihalyi, Mihaly. (2000). Positive Psychology. *American Psychologist, 55* (1), 5-14.

Shanbhag, Vivek. (1999). *A Beginner's Introduction to Ayurvedic Medicine: The science of natural healing and prevention through individualized therapies.* New Canaan, CT: Keats Publishing, Inc.

Sharma, Arvind. (1995). *The Philosophy of Religion and Advaita Vedanta: A Comparative Study in Religion and Reason.* University Park, PA: The Pennsylvania State University Press.

Singer, June. (1977). *Androgyny: Toward a New Sexuality.* New York, NY: Doubleday Books.

Singer, Peter. (1983). *German Philosophers: Kant, Hegel, Schopenhauer and Nietzsche.* New York, NY: Oxford University Press.

Sinha, Jadunath. (1958). *Indian Psychology, Volumes 1-3*. Delhi, India: Motilal Banarsidass Publishers.

Sinha, Jadunath. (1971). *Indian Philosophy, Volumes 1-3*. Delhi, India: Motilal Banarsidass Publishers.

Spencer, Lloyd & Krauze, Andrzej. (1996). *Introducing Hegel*. New York, NY: Totem Books.

Spitler, Harry. (1941). *The Syntonic Principle*. The College of Syntonic Optometry.

Suzuki, D.T. (1963). *Outlines of Mahayana Buddhism*. New York, NY: Shocken Books.

Suzuki, D. T. (1964). *An Introduction to Zen Buddhism*. New York, NY: Random House, Inc.

Svoboda, Robert & Lade, Arnie. (1995). *Tao and Dharma: Chinese Medicine and Ayurveda*. Twin Lakes, WI: Lotus Press.

Tillich, Paul. (1984). *My Search for Absolutes: A Credo Perspective*. New York, NY: Simon & Schuster.

Tisserand, Robert. (1983). *The Art of Aromatherapy: The Healing and Beautifying Properties of the Essential Oils of Flowers and Herbs*. Rochester, VT: Inner Traditions International.

Unknown Author. (1946). *The Cloud of Unknowing*. London, England: John M. Watkins Publisher.

Walker, Brian Browne. (1995). (Translator) *The Tao Te Ching of Lao Tzu*. New York, NY: St. Martin's Press.

Walker, Brian. (1992). (Translator*)* *Hua Hu Ching, The Unknown Teachings of Lao Tzu*. San Francisco, CA: Harper Collins.

Walsh, Roger, & Vaughan, Frances. (1980). *Beyond Ego: Transpersonal Dimensions in Psychology*. Los Angeles, CA: J. P. Tarcher, Inc.

Warrier, G., Verma, H. & Sullivan, K. (2001). Secrets of Ayurveda. New York, NY: DK Publishing, Inc.

Watanabe, K., et al. (2001). Effect of music therapy for patients with dementia: Using the Ehime Music Therapy Scale for Dementia. *Seishin Igaku Clinical Psychiatry*, 43 (6), 661-665.

Weinberg, L. (1991). Infant Development and the Sense of Self: Stern vs. Mahler. *Clinical Social Work Journal*, 19 (1), 9.

Wilber, Ken. (1977). *Spectrum of Consciousness*. Wheaton, IL: The Theosophical Publishing House.

Wilber, Ken. (1980). *The Atman Project: A Transpersonal View of Human Development*. Wheaton, IL: Quest Books.

Wilber, Ken. (1981). *Up From Eden: A Transpersonal View of Human Evolution*. New York, NY: Shambhala Publications, Inc.

Wilber, Ken. (1995). An Informal Overview of Transpersonal Studies. *Journal of Transpersonal Psychology,* 27(2), 107-129.

Wilber, Ken. (1998). *The Marriage of Sense and Soul*. New York, NY: Random House.

Wilber, Ken. (2000). *Integral Psychology*. New York, NY: Shambhala Publications, Inc.

Wilber, Ken. (2001). *Quantum Questions: Mystical Writings of the World's Great Physicists*. Boston, MA: Shambhala Publications, Inc.

Wilheim, Richard. (1931). *The Secret of the Golden Flower: A Chinese Book of Life*. Orlando, FL: Harcourt Brace & Company.

Ziyin, Shen & Zelin, Chen. (1994). *The Basis of Traditional Chinese Medicine*. Boston, MA: Shambhala Publications, Inc.

Zukav, Gary. (1980). *The Dancing Wu Li Masters*. New York, NY: Bantam Books.

Zukav, Gary. (1989). *The Seat of the Soul*. New York, NY: Simon & Schuster, Inc.

Printed in the United States
24166LVS00003B/7

9 781413 715798